CANADIAN ANNUAL REVIEW OF POLITICS
AND PUBLIC AFFAIRS 1997

Canadian Annual Review
of politics and public affairs
1997

EDITED BY DAVID MUTIMER

Published with the support of York University by
University of Toronto Press
Toronto Buffalo London

ISBN 0-8020-8803-1

Printed on acid-free paper

Canadian annual review of politics and public affairs

1971–

ISSN 0315-1433
ISBN 0-8020-8803-1 (1997 issue)

1. Canada – Foreign relations – 1945–   . – Periodicals.
2. Canada – Economic conditions – 1945–   . – Periodicals.
3. Canada – Politics and government – 1945–   . – Periodicals.

FC2.C36   320.9′71′064   C90-032166-0 rev

University of Toronto Press acknowledges the financial assistance to its publishing program of the Canada Council for the Arts and the Ontario Arts Council.

This book was published with the support of York University.

University of Toronto Press acknowledges the financial support for its publishing activities of the Government of Canada through the Book Publishing Industry Development Program (BPIDP).

Copies of the *Canadian Annual Review* published annually for 1960 to 1982, and 1984 to 1997 are available.

Contents

Contributors ix

Canadian calendar 1997 xi

Editor's introduction – the year in review 3

THE FEDERAL PERSPECTIVE

Parliament and politics *by Robert Everett* 11

THE 1997 GENERAL ELECTION 13
An early election? 13; The writs are issued 13; The Liberal
Party 15; Bloc Québécois 17; Reform Party 18; New Democratic
Party 19; Progressive Conservative Party 20; Other parties and
independents 21; The campaign 22; Results and aftermath 24;
The new cabinet 27

FIRST SESSION OF THE THIRTY-SIXTH PARLIAMENT 30

NATIONAL INSTITUTIONS 32
Senate 32; Supreme Court 33; Auditor general's reports 34

CONSTITUTIONAL QUESTIONS AND NATIONAL UNITY 35
The Calgary Declaration 35; Reference to the Supreme Court 37;
Partition, negotiation, and other issues 38

THE NATIONAL ECONOMY 39
Economic indicators 39; The spring budget and autumn economic
statement 40

MAJOR POLICY FIELDS AND INITIATIVES 41
Pension reforms 41; Child poverty 42; The troubled fisheries 43;
Tobacco control legislation 45; Helicopter purchase 45; Postal
dispute 46; Canadian Wheat Board 46; 'Anti-biker' legislation 47

COMMISSIONS AND INQUIRIES 47
Krever Commission 47; Somalia inquiry 49

PERSONALITIES AND CONTROVERSIES 51

Ottawa and the provinces *by Michael Howlett* 54

THE QUEBEC-OTTAWA PHONY WAR 54

QUEBEC: FROM PLAN B TO THE CALGARY DECLARATION 54

DEBTS AND DEFICITS — THE CONTINUING STRUGGLE OVER
FISCAL POLICY 60

NEW BUSINESS 62
Children and youth 62

OLD BUSINESS 63
Native affairs 63; The BC fishery 63; Health care 64; GST 65

Foreign affairs and defence *by Dean F. Oliver* 67

THE FEDERAL ELECTION 69

FOREIGN AFFAIRS 69
United States 69; Central and South America 72; United
Nations 73; Trade and culture 73; Europe 74; The North Atlantic
Treaty Organization 75; The Middle East 77; Asia-Pacific 78;
Africa 81

DEFENCE 82
Arms control 82; Defence policy 84; Defence budget, military
equipment, and training 85; Somalia inquiry 86; Other
scandals 94; Organization and personnel 95; Domestic
emergencies 96

THE PROVINCIAL PERSPECTIVES 99

ONTARIO *by Robert Drummond* 99
Education 101; Health 107; Municipal affairs 111; Crime and
punishment 118; The economy and the budget 121

QUEBEC *by Jocelyn Coulon* 123
Politics 123; Federal-provincial relations 134; Other significant
events 135

NOVA SCOTIA *by Robert Finbow* 136
Politics 137; The legislature 139; The economy 141;
Intergovernmental affairs 144

NEW BRUNSWICK *by Richard Wilbur* 146
Public-private partnerships 146; The spring legislative session 148;
Mounting problems for NB Power 150; The politics of education 151;
Fighting amalgamation and changes to policing 152; Changing
political leaders ... and members 153; The general economic
picture 154; The fall legislative session 155

MANITOBA *by Geoffrey Lambert* 156
The economy 156; Politics and political parties 158; The 'flood of the
century' 160; The legislative session 162

BRITISH COLUMBIA *by Carey Hill* 164
Pacific salmon treaty 165; APEC 168; Federal-provincial
relations 169; National unity 170; Federal election 173; Court
challenge and recall 176; The economy 176

PRINCE EDWARD ISLAND *by Peter E. Buker* 178
The economy 178; Fiscal events 181; The legislature and
politics 182; Other events 185

SASKATCHEWAN *by Joseph Garcea* 188
The legislature and government 188; Parties and elections 190; The
budget and economy 196; The Calgary Declaration 200; Aboriginal
affairs 201; Justice sector 203

ALBERTA *by Harold Jansen* 204
The provincial election 204; Sorting out the future 209; The
legislature 213; The federal election in Alberta 216; The
economy 218; Miscellaneous 220

NEWFOUNDLAND AND LABRADOR *by Raymond B. Blake* 221
The budget and the economy 221; The fishery 225; Politics 227;
Education and social issues 229

YUKON AND NORTHWEST TERRITORIES *by James Lawson* 231
The territories in Confederation and the world 231; Yukon:
Economy 233; Yukon: Government policy and politics 234;
Yukon: Aboriginal affairs and constitutional development 235;
Yukon: Society 236; Northwest Territories: Economy 236;
NWT: Government policy and politics 239; NWT: Aboriginal affairs
and constitutional development 240; NWT: Society 241

Obituaries 243

Index of names 247

Index of subjects 259

Contributors

RAYMOND B. BLAKE, Assistant Professor, Centre for Canadian
Studies, Mount Allison University

PETER E. BUKER, Assistant Professor, Department of Political
Studies, University of Prince Edward Island

JOCELYN COULON, Journalist with *Le Devoir*, 1985–99

ROBERT DRUMMOND, Associate Professor, Department of Political
Science, York University

ROBERT EVERETT, University Secretariat, York University

ROBERT FINBOW, Associate Professor, Department of Political
Science, Dalhousie University

JOSEPH GARCEA, Associate Professor, Department of Political
Science, University of Saskatchewan

CAREY HILL, Doctoral Candidate, Department of Political Science,
University of British Columbia

MICHAEL HOWLETT, Associate Professor, Department of Political
Science, Simon Fraser University

HAROLD J. JANSEN, Assistant Professor, Department of Political
Science, University of Lethbridge

GEOFFREY LAMBERT, Professor, Department of Political Studies,
University of Manitoba

JAMES B. LAWSON, Doctoral Candidate, Department of Political
Science, York University

DEAN OLIVER, Post-Doctoral Fellow, The Norman Paterson School of
International Affairs

RICHARD WILBUR, Fundy Promotions, St Andrews, New Brunswick

Canadian calendar 1997*

*Compiled by J. Marshall Beier

JANUARY

3 Citing inadequate financial support from the anglo-
phone community, English-rights activist Howard
Galganov announces the dissolution of his Quebec
Political Action Committee.

4 New Unemployment Insurance rules go into effect.
Among the reforms is a change in the basis of eligibility requirements from number of weeks to total hours
worked and a new name: Employment Insurance.

6 A settlement is announced in the $50 million libel suit
brought by former prime minister Brian Mulroney
against the federal government over the RCMP's handling of the Airbus affair.

9 Daniel Turp becomes the sixth contender to announce
his candidacy for the leadership of the Bloc Québécois.

– Bombardier Inc. announces a record $825 million sale
of Canadair Regional Jets to Southwest Airlines.

10 Defence Minister Doug Young forces an early halt to
the Somalia inquiry, ordering it to conclude hearings
by 31 March and submit its report by the end of June.

– Air Canada's regional airlines are hit by a pilot strike
only five days after Air Ontario's flight attendants
walked off the job seeking wage parity with their Air
Canada counterparts.

12 Somalia inquiry chair Mr Justice Gilles Letourneau
says the early conclusion ordered by Defence Minister
Doug Young two days earlier will preclude investiga-

tion of the post-deployment phase and allegations of a cover-up at the Department of National Defence.

13　Ontario's Conservative government announces sweeping reforms that will see it take direct control of elementary and secondary education in the province.

14　Reform Party MP Stephen Harper resigns his Commons seat to assume the vice-presidency of the National Citizens' Coalition.

−　Overturning a lower court ruling, the Federal Court of Appeal unanimously allows deportation proceedings against three men implicated in Nazi war crimes.

−　A human rights tribunal orders the Canadian Forces to pay compensation for age discrimination to former pilots and flight attendants terminated in 1985 on grounds that they were too old.

15　Ontario's Conservative government adds transportation infrastructure costs to the social services passed to the province's municipalities a day earlier, for a total of $6.4 billion in downloaded expenditures.

16　Former Trudeau cabinet minister Paul Hellyer inaugurates the Canadian Action Party as Canada's newest political party.

−　Bloc Québécois MP Pierrette Venne announces her run for the party's leadership.

17　The Federal Court of Appeal rules unanimously to allow the Krever Commission to assign blame in its final report on Canada's tainted blood scandal.

−　As Ottawa prepares for the closing of the federal Prison for Women in Kingston, plans are announced to move twenty to twenty-five female prisoners into the men's maximum security Kingston Penitentiary.

−　An inquiry report finds that Canada's first female infantry officer suffered harsh treatment and harassment in the military because of her sex. The same report fails to find support for allegations that she was beaten by other soldiers during a training exercise in 1992.

−　Retired colonel Geoff Haswell is found not guilty by a court martial hearing allegations that he ordered the destruction of documents related to the Somalia affair in September 1995.

22 Foreign Minister Lloyd Axworthy wraps up a two-day visit to Cuba at which he and Fidel Castro agreed to a number of cooperative measures to improve human rights.

23 Two former lawyers for convicted killer Paul Bernardo are charged with obstructing justice and possession of child pornography after they withheld videotapes of Bernardo's crimes, which they took from his home in 1993. Before learning of the tapes' existence, prosecutors allowed Bernardo's wife and accomplice, Karla Homolka, a twelve-year sentence in exchange for her testimony.

24 Conservative Senator Eric Berntson resigns from caucus and as his party's deputy leader in the Senate after the RCMP charged him in connection with a broader scandal involving misuse of funds by members of Grant Devine's Conservative Saskatchewan government in the late 1980s.

– Ontario Attorney General Charles Harnick announces $1.25 million in compensation to be paid to Guy Paul Morin and his parents in return for their agreeing to drop a $17-million law suit against police and prosecutors. In 1995 DNA evidence showed that Mr Morin had been wrongfully convicted of the 1984 murder of Christine Jessop.

– The Canada Mortgage and Housing Corporation reports that new housing starts in 1996 were up 12.4 per cent over the very poor showing a year earlier.

29 Industry Canada announces that personal and business bankruptcies in Canada hit a record high in 1996.

30 Lise Thibault is sworn in as Quebec's first female lieutenant-governor.

31 Andrew Petter, British Columbia's finance minister, admits that election campaigning moved the NDP government to promise a balanced budget it would not be able to deliver.

FEBRUARY

4 A report by the Canadian Security Intelligence Service says industrial espionage is a growing concern with foreign governments spying on Canadian firms.

5 A Health Canada report warns that the number of AIDS cases in Canada could double over the next three years.

6 A controversial 5–4 ruling by the Supreme Court upholds the right of an accused to access the private records of sexual assault victims.

– The federal government announces that Canada will be sending ten human rights observers to Rwanda as soon as the Canadian International Development Agency can offer assurances as to their safety while in that country.

7 Security on Parliament Hill is called into serious question after a disturbed Quebec man drives his SUV up two flights of steps in front of the Peace Tower.

8 The federal Human Resources Department reports that student debt levels are rising dramatically. Meanwhile, record numbers of students have been declaring personal bankruptcy.

10 A report issued by the National Council of Welfare says that some welfare recipients have had their benefits cut nearly in half over the past decade as a consequence of provincial cost-cutting.

11 Alberta Treasurer Jim Dinning hands down a pre-election budget projecting a $144 million surplus.

– Ontario Correctional Services Minister Bob Runciman announces that an unused prison farm will be privately operated as a strict discipline facility for young offenders.

12 Federal Human Resources Minister Pierre Pettigrew unveils the Liberal government's long-awaited youth employment strategy, which will see $255 million dedicated to internship programs and the creation of summer jobs.

– British Columbia Attorney General Ujjal Dosanjh announces that nearly 10 per cent of the province's courthouses will be closed as a cost-saving measure.

14 Finance Minister Paul Martin introduces legislation designed to save the Canada Pension Plan. The scheme will increase contributions over the next six years while cutting benefits by nearly 10 per cent.

17 Statistics Canada reports that in 1995 Canadians

invested more in Registered Retirement Savings Plans than in registered pension plans.

18 A pre-election budget tabled by Finance Minister Paul Martin promises deficit reduction with no new tax hikes.

20 Treasury Board President Marcel Masse tells the Commons that an accumulated surplus will see the Employment Insurance fund double to $12 billion by the end of the fiscal year.

21 The World Trade Organization sides with U.S. magazine publishers against their Canadian counterparts in the dispute over so-called split-run periodicals.

24 Assembly of First Nations National Chief Ovide Mercredi announces plans to slow traffic on the Trans-Canada Highway to protest the federal government's failure to respond to recommendations contained in the report of the Royal Commission on Aboriginal Peoples.

– Citing the federal government's improved fiscal outlook, New York-based debt rating agency Standard and Poor's raises Canada's foreign currency debt rating to AA+.

– The Ontario Health Services Restructuring Commission announces that the province's only French-language hospital is among those slated for closure during the next two years. The Montfort Hospital is one of four Ottawa area hospitals on the Commission's list.

26 Canadian Airlines International strikes a tentative deal with its creditors for the implementation of a restructuring plan giving the financially troubled airline six months to improve its fiscal outlook.

27 British Columbia's Supreme Court authorizes a citizens' group to proceed with its lawsuit alleging fraud by the NDP government in connection with election promises of a balanced budget.

– The T. Eaton Company announces that it has been granted bankruptcy protection from its creditors while it works to restructure in the wake of a $128-million operating loss in 1996.

28 The federal government's position that Quebec seces-

sion can only proceed through the Constitution is presented before the Supreme Court of Canada.

MARCH

3 Voters in Metropolitan Toronto overwhelmingly reject a provincial government proposal to merge the six existing municipalities into a single so-called Megacity.

4 A military doctor who examined the body of a Somali civilian shot dead by Canadian soldiers on 4 March 1993 testifies before the Somalia inquiry, alleging that officers began to orchestrate a cover-up within hours of Ahmed Aruush's death.

5 Quebec orders a police investigation into allegations that some provincial government employees have been selling information collected from police files, medical records, and tax documents on the black market.

6 A federal government anti-smoking bill, which will limit tobacco company sponsorship of sporting and cultural events, passes the Commons by a vote of 139–37.

— A study released by the National Cancer Institute of Canada, Health Canada, and Statistics Canada reports a doubling in the number of lung cancer deaths among women over the last ten years.

— British Columbia drops its controversial welfare residency rule after the federal government pledges $67 million over three years to aid in the settling of new immigrants in the province.

— Ontario's Health Services Restructuring Commission recommends that ten Toronto hospitals be closed and that two others be reduced to walk-in clinics.

11 Circumventing the normal nomination process, Prime Minister Jean Chrétien handpicks four women to run as Liberal candidates in the next federal election.

— Alberta Premier Ralph Klein's Conservative government handily defeats the opposition Liberals, improving its majority from fifty-four to sixty-three of the legislature's eighty-three seats. Grant Mitchell's Liberals are reduced from twenty-nine to eighteen seats. The NDP returns to the legislature with two seats after a four-year absence.

12   As part of its restructuring plans, the T. Eaton Company notifies employees of its intention to close thirty-one of its eighty-five department stores.

14   Manitoba's Conservative government announces the first payment against the province's debt since the 1950s.

15   Gilles Duceppe wins the leadership of the Bloc Québécois.

20   The Canadian Human Rights Commission warns the federal government not to ignore the recommendations contained in the Report of the Royal Commission on Aboriginal Peoples.

–   The House of Commons passes a bill to implement the Harmonized Sales Tax in Newfoundland, New Brunswick, and Nova Scotia effective 1 April.

–   Nova Scotia Premier John Savage resigns in the hope that his Liberals' re-election chances will be buoyed with a more popular leader.

–   As part of its efforts to balance the provincial budget, Newfoundland Premier Brian Tobin's Liberal government announces the elimination of 1,600 public-sector jobs.

25   A preliminary report of the Ontario Child Mortality Task Force says that inadequate investigative methods and poor inter-agency coordination between the province's Children's Aid Societies are to blame for their failure to prevent deaths.

26   Calgary's Bre-X Minerals admits that estimates of the amount of gold in its Indonesian deposit might have been inflated.

27   The Federal Court of Canada rules that the federal government exceeded its authority in imposing deadlines for the Somalia inquiry to complete hearings and submit its final report.

–   Statistics Canada reports a range of positive indications that the economy is regaining vitality after several years of unspectacular growth following the recession of early 1990s.

30   Defence Minister Doug Young insists that deadlines

imposed on the Somalia inquiry will stand in spite of a Federal Court ruling that he overstepped his authority in ordering them.

APRIL

1 A promised pay raise for Canadian Forces personnel goes into effect.

2 The Quebec Superior Court rules that the province's chief electoral officer does not have jurisdiction over infractions of Quebec's election laws committed elsewhere in Canada. The Court throws out charges against Ontario groups and individuals who transported people to a federalist rally three days before the 1995 sovereignty referendum.

8 A report by the Official Languages Commissioner finds increasing polarization between the country's principal language communities. While francophone communities outside Quebec are in decline, the number of anglophones in Quebec is falling.

9 Addressing Washington's National Press Club, Prime Minister Jean Chrétien suggests that the United States should either pay its United Nations dues or allow the UN to move from New York to Montreal.

10 The federal government introduces legislation to create a national DNA database for use by law enforcement.

– The Canadian Coast Guard announces that it has billed New Brunswick's Irving conglomerate $42.2 million for the raising of its oil barge, the *Irving Whale*, which sank off Prince Edward Island in 1970.

14 Former prime minister Brian Mulroney publicly attacks the federal Liberals' handling of national unity, calling for the transcendence of partisanship in order to find a constitutional solution.

– Citing violations of NAFTA, a U.S. firm files suit against the federal government five days after the Senate passed a bill banning the use of a gasoline additive linked to health concerns.

15 Statistics Canada reports that Quebec accounts for less than 25 per cent of the total population of Canada for the first time since Confederation.

16 In an out-of-court settlement, the federal government agrees to pay the Pearson Development Corporation $60 million in compensation for its cancellation of a contract signed by the Conservative government of Kim Campbell that would have seen the group renovate and operate two terminals at Toronto's Pearson International Airport.

17 Hopes for a Senate inquiry into the Somalia affair are dashed when Conservative senators walk out of an organizational meeting and promise to boycott hearings scheduled to begin on 21 April.

– Federal Fisheries Minister Fred Mifflin announces the opening of a limited East Coast cod fishery effective 1 May.

– Nova Scotia Finance Minister Bill Gillis tables a budget projecting the province's first surplus in a quarter century.

18 After Prime Minister Chrétien declines to meet with aboriginal leaders, Assembly of First Nations National Chief Ovide Mercredi promises to keep aboriginal issues at the fore throughout the federal election campaign.

26 A bill amending the Criminal Code of Canada in a bid to halt biker-gang violence in Quebec receives royal assent.

27 Prime Minister Chrétien calls a federal election, to be held on 2 June.

28 An Ontario Provincial Police officer is found guilty of negligence causing death in the 1995 shooting of aboriginal protestor Dudley George at Ipperwash Provincial Park.

– Prime Minister Chrétien announces that the Liberals will cancel additional scheduled cuts in transfers to the provinces.

MAY

1 New Democratic Party leader Alexa McDonough unveils her party's election platform, the centrepiece of which is a promised $19-billion increase in social spending over five years to be funded in part by tax increases for big corporations and the wealthy.

2   The Red River begins five days of crest levels, causing extensive flooding in southern Manitoba that is the worst in a century.

4   A report by Strathcona Mineral Services exposes the Bre-X gold deposit in Indonesia as a deliberate hoax.

5   *Time* magazine lauds the virtues of order and prosperity that have made Canada the United Nations' first pick as the best country in which to live.

–   A coalition of Canadian broadcasters and cable operators proposes a new voluntary content rating system that would enable parents to exercise greater control over their children's television viewing.

7   With less than a month to go before the federal election, Finance Minister Paul Martin announces that tax cuts are in the offing as the government's deficit reduction measures exceed their targets.

–   Halifax doctor Nancy Morrison is charged with first-degree murder in connection with the death of a terminally ill sixty-five-year-old cancer patient. The case promises to reopen the national debate on mercy killing.

–   The Toronto Stock Exchange delists Bre-X. The company's stocks are down 99.7 per cent from their value of just eight months ago.

13   Canadian Forces units are cheered in Winnipeg for their work in providing relief in flood-ravaged areas. The deployment has been the Forces' largest ever peacetime operation.

–   Ontario's Centre of Forensic Sciences begins a formal review of murder and manslaughter cases investigated by scientists involved in the investigation that culminated in the wrongful conviction of Guy Paul Morin.

15   Federal Health Minister David Dingwall voices strong opposition to a private health-care facility planned for Calgary, warning that it could lead to a two-tier health system.

–   Standard and Poor's downgrades British Columbia's bond rating from AA+ to AA only one week after a similar move by Moody's Investors Service.

20   A British Columbia court finds aboriginal activist William Jones Ignace (Wolverine) guilty of mischief

endangering life for his part in the Gustafsen Lake
stand-off two years ago.

22   In what promises to be one of the federal election campaign's most memorable lines, New Democrat leader
Alexa McDonough responds to the other candidates'
fixation on national unity with the exclamation, 'It's
about jobs, stupid.'

–   Nearly half of the gun registry unit of the Metropolitan
Toronto police force faces charges arising from allegations that they used their positions to buy and sell firearms.

29   The annual review of the Bank of Canada reveals that
Canadian household debt rose to record levels in 1996.

31   The Confederation Bridge connecting Prince Edward
Island to the mainland opens to traffic.

JUNE

2   The federal election sees Jean Chrétien's Liberals
returned to power, though with a greatly reduced
majority after the loss of twenty-two seats. The Bloc
Québécois loses its tenuous hold on the Official
Opposition, which falls to Reform. Both the New
Democrats and the Conservatives make considerable
gains over their dismal showings of 1993, easily
regaining official party status.

3   As the impact of massive provincial restructuring
begins to be felt, Ontario's Conservative government
moves to limit the ability of public sector unions to
strike.

4   Ontario Transportation Minister Al Palladini tables a
bill intended to curb the problem of unsafe trucks on
the province's highways. Four deaths have been
caused in the last two and a half years by wheels flying
off moving transports.

5   British Columbia's New Democrats introduce child
custody and maintenance legislation under which
same-sex couples would be treated as legal spouses.

6   The Quebec National Assembly votes 63–24 in favour
of allowing a return of the Commission de protection
de la langue français, decried by anglophones as the
'language police.'

8   Alberta Safeway employees return to work after a bit-
     ter ten-week strike at the province's largest grocery
     chain.

13   Ontario Education Minister John Snobelen introduces
     tough new standards for elementary school students,
     which will demand better performance earlier. Those
     not making the grade will be held back.

16   British Columbia will bring in legislation that will
     enable it to seek compensation from tobacco compa-
     nies for smoking-related health-care costs, according
     to Premier Glen Clark and Health Minister Joy
     MacPhail.

17   Over the objections of conservationists, a joint federal-
     provincial panel recommends that the controversial
     Cheviot mine be allowed to proceed with coal mining
     operations near to the ecologically sensitive Jasper
     National Park.

19   Quebec Premier Lucien Bouchard says that, in light of
     shared debt and trade considerations, the rest of Can-
     ada would have no alternative but to conclude a part-
     nership agreement with an independent Quebec.

20   Amid charges of hypocrisy, Reform leader Preston
     Manning cites public demand as the reason for revers-
     ing himself and accepting Stornoway, the official
     residence of the leader of the Opposition.

22   The so-called Summit of the Eight wraps up three days
     of meetings in Denver. Prime Minister Chrétien leaves
     without having persuaded U.S. President Bill Clinton
     to support a ban on anti-personnel land-mines.

24   In what is becoming something of an unwanted tradi-
     tion, Quebec's annual Fête Nationale is once again
     tainted by the violence and vandalism of unruly mobs.

27   Fisheries Minister David Anderson announces unilat-
     eral Canadian quotas for the Pacific salmon catch in
     the wake of further failed efforts to reach an agreement
     with the United States. The second highest-ever
     Canadian quota means that most of the salmon will
     never reach U.S. waters.

30   Statistics Canada reports the best performance by the
     Canadian economy in nearly three years. Renewed con-
     sumer spending is credited with the improved outlook.

JULY

2 The Somalia inquiry issues its report, which is highly critical of senior military officers who, it says, too readily blamed subordinates for their own failings. The report also alleges a cover-up in Somalia and at National Defence Headquarters.

3 Ontario's road safety bill passes in an emergency sitting of the legislature. In addition to truck safety provisions, the new legislation includes stiffer penalties for drunk driving and for motorists who illegally pass a stopped school bus.

4 As part of a plan to reduce the size and expense of government in the province, Alberta Treasurer Stockwell Day announces that the legislature will henceforth sit for only one session per year.

8 It is reported that a court martial has fined and severely reprimanded a Canadian military officer for a December 1996 incident in which he brandished a pistol while attempting to break up a traffic jam in Haiti.

9 Officials at Foreign Affairs confirm that they are considering legal means to block British Columbia Premier Glen Clark's threat to evict the U.S. Navy from a Vancouver Island torpedo testing range if a deal is not reached on Pacific salmon.

– Nova Scotia doctors accept a deal with the province that will see their billing rates increase in each of the four years that it is in effect.

10 Calls for a public inquiry into the killing of aboriginal protestor Dudley George come in response to news that the police officer convicted of the shooting has been spared jail time.

11 Canada-U.S. relations seem not to have suffered any serious harm after a live microphone catches Prime Minister Chrétien making disparaging remarks about U.S. President Bill Clinton and the American political system while at a NATO summit in Madrid.

12 Russell MacLellan becomes premier-designate of Nova Scotia after the governing Liberals elect him as their new leader in a phone-in vote.

18 A Federal Court of Appeal ruling upholds the federal

government's right to force an early end to the Somalia inquiry.

– After DNA evidence confirms that David Milgaard was not the person who raped and killed nursing student Gail Miller in 1969, the Saskatchewan government apologizes for his wrongful conviction.

– Bell Canada announces that a workforce reduction of 2,200 will be added to the 10,000 jobs the company has already eliminated over the last three years.

19 Angry British Columbia fishers blockade an Alaskan ferry in the Prince Rupert harbour in an effort to bring attention to what they claim is Alaskan overfishing of Pacific salmon stocks.

22 The European Union lifts its ban on Canadian furs in return for a pledge that steel-jawed leghold traps will be phased out over the next two and a half years.

24 An Ontario Court judge rules that the provincial government's so-called Megacity law does not violate the Constitution.

29 The Canadian Coast Guard files suit against New Brunswick's Irving conglomerate for the costs of recovering the sunken oil barge *Irving Whale*.

30 Statistics Canada reports that while homicides were up in 1996, overall crime rates fell.

AUGUST

1 Phil Fontaine, head of the Assembly of Manitoba Chiefs, is sworn in as the new national chief of the Assembly of First Nations, replacing Ovide Mercredi.

7 Canada imposes trade sanctions on Burma in hopes of persuading that country to improve its human rights record.

11 A British Columbia Human Rights tribunal rules that breast-feeding children in public is a fundamental right, which cannot be prohibited.

13 Ontario's Health Services Restructuring Commission bows to mounting political pressure, announcing that Ottawa's French-language Montfort Hospital will be spared.

14 The federal government begins a lawsuit against British Columbia in a bid to prevent BC Premier Glen

Clark from following through on his threat to close a
U.S. Navy torpedo testing range.

18 The federal government agrees to buy a parcel of land
from the Quebec community of Oka in an effort to
resolve one of the outstanding issues from the 1990
Mohawk crisis.

21 The Saskatchewan Party, recently created by a small
group of Conservatives and Liberals, is recognized as
that province's Official Opposition.

22 David Milgaard accepts $250,000 compensation from
the Saskatchewan government for the nearly twenty-
three years he served in prison after being wrongfully
convicted of murder.

– Ontario Environment Minister Norm Sterling
announces that the province will become the second in
Canada to require mandatory emissions testing for
automobiles.

25 A World Trade Organization ruling strikes down the
European Union's ban on beef produced with growth
hormones, opening a $100-million annual market to
Canadian beef producers.

– Psychiatrist Vivian Rakoff admits that his assessment of Quebec Premier Lucien Bouchard, whom he
has never met, was unscientific and likely influ-
enced by his own federalist views. Rakoff has been
at the centre of a scandal since it came to light
that he was hired by a Liberal MP to profile Mr
Bouchard in the wake of the 1995 Quebec sovereignty referendum.

26 Labrador Innu and Inuit secure a court injunction
halting work at the Voisey's Bay nickel and copper
mining project.

28 Newfoundland's Terra Nova offshore oil project
receives environmental approval.

– The annual meeting of the Canadian Police Association passes a resolution calling for a return to the death
penalty for murderers.

– A planned event to inaugurate Ontario's new privately
run strict discipline youth detention facility is cancelled after two teenage inmates escape and two others
assault a guard.

SEPTEMBER

9   Finance Minister Paul Martin responds to critics of the growing Employment Insurance surplus saying that a $15-billion surplus has been recommended in order that the next economic downturn will not force an increase in premiums.

10   Northern Telecom announces a major expansion of its Montreal operations that will create 1,000 new jobs.

–   Toronto police make twenty-two arrests after uncovering an international sex-slave ring that sold Asian women into servitude as prostitutes while they worked off debts.

11   British Columbia Premier Glen Clark accuses the federal government of treason for its interference with the province's attempts to force a resolution of the Pacific salmon dispute with the United States.

–   A government-appointed commission finds that cuts to Ontario's legal aid system have compromised the province's court system as poor people are forced to go without representation.

15   Assembly of First Nations National Chief Phil Fontaine says Canada's aboriginal peoples are being denied sufficient voice in national unity discussions.

–   An Ontario Divisional Court ruling upholds the right of the Health Services Restructuring Commission to order the closing of Ontario hospitals.

17   Foreign Minister Lloyd Axworthy is credited with playing a leading role in the conclusion of an eighty-nine-country agreement to ban anti-personnel landmines.

–   The International Monetary Fund predicts that Canada will lead the industrial world in economic growth for the next two years.

–   Army General Maurice Baril is named new Chief of Defence Staff, replacing acting chief Vice-Admiral Larry Murray.

–   Vancouver sanitation workers return to work after a six-week strike, which saw garbage pile up on city streets.

21   After only fifteen months in the skies, financially troubled discount airline Greyhound Air ceases operations.

22 In a measure designed to address the problem of gambling addiction, New Brunswick imposes a 2:30 a.m.–10:00 a.m. shutdown on video lottery terminals in the province.

23 The federal Liberals' Throne Speech pledges assistance for unemployed youth and low-income families.

24 Prime Minister Chrétien announces a new federal scholarship fund for post-secondary students, to be implemented at the new millennium.

25 Finance Minister Paul Martin tables legislation that includes a retroactive premium increase and a number of other measures designed to guarantee the future of the Canada Pension Plan.

26 The Supreme Court rules against a Red Cross challenge of an earlier decision allowing the Krever Commission to lay blame in Canada's tainted blood scandal.

–   Conservative Senator Pat Carney steps into controversy, suggesting that British Columbia ought to threaten secession in order to press a renegotiation of its place in Confederation.

29 In a gesture that is compared with Charles de Gualle's 1967 'Vive le Quebec libre' exclamation, French President Jacques Chirac tells Quebec Premier Lucien Bouchard that France will back Quebec in whatever path its chooses.

OCTOBER

1   Michel Bastarache, a noted federalist judge from the New Brunswick Court of Appeal, is appointed to the Supreme Court of Canada.

2   Canada's ambassador to Israel is recalled for consultations after reports that Israeli Mossad agents used counterfeit Canadian passports in intelligence operations.

–   A racial brawl at Nova Scotia's Cole Harbour District High School is the third in less than a year.

7   An arbitrator rules that the RCMP must pay former prime minister Brian Mulroney more than $2 million plus interest to cover legal expenses arising from the Airbus affair.

– Frank McKenna resigns after a decade as Liberal premier of New Brunswick.

8 The Auditor General's report is tabled in the Commons. Among the targets of criticism is the TAGS program, which has not achieved its objective of restructuring the Atlantic cod fishery in spite of its $1.9-billion price tag.

9 Fisheries Minister David Anderson promises Atlantic fishers that federal support will continue beyond the expiry of the TAGS program next year.

– The Supreme Court rules that provisions in Quebec's referendum law limiting spending are unconstitutional.

10 Foreign Minister Lloyd Axworthy tells the Commons he has received assurances that Israeli agents will not use Canadian travel documents in the future.

14 Defence Minister Art Eggleton tells a news conference that while the military accepts most of the recommendations of the Somalia inquiry, it will not conduct any further investigations into wrongdoing in Somalia or in other incidents subsequent to Somalia.

15 The RCMP concludes its investigation of alleged Liberal fund-raising irregularities. Liberal organizer Pierre Corbeil is charged with influence-peddling.

20 An Ontario Court judge rules that police may not pluck hairs from criminal suspects in order to conduct DNA analysis.

22 Quebec Health Minister Jean Rochon says Quebec will manage its own blood supply rather than join the other provinces in becoming part of the new agency slated to replace the Red Cross.

23 Standard and Poor's upgrades Alberta's credit rating to AA+, the highest of any Canadian province.

29 The owners of New Brunswick's Potacan potash mine confirm that it will be shut down at a cost of 500 jobs after it was flooded with water.

27 Ontario's 126,000 primary and secondary school teachers walk off the job to protest the provincial government's education reforms.

30 Justice Minister Anne McLellan unveils the details of the Firearms Act, under which gun owners will be required to register their firearms.

31   The Supreme Court refuses to recognize a fetus as a
     person with legal rights in connection with a case in
     which a pregnant Winnipeg woman was ordered to
     undergo treatment for solvent addiction in 1996.
–   Citing the right of an accused to a fair trial, the
     Alberta Court of Queen's Bench strikes down Can-
     ada's rape shield law, which protected sexual assault
     victims from having their personal records intro-
     duced in court.

NOVEMBER

3   The last of the Canadian military's arsenal of anti-
     personnel land-mines is destroyed in the presence of a
     group of dignitaries active in the campaign for a treaty
     banning the weapons.
4   The New Brunswick Court of Queen's Bench rules
     that aboriginal people enjoy an unrestricted right to cut
     trees on Crown land. Moreover, the ruling says that
     aboriginal property rights over the trees have never
     been relinquished.
5   In a preliminary land-claims settlement, Newfound-
     land agrees to transfer 5 per cent of the territory of
     Labrador to Inuit control.
–   The British Columbia Supreme Court throws out a
     lawsuit alleging fraud by the NDP government in the
     last provincial election, but allows related actions to
     proceed against three individual NDP members of the
     legislature.
6   Prime Minister Chrétien signals would-be Liberal con-
     tenders for his job that he has no intention of retiring
     soon but will remain at least until after the next federal
     election.
–   Ontario Energy Minister Jim Wilson announces that
     Ontario Hydro, North America's largest utility, will be
     broken up and the market opened to competition.
9   Still reeling from scandals dating from Grant Devine's
     government of the 1980s and the defection of mem-
     bers to the new Saskatchewan Party, Saskatchewan's
     Conservative Party votes itself out of existence.
10   The British Columbia Court of Appeal rules that as
     long as outstanding aboriginal land claims remain

unresolved the province does not enjoy rights of
exclusive control over its forests.

- The U.S. Congress votes to delay by one year a plan
that would impose tighter control over the Canada-
U.S. border, threatening to make crossings by Canadians much more difficult in the process.

- Ontario teachers end their province-wide strike but not
their opposition to the provincial government's education reforms.

15 A 45-kilometre stretch of the Trans-Canada Highway
in Nova Scotia opens as a toll road in a controversial
partnership between the provincial government and
Atlantic Highways Corp.

17 Newfoundland's celebrated Hibernia offshore drilling
operation pumps its first barrels of oil.

18 At a meeting in Winnipeg, a majority of provincial
premiers agree to have aboriginal leaders add their
input to discussions on national unity.

- The House of Commons passes a constitutional
amendment that will enable Quebec to replace denominational school boards with linguistic ones.

19 The Canadian Union of Postal Workers strikes over
wages and other issues, bringing Canada Post to a
standstill.

25 In what many describe as an excessive use of force,
Mounties use pepper spray to disperse protestors at the
APEC summit in Vancouver.

26 The report of the Krever Commission into Canada's
tainted blood scandal is released. The report, which
describes the blood system as poorly funded and lacking clear policy guidance, also calls for compensation
for victims of contaminated blood.

- Buttressing his party's control of the Senate, Prime
Minister Chrétien appoints two prominent Liberals to
the upper house. The appointees are former Trudeau
cabinet minister Serge Joyal and Alberta Métis leader
Thelma Chalifoux.

- Prince Edward Island Premier Pat Binns announces that
his government will pay $750,000 in compensation to
seasonal workers who claim to have been dismissed for
political reasons after the 1996 provincial election.

27 Federal legislation banning anti-personnel land-mines receives royal assent.

DECEMBER

1 Disabled-rights activists are outraged as a Saskatchewan judge sentences Robert Latimer to two years less a day for the 1993 mercy killing of his severely disabled daughter Tracy.

– The long-awaited report of the inquiry into Nova Scotia's Westray Mine disaster is released. The report is critical of company officials, safety inspectors, and even former premier Donald Cameron, who actively promoted the mine.

2 Defence Minister Art Eggleton announces that Canadian troops will remain in Bosnia-Herzegovina for at least another six months.

– The head of Canada's Labour Relations Board is fired in the wake of harsh criticism of Board spending contained in the Auditor General's report.

3 Ontario Attorney General Charles Harnick apologizes to the surviving Dionne quintuplets for their treatment as children, but stops short of promising compensation for the years they were separated from their family and treated as a tourist attraction.

4 The convention banning anti-personnel land-mines is signed by 121 countries in Ottawa.

5 Postal workers return to the job a day after back-to-work legislation, which imposes wage terms but leaves other issues unresolved.

7 Prime Minister Chrétien tells reporters in Quebec City that Quebec would have to negotiate the terms of separation with the federal government after a separatist referendum victory and that a unilateral declaration of independence would likely be illegal.

10 An Ontario Court judge finds parts of Canada's marijuana laws to be unconstitutional, opening the way for a renewed debate about the medicinal use of the drug.

11 A historic ruling by the Supreme Court of Canada with sweeping implications finds that aboriginal peoples who have never signed away title to their ancestral

lands have a constitutional right to use them in almost any way they wish.

– The lawyer for four students who allege their civil rights were violated by police as they protested at the APEC summit announces that they are suing the RCMP.

12 A deal struck between Ottawa and nine provincial premiers for the negotiation of new terms for the country's social programs is denounced by Quebec Premier Lucien Bouchard as a federal power grab.

– Federal Indian Affairs Minister Jane Stewart announces that $10.1 million in federal and provincial compensation will be paid to British Columbia's Osoyoos Indian Band for lands improperly taken from them 120 years ago.

16 The federal government announces a three-and-a-half-month extension of support for unemployed fishers under the TAGS program.

17 Ottawa announces that Canada will settle and protect witnesses who testify about war crimes in Bosnia and are consequently unable to return to their homes.

19 Corrections Canada announces that the Prison for Women will remain open to house a small number of inmates whose transfer to the men's Kingston Penitentiary or regional women's facilities had been contemplated.

22 Brazil threatens to suspend trade talks between Canada and the Mercosur customs union after Bombardier Inc. won a major contract to supply aircraft to Canada's NATO pilot training program. Brazilian aircraft manufacturer Embraer had been expected to win the deal.

23 Saskatchewan's Potash Corp. announces that it hopes to buy the flooded New Brunswick Potacan potash mine and to make it operational again.

CANADIAN ANNUAL REVIEW OF POLITICS
AND PUBLIC AFFAIRS 1997

EDITOR'S INTRODUCTION –
THE YEAR IN REVIEW

The Liberal government had been elected in 1993 on a series of promises designed to eliminate the federal deficit and build the foundation for long-term growth in an era of budget surpluses. By 1997, it appeared that era was at hand. The government was on the verge of a balanced budget, inflation seemed to have been tamed, and so the leading economic policy question was, How should the surpluses, which the government expected to begin accumulating, be spent? In this context, despite there being nearly sixteen months left in its mandate, it is not surprising that, on 27 April, Prime Minister Chrétien dropped the writs for a 2 June election. The Prime Minister's intention was to campaign on the government's economic record and invite Canadians to enter into the politically pleasurable task of dividing up the spoils of years of fiscal restraint, but the campaign was dominated by the issue of national unity. Despite this shift in the campaign's terrain, and the general feeling that the Reform Party won the national unity issue and the Tory leader, Jean Charest, won the lone debate, Mr Chrétien won the election, although returning with a much reduced majority. The Liberals lost twenty-two seats, leaving them with a majority of only four. Both the Conservatives and the NDP regained their party status in the House, and the Reform Party became the Official Opposition in place of the Bloc Québécois, now led by Gilles Duceppe.

The fact that the federal election campaign was dominated by the constitutional question reflected the continuing fallout from the narrow victory of the federalists in the 1995 Quebec referendum. In 1996, the federal government had launched an aggressive new, two-pronged strategy for dealing with Quebec's constitutional ambitions. Plan A, wooing Quebec with the lucrative possibilities of a renewed federalism, was balanced with the more hard-line Plan B. The centrepiece of Plan B was a constitutional reference to the Supreme Court in 1997 on the legality of provincial separation from Canada, and the obligations of the federal government in the case of a successful separatist referendum. The

Supreme Court delayed its consideration of the reference because of two vacancies on the Court's bench, and into this pause stepped the provincial and territorial leaders. Meeting in Calgary for their annual session in September, the premiers and territorial leaders held a long session debating constitutional reform. The result of this deliberation was the Calgary Declaration, a seven-point set of what were primarily platitudes aimed at providing the principles on which constitutional change might be built. The Declaration recognized the 'unique character' of Quebec society, and the role of the Quebec government in protecting and promoting that character, but also asserted that any constitutional change conferring new powers on a province must be available to all the provinces. Not surprisingly, the Declaration was issued by only nine of the premiers together with the two territorial leaders; Quebec's Lucien Bouchard called the principles 'insipid,' and rejected any constitutional change that did not recognize the Québécois as a people and further recognize that people's right to sovereignty and self-determination.

Beyond the arena of constitutional debate, 1997 also saw the reporting of a number of commissions on important scandals. In January, the government announced that the inquiry into the Canadian military's involvement in Somalia would be halted in June. This decision was somewhat controversial, as the commission complained that the arbitrary end date would compromise its ability to conduct a comprehensive investigation. The government stuck to its guns, and then compounded the problem, in some eyes, by arranging for the final report to be released on the Canada Day weekend, effectively hiding it from intensive media scrutiny. Nevertheless, the report was damning, as it ran to 1,700 pages and constituted a severe condemnation of military mismanagement and poor leadership. In September, the way was finally cleared for the Krever Commission into the tainted blood scandal to release its report. It had been delayed by a court challenge to its ability to release names in the report, but once the Supreme Court upheld its right to do so, the report was released in November. The report was something of an anticlimax, however, as it did not ascribe culpability, and governments had already instituted much of what it recommended. Finally, in December, the provincial inquiry into the Westray Mine disaster in Nova Scotia reported, despite not having heard from the mine's managers. The report condemned the company for ignoring workers' safety in the pursuit of profits and further charged the Department of Natural Resources as 'wilfully blind' and the inspectors of the Department of Labour as 'incompetent.'

Nova Scotia's neighbour lost its popular and long-serving premier in

1997. When he was first elected, performing a clean sweep of the province's ridings, New Brunswick Premier Frank McKenna had said that ten years was long enough for anyone to be premier. The ten-year anniversary of Mr McKenna's stunning defeat of the Conservatives under Richard Hatfield was marked on 10 October, and despite having denied rumours of his departure throughout the year, it also marked the end of his tenure in the Premier's Office. No other provincial premier left office in 1997, although Alberta's Ralph Klein did put himself before the voters in a general election on 11 March. The Conservative victory in that election was never in doubt; the only real questions were whether the Opposition would splinter and what the size of Mr Klein's majority would be. In the end, the Conservatives took 51 per cent of the vote, and sixty-three of the eighty-three seats in the provincial legislature.

The spring also saw the worst flooding in Manitoba in more than a century, with waters reaching levels not seen since 1826. The Red River rose to these unprecedented levels in April and May, leading to a massive effort to protect people and property from the waters – an effort aided by the military providing its 'aid to the civil power.' As the waters were rising, the federal government called its general election, to the genuine anger and disgust of many in Manitoba. It was seen as another indication of the how the Liberals ignored the needs of Western Canada in general and Manitoba in particular. There was some call for the election to be postponed in the most heavily affected ridings, but the Elections Commissioner visited the areas and said that the vote could go ahead as planned. Mr Chrétien did not help his cause – when he visited Winnipeg, he was handed a single sandbag and was heard asking what to do with it! It is unclear whether the timing hurt the Liberals in Manitoba, although they did lose six of the twelve seats they had held at dissolution.

While the Canadian economy appeared to be quite robust in the year, riding on the tails of a buoyant U.S. economy which was powering global growth, 1997 did see a real shock hit some of the world's economies. The Asian economies, which had been growing faster than any others, fell into a financial crisis. The full effects of the crisis were not felt during the year, but it was a sobering reminder of the fragility of the economic good fortune that was leading to record revenues and the return of fiscal surpluses. The crisis also had a differential effect across the country, as some regions were more closely tied to the Asian markets.

In the midst of this crisis, Canada played host to the leaders of the APEC in Vancouver. The summit was marked by demonstrations by those opposed both to the practices of global economic neo-liberalism and to the human-rights records of some of the APEC guests, in particular, President Suharto of Indonesia, who was the target of human-rights protesters. The federal government chose to impose very severe security restrictions on the meetings and on the protesters around the meetings. There was considerable concern that the government was stifling the free expression of political dissent in Vancouver in the interest of not embarrassing President Suharto. The concern was even more pronounced when the RCMP used what seemed to be excessive force against some of the protesters. In particular, there was an outcry when an RCMP officer was shown spraying a fire-extinguisher sized cannister of pepper spray into the face of a student protester. The Prime Minister again did not help matters by belittling the effect of pepper spray, referring to it as a condiment rather than a riot-control chemical.

British Columbia was also at the heart of the principal issue in Canada's relationship with its U.S. neighbour in 1997, when the long-simmering dispute over Pacific salmon fishing off the BC coast flamed up. The conflict was marked by rancorous international negotiations. Talks with the United States broke down several times during the year, with the United States refusing to refer the issue to an international court for settlement. It was also marked by rancour within the country. BC Premier Glen Clark took on the federal government, exasperated at the failure to reach an agreement with the United States. Things only got worse in the summer when BC fishers blockaded an Alaskan ferry in the Prince Rupert harbour as retaliation for apparent overfishing.

Otherwise, Canada's international affairs were rather more productive. The new foreign minister, Lloyd Axworthy, continued to be an extremely active force in the world, promoting his agenda of human security. In 1996, he had issued a challenge to world leaders to negotiate a treaty to ban the manufacture and use of anti-personnel land-mines, and had invited those same leaders to gather in Ottawa in December 1997 to sign the treaty. The goal was far-reaching and ambitious. Mr Axworthy sought to lift the issue of a ban on land-mines out of the multilateral arms control forum, in which it had stagnated, and create a major international convention in the space of a year. He succeeded. In what is likely to be seen as the crowning achievement of his time as foreign minister, Mr Axworthy was able to welcome 122 nations to sign the Ottawa Convention, although the United States was not among them. Perhaps as important was that the process which had gone on over the course of the year to produce this outcome was quite different to conventional treaty negotiations, particularly on arms control. Non-government organizations, notably the International Campaign to Ban Landmines, played a central role in the negotiating process. Indeed, the

ICBL and its head, Jodi Williams, would beat out Mr Axworthy for the Nobel Peace Prize for its efforts. However, the more important consequence is the example of productive collaboration between state and NGOs in the creation of a global security convention.

In Europe, the North Atlantic Treaty Organization continued its drive to renew its relevance in the post–Cold War world. Since the fall of the Berlin Wall and the collapse of the eastern European regimes, the newly democratic states of east and central Europe had been seeking admission to the Alliance. While never ruling it out, NATO had tried throughout the first half of the 1990s to put off the applicants with various programs short of membership. By 1995 this strategy had run its course, and the Alliance had decided to open itself to eastern European members. In 1997, NATO issued its first invitations for membership to the Czech Republic, Poland, and Hungary, with the expectation that they would join the Alliance in 1999, in time for the organization's 50th anniversary.

The federal perspective

ROBERT EVERETT

Parliament and politics

Trends in long-term tracking by pollsters strongly suggested that the outcome of the 1997 general election was all but sealed long before the campaign began. After earning a majority victory in 1993, the Liberal Party had maintained a degree of public support that foreshadowed an easy reprise. Although the Liberal record in power was not unblemished or uncontestable, the government of Jean Chrétien could point to accomplishments such as reducing annual budget deficits to the point where they would soon be a memory, and generally conducting its affairs in a low-key manner. The party was poised to cultivate support in every region of the country, a boast that no other party could make in the otherwise regionalized political culture of Canada. All of the opposition parties lagged well behind the front-running Liberals. It seemed as if the 'natural' governing party was truly reinstalled after the Progressive Conservative interregnum of 1984–93.

When viewers settled in front of their televisions on the evening of 2 June, however, the first results from the polls were startling. New Democratic Party candidates had picked off previously elusive Nova Scotia ridings in a wave of repudiation for the Liberals. The Progressive Conservatives had also defeated Liberal candidates in Atlantic Canada (including high-profile cabinet ministers). Was an upset in the making? Breathless commentators were basking in the possibility of a dramatic, made-for-television story written by Canadian voters. As it turned out, the comeuppance dealt to the Liberals on the East Coast was an isolated phenomenon. The party's candidates were returned in sufficient numbers to reclaim a majority in the House. In large part this reprieve was a gift from steadfast Ontario, where all but two ridings fell to the Liberals. But the size of the overall lead in the House was narrow, and the evening-ending tally of votes in the western part of the country made for a nail-biting finale.

There were consolations for all of the established parties, yet emotions were mixed and the celebrations were muted all around. It was by no means the sternest rebuke suffered by a ruling party, as the *Ottawa Citizen* rightly noted in a morning-after editorial (3 June), and Liberal strategists had anticipated some slippage in popular votes and seats. Even so, the mood in party headquarters was one of relief rather than exultation. The Liberals retained their pre-eminence and maintained their majority, but the caucus looked to have some craggy edges that might need careful tending by the whips. There would also be a slender wall of votes with which to rebuff a concerted Opposition siege.

Reform took a potentially momentous step in its evolution by emerging as the Official Opposition. Despite this lift, Preston Manning's party once again failed to make any gains east of Manitoba. More than that, the party surrendered its solitary Ontario outpost to the Liberals. For the Bloc Québécois, the loss of Official Opposition status smarted; but, if nothing else, the party under leader Gilles Duceppe recovered from a dismal start to the campaign and clung to first place on its home turf. While the New Democrats and Alexa McDonough rejoiced at the historic breakthrough in the Atlantic provinces, the harvest in the East was offset by the grim results in Ontario. The heartland remained barren electoral terrain for the party, especially for a handful of star candidates in Toronto and the southwest. It was equally frustrating that erstwhile NDP voters in the West continued to flirt with Reform rather than coming home to roost. Progressive Conservatives surged in New Brunswick and claimed a smattering of victories in Quebec. Voters elsewhere proved much more fickle towards Jean Charest's team, and Tory blue faded as votes elsewhere were tallied.

Looking back on the year, some commentators felt that it was one of the least consequential in the recent life of Parliament. Although punctuated by the election, the rhythm of politics seemed predictable and dull. Perhaps this feeling was caused by the fact that House sittings were interrupted and truncated by the campaign. It might have been engendered by the sense that much of the business finished in the weeks before the election was actually carried over from the previous year, and that many bills introduced in the autumn still awaited final passage as 1997 closed. There was also a vivid impression that the Liberals were staying the course, contentedly taking care of Parliament in the absence of any semblance of concerted Opposition. In the view of many, the party was safely ensconced by default because of the multiparty, regional political landscape (a perception that helped amplify calls for a 'united right' merger of Reform and the Tories to challenge the Liberals).

Dramatic initiatives, it is true, seemed few and far between. Yet the year was not without consequence. Some of the legislation passed – or derailed – touched on matters of vital interest. The debate over how to use the windfall from budget surpluses was especially sharp, even if it was not fully resolved. A tricky reference to the Supreme Court on the constitutionality of a unilateral declaration of sovereignty by Quebec was in the offing. As briefs arrived at the Court, the political arguments – far more important to the future of Confederation – continued. Observers may have felt that there was little vision in the realm of political discourse, but this was a deception.

The 1997 general election

An early election?

Liberal fortunes had been soaring since the 1993 election. A long run of consistently favourable approval ratings for the party was almost unprecedented. Both the government and Prime Minster Chrétien maintained their popularity. As 1996 gave way to a new year, the only downside was a perceptible erosion of confidence in Mr Chrétien's performance. This fuelled media conjecture about the possibility of a quicker-than-normal return to the polls. Although the Liberals were just over three years into the maximum five-year mandate, the time might be right to face the electorate before attitudes hardened against the government or voters took a shine to one of the fractious Opposition parties. The only rival on the rise was the Progressive Conservative Party led by Jean Charest. Yet the Tory revival was incomplete, despite the lift derived from having a popular leader, and the party had not yet broken through the 20 per cent threshold in opinion polls. Reform and the New Democratic Party trailed the Conservatives, while the Bloc Québécois, competitive in its home province, was confined within Quebec's borders. The calculus of election calls is difficult to master, but hints dropped by the Liberals in the early months of the year suggested that they were gearing up for a campaign that would come sooner rather than later.

The writs are issued

Mr Chrétien announced the dissolution of the House on 27 April. Even though the government's mandate was not due to expire for another sixteen months, ballots would be cast on 2 June. With Canada at a crossroads, said Mr Chrétien, and in need of a government capable of positioning the country for the new century, the time had come to consult voters again. The Prime Minister insisted that his cabinet had fulfilled most of the Liberal promises made during the 1993 election campaign and needed a fresh mandate. Other parties were critical of the timing. Tory leader Jean Charest argued that, with more than a million unemployed Canadians, the House should be concentrating on economic revival. Reform's Preston Manning described the early call as an 'abuse of process' and argued for U.S.-style fixed-term mandates.

Optics were bad for the Liberals on another score. The day before the call came, Mr Chrétien flew into Winnipeg for a quick tour as the waters of the Red River swelled. It appeared as if the Prime Minister had organized an unseemly photo opportunity on the eve of what became one of the most devastating floods in Canadian history. Controversy crested long after the floodwaters receded. Many Manitobans thought that the election should be suspended for ninety days (permissible in emergency circumstances under the Election Act). Mr Chrétien deferred to the chief electoral officer, Jean-Pierre Kingsley, who eventually determined that the count should go ahead despite the clean-up (Canadian Press Newswire, 4 May). It was only when Winnipeg Mayor Susan Thompson publicly thanked the Prime Minister for providing material assistance and military personnel that the criticisms abated, for the mayor was a known Conservative.

The approaching campaign led to a flurry of activity on the Hill. The month of April saw the House and Senate busily tidying up a number of critically important pieces of legislation. The pace was particularly rapid for the approval of the so-called anti-biker legislation aimed at curbing motorcycle gang violence and the dispute over territory that had unleashed a reign of terror and death in Quebec. Among other bills cleared for royal assent in the last days of Parliament were ones sanctioning free trade between Canada and Chile, banning the importation and interprovincial traffic in the gasoline additive MMT, limiting the advertisement of tobacco products, and establishing a new regime for copyright.

In the rush some bills were crowded out. One piece of legislation that lapsed was a private member's bill that nearly made it all the way to royal assent. Bill C-261 was crafted to ban the practice of negative option billing when new television services were added by cable companies. Sponsored by Liberal backbencher Roger Gallaway, the legislation had its origins in the 'cable revolt' of 1995 when subscribers balked at being automatically signed up for a package of new domestic channels unless they returned a form mailed by cable services. The bill made it through the House despite the cabinet's hardened attitude. Passage was assured when a clutch of Liberals broke ranks with the leadership. The ride in the Senate was rougher. Lobbyists worked hard to defeat the bill, which, it was feared, would make it difficult to sustain French-language and less-popular programming without bundling services together. An amended version was sent back to the House, where the Bloc refused to expedite consideration and thereby consigned the bill to oblivion.

Mr Gallaway's bill was not the only one to slip out of the parliamentary net. Several major government bills were stranded on the order-paper. They included changes to the Indian Act (opposed by the Assembly of First Nations), which would give some bands more say in reserve management. The campaign also interrupted the legislative life of bills aimed at amending the Canada Labour Code on the question of how to determine if the use of strikebreakers would be permitted; extending federal government powers over the preservation of some endangered species; establishing a national DNA bank for convicted violent offenders; regulating and restricting numerous reproductive technologies; and setting up a network of local authorities to take the place of federal authorities in the operation of major ports.

At the end of the Thirty-fifth Parliament there were one hundred and seventy-four Liberals in the House. Reform and the Bloc were tied with fifty seats each. The New Democrats and the Progressive Conservatives had nine and two members respectively. Three seats were vacant and, in the wake of a series of shake-outs and resignations, there were six independents.

The Liberal Party

The Liberal platform was officially released on 30 April. Unfortunately for Mr Chrétien, Preston Manning had impishly leaked the contents of Red Book Two four days earlier. The Reform leader took the occasion to lampoon the governing party for plotting a course for an old-fashioned, big-government spending spree once the post-deficit era arrived. Although the manifesto was not exactly penurious, it was largely perceived as cautious. In terms of budget surpluses, the Liberals favoured a fifty-fifty split of the dividends between new program spending and tax and debt reduction. Some of the key planks had already been announced or implied in government initiatives (such as an infusion of $6 billion in health funding transfers to the provinces and money for, and an extension of, a grant program for research into the cause and treatment of AIDS).

Among other promises outlined in the revised Red Book were the following:

– serious and sincere negotiations aimed at constitutinal recognition of Quebec's 'uniqueness';
– tax credits for in-home family care of elderly parents; and,
– funding for a national 'pharmacare' program in conjunction with the provinces.

Within the Liberal camp, a number of incumbents decided that they had fought their last campaign. One-time cabinet minister and periodic maverick Warren Allmand resigned from one of the safest Liberal seats in the country in order to succeed Ed Broadbent (an NDP leader in the 1970s and early 1980s) as head of the International Centre for Human Rights and Development. Indian Affairs Minister Ron Irwin announced that he would not seek election. In Nova Scotia, Russ MacLellan gave up federal politics to seek the leadership of the provincial party (he succeeded). Jack Anawak retired from the House after fifteen years in order to serve as the first commissioner for the newly created territory of Nunavut. Kitchener area MP John English pulled out of the campaign so that he could care for his wife as she battled cancer.

One Liberal incumbent left the scene unwillingly. In St John's, Jean Payne lost her bid for re-nomination thanks to a dark cloud hanging over an RCMP investigation into a government loan received by one of her businesses. The police ultimately decided not to proceed with charges on 12 May, too late for Ms Payne. Another East Coast Liberal, Nova Scotian Roseanne Skoke, also departed in ignominious circumstances. Ms Skoke was an ardent (and, for the government, embarrassing) foe of human-rights legislation guaranteeing equal treatment of gays and lesbians. Local riding members obligingly saved the national office from having to refuse to sign Ms Skoke's papers, as had been rumoured. Later in the year the former MP vied for the leadership of the Nova Scotia party against Mr MacLellan. She was trounced.

As he had done in 1993, Mr Chrétien exercised his discretionary powers to bypass customary selection processes and selected candidates in several ridings. Once again all of those handed a free pass to the campaign were women. The rank and file were mightily aggrieved, at least in some ridings, by Mr Chrétien's actions in 1993. This time around the anointments caused less of a stir. Those selected by Mr Chrétien were former Ontario cabinet minister Elinor Caplan (in Thornhill); municipal councillor Judy Sgro in the Toronto riding of York–

South Weston; local politician Judi Longfield in Whitby–Ajax; Sophia Leung in Vancouver–Kingsway; and Karen Redman in Kitchener. Ms Sgro was the designated rival of the popular incumbent, independent member John Nunziata. It was bound to be a scuffle given Mr Nunziata's break with the Liberals over the failure of the government to keep its word to abolish the Goods and Services Tax and the party's fervent wish to see him gone. The designations meant that the Liberal Party exceeded its goal of 25 per cent female candidates across the country. The NDP had the highest proportion of female candidates while Reform had the fewest.

Bloc Québécois

The first order of business for the Bloc Québécois was to elect a successor to Michel Gauthier. The whipsawed former leader had quit in late 1996 after coming under pressure from within the caucus and the broader sovereignty movement. One of the first announced contestants was a former Bloc MP, Jean Alfred. His candidacy was nullified when he failed to deliver the minimum number of required nomination signatures. This left the field to three sitting MPs, a pair of former Quebec cabinet ministers and a well-known Bloc adviser and media commentator. Emerging from within caucus were Gilles Duceppe, Francine Lalonde, and Pierrette Venne. Mr Duceppe was the best-known individual among this trio, having been the first Bloc member elected to the House and one of the more active participants in debates. Ms Lalonde had lost to Mr Gauthier in a two-person contest in 1996 but was not considered a front runner. Chances were also slight for Ms Venne, a onetime Progressive Conservative MP who entered the fray late in the day.

Facing off against this group were ex-Parti Québécois cabinet ministers Rodrique Biron and Yves Duhaime. Both enjoyed a degree of celebrity within Quebec, but Mr Duhaime, who was preparing to take on Jean Chrétien in the Prime Minister's riding, was considered a front runner for the leadership. Rounding out the slate was Daniel Turp. Easily distinguished by his bow-tied bonhomie on frequent television appearances, Mr Turp was a seasoned Bloc adviser who, many suspected, helped engineer the downfall of Mr Gauthier.

The convention was held on 15 March. In 1996 Mr Gauthier was chosen by a small cadre of invited party elites. This time around the process was more elaborate, the electorate was much more representative and the setting was reminiscent of a conventional party gathering. It took just two ballots for Mr Duceppe to win the leadership. As predicted, his triumph was thought to be tragic by a number of Bloc members. After all, Mr Duceppe had steered clear of the 1996 contest after being convinced that his selection would be divisive. Now that he was installed as the head of the Bloc, ripples of discontent broke the surface. Backbencher Nic Leblanc resigned from caucus to sit as an independent while the runner-up, Mr Duhaime, wondered aloud if he should run in Chicoutimi after all (he eventually did). It was too soon to tell how Mr Duceppe's leadership might impact on the Bloc's electoral success. Some observers predicted that he would be a liability, given his wooden public personality and a tendency to improvise. To be fair, it would be difficult for anyone to succeed, even at a remove, the estimable Lucien Bouchard.

The Bloc's platform was unveiled on 26 April. Uncharitable commentators considered the platform an incoherent hodgepodge that reflected the wide ideological spectrum embraced by the nationalist movement. To be sure, the Bloc called for an end to the heritage ministry's unity 'propaganda' campaigns and affirmed that it would lend whatever assistance it could towards realizing the sovereignty project. Apart from its independence agenda, the Bloc pledged to work for a cut in Employment Insurance premiums and for a national policy on job sharing. Both planks were designed to stimulate the economy, as was a plan to allow unemployed individuals to draw on their Registered Retirement Savings without penalty if they used the funds for new business ventures.

Bloc member André Caron died on 10 January. This left the Bloc and Reform tied at fifty members each, and Mr Manning tried once again to persuade the Commons that his party should assume the role of Official Opposition. This effort was once again thwarted by other parties, and speaker Gilbert Parent, who had previously done so in a similar circumstance, ruled that the Bloc should retain its status on the principle that incumbency takes precedence in the event of a tie. The Bloc headed into the election as the Official Opposition Party, but its chances of retaining this status looked dim at the outset.

Reform Party

Reform would also head into the election without some leading incumbents. Stephen Harper resigned on 14 January. The bilingual Mr Harper, considered a leader-in-waiting by many in the rank and file, immediately took up the position of vice-president of the National Citizens Coalition, a right-wing anti-tax lobby group. If all went according to plan,

Mr Harper would inherit the presidency from the Coalition's founder, David Sommerville. On 9 March, Bob Ringma bowed out of federal politics. The BC Reformer had been at the centre of a maelstrom in 1996 when he made comments that were decried as racist and homophobic. The ensuing strife within the caucus led to his suspension and the departure of Alberta MP Jan Brown. Other Reform MPs bowed out in 1996. Among those who declined to seek another term were Jim Silye, Ray Speaker, Herb Grubel, and Ontario's Ed Harper, the lone incumbent east of Manitoba.

Reform's platform was outlined in its Fresh Start campaign launched in October 1996. Mr Manning refreshed memories on 4 February. Reform emphasized themes of law and order, tax reduction, and 'traditional' values. Tax reduction was a pivotal objective. By the year 2000 every taxpayer would receive a break of $2,000. A Reform government would balance the budget within two years, after which the tax cuts would kick in. To preserve so-called traditional family values, Reform would increase tax credits for spouses, institute new credits for parents who cared for children in the home, and crack down on domestic violence, child prostitution, and pornography. Other promises included adopting tougher sentencing guidelines, applying stricter parole, and protecting victims' rights; establishing a more decentralized federation and providing a detailed response to Quebec's demands; and providing greater accountability in the political system through devices such as free votes in the House, recall petitions, and referenda.

New Democratic Party

The New Democratic Party was one of three established parties that would enter the election with a new leader. Alexa McDonough had led the Nova Scotia NDP on the provincial hustings but this was her first attempt at the federal level. Although she did not have a seat in the Commons, and was not as prominent as the leaders of other parliamentary parties, Ms McDonough had travelled far and wide to galvanize the party faithful. Meanwhile, her predecessor, Audrey McLaughlin, announced that she would not run again in the Yukon. Ms McDonough disappointed some NDP loyalists by conceding the election to the Liberals during a 12 April address to a national convention in Regina. Most Canadians expected the Liberals to triumph again, she said. Therefore the main objectives for the party were to reclaim official party status and to return a 'record number' of NDP members. As she opened the party's campaign, Ms McDonough said that the NDP wanted to be a vehicle for expressing the 'priorities of the people, not the powerful' (*Toronto Star*, 13 and 28 April).

The NDP platform was previewed at the Regina assembly and officially unwrapped on 1 May. The party's manifesto, entitled *A Framework for Canada's Future*, illuminated the uniqueness of the NDP's approach. Unlike other parties, fixated as they were on tax reductions, the NDP actually contemplated a few select but substantial tax rises. The party proposed to apply new taxes on the income and wealth of affluent Canadians and profitable corporations. The dividend would be invested in social programs. According to the party's formula, an immediate infusion of $9 billion would lay the foundation for additional spending, amounting to $19 billion over five years. At the other end of the income scale, there would be relief for taxpayers. This would be accomplished through a combination of measures such as removing the Goods and Services Tax from certain items (such as books, magazines, and children's clothing), eliminating the personal income surtax on lower- and middle-income earners, and enhancing tax credits for those in need. The NDP also wanted to see national programs for child care and pharmacare.

The NDP's central campaign theme turned on employment creation and job stability. The party wanted to set an unemployment target of not more than 5.4 per cent by the year 2001. This goal would be enshrined in a National Employment Act that would enforce job creation priorities. Another NDP idea designed to increase the size of payrolls was the development of a national environment program by which the government would fund capital projects for public transit, sewage facilities, and water treatment.

Progressive Conservative Party

The Tories were led by Jean Charest. Although no stranger to Parliament and governance, Mr Charest was a neophyte at the helm. Despite his evident popularity (he was especially well liked in Quebec), Mr Charest had inherited the mantle of leadership by default. The Progressive Conservatives had been reduced to a rump in the drubbing of 1993, and Mr Charest was the sole Tory willing and able to take on the exceedingly daunting task of rebuilding a party weighed down by heavy debts and suffering from a tarnished image. Some high profile campaigners did offer themselves as candidates. Former major-general Lewis McKenzie, who helped coordinate international peacekeeping efforts in Bosnia, won the nomination in Ontario's Parry Sound–

Muskoka riding. Independent MP Jan Brown adopted the Tory banner in a bid to unseat Reform Leader Preston Manning, her former boss.

The Conservative Party's platform was published on 18 March. Entitled *Let the Future Begin*, the document's key planks emphasized themes first trumpeted at the party's 1996 policy convention. The Tories promised to balance the books by the year 2000 (a safe bet), but would do so while cutting personal taxes by 10 per cent and chopping Employment Insurance premiums. Health and education transfers to the provinces, reduced by the Liberal government, would be restored to the $14 billion level, up some $1.4 billion. The Progressive Conservatives also pledged to repeal the Liberal's gun control legislation and enact a victim's bill of rights. Although the platform tilted to the right (and Reform accused the Tories of poaching its ideas), Mr Charest softened the message sent to the Tory rank and file during his campaign sojourns.

Other parties and independents

The general election of 1997 featured some 1,672 candidates (down from 2,155 in 1993) vying for 301 seats (up from 295). Most were obscure in the minds of the voters and certainly in the media. Ten parties managed to clear the new higher hurdles for designation on ballots. In addition to the parties represented in Parliament at dissolution, citizens could also cast votes for candidates of the Natural Law, Green, Marxist-Leninist, Canada Action, and Christian Heritage parties. All other candidates were designated as unaffiliated even if they were not strictly independent. The Communist Party challenged the criteria for party status in the courts. It lost. The newest formation on the scene was the Canada Action Party. Founded by former Liberal cabinet minister Paul Hellyer, who later went on to contest the Conservative leadership, the party was introduced to voters by means of a widely distributed comic book in which Mr Hellyer offered his populist economic diagnosis and remedies.

Among sitting independent members, Gilles Bernier decided not to contest the election. By stepping aside he created an opening in the Beauce that the Liberals exploited. Mr Bernier, a one-time Tory MP, was rewarded with the ambassadorship in Haiti after the election. Jan Brown cast her lot with the Conservatives. John Nunziata announced that he would run again in the Toronto area riding of York South–Weston. Although he would face formidable opposition in the person of Judy Sgro, it appeared that the maverick former Liberal had a very real chance to equal Mr Bernier's 1993 feat of running successfully without party affiliation. Meanwhile the campaign of Jag Bhaduria was quixotic at best. The disgraced former Liberal had little hope of winning against the regular party candidate in Markham.

The campaign

As it turned out, the election of 1997 was dominated by questions of national unity. Mr Chrétien helped set the stage when he indicated, just before the campaign got under way, that national unity was always the main priority of any government. Although the constitutional future of Canada and Quebec was front and centre, the debate was often conducted on vague terms. There was little talk of substantive initiatives. Instead the focus was on broad approaches to the constitutional order. By most accounts, Reform seized control of the agenda with its distinctive combination of strict equality for all ten provinces and decentralization of powers. The Bloc Québécois – which Mr Chrétien referred to as the other side of the Reform coin – also featured prominently in the coverage of the issue.

Ironically, the Bloc stumbled out of the gate. En route to a campaign stop, the press party, following Mr Duceppe and his entourage, found themselves in the company of a bus driver with poor navigational skills. Lost on the road, the journalists had a field-day with the mix-up. The driver was fired. Mr Duceppe might have wished he had never made his way to a photo-opportunity tour of a cheese factory earlier in the opening fortnight. Required to don sanitary garb, including a floppy hairnet, Mr Duceppe was snapped in an unbecoming pose that delighted editorial cartoonists in Quebec and elsewhere. Worse for Mr Duceppe, who was not exactly a charismatic campaigner, it proved difficult to emerge from the shadow cast by Lucien Bouchard. Mr Duceppe's predecessor, now installed in the Premier's Office in Quebec City, 'invited himself' to the leader's nomination meeting. This gave rise to accusations that the Bloc was little more than a junior partner to the Parti Québécois. It did little to help when the director-general of the PQ was summoned to replace the Bloc's original campaign director, who had bowed out amid concerns about organization.

Another blow for the Bloc came on 8 May. That was the day when former Quebec premier Jacques Parizeau published his book entitled *Pour un Québec souveran*. In a media interview with Michel Vastel, the former premier revealed that the Parti Québécois government had planned to issue a declaration of sovereignty immediately after the 1995 referendum if the 'yes' side had won. This bluntly contradicted assurances that the referendum would animate a negotiation process and that any settlement would be submitted for ratification in a second referendum. Mr Parizeau claimed that he had been misunderstood. He meant to say that such a declaration would be suspended during the consultation round. Nevertheless the damage was done.

One of the outcomes of the Bloc's travails was an intensification of the focus on national unity and Quebec's future. The customary leader debates reinforced attention on this issue. The first debate was conducted in English on 12 May. Mr Chrétien was the unwanted centre of attention as the other debaters excoriated him from all sides. Mr Charest was thought to have handled himself well, earning the evening's only spontaneous applause with his passionate commitment to bequeath his children the country he had inherited from his parents. The French-language debate was held, or at least started, one night later. Just as the crucial topic of national unity was about to be broached, the event's moderator, Claire Lamarche, passed out at her desk. Ms Lamarche, who had a history of fainting due to low blood pressure, recovered nicely. Several nights later the leaders picked up where they left off with a forty-five-minute discussion of unity and sovereignty.

There was a third major debate during the campaign, but Alexa McDonough was the only leader to attend the event sponsored by the National Action Committee on the Status of Women (NAC). Other parties were represented by sitting MPs or candidates. Ms McDonough enjoyed the warmest reception while Reform's Nancy Branscombe received hostile reactions from the audience.

Not everyone was pleased that the campaign narrative featured unity. For her part Alexa McDonough was concerned that the dominance of the issue overwhelmed the NDP's insistence that job creation should be the pre-eminent political priority. In a paraphrase of the 1992 presidential campaign of Bill Clinton, Ms McDonough insisted that the election was 'about jobs, stupid.' While other issues did come to the fore, such as the advent of budget surpluses and how they should be used, unity invariably bounced back into the headlines. Reporters peppered the leaders with questions about the threshold required in any referendum on sovereignty (Mr Chrétien maintained that a 50 per cent plus one vote was not necessarily a sufficient precondition for a dramatic change) and the fate of the Canadian union.

National unity was pivotal because, in part, it captured some essential differences between the parties. Reform was particularly interested in keeping the issue alive given the party's origins in opposition to previous strategies for dealing with Quebec sovereignty and national unity.

Some said that the party hijacked the campaign agenda. To take one example, a new batch of Reform advertisements appeared on 23 May. In them Reform decried the domination of the unity agenda by Quebec. They also lumped Mr Chrétien and Mr Charest in with sovereignists on the national and provincial stages by implying that national unity affected everyone, not just 'Quebec politicians.' Denunciations of this tactic were swift and sharp. Reform took heat from all sides for sowing division with a message that some argued verged on racism.

Meanwhile, Mr Duceppe, who appeared to have rebounded from the disastrous early days of the campaign, stumbled in an interview televised on 28 May. Responding to a question about the possibility of internal partitions if Quebec separated from the rest of Canada, Mr Duceppe argued that this was both unimaginable and untenable. Why would it not be possible for some parts of Quebec to remain within Canada? Well, said Mr Duceppe, the Constitution protects Canada against partition. The Bloc leader was painted as a hypocrite by federalists for this improbable analysis.

As the campaign wound down it was clear that the support for the Liberals had trailed off from the heady days prior to the election call. It was not clear how much impact this would have, but Mr Chrétien, taking no chances, began asking voters for a Liberal majority. A minority government in Ottawa would have difficulty steering through rocky constitutional shoals and economic challenges.

Results and aftermath

When the votes were tallied, the Liberals had won the majority they so desperately wanted. Down by twenty-two ridings, they clung to a four-seat cushion. Erosion of the Liberal vote resulted in a House in which there would be five official parties. The Tories and NDP exceeded the threshold of a dozen members and restored their eligibility for time allocation during question period, research funds, and other perquisites. Reform took over as the Official Opposition. The political map was decidedly regional in orientation. Although the Liberals had clung to their majority (a fortunate happenstance, said some observers, considering that instability might equate with vulnerability on the national unity front) and garnered seats in every part of the country, there were unmistakable geographic divisions. Reform dominated in British Columbia, Alberta, and Saskatchewan. The Bloc held onto a majority of ridings in Quebec. The NDP was anchored in pockets of the West and inherited custody of alienation in Nova Scotia.

TABLE 1
Projected and actual voting results, by party (Various Gallup Reports)

Party	28 January % Votes	25 April % Votes	16 May % Votes	29 May % Votes	Actual Results % Votes
Liberal Party	53	55	46	41	38
Reform	10	10	14	16	19
Progressive Conservative Party	18	15	19	22	19
New Democratic Party	9	9	9	11	11
Bloc Québécois	9	11	11	9	11
Bloc (Quebec only)	38	44	43	33	44
Other parties	1	1	1	<1	2

The electoral waves that buffeted the Liberals in Atlantic Canada dragged down two prominent cabinet members. In Nova Scotia, Health Minister David Dingwall was trumped by the NDP, and Defence Minister Doug Young lost in New Brunswick. Both were stunned by their defeats, but Mr Young quickly rebounded to form a consulting firm in Ottawa along with another toppled Grit, Paul Zed. A third cabinet member, Science Minister Jon Gerrard, was unseated in Manitoba. Prominent backbencher Mary Clancy lost to Alexa McDonough in Halifax, but landed on her feet in Boston, where she would serve as Canada's consul. Among independents, only John Nunziata managed to pull off a rare victory. A total of sixty-two women were elected, a figure that translated into just under 20 per cent of the House membership. In terms of party representation, thirty-six women were Liberals, eleven were members of the Bloc, eight ran as New Democrats, three were in the Reform caucus, and two were Progressive Conservatives. Voter turnout continued to fall. Ballots were cast by just 67 per cent of eligible voters in 1997, down from 75 per cent in 1988 and 70 per cent in 1993.

For Jean Charest the campaign was something of a personal triumph. He was credited with a stellar performance despite the party's disappointingly partial comeback. Although Mr Charest was stoical and upbeat in public, some party insiders whispered that life out of the political spotlight was dispiriting for the leader. There was also mounting speculation that he could be open to a summons to head up the provincial Liberal Party in Quebec. An Angus Reid / Société Radio Canada poll published on 9 December indicated that the Charest-led Liberals would defeat the Parti Québécois. For the moment, Mr Charest had 'no intention' of abandoning the House in order to don the mantle of saviour.

TABLE 2
Distribution of seats and share of votes by party and province

	Liberal Party		Reform		Block Québécois		New Democratic Party		Progressive Conservatives	
	Seats	% Votes	Seats	% Votes	Seats	% Votes	Seats	% Votes	Seats	% Votes
Newfoundland	4	37.9	0	2.5	0	0.0	0	22.0	3	36.8
Prince Edward Island	4	44.8	0	1.5	0	0.0	0	15.1	0	38.3
Nova Scotia	0	28.4	0	9.7	0	0.0	6	30.4	5	30.8
New Brunswick	3	32.9	0	13.1	0	0.0	2	18.4	5	35.0
Quebec	26	36.7	0	0.3	44	37.9	0	2.0	5	22.2
Ontario	101	49.5	0	19.1	0	0.0	0	10.7	1	18.8
Manitoba	1	34.3	3	23.7	0	0.0	4	23.2	1	17.8
Saskatchewan	2	24.7	8	36.0	0	0.0	5	30.9	0	7.8
Alberta	2	24.0	24	54.6	0	0.0	0	5.7	0	14.4
British Columbia	6	28.8	25	43.1	0	0.0	3	18.2	0	16.2
Yukon	0	22.0	0	25.3	0	0.0	1	28.9	0	13.9
Northwest Territories	2	43.1	0	11.7	0	0.0	0	20.9	0	16.7
Canada	155	38.5	60	19.4	44	10.7	21	11.0	20	18.8

Meanwhile Reform leader Preston Manning did an about-face on a 'no intention' stance of his own. On 20 June he announced that he would move into the Opposition leader's residence of Stornoway after all. The leader withstood an avalanche of criticism for his apparent hypocrisy.

The results also led to renewed calls for a united right-wing alternative to the Liberals. The combined votes for Reform and Tory candidates equalled the Liberal tally across the country. On 3 March, Ontario Premier Mike Harris added his voice to those favouring a serious think about the possibility. Mr Charest was even more adamant about a merger than his departure. Reform leader Preston Manning was far more inclined to entertain the possibility of a fused right-wing formation. A member of the caucus was designated to help build bridges and the party planned to confront the possibility squarely if cautiously.

The fate of the Bloc Québécois also hung in the balance. Now that the prestige and privileges of the Official Opposition status had passed to Reform, the raison d'être of the Bloc was harder to fathom, even for sovereignists. The power to dictate the course of events leading to a third referendum resided in the Assemblée nationale, and Bloc members seldom pretended to speak for all Canadians, as they did in the days of Official Opposition. However, on 11 December, Bloc leader Gilles Duceppe confirmed that the Bloc would not disband even if the voters of Quebec opted for sovereignty. It was important, he said, that negotiations between the province and Ottawa not be controlled entirely by federalists.

As for Jean Chrétien, speculation about his future began on the morning after the election when some headline articles forecasted that pressure would mount for him to resign before the next campaign. He had long been branded as 'yesterday's man' by opponents. After such a close race there were rumours that he would step aside for a younger, more dynamic leader. The name of Finance Minister Paul Martin inevitably came to mind when the subject of Mr Chrétien's departure came up. The Prime Minister refuted any such suggestions (to do otherwise would have made him seem a lame duck) and insisted that he was looking forward to greeting the new millennium from the Prime Minister's Office. Across the floor, Alexa McDonough was just beginning her career in the House. While secure in her position, she suffered a fate often dealt to NDP leaders, that of virtual invisibility in the media.

The new cabinet

Renovations to the cabinet began promptly, as did media curiosity about the changes. Resignations and defeats opened up a handful of

TABLE 3
Party standings after recent elections

	1988 (Total seats 289)	1993 (Total seats 295)	1997 (Total seats 301)
Liberals	83	177	155
Progressive Conservatives	163	2	20
New Democratic Party	43	9	21
Bloc Québécois	0	54	44
Reform	0	52	60
Independent	0	1	1

positions. More importantly, Ottawa journalists were anxious to see if the composition of the new inner circle would tip off how the Liberals planned to deal with the coming surplus. Ontario MP Carolyn Parrish predicted a 'left-wing' tilt, while others were convinced that the new cabinet would have a more 'beneficent face' (*Globe and Mail*, 8 June). If anything the line-up introduced on 11 June appeared to reflect a disposition to stand pat. This was undoubtedly true of the key economic portfolios of finance, industry, and the treasury board, and in the sensitive areas of intergovernmental and foreign affairs. It was perhaps less obvious in the other choices, but there were only five fresh faces from the Commons (along with Senator Alisdar Gillespie). Mr Chrétien decided not to recruit highly touted prospects such as Elinor Caplan, a former minister in Ontario. He also bypassed the brace of new members from Quebec despite the consequence of hearing charges that the province was slighted in the formation of the cabinet. The size of the inner cabinet grew from twenty-three to twenty-seven members. In addition there were nine secretaries of state. One secretary position went unfilled for a week, time enough for a judicial recount to confirm the election of Gilbert Normand.

No change in portfolio:

- Prime Minister: Jean Chrétien
- Minister of Foreign Affairs: Lloyd Axworthy
- Minister of Transport: David Collenette
- President of the Queen's Privy Council and Minister of Intergovernmental Affairs: Stéphane Dion
- President of the Treasury Board and Minister Responsible for Infrastructure: Marcel Massé
- Minister of Industry: John Manley

- Minister of Finance: Paul Martin
- Minister of Human Resources Development: Pierre Pettigrew
- Minister of Citizenship and Immigration: Lucienne Robillard

Continuing with a new portfolio:

- Deputy Prime Minister: Herb Gray (from Government Leader in the House)
- Leader of the Government in the House of Commons: Don Boudria (from International Development and la Francophonie)
- Minister of Canadian Heritage: Sheila Copps (loses Deputy Prime Ministership)
- Minister for International Trade: Sergio Marchi (from Environment)
- Minister of Natural Resources and Canadian Wheat Board: Ralph Goodale (from Agriculture)
- Minister for International Cooperation and for la Francophonie: Diane Marleau (from Public Works)
- Minister of Fisheries and Oceans: David Anderson (from Transport)
- Minister of National Defence: Art Eggleton (from International Trade)
- Minster of Justice and Attorney General of Canada: Anne McLellan (from Natural Resources)
- Minister of Health: Allan Rock (from Justice)
- Minister of Public Works and Government Services: Alfonso Gagliano (from Labour)
- Minister of Veterans Affairs and Atlantic Canada Opportunities Agency: Fred Mifflin (from Fisheries)
- Minister of Labour: Lawrence MacAulay (from Veteran's Affairs)
- Minister of Indian Affairs and Northern Development: Jane Stewart (from Revenue)

Promoted from the secretary of state level:

- Minister of the Environment: Christine Stewart

Promoted from the backbench:

Minister of Agriculture and Agri Food: Lyle Vanclief
- Minister of National Revenue: Herb Dhaliwal
- Solictor General of Canada: Andy Scott
- Leader of the Government in the Senate: Alasdair Graham

Continuing at the secretary of state level:

- Secretary of State (Children and Youth): Ethel Blondin-Andrew
- Secretary of State (Asia-Pacific): Raymond Chan
- Secretary of State (Federal Office of Regional Development – Quebec): Martin Cauchon
- Secretary of State (Multiculturalism) (Status of Women): Hedy Fry
- Secretary of State (Latin America and Africa): David Kilgour

Secretaries of State promoted from the backbench:

- Secretary of State (International Financial Institutions): James Peterson
- Secretary of State (Science, Research, and Development and Western Economic Diversification): Ronald J. Duhamel
- Secretary of State (Parks): Andrew Mitchell
- Secretary of State (Agriculture and Agri-Food Canada and Fisheries and Oceans): Gilbert Normand

First session of the Thirty-sixth Parliament

As MPs old and new gathered on the Hill in anticipation of Parliament's opening, their first chore was to elect a Speaker of the House. Gilbert Parent wanted to keep the job he had won in 1994, but re-election was by no means assured. Two other backbench Liberals also openly coveted the position: Roger Gallaway from Ontario and Quebec's Clifford Lincoln. Mr Gallaway campaigned hard and even allowed cameras from the Cable Public Affairs Channel to follow along as he toured the corridors of Parliament Hill in search of votes. There was an intriguing fourth candidate, none other than John Nunziata, the former Liberal now elected as an independent. The slate of candidates, coupled with a secret ballot, ensured that the voting process was a long one. Mr Nunziata's candidacy also offered an irresistible invitation to make the government squirm, and it was clear that even some Liberal backbenchers cast their lot with Reform in backing Mr Nunziata. For all of his exertions, Mr Gallaway was eliminated on the second ballot. Mr Lincoln suffered the same fate in the next round. In a head-to-head finale, Mr Parent edged out Mr Nunziata.

Business began in earnest with the reading of the Speech from the Throne by Governor General Romeo Leblanc on 23 September. If there was a unifying theme in the government's plans it was the intention to make 'strategic investments' once the deficit was fully eradicated, a moment expected to arrive in 1999. Funds would be invested in the welfare of children and youth, the health-care system, and local communities. In general, the Chrétien government planned to devote one-half of the surplus in this mandate to addressing the social and economic needs of Canadians, while the other half would go to a combination of reducing taxes and the national debt.

Another priority outlined by government was fostering 'knowledge and creativity' through measures such as creating a national student assistance program for post-secondary students and increasing funding for the Canada Council. Some of the objectives set out in the Speech would require cooperation with the provinces. They included a national prescription drug plan (or 'pharmacare') and pan-Canadian efforts to bring down youth unemployment and increase support for children. On national unity questions the government would press for 'frankness and clarity' from Quebec. The Liberal cabinet also pledged to support projects associated with celebrations for the new millennium. No doubt some of these would be geared towards promoting unity.

Fifty sitting days after the Speech the Commons adjourned on 11 December. In the course of just over two months the House received twenty-eight bills, twelve of which passed before the new-year recess. Many of the bills that lapsed at the dissolution of the House were brought back to the floor quickly. On 25 September the government reintroduced legislation affecting the Canada Pension Plan (C-2), mandatory DNA identification of convicted criminals (C-3), and the Canadian Wheat Board (C-4). The House and Senate expeditiously approved the terms of the International Convention to Ban Anti-personnel Mines (a treaty that owed much to Canadian leadership). As the session closed, the House approved the erection of a statue on the grounds of Parliament Hill commemorating the five Alberta women who, in the 1920s, successfully argued that the term 'person' in legal documents and definitions applied to all Canadians. Some members (especially John Nunziata) argued up to the end that statuary on the Hill should be reserved for likenesses of monarchs and former prime ministers.

Just after Parliament adjourned for the holidays, Mr Chrétien welcomed the premiers to a federal-provincial first ministers' conference. The agenda for the meeting, held on 11 and 12 December, was designed to foster discussion about issues such as youth unemployment, health care, and social policies. Ralph Klein of Alberta let it be known that he would begin by criticizing the federal government's handling of negotiations over international action on climate change just concluded in

Kyoto, Japan. The Premier was angered that Canadian delegates agreed to more ambitious guidelines than had been accepted at a federal-provincial summit of energy ministers. This struck him as a violation of the spirit of cooperative federalism that had characterized recent constitutional initiatives.

The biggest news coming out of the conference had to do with an agreement on a framework for developing a 'social union,' which 'respected each other's constitutional jurisdiction and powers.' As summarized by *The Globe and Mail* on 13 December, the agreement entailed the following objectives in the domain of social policies:

- establishment of a set of principles to frame federal-provincial initiatives;
- development of collaborative 'approaches' to the use of the federal government's spending power (the constitutional provision that permitted Ottawa to enter into domains normally assigned to the provinces);
- agreement on new ground rules for intergovernmental cooperation; and,
- clarification of the roles and responsibilities of various levels of government.

What did it all mean? For Quebec's Lucien Bouchard, who refused to subscribe to the consensus, the agreement was fundamentally symbolic in nature, an empty vessel for 'flexible federalism.' Some premiers thought they had secured a commitment for a complete overhaul of legislation such as the Canada Health Act and a promise by Ottawa to curb its unilateral spending power. Others denied having gone quite that far. Discussions, and probably disagreements, would pick up again in 1998.

National institutions

Senate

Mr Chrétien had an opportunity to appoint a number of new senators during the course of 1997. Without exception, he chose Liberals. The first vacancy was created when former Senate speaker, Maurice Riel, reached the mandatory retirement age of seventy-five on 5 April. Three days later Lucie Pépin was named as his replacement. Ms Pepin, a pioneer in birth planning in Canada according to her biography, had been a Liberal MP between 1984 and 1988.

A quartet of Liberals was summoned to the upper chamber on 23 September. Among them was Sister May Alice Butts of Nova Scotia. A former professor in Cape Breton, the new senator tried to downplay her partisan past, but she was a recognized Liberal enthusiast. Joining her was Marisa Ferretti Barth, an organizer in the Italian-Canadian community of Quebec. Neither of the two had held elected office. The other appointments went to former Liberal MPs. Catherine Callbeck served in the House from 1988 to 1993 before returning to provincial politics in her native Prince Edward Island. In March 1993, she became the first woman to lead a provincial party to victory at the polls. Her premiership was short-lived, lasting three and a half years, and was marred by turmoil within the Liberal caucus. Rounding out the group was Fernand Robichaud. The New Brunswick senator held two secretary of state postings in the Chrétien cabinet. He had also been rewarded with the job of special assistant to the Prime Minister after gallantly resigning his Commons seat in favour of Mr Chrétien in 1990.

Two more senators were named on 26 November. Former Trudeau-era cabinet minister Serge Joyal was summoned to fill a vacancy in Quebec. In a move that exercised Reform, Mr Chrétien named prominent Métis leader Thelma Chalifoux to represent Alberta. Ms Chalifoux's selection was singled out for condemnation by the Reform given its zealous commitment to create an elected Upper House, a sentiment shared by Alberta Premier Ralph Klein.

There was another vacancy of sorts in the Senate, but one that went unfilled. Long-time Senator Andrew Thompson continued to shy away from the Hill but refused to resign. Citing health difficulties, the truant was spending most of his time at a villa in Mexico where he was tracked down by photographers. As his absence lengthened, calls for Mr Thompson's dismissal grew louder. Senators of all stripes worried that public mockery would foster cynicism and further discredit an institution under siege. Liberals expelled him from the caucus. Then, on 16 December, the Senate stripped him of his office and staff. Frustrated colleagues warned Mr Thompson that he would be expelled if he did not show up for work by February 1998.

Supreme Court

Mr Justice Gerard La Forest resigned from the Court on 26 August. Appointed in 1985, the former law professor was considered a leading jurist in the field of privacy law. At the age of seventy-one, Justice La Forest planned to take up his pen upon returning to New Brunswick.

He was also in a mood to talk, and surprised some when he suggested that it could be time to open up the process leading to the selection of Supreme Court members. While he had no objections to the fact that the Prime Minister makes the selections, Justice La Forest thought it might be constructive to engage in a more elaborate consultation process. With this departure, Mr Chrétien had an opportunity to make his first appointment after four years in office.

The succession appointment was important given that the Court would hold critical hearings on the federal government's constitutional reference. For this reason, the person chosen by the Prime Minister raised eyebrows and ire. The new justice was Michel Bastarache, a New Brunswick Court of Appeal judge. Mr Bastarache served as chair of the national 'yes' committee during the 1992 Charlottetown Accord referendum. He had also been a colleague of Mr Chrétien at the law firm of Lang Michener (a fact that caused Reform to denounce the appointment as partisan). Reaction from Quebec was harsh. In the Commons, Bloc leader Gilles Duceppe asked 'does the prime minister find this acceptable for the credibility of the Supreme Court?' (Canadian Press Newswire, 1 October.)

Mr Justice John Sopinka died on 24 November from illness related to an undisclosed blood condition. He was sixty-four years of age. His tenure began in 1988 after a career in professional sports and legal defences. Speculation about who would fill the Ontario vacancy on the bench was intense. According to some sources, lobbying for the job was also vigorous and nasty. Insiders claimed that the backers of ostensibly leading candidates had launched campaigns to discredit rivals. Madam Justice Louise Arbour was thought to be another possibility. As Canada's representative on the war crimes tribunal dealing with war crime cases in the former Yugoslavia being held in the Netherlands, she was considered to be on the inside track. If there was an obstacle in the way of her appointment, it was the reluctance of Mr Chrétien to recall her from a sensitive posting.

Auditor general's reports

Auditor General Denis Desautels produced a series of reports on the state of the government's books during the year. The April/October installment was tabled in Parliament on 7 October. Mr Desautels commented on some troubling overall trends. For example, he was critical of the government's reluctance to establish explicit objectives and performance indicators for new initiatives. This made it difficult for citizens to understand and assess programs. Mr Desautels was also concerned that a beleaguered public service was shrinking and aging at a time when demands from the public were rising. Several specific programs were targeted for criticism. The auditor general concluded that the 'TAGS' strategy for restructuring the fisheries had fallen far short of expectations despite a substantial investment of time and money. Neglect on the part of Health Canada meant that physicians were over prescribing medication for many aboriginal patients and, ironically, compounding drug abuse problems in the First Nations population. Environment Canada was criticized for failing to properly monitor the shipment and storage of toxic waste and for tardiness in developing the means by which to promote and document treaty-set reductions in the release of gases implicated in global warning.

A second canvass was issued on 2 December. This time around the Immigration and Refugee Board (IRB) caught the auditor's eye. It seemed that the IRB, launched in 1989, was unable to redeem the promises made by the Mulroney government to streamline and accelerate the process. Indeed, the backlog of cases was higher than in 1989, and only one-quarter of those who had been unsuccessful in their applications to settle in the country had actually left Canada. Over at Revenue Canada, Mr Desautels turned up some serious anomalies in the awarding of licences to duty-free operators. At Industry Canada, it was determined that losses on small-business loans issued between 1993 and 1995 would total $210 million (the department had projected a $72-million surplus for the same period). The Department of Fisheries and Oceans was criticized for failing to adequately measure the loss of habitat for Pacific salmon.

One finding in the report led to the sacking of the chair of the Canadian Labour Relations Board in early 1998. Assigned to review the board's accounts in April, Mr Desautels concluded that Ted Weathergill had misappropriated expenses to the tune of $50,000 or more since 1989. The chair's extravagant meals put his claims well beyond the limit imposed under Treasury Board guidelines. Labour Minister Lawrence MacAulay started the process to force the chair's ouster, but Mr Weathergill dug in his heels and was testing various legal manoeuvres as the year ended.

Constitutional questions and national unity

The Calgary Declaration

For some time, Prime Minister Chrétien had tried to deflect criticism of his government's strategy for dealing with Quebec by noting that provincial governments had been slow to seize the issue. Nine premiers took up the gauntlet during their annual meeting in September. With the two territorial leaders in attendance, and Ralph Klein acting as host, the premiers came up with a Declaration after an extended session that ended late in the night on 14 September. Some seasoned constitutional hands, such as Saskatchewan's Roy Romanow, were said to have argued in favour of responding directly and clearly to Quebec's concerns. In the other camp were leaders like Mr Klein and British Columbia's Glen Clark who wanted to arrive at a comprehensive accord rather than embark on an exercise that would inevitably falter unless it addressed broader concerns.

The Declaration had seven parts. They were partly platitudes and partly principles. References to Quebec were downplayed in the package, which was emphatic about the 'equality' of the provinces and the availability to all of any power granted to one. The premiers abandoned the phrase 'distinct society' when characterizing Quebec (with its echoes of past constitutional debates), choosing instead to underline the province's 'unique character.' The full text of the Declaration was as follows:

1 All Canadians are equal and have equal rights protected by law.
2 All provinces, while diverse in their characteristics, have equality of status.
3 Canada is graced by a diversity, tolerance, compassion and an equality of opportunity that is without rival in the world.
4 Canada's gift of diversity includes Aboriginal peoples and cultures, the vitality of the English and French languages and a multicultural citizenry drawn from all parts of the world.
5 In Canada's federal system, where respect for diversity and equality underlies unity, the unique character of Quebec society, including its French speaking majority, its culture and its tradition of civil law, is fundamental to the well-being of Canada. Consequently, the legislature and Government of Quebec have a role to protect and develop the unique character of Quebec society within Canada.
6 If any future constitutional amendment confers powers on one province, these powers must be available to all provinces.
7 Canada is a federal system where federal, provincial, and territorial governments work in partnership while respecting each other's jurisdictions. Canadians want their governments to work co-operatively and with flexibility to ensure the efficiency and effectiveness of the federation. Canadians want their governments to work together particularly in the delivery of their social programs. Provinces and territories renew their commitment to

work in partnership with the Government of Canada to best serve the needs of Canadians.

The premiers' blueprint was welcomed in Ottawa and other places where federalist elites were waiting for some kind of overture from the premiers. The reaction from Quebec Premier Lucien Bouchard to all this was not difficult to predict. He called the principles 'insipid' and rejected any constitutional overture that was not predicated on recognition of Quebecers as a 'people' with the sovereign power of self-determination. The next step in the process called for the premiers to submit the seven-part Declaration to provincial legislatures for approval after public consultations. Beyond that, the intended constitutional status of the Declaration was not at all clear.

Reference to the Supreme Court

Although formal arguments would not be heard until early in 1998, preparations accelerated in advance of the Supreme Court's consideration of a reference from the federal government on the constitutional path to Quebec sovereignty. In September of 1996, the cabinet asked the Court to answer a series of three questions concerning the legality of a unilateral declaration of sovereignty. The undisguised hope was to secure the Court's agreement that secession could only be affected in accordance with the Constitution and international law. The Parti Québécois government refused to recognize the legitimacy of the reference, dismissing it as a meaningless legal opinion on issues that were wholly political and subject to democratic processes. Faced with this indifference, the Court appointed an *amicus curiae* (a friend of the Court) to argue the case against the government (Canadian Press Newswire, 14 July). In his first major brief, André Joli-Coeur also challenged the authority of the court (18 December). Describing the Supreme Court as merely a 'general court of appeal,' Mr Joli-Coeur contended that it had no jurisdiction in hypothetical questions. This argument was almost certainly doomed thanks to the Court's established history of offering 'advice' to governments on request.

All but two provinces, Saskatchewan and Manitoba, preferred to sit on the sidelines. Other governments were wary of stepping into a potential political quagmire. There were other eager intervenors. The most visible was Guy Bertrand. The erstwhile separatist turned arch-federalist won something of a victory when, on 2 September, the Supreme Court ruled that he could submit resolutions adopted by municipal councils on the matter of 'partitioning' Quebec in the event of separation. This was the thorniest question of the day. Could regions that rejected sovereignty remain a part of Canada, and could First Nations likewise opt out? Sovereignist scholars and politicians insisted that Quebec was an indivisible entity.

Partition, negotiation, and other issues

While lawyers geared up for the Supreme Court, Mr Chrétien attracted front-page coverage with his confession that Ottawa would enter 'a negotiation' with Quebec in the event that citizens of the province endorsed sovereignty in a referendum (Canadian Press Newswire, 7 December). While this was purported to be the first public concession to a negotiated process by the prime minister, as *The Toronto Star* reported the next day, there were strict prior conditions to be met before talks would proceed. The sentiment would have to be expressed strongly and clearly. A unilateral declaration of independence, said Mr Chrétien and senior cabinet ministers, would be illegal.

Early in the year the Quebec government came calling on Ottawa for a favour. The province needed to procure an amendment to the Constitution so that primary and secondary education could be organized on language lines rather than religious ones. The province of Newfoundland had recently petitioned Ottawa for bilateral constitutional changes aimed at secularizing public education (and would do so again in 1997). In the politically charged atmosphere of Quebec, some sovereignists fretted about the spectre of the province tacitly acknowledging the legitimacy of the Constitution. To this sort of fear Premier Lucien Bouchard replied that the change entailed an amendment to clauses in the British North America Act of 1867 rather than the Constitution Act 1981, a document which Quebec refused to formally ratify.

Meanwhile a Quebec judge halted proceedings in a case involving alleged violations of the province's electoral laws during the run-up to the referendum. Just prior to voting day, a large pro-unity rally took place in Montreal. Many in the crowd were from elsewhere in Canada and, in some cases, had taken long (and sometimes subsidized) journeys so that they could wave the Maple Leaf. The event had not been sanctioned by any one of the campaign's organizing committees, and charges were laid against a student group from Ottawa's Algonquin College, two individuals, and a travel company. The case was dismissed on the grounds that Quebec's laws could not reach beyond provincial borders.

The national economy

Economic indicators

The Canadian economy performed with wondrous ambivalence during 1997. Most key indices tended to show that growth was reasonably robust and that, at last, unemployment was dropping. Inflation had been wrung out of the system, and there was little chance that it would reappear in the near term. Annual federal government deficits would soon be a thing of the past. Yet the dollar came under attack and interest rates rose during the year.

Inflation fell to 0.7 per cent in December. This meant that the annual rise was 1.6 per cent, the same as the previous year. Despite this the value of the dollar dropped over a twelve-month span from 74.85 cents in U.S. currency to a floor that was very near the historic nadir of 69.17 cents. On the last day of the year the loonie 'rallied' to close at 69.91 cents. Analysts attributed part of the dollar's dilemma to an economic plunge that had suddenly caged the 'Asian Tiger' economies. Some of the hottest markets in the Far East had cooled to the point of collapse, especially in South Korea, and uneasy investors stocked up on safe U.S. dollars. It was also true that a number of domestic banks were exposed in the Asian lending markets.

It was not just the dollar that felt the shocks. Although stock prices were up by 13 per cent on the Toronto Stock Exchange overall, they fell off from a peak reached on 7 October. With the dollar in decline, the Bank of Canada boosted interest rates on four occasions. The final increment of the year came on 12 December when the bank pegged the rate at which it loaned money to financial institutions at 4.5 per cent. This figure translated into a prime lending rate of 5.5 per cent for preferred customers and even higher charges for holders of personal loans and home mortgages. Home-owners had seen rates dip to a thirty-year low during 1997, but the trend was now climbing.

The unemployment rate dipped below 9 per cent, the lowest it had been since 1990. It ended the year at 8.6 per cent. Although the federal government took the occasion to indulge in a little crowing, the news was not all good. Growth in jobs had enticed more Canadians into the labour pool and this blunted the effect of job creation. Wages remained stagnant, even though the proportion of full-time jobs created was rising. A report released by Statistics Canada indicated that brighter economic prospects were not shared by all Canadians. Average incomes were up by 1 per cent in 1996 but were still off by 3.9 per cent from

1993. In addition, 17.9 per cent of Canadians were living in poverty. Meanwhile the richest 20 per cent of the population had enjoyed an increase of $2,052 in average income in 1996. The inescapable conclusion drawn from the data was that the gap between rich and poor Canadians had grown even as the economy rebounded.

In what was becoming an annual tradition, Mr Chrétien led a delegation of provincial premiers, federal officials, and business representatives on a 'Team Canada' trade junket. The 1997 itinerary saw the group touch down in South Korea, the Philippines, and Thailand. The value of contracts signed along the way (estimated at $2 billion) was lower than on previous pilgrimages. The team was also dogged by accusations that Canada was cooperating with repressive regimes. The entourage arrived in Seoul shortly after labour laws had been curtailed, and other visits appeared to legitimize policies that countenanced child labour and poverty wages for workers.

The spring budget and autumn economic statement

Amid rampant speculation that the Liberals were far ahead of their self-imposed deficit-reduction schedule, Finance Minister Paul Martin readied to deliver his fourth budget speech. The date for his address was set at 18 February, somewhat earlier than customary. The deficit for the current year was reckoned to be 'no greater than $19 billion.' This was at least $5.4 billion below the target set in the 1996 budget. Mr Martin's words were carefully chosen. Analysts outside of government were convinced that the final figure would be much lower. For public purposes, however, the official forecast anticipated that the deficit would dip to $17 billion in 1997–8 and to $9 billion in 1998–9.

With the election out of the way, Mr Martin donned the mantle of the finance minister with money to spend. For the first time in decades the federal coffers would be spilling over the brim. How should the Liberals handle the surplus? According to the party's Red Book manifesto of 1993, half of each extra dollar would be invested in program spending with the remainder used to pay down the debt and lower taxes.

Mr Martin continued to come under fire over the government's Employment Insurance policies. Acting on the advice of external examiners, the government was keen to build a nest egg of $15 billion to enure that EI funds were adequate when the next recession came. Or so it was said. In truth, the premium surplus had been diverted to general revenues in order to hasten the demise of the deficit. The draw was on the order of $5 billion annually. Mr Martin attracted criticism from all sides. Business groups wanted premiums to drop, dramatically, to spur investment and job creation. For their part, labour organizations were lobbying for the restoration of benefits diminished in 1995. Rules introduced that year had slashed the value of benefits, lessened the length of the eligibility period, and made it more difficult for part-time workers to file a claim. The finance minister was having none of it. Premiums would stay high and untouched until the rainy-day stash had been tucked safely away.

Mr Martin dutifully appeared before the House Committee on Finance for his annual autumn budget update on 15 October. He announced that the final deficit figure for the fiscal year ending 31 March was $8.9 billion, the lowest it had been in twenty years. Program spending was down by $7.2 billion while revenues had grown by $10 billion during the year. Mr Martin echoed the views of the Prime Minister in stating that the dividend would be modest when it kicked in, and would take time to amass in significant quantity. It was also noted that the debt-to-gross-domestic-product ratio was still high at 73 per cent. This was the Liberal way of deflating expectations. Few economists believed that the surplus would be as modest or as slow-growing as the government contended.

Major policy fields and initiatives

Pension reforms

The government of Canada faced the worrisome prospect of a bankrupt Canada Pension Plan. By the year 2010, the funding pool would dry up unless significant infusions of money were found. The first step towards pension reform involved meetings between the federal and provincial governments. An agreement was hammered out on 14 February. Premiums would rise sooner than originally imagined in order to cushion the effect of even larger rises if delayed. Benefits would also go down over time. Most Canadians would take home 10 per cent less if they retired in the third decade of the next century. Two provinces refused to sign the deal. British Columbia and Saskatchewan felt that the increased premiums were the wrong way to go. Reform and some others thought the solution was to introduce greater personal choice in selecting and managing funds. They likened the deal to a punitive, hidden tax on Canadians. Mr Martin insisted that the rate hike was an 'investment in the retirement of Canadians' rather than a tax. The idea of creating a plan that would permit opting-out was also stoutly resisted by those who worried that such a move would undermine the principle of universality.

Legislation was introduced to the House on 25 September. Bill C-2 called for gradual increases in employer and employee contributions. Between 1 January 1998 and the year 2003, premiums would rise from 5.85 per cent of earnings to 9.9 per cent. A cap would remain in place that limited contributions to the first $35,000 of earned income. Over in the Senate, members of the Progressive Conservative caucus threatened to stall the legislation. Their stated concern turned on the role and public accountability of a new Canada Pension Investment Board. The bill passed once Finance Minister Paul Martin agreed to delay the board's establishment in order to give senators a chance for further study of the board. The bill came into law following the Senate's concurrence on 18 December.

Child poverty

A report issued by Campaign 2000 (so named because the House voted in 1989 to eradicate child poverty by the new millennium) indicated that the situation had in fact deteriorated (Canada Press Newswire, 27 November). According to the group, nearly 1.5 million children lived in poverty in the year 1995. This represented a 58 per cent increase in the number of poor Canadian children since 1989. These data painted a damning picture of an affluent society.

Against this backdrop, Human Resources Minister Pierre Pettigrew met with provincial counterparts in a series of high-profile encounters. A meeting in Toronto during the first month of the year produced an agreement to jointly pursue a 'national children's agenda' (Canada Press Newswire, 29 January). Mr Pettigrew pledged that significant additional sums would be devoted to the federal child tax credit (and, in the February budget, Finance Minister Paul Martin announced that a further $80 million would be devoted to the $5.1 billion program). This was not enough for provincial ministers. At a meeting in St John's beginning 8 October, they pressed for more money and greater specificity in how it was to be used. The general objective was to create a blended national system whereby funds made available to families with children through tax credits would help boost family income for the working poor. Another goal was to encourage parents to move off welfare: provinces planned to cut welfare payments and invest the differential in dedicated programs such as school lunches. The October conference also saw the unveiling of a draft report prepared by officials from all three levels of government. In its pages, the report covered possible programs geared to various stages of childhood, from prenatal nutrition to improvements in the monitoring of students who were having difficulty in school.

Another way to help children was to adopt stricter measures to ensure that parents complied with the terms of support decrees arising from judgments and settlements in divorce proceedings. Women's groups had effectively demonstrated that fathers were rampantly dodging support payments. The government finally took action. In November 1996, the House approved legislation that amended the Divorce Act, the Family Orders and Agreements Enforcement Assistance Act, the Garnishment, Attachment and Pension Diversion Act, and the Canada Shipping Act. As suggested by the list of acts covered by Bill C-41, the government wanted to use various powers to enforce payment of support by 'delinquent dads.' The legislation also established a formulaic way of calculating payments on the basis of need and income. The bill was treated harshly in the Senate. Conservative members in the Upper House considered it far too harsh on parents. They had an ally in the unpredictable Liberal Anne Cools. She campaigned against the legislation outside the environs of the Hill and in the media. The impasse was resolved on 13 February when Justice Minister Allan Rock accepted amendments that would eliminate non-custodial parents' obligatory assistance with the cost of post-secondary education for their children, and reduce the amount of money paid if a parent was granted access and custody rights of 40 per cent or more. The government also agreed to ask a Joint House-Senate Committee to review custody and access implications of the Divorce Act.

The troubled fisheries

Time was running out for The Atlantic Groundfish Strategy (or TAGS). The program was designed to compensate workers in Atlantic Canada who had lost their jobs because of the devastation of the fishing industry. Funds were scheduled to dry up by May 1998, even though 20,000 individuals (about half the original total) were still receiving disbursements. At year's end, Human Resources Minister Pierre Pettigrew announced that the program would be extended until the end of August 1998. At the same time, Fisheries Minister David Anderson announced the commercial cod quota for 1998. The take would be limited to just 9,300 tonnes, down from 13,000 in 1997.

On the West Coast, problems continued to plague the salmon fisheries. It was a complex dispute, pitting British Columbia and the federal government against adjacent U.S. states and the White House. The government of Premier Glen Clark was also at odds with Ottawa over strategies. At the heart of the matter was an assertion that Americans were increasing their hauls of Canadian-spawned salmon while British Columbia operators were scaling back on their catches. Allocations and conservation issues went unresolved because there was no agreed-upon framework in place. Talks aimed at renewing the Pacific Salmon Treaty (a tortuously negotiated 1985 accord that lapsed in 1992) were stalled. Successive attempts at restarting them proved desultory.

The cross-border stand-off proved extraordinarily frustrating. Tensions arose between Ottawa and Victoria. In 1996, the federal government had laid down new licensing regulations designed to restructure the industry. Under the plan, Ottawa had managed to buy back some 1,300 licences and cut the fleet by 30 per cent. One element of the package that riled the provincial government was a provision that permitted licence 'stacking,' which allowed operators to purchase a licence for more than one area. This had the effect, said Mr Clark, of driving out smaller licence holders.

Reflecting the growing anger with the impasse, a small fleet of fishing boats surrounded an Alaskan ferry docked in the port of Prince Rupert. The vessel was trapped for three days by protesting fishery workers who argued that Alaskan counterparts were harvesting four times the permissible tonnage of salmon in northern waters. The action led to legal proceedings. It also alarmed Ottawa and Washington. Three days after the ferry's release the federal government named David Strangway, the retiring president of the University of British Columbia, as Canada's special negotiator (Canada Press Newswire, 25 July). Across the table would be a high-level Clinton administration appointee, William Ruckleshaus, the Nixon-era head of the Environmental Protection Agency. The seniority of these individuals was supposed to symbolize the will to find a just resolution. The task remained a difficult one.

Canada did adopt a 'Canada-First' strategy, which resulted in higher yields of Fraser River sockeye and, said proponents, demonstrated to the Americans that the price for failing to renew the accord would be high. In other respects, the goal was to find an acceptable bilateral approach. Impatient, the province filed suit against the United States, Alaska, and the state of Washington (Canada Press Newswire, 8 September). A U.S. court was asked to agree with British Columbia's claim that quotas imposed under the Pacific Salmon Treaty had been ignored. The province also sought damages of $300 million in compensation for U.S. overfishing. Mr Clark was livid when, shortly after the suit was filed, officials in Foreign Affairs drafted an advisory memorandum predicting that the case would be dismissed. The Premier went so far as to say that the opinion was 'treasonous.' In another feud, Mr Clark threatened to terminate the U.S. lease on the Nanoose Bay torpedo testing site in retaliation for injustices. Ottawa, convinced that the action was groundless, responded with threats of legal action.

Tobacco control legislation

With support from all but one opposition party, the government managed to enact legislation curbing advertisements for cigarettes and other tobacco products. Bill C-71 passed the House on 6 March on a vote of 139–37. Only the Bloc Québécois opposed the measures in the Commons. It took the stance that any restrictions on the sponsorship of cultural and sporting events by tobacco companies would jeopardize events like the Montreal Grand Prix. Then, on 17 April, Health Minister David Dingwall and Justice Minister Allan Rock announced that automobile racers would be allowed to wear the corporate logos of tobacco manufacturers. Health advocates sharply criticized the about-face while tobacco companies vowed to continue their confrontation with the government by whatever means possible.

Helicopter purchase

One of the first acts of the Liberal government when it came to power in 1993 was to cancel an order for fifty EH-101 helicopters (thirty-five of which were ship-borne) placed by the defence department. The deal, worth $4.3 billion, had been signed by the governing Progressive Conservatives under a cloud of controversy, and the Liberals acted despite paying a $500-million cancellation penalty. Still, the armed forces pleaded for better search-and-rescue capabilities than could be provided by a fleet of aging and nearly obsolete Labrador helicopters. Any decision was bound to incite a new round of controversy. As a result, Mr Chrétien began to explain that the original deal was too costly, given the extent of the budget deficit. Now, with the deficit virtually gone, the purchase seemed plausible.

In September, the media began tracking the story of the acquisition in earnest. Although manufacturers such as Boeing Canada, Eurocopter Canada, and Sikorsky were interested in a deal, word out of the defence department was that the favourite was an Italian-British consortium led by EH Industries, that same group that had won the cancelled contract. This time the consortium was offering Canada a stripped down version of the EH-101 called the AW-520 Cormorant. At $790 million for all fifteen Cormorants, the sticker price was 40 per cent less than that of the

EH-101, and the consortium included Canadian partners. If successful, EH would also enjoy a considerable advantage when the government later turned to finding a replacement for ship-borne Sea King helicopters. Unable to make up its mind on the search-and-rescue helicopter, cabinet assigned the final selection to a committee of ministers and senior armed forces officials. As the year ended they had not formally announced a decision, even though it seemed likely that the Cormorant would get the nod, to the consternation of rival bidders. The prospect of reviving the EH-101 secretly delighted the opposition parties, who sensed that the Liberals would have to weather a political battering over the affair.

Postal dispute

Members of the Canadian Union of Postal Workers set up picket lines on 19 November after talks with Canada Post broke off. On 24 November, Public Works Minister Alfonso Gagliano implied that back-to-work legislation was being readied. The spectre of a forced return prompted CUPW officials to declare that the strikers would respond with an unprecedented level of civil disobedience, which might include closing highways, bridges, and airports. Labour Minister Lawrence MacAulay cooled the situation by offering the services of Warren Edmondson, the director-general of federal mediation and conciliation services. The parties accepted.

Even with a top mediator on duty, talks proved inconclusive. When negotiations broke off, the government moved to end the dispute with back-to-work legislation. On 2 December the House passed Bill C-24 by a vote of 198–56. The Bloc and NDP dissented, even though they accommodated swift passage though the three readings of the bill in a single day. Reform and the Progressive Conservatives supported the bill despite the fact that they, too, had qualms about certain provisions, particularly the wage increase of 5.15 per cent over three years. This was actually less than Canada Post's final offer.

Canadian Wheat Board

One of Ralph Goodale's first duties as the minister responsible for the Canadian Wheat Board was to resuscitate legislation aimed at restructuring and expanding the powers of the board. Bill C-4 was read for the first time early in the session and once again ignited the sort of controversy that surrounded a similar bill that lapsed on the order-paper in April. The government proposed to abolish the existing board, an all-appointed ten-member body, and substitute a fifteen-person board. Ten representatives would be elected by prairie farmers while others, including the president, would be chosen by the government. Critics were especially concerned by provisions of the bill, which would permit the board to extend its monopoly over other grains or to exclude some from its oversight. The bill was scheduled for a final vote early in 1998. Late in the year, the government appointed former Supreme Court justice Willard Estey to conduct a review of the shipment of grains from the field to shipping harbours (Canada Press Newswire, 18 December). Mr Estey would need to muster diplomatic skills to resolve a disagreement between the board and the railways over who was responsible for delaying transportation and costing farmers money.

'Anti-biker' legislation

The government of Quebec was in a quandary. Members of motorcycle gangs were embroiled in an all-out territorial battle that had left more than thirty individuals dead. Counted among the victims was an innocent young child. Originally reluctant to call for federal help, the feuding had grown so intensely violent that Lucien Bouchard's government joined calls for stern penalties for gang-related crimes. Justice Minister Allan Rock was equally wary in the matter. He was concerned that some proposed measures – such as making membership in a criminal organization illegal – would fail legal tests. The justice minister wondered if it was appropriate to press forward if guilt by association would be rejected by the courts.

The government finally acceded. Bill C-95 was swiftly drafted, debated, and approved in the span of just nine days. The law, unveiled on 17 April and given royal assent on 26 April, contained several measures to curb biker-gang violence. In addition to making membership in a criminal organization illegal, the bill granted the police seizure of the spoils of crime. Parole for gang members could be delayed. The bill also raised the penalty for possession of explosives (which were featuring prominently in the raging street battle).

Commissions and inquiries

Krever Commission

Mr Justice Horace Krever finally released his bedevilled and delayed report on how so many Canadians had come to be infected by tainted blood starting in the 1980s. Although Justice Krever was poised to submit the results of his inquiry sometime in the spring, the Supreme Court agreed to hear an appeal against a lower court ruling defending the right of inquiries to assign blame. The final barrier was lifted when, on 27 September, the Court affirmed previous decisions. The Court rejected arguments made by the Red Cross, two pharmaceutical companies, and a dozen individuals that an assessment of blame by Justice Krever would amount to a trial by inquiry. In a unanimous verdict, the Court concluded that damaged reputations 'may be the price which must be paid to ensure that if a tragedy such as that presented to the commission ... can be prevented, it will be.' It was nearly a moot point given that Justice Krever had let it be known that he was not inclined to point the finger at individuals.

Freed at last from legal entanglements, the report was issued on 26 November. As expected, Justice Krever did name names; but nowhere in his 1,138-page chronology did he attribute personal wrongdoing to any individual. The burden of this argument was that the real fault for the calamity lay with a breakdown in oversight of an overly complex system. As a result, weak coordination and poor planning led to the acquisition of HIV and hepatitis-C by thousands of Canadians. Just how many people had been exposed to such infections through transfusion was in dispute, and Justice Krever drew the startling conclusion that 29,000 individuals had contracted hepatitis-C rather than previous estimates of 12,000. Among the fifty recommendations in the report was a call for 'no-fault' compensation for the victims of all past and future blood contaminations. Justice Krever also endorsed the creation of a national system for blood collection and distribution with a clear mandate and reliable means of accountability. He also argued that a database was needed to compile information about donors, donations, and recipients. None of these proposals was costed. When the report was released the Red Cross issued an apology, as did Health Minister Allan Rock. Speaking on behalf of the federal government, Mr Rock pledged to ensure the implementation of key recommendations.

Justice Krever's diffidence perplexed some observers. A *Toronto Star* editorial asked if the effort amounted to a 'waste of four years and $15 million' (27 November). The report also seemed to come after the fact. Prior to the release of the report, provincial health ministers reached an important stage in planning for a new blood agency (*Toronto Star*, 11 September). After securing a pledge of $81 million from Ottawa, nine provinces – Quebec having decided to go its own way – agreed to proceed with the creation of a 'national blood authority.' The ministers also agreed on a transition bureau to oversee the hand-off from the Red Cross. It was anticipated that the new authority would be fully operational by September 1998. Justice Krever's 'recommendations' amounted to an endorsement.

In the days following the release of the report, the NDP joined others in calling for a criminal investigation. RCMP commissioner Phillip Murray responded by saying that the Mounties would be 'pro-active' in an investigation even if it had not been asked to launch a formal probe (*Hamilton Spectator*, 28 November). The creation of an RCMP task force was announced on 22 December. Shortly thereafter the justice ministry indicated that it would move for changes to clauses in the Criminal Code stipulating that death must occur within one year of the commission of a crime in order to be judiciable.

Somalia inquiry

In the spring of 1995 the government established an inquiry into the incidents that marred Canada's peacekeeping mission in strife-torn Somalia. The three-person panel was asked to report by December of that year on the deaths of two young Somalia men while in the custody of soldiers from the Canadian Airborne Regiment. It was also asked to look into how senior political and military staff handled the matter. Unable to complete its task on time, the inquiry twice received permission to extend its deadline, first to June 1996 and then to June 1997. By December of 1996, the inquiry had only touched on the events surrounding the death of one man and had yet to hear from many important witnesses. The inquiry, headed by Mr Justice Gilles Letourneau, asked for another delay, indicating that December 1997 would be a more realistic target date. This time the government said no. Defence Minister Doug Young maintained that it was time to wrap up the inquiry so that Canadians would know what happened during the mission and so that the military could begin making the changes necessary to prevent a recurrence of the events. The impatient minister argued that the inquiry had assembled sufficient evidence to figure out how Shidane Arone had met his death. He would brook no more postponements.

Thus began six months of ill-tempered spats in front of the commission, legal jousting about the fate of the inquiry, and a free-flowing exchange of barbs among various parties. The tone in the hearing room was typified by the testimony of Vice Admiral Larry Murray. Justice Letourneau was openly exasperated by the length, tone, and intemperance of the acting chief of defence's testimony. At one point, he issued a stern admonishment: 'I'm warning you for the last time, you're not supposed to talk when the chairman is talking.'* Inquiry members were not just concerned about the lack of etiquette on the part of those testifying. They were plainly troubled by testimony that they considered less than forthcoming.

The government's plug-pulling act was subjected to litigation. On 27 March, a Federal Court judge in Vancouver ruled that the cabinet's decision to shut down the Somalia inquiry was unlawful. Madam Justice Sandra Sampson concluded that the cabinet had exceeded its authority when it ordered a halt to the proceedings without formally revising the mandate. Left with no choice, the government revised the inquiry's terms of reference on 3 April.

The report was finally released on 2 July. Entitled *Dishonoured Legacy: The Lessons of the Somalia Affair*, it was a damning indictment of military structures, management, and procedures. Justice Letourneau and his colleagues did not shy from singling out individuals for blame. The commission was convinced that the Canadian Airborne Regiment was unfit for the duties it had been assigned. Training was inadequate and discipline was lax. Moreover, in the days after the death on 4 March 1993, personnel in Somalia and in Ottawa launched a cover up. Over time, documents had been tampered with and destroyed, and military leaders had lied and engaged in stalling tactics. The testimony of former chiefs of staff John de Chastelain and Jean Boyle was dismissed as not credible; and Vice-Admiral Murry was considered unsuitable to take permanent responsibility. It was suggested that the transcript of the hearings should be studied for indications that perjury may have been committed by various witnesses.

The inquiry deposited a series of recommendations. To start, an inspector general should be given the task of investigating problems and protecting whistle blowers. If Canada was to continue to offer peacekeeping assistance, the military would need clearer criteria for decision making, improved guidelines for carrying out orders, better training, an enhanced intelligence-gathering capacity, and superior planning and preparation. It was essential to vet prospective leaders and to actively ferret out pockets of unruly behaviour, insubordination, and racism.

The report was notable for what it did not say. Because it had been cut off, the inquiry was unable to address a range of issues. A Canadian Press story on the wires of 21 March identified some of the questions

---

*Commission of Inquiry into the Deployment of Canadian Forces to Somalia, Hearing Transcripts.

that would be left unanswered: 'Was there an effort to keep details of the March 16, 1993, torture-murder of a teenager away from the office of then-defence minister Kim Campbell? Did bureaucrats try to smooth Campbell's Tory leadership campaign by downplaying events in Somalia? Was there an effort to obstruct a military police investigation of the Somalia affair? Are there institutional problems in the military that made the Somalia affair inevitable?'

The testy tone and unrelenting critical edge of the document was rejected by the government. Defence Minister Art Eggleton called it 'excessive' and 'insulting.' The Prime Minister concurred. Although reluctant to express full confidence in Vice-Admiral Murray, it was clear enough that Mr Chrétien did not accept the harsh depictions of the chief of staff rendered by the inquiry. The government did agree to follow up on recommendations arising from the report. However, it took some time to iron out the implementation process. It was not until 14 October that the process was clarified. Former Supreme Court justice Willard Estey was named to head an eight-person committee to oversee the implementation of recommendations. The group was given two years to complete its task and would file quarterly reports on its progress. Its mandate was set out in a blueprint called *A Commitment to Change*. One remedy was notably absent from the report. The government turned down the idea of appointing an inspector general. Instead, said Mr Eggleton, the present system could work well with 'refinements,' such as the appointment of an ombudsman. A powerful inspector general could create a separate chain of command.

On 19 March the government agreed to refer the affair to a special Senate committee. Critics contended that the decision confirmed that the government had come to realize that it was in error when it stopped the inquiry. Former MP William Romkey was picked to head the probe. The plan blew up when Progressive Conservatives bolted from preliminary planning sessions for the special committee and denounced the government's continued efforts to narrow the scope of inquiries. They would not participate in a 'whitewash' (*Toronto Star*, 17 April).

Personalities and controversies

On 6 January the government abandoned its defence against a lawsuit filed in November 1995 by former prime minister Brian Mulroney. The action was launched by Mr Mulroney in response to the publication of a letter, written by justice department officials, requesting the assistance of Swiss authorities in an investigation of alleged improprieties surrounding the sale of Airbus planes to Air Canada. In the scenario sketched by Canadian officials by way of explaining the need for cooperation, it was suggested that Mr Mulroney might have been involved in a kickback scheme along with his close friend and former Newfoundland premier Frank Moores and a business associate, Karl-Heinz Schreiber. On the eve of a formal trial, the government agreed to pick up the tab for legal expenses estimated at $1 million and to offer a written apology to Mr Mulroney. In the text of the apology the government conceded that 'based on the evidence to date, the RCMP acknowledges that any conclusions of wrongdoing by the former prime minister were, and are, unjustified.' Mr Moores and Mr Schreiber also received apologies but no compensation (*Toronto Star*, 7 January).

Justice Minister Allan Rock confirmed that the government backed out of the trial because of an admission by lead RCMP investigator Fraser Fiengerwald that he had leaked word that Mr Mulroney was under suspicion. In addition, a 3 January ruling in the case widened the scope of permissible testimony in ways that went against the government. Yet it was clear that criticisms of the government were taking a toll on Liberal popularity.

Although the document issued by the government's lawyers insisted that the justice department and RCMP investigators acted 'within their legitimate responsibilities,' Mr Mulroney was quick to claim that his vindication was complete and final. Nevertheless Justice Minister Allan Rock, who had come under fire for his handling of the affair, refused to state categorically that the former prime minister was no longer the subject of a probe. Mr Rock was not the only cabinet minister who was caught in the political fall out from the matter. Solicitor General Herb Gray and Prime Minister Chrétien were also forced to deny any partisan motivation in the investigation or political management of the subsequent controversy.

Details of the financial compensation for Mr Mulroney were made known on 6 October. The settlement was pegged at just over $2 million. There was money enough to pay all of the former prime minister's bills, including a public relations tab estimated at $600,000. All in all, the legal saga cost the federal government some $3.4 million (*Globe and Mail*, 7 October).

The Liberals faced another drawn out affair as opposition parties hammered away with charges of influence peddling. The controversy began in March when Human Resources Minister Pierre Pettigrew forwarded allegations about the activities of Pierre Corbeil, a Liberal fund-raiser, to the RCMP. According to legal documents, Mr Corbeil cited his connections to the government while looking for money from companies eligible for grants under the Transitional Jobs Fund program. On 12 June the RCMP, acting with judicial permission, entered the Quebec headquarters of the Liberal Party in a search for evidence implicating Mr Corbeil. Officers seized a day-planner and other documents. On 9 October, Tory MP Peter McKay inquired about a second warrant, this one to enter the office of Treasury Board president Marcel Massé in Montreal. Mr Massé, who had been under scrutiny because of his role as the senior political minister in the province, insisted that the warrant was signed but never executed. Reform insisted that there was 'something fishy' about the awarding of contracts to firms doing business with the federal government in Quebec and that Mr Corbeil appeared to have inside help in targeting prospective donors.

The RCMP announced an official end to its investigation on 15 October, one day after charges were laid against Mr Corbeil. He alone would face criminal proceedings in the matter. Opposition members were angered by the loose threads left dangling. It seemed improbable to them that Mr Corbeil could have acted alone in targeting specific companies. In the words of Tory MP André Bedard, there was still a 'missing link' between Mr Corbeil and the party. It was still not clear why Mr Massé had volunteered information about the mysterious unexecuted warrant.

Charges were laid again Senator Eric Bernston on 23 January. The proceedings stemmed from an ongoing RCMP investigation into allegations of misuse of caucus funds and legislative allowances by members of Saskatchewan's Progressive Conservative provincial caucus. With the charges against Mr Bernston and five others, a total of nineteen individuals had been charged. One day after the charges were laid, Mr Bernston surrendered his post as deputy leader of the Tories in the Senate and resigned from the party's caucus. Bloc Québécois MP Bernard Saint-Laurent also removed himself from caucus after being convicted of eavesdropping on a former member of his staff. The criminal conviction carried with it a fine of $1,000 and a sentence of probation.

The year 1997 marked the passing of Stanley Knowles. Often referred to as the 'conscience of Parliament,' Mr Knowles spent the final years of his life as a special officer of the House. Although nearing the age of ninety when he died, Mr Knowles was faithful in his attendance, taking in the proceedings from his chair at the clerk's table. Gerard Pelletier, a friend, adviser, and cabinet colleague of Pierre Trudeau also died during the year. One of the 'three wise men' in the Trudeau circle, Mr Pelletier helped design the brand of liberal federalism that stood opposed to nationalism in Quebec.

MICHAEL HOWLETT

Ottawa and the provinces*

The Quebec-Ottawa phony war

After many years of loud public clashes and conflicts over the Constitution, 1997 proved to be the second year in which quiet but intense
struggles between Ottawa and Quebec City occurred largely outside of
the public spotlight. Both sides struggled to score public relations' points
on a variety of issues, but compared with the almost-decade-long contest
over the Meech Lake and Charlottetown Accords, and the Halloween
1995 Quebec referendum, these fights seemed picayune and pedantic.

This lull in the storm in 1997 allowed Ottawa to continue its agenda
of deficit reduction and consensual federalism. Few major new issues
arose in the federal-provincial sphere, and relations between the two
spheres of Canadian federalism warmed considerably as the federal
government surpassed its deficit targets, promising to usher in a new
round of spending. Much of the spending was undoubtedly to be targeted to areas such as health, social welfare, and education – all areas of
provincial jurisdiction.

Quebec: From Plan B to the Calgary Declaration

Quebec-Ottawa relations began the year on an up note when Quebec
Premier Lucien Bouchard agreed to accompany the Prime Minister and
other provincial leaders on a 'Team Canada' trade mission to East Asia.
Breaking the pattern set by his Parti Québécois predecessor Jacques
Parizeau, who refused to take part in earlier missions, Bouchard argued
that the mission's potential benefits to the province outweighed the symbolic aspects of Quebec's participation (*Globe and Mail*, 8 January).

However, on a variety of other issues, the two governments contin-

*Thanks to Evan Jones for research assistance on this chapter.

ued to wage publicity battles over largely symbolic points. In January, for example, the Quebec government demanded that Ottawa transfer $360 million in Employment Insurance funds in order to cover elements of its planned day-care and maternity-leave expansion (*Globe and Mail*, 24 January and 6 August). Ottawa balked at this demand, and talks continued on this subject throughout the year. The proposal, however, was only a small part of a much larger project to have Ottawa hand over to Quebec responsibility for $2.7 billion in job-training programs. Faced with the need to appear flexible and responsive to the 'real' concerns of Quebecers, Ottawa acceded to this demand and an agreement was reached in April. Prime Minister Chrétien argued that the job-training scheme was proof positive that Canadian federalism could work (21 and 25 April). The PQ government was quick to respond that this had been the subject of Quebec demands since 1965 and pointed to the thirty-two-year delay encountered in accomplishing its goal as proof positive that it could not.

Another heavily symbolic issue arose when the province proposed a constitutional amendment to abolish the provincial system of denominational schools and replace it with a system organized along linguistic lines (*Globe and Mail*, 24 January). This latter proposal immediately raised a set of issues around whether or not the proposal amounted to de facto recognition of the existing constitutional order on the part of the Quebec government.

The school question lingered throughout the spring, as uneasy anglophones in Quebec asked for various assurances that the new proposal would not lead to the underfunding or elimination of their schools. The federal government, put in the position of having to demonstrate that the existing constitutional system *was* flexible and could accommodate legitimate change, argued that a consensus would have to emerge in the province before it would approve of any amendment (*Globe and Mail*, 12 and 13 February, and 25 March). The provincial government attempted to have Ottawa debate the proposed amendment prior to its passage in Quebec, but soon backed down on this demand. The provincial Liberal opposition at first opposed the amendment, but the PQ government agreed to negotiate minor changes to it in order to gain their support, and in April the proposed amendment passed the National Assembly in a unanimous vote (12 and 16 April).

Ottawa then agreed to move fast on the proposed amendment (*Globe and Mail*, 17 April), at least partially due to its own desire not to have it become an issue in the impending federal election. The amendment was not introduced as soon as expected, however, and the Prime Minister was forced to admit that it was unlikely to pass before the election was called (19 and 23 April). When it was finally introduced in October, it was joined by a similar proposal from Newfoundland, following a provincial referendum in September in which 73 per cent of voters endorsed a provincial plan to abolish denominational school systems (25 August and 28 October). The referendum prompted a second bid by the province to abolish the schools, its first effort in 1996 having been undone by a court challenge.

Although the Quebec government wanted rapid passage of the amendment, it was referred to a federal committee for study and did not emerge until November. It was finally passed 18 November, by a 204–59 free vote in the House of Commons. In December, the Newfoundland amendment also passed in a free vote, this time by a 212–53 vote (*Globe and Mail*, 8 November and 10 December).

The major development which threatened to end the federal-provincial phony war occurred at the end of February when the federal government began its arguments before the Supreme Court in the reference on unilateral secession (*Globe and Mail*, 28 February). In 1996, the federal government had begun its policy of publicly pointing out the difficulties and costs associated with Quebec independence. The so-called federal Plan B included veiled threats of partition and the redrawing of provincial boundaries; declarations that Quebec would have difficulty entering into trade pacts such as NAFTA without Canadian approval; and dire warnings about the difficulties of negotiating any new post-sovereignty social, political, or economic arrangements with Canada. The most overt act in this new federal play, however, was to move the debate from the streets to the courts as the government supported renegade Parti Québécois cabinet minister Guy Bertrand's challenge to Quebec's right to alter the Constitution unilaterally.

In September 1996, the federal government asked the Supreme Court to rule on three questions: (1) Does the Canadian Constitution allow the National Assembly of Quebec to unilaterally secede from Canada? (2) Does international law allow it to do so? (3) If the two conflict, which would take precedence in Canada?

The Bertrand case was boycotted by the Quebec government, which argued that the question of self-determination of peoples was a political and not a judicial matter. The case nevertheless began to be heard by the Supreme Court in 1997. Ottawa opened its case at the beginning of March, and argued in its formal written brief to the Court that the procedures to amend the Canadian Constitution must be used in all circumstances, including secession, even if the document itself did not specifically mention or deal with that possibility (*Globe and Mail*, 1 March). This immediately brought forth a negative reaction from the federal Conservative Party. Former prime minister Joe Clark and current party leader Jean Charest both argued that the federal Plan B strategy would needlessly antagonize Quebecers and result in further confrontations and antagonisms (3 March). Later, former Conservative prime minister Brian Mulroney joined them, arguing that Plan B would inevitably fail to accommodate the legitimate demands of Quebecers within Confederation and thus lead to the demise of Canada (15 April).

However, not all of the reaction was negative, as provincial governments in Saskatchewan and Manitoba both filed documents with the Supreme Court endorsing the federal position. For his part, Bertrand argued that both the federal and provincial governments, in contemplating secession, violated the constitutional rights of Canadians (*Globe and Mail*, 12 and 14 April). Although the Court initially expected to hear the case in December, the death of Supreme Court Justice John Sopinka and the resignation of Justice Gerard LaForest led Chief Justice Antonio Lamer to delay hearing the case until 1998 when a full complement of nine justices would be present (19 September).

The unity issue played a minor role in the late-spring federal election campaign, as federal party leaders were forced to grapple with release of the memoirs of former PQ premier Parizeau and the revelation that he had intended to issue a unilateral declaration of independence if the Halloween eve 1995 referendum had succeeded. For his part, Prime Minister Chrétien argued that the revelations underlined the wisdom of his government's referral of the issue to the Supreme Court. Conservative leader Charest, however, argued that the unilateral declaration would have emerged, Supreme Court ruling or not (*Globe and Mail*, 9 May).

Although most of the federal parties attempted to focus on other issues, such as employment and job growth, the Reform Party continued to hammer away at the national unity issue, which played well with anti-Quebec elements in Western Canada but fell on deaf ears in Ontario and Eastern Canada. The strategy did succeed in drawing out some missing elements of the federal Liberal position, however, such as the explicit statement made by the Prime Minister for the first time during the campaign, that a simple majority vote on a referendum would not be considered adequate to legitimize Quebec sovereignty (*Globe and Mail*, 22 and 26 May).

After the election, and the accompanying loss of Official Opposition status by the federal Bloc Québécois, federal-provincial squabbling continued. In June, Canada blocked Quebec's bid to have its representative at the United Nations obtain special status (*Globe and Mail*, 21 June). However, the main event – public hearings by the Supreme Court in the Bertrand case – continued to garner most of the attention. In July, speculation increased as to what strategy would be adopted by André Joli-Coeur, the amicus curiae (friend of the court) appointed to argue the position of the absent Quebec government (17 July).

Not everyone was content to allow the national unity agenda to be developed by the Court, however. In August, the provincial premiers debated a suggestion put forward by the Business Council on National Issues that they assume the lead in attempting to continue Plan A – the attempt to accommodate Quebec's demands in Confederation. Even this attempt, however, was soon embroiled in the negative hardball of Plan B, when a letter from New Brunswick Premier Frank McKenna to a group urging municipalities in Quebec to endorse the partition of the province was seized upon by Premier Lucien Bouchard as unwarranted interference in the internal affairs of the province (*Globe and Mail*, 7 August). Jumping into the fray, federal Intergovernmental Affairs Minister Stéphane Dion blasted the Quebec premier for misrepresenting the legal position of the province and its ability to determine the nature of its borders in the event of secession. After a tit-for-tat exchange of letters with Deputy Premier Bernard Landry, Mr Dion asserted that there was no question that the nature of Quebec's boundaries would be a subject of negotiation in any talks following or accompanying secession (12, 27, and 28 August).

Despite the uproar, the premiers pressed ahead with their plans to debate the national unity issue at a set of meetings scheduled for Calgary in September. Behind the scenes, meetings of premiers and officials continued, with Ontario Premier Mike Harris emerging from the shadows for the first time to debate the unity issue. They were joined by talks between provincial premiers and the Prime Minister, who urged the premiers to develop a common position on the unity portfolio (*Globe and Mail*, 4 and 5 September).

After their meetings in Calgary, the premiers emerged with their own unity plan. The Calgary Declaration contained the seven following points: (1) the affirmation that all Canadians are equal before the law; (2) that all provinces have equal status; (3) that diversity is of benefit to the nation; (4) that diversity includes aboriginal peoples, English and French languages, and a multicultural citizenry; (5) that within Canadian federalism Quebec is unique in its language, culture, and legal system; (6) that future constitutional changes affecting one province must make those powers available to all of the others; and (7) that

Canada's federal system is a cooperative partnership (*Globe and Mail*, 15 September). The premiers also promised to hold public hearings on the Declaration and planned to meet with aboriginal leaders to discuss its content. The meeting was held in November and resulted in a commitment by the premiers to endorse aboriginal desires for a separate order to government (19 November).

The Prime Minister was quick to praise the Calgary Declaration and stated that if it was adopted by the provinces and territories, he would have it endorsed by the federal Parliament. The Declaration was also quickly endorsed by the federal Conservative Party, although Progressive Conservative leader Jean Charest argued that the federal government should have taken a leadership role in the development of the proposal and not have left the issue up to the provinces to resolve. In Quebec, however, the Parti Québécois government heaped scorn on the use of the word 'unique,' noting that this was only the latest effort to distance the country from the use of the 'distinct society' clause contained in the failed Meech Lake Accord. The provincial Intergovernmental Affairs Minister Jacques Brassard called the Declaration 'another plunge into nothingness and insignificance' (16 September). He continued to insist that Quebec's demands and concerns would only be taken seriously by the rest of the country after a 'yes' vote on a sovereignty referendum. This prompted the Prime Minister to threaten to hold a federal consultation process on the Declaration in Quebec should it be adopted throughout the rest of the country (25 September).

In November, the House of Commons endorsed the Calgary Declaration and the Reform Party sponsored a motion calling for it to lead consultations in Quebec on the contents of the document. Soon after, the Declaration was endorsed by the Legislature of Saskatchewan, beginning a process of formal provincial ratifications (*Globe and Mail*, 26 November and 1 December).

By year's end, Quebec Premier Lucien Bouchard began back-pedalling on the hardball language used by his government. Chastened by three by-election losses in October, the Premier told the Canadian Alliance of Manufacturers and Exporters that a unilateral declaration of independence would not be necessary after a referendum, since 'common sense' and the democratic tradition in Canada would lead to meaningful negotiations following a 'yes' referendum victory (*Globe and Mail*, 7 October). This view was echoed by the Prime Minister, who stated that if the provincial government won a clear victory on a clear referendum question then the federal government would negotiate with the province (8 December). Although Mr Bouchard went into a first ministers' meeting in Ottawa complaining about federal incursions into areas of provincial jurisdiction, unlike many of his predecessors he at least attended it. His government made its points, in key areas such as housing and research and development spending but displayed some pragmatism in bargaining with Ottawa (12 and 17 December).

Debts and deficits – the continuing struggle over fiscal policy

The 1995 federal budget created a new federal transfer, the Canada Health and Social Transfer (CHST), to replace the Pearson-Trudeau era Canada Assistance Plan (CAP) and Established Programs Financing Act (EPF). The combined payments made to the provinces under the new scheme would be cut substantially over the next several years; with $2.5 billion in cuts coming in 1996–7 and a further $4.5 billion in 1997–8.

In 1996 the federal government stuck to its deficit targets and achieved some success in getting its fiscal house in order. In the March budget, Finance Minister Paul Martin announced the government had met its target of reducing the deficit to $32.7 billion in 1995–6 and forecasted it would exceed its target of $24.3 billion in 1996–7. He also announced that federal-provincial transfers would be cut by an additional $700 million prior to their stabilization in 1999–2000.

Most of these cuts would begin to take affect in 1997. Combined with increases in payroll taxes for Employment Insurance and other measures, the effect of the federal deficit-cutting measures gobbled up a variety of tax cuts made by the provinces in earlier years. Although the federal government tried to soften the blow by offering to renew the $1.8-billion infrastructure program it had created after the 1993 federal election (*Globe and Mail*, 1 and 7 January), the provinces were not amused. In February they secured the agreement of Finance Minister Paul Martin to reduce Employment Insurance premiums in exchange for their agreement to renegotiate elements of the Canadian Pension Plan (CPP). Although the New Democratic Party governments of British Columbia and Saskatchewan refused to go along with the federal CPP restructuring proposals, which they felt would adversely affect low-income and disabled recipients, changes to the plan only required approval of two-thirds of the provinces (14 and 15 February). The new proposals called for a doubling of CPP contribution rates over an eight-year period in order to finance the increasing number of baby-boomer retirees.

Having successfully reformed most elements of Canada's major federal spending programs, Mr Martin was able to introduce a new pre-election budget in February, which promised the lowest deficit in fif-teen years as well as over a billion dollars in new spending on job cre-ation and social policy initiatives (*Globe and Mail*, 19 February).

Although the finance minister continued to forecast a multi-billion dollar deficit, commentators were quick to point out that the budget contained numerous contingency funds as well as very conservative estimates of economic growth and performance. Many felt the deficit problem, which had been such an issue in the 1993 federal election and subsequent Liberal budgets, would be completely eliminated by 1998 – ushering in an new era of budgetary surpluses as interest paid on out-standing debt continued to decline.

This situation was partially confirmed during the federal election campaign in May, when Prime Minister Chrétien said the federal gov-ernment would not proceed with the last two phases of a planned $1.5-billion cut in cash transfers to the provinces. In August, the provincial premiers, at their annual meeting in St Andrews, New Brunswick, made it clear they expected a large part of any future surplus to be devoted to the restoration of cuts to federal-provincial transfer pay-ments (*Globe and Mail*, 8 August).

Nevertheless, in the short term, the devolution of federal responsibil-ities to the provinces, and provincial off-loading of costs onto munici-palities, continued apace. In February, Ottawa offered to relinquish some of its control over immigration to Ontario, British Columbia, and Alberta, matching a deal made with Quebec in 1991 (*Globe and Mail*, 27 February and 22 March). In June, Ottawa intervened in provincial efforts to download responsibility for social housing to the municipal level. Public Works Minister Diane Marleau warned the Ontario govern-ment that Ottawa would have to be consulted in any moves affecting housing built under joint federal-provincial plans (7 June). Ontario offi-cials, however, noted that Ottawa had already agreed to devolve respon-sibility to the provinces and had signed deals with Newfoundland, Saskatchewan, New Brunswick, and the Northwest Territories to that effect. For their part, the municipalities denounced both senior levels of government for evading their responsibility to maintain existing pro-grams (*Globe and Mail*, 10 June and 22 July). In July, new Public Works Minister Alfonso Gagliano said that all future deals with the provinces would include a clause requiring them to honour existing funding arrangements (24 July).

By year's end, as the premiers prepared to meet for a first ministers' conference in Ottawa, they remained uncertain whether they would meet the old, devolutionist federal government or a new one prepared to reinvigorate the role of the federal government in Confederation (*Globe and Mail*, 9 December). While provincial finance ministers continued to make the case that any surplus should be used to restore federal-provincial transfers, the premiers, including Quebec's Bouchard, agreed that major programs in areas such as health care had been badly hit by cuts and needed additional funding (*Globe and Mail*, 10 and 13 December). The federal government insisted on its right to govern, including the ability to design and implement new spending programs, and refused to commit any additional funds to offset federal-provincial transfer payment cuts. It did agree, however, to allow the provinces to design their own personal-income-tax systems, providing they compensated Revenue Canada for any increased costs associated with the new system (*Globe and Mail*, 11 and 13 December).

New business

Children and youth

While most of the federal-provincial scene in 1997 centred on constitutional squabbles and fiscal problems, one area received unanimous approval and a new injection of funds: child poverty. Led by Human Resources Minister Pierre Pettigrew, the federal government began an initiative in early January aimed at improving the conditions of poor children in Canada (*Globe and Mail*, 14 January).

Child advocacy groups put the price tag for substantially improving the conditions of children at over $2 billion. Although Mr Pettigrew claimed that 'present fiscal circumstances' would not allow a commitment of that size, he said up to $600 million could be provided by Ottawa for new programs (*Globe and Mail*, 28 January). The plan was backed by the provinces, which proposed the extension throughout the country of a new child benefit program developed by the NDP government of British Columbia. They placed the cost for such a program, however, at $1.2 billion (29 January).

BC Premier Glen Clark called on Finance Minister Paul Martin to pony up the additional $600 million required for the program. The federal budget, however, included only a $600-million commitment, although Mr Martin noted that a further $250 million allocated in the 1996 budget had not yet been spent and would also be directed towards the new program (*Globe and Mail*, 15 and 19 February).

The provinces did not give up on the idea of an expanded program, however, and a two-day conference of Western premiers in May

attempted to place the issue on the electoral stage. It was only successful in having Ottawa agree to develop measures to test the performance
of the new benefit in future years (*Globe and Mail*, 28 May, 23 September, and 7 October).

By the time the premiers met for their annual conference in August,
they had moved onto the issue of youth unemployment and began to
develop plans for job training and educational programs aimed at ame-
liorating the 16 per cent unemployment rate among youths – about double the national average (*Globe and Mail*, 8 August). Ottawa promised
action on a variety of issues, largely relating to education. These
included proposals to ease student debt loads and create a new federal
university scholarship fund, which prompted some observers to suggest
that the 1998 federal budget would be an 'education' budget (24 September and 29 November).

Old business

Native affairs

The year 1997 saw little progress made on issues relating to Canada's
First Nations. The federal government did not respond to the many
issues raised in the multi-volume report of the Royal Commission on
Aboriginal Peoples, and the issues that did emerge tended to be
regional rather than national in scope.

One such issue concerned the continuing question about the future
of First Nations in Quebec, given the possibility of the province sepa-
rating from Canada. While Quebec's Native population had voted in
1995 to remain within Canada, in 1997 it was the turn of the province's
Inuit population. At meetings in Kangiqsualujjaq, about 1,800 kilometres north of Montreal, Inuit representatives began to debate whether to
separate from the province should it declare independence. Citing a
'special relationship' they enjoyed with the federal government, their
preference was to join the new federal territory of Nunavut in the event
of Quebec's secession (*Globe and Mail*, 8 April).

The BC fishery

A major irritant in federal-provincial relations in 1997 was the fishery,
especially the simmering dispute between British Columbia and Alaska
over the Pacific salmon fishery that threatened overall U.S.-Canada
bilateral relations.

In the run-up to the June election, the federal government moved to assuage BC, which had argued that Ottawa had not done enough to assert Canada's rights in 1996. Prime Minister Chrétien flew to Vancouver in March and promised the province greater input into the fishery's management (*Globe and Mail*, 7 March). In April, BC Premier Clark flew to Ottawa to sign a new Canada-British Columbia Agreement on the Management of Pacific Salmon Fishery Issues, which, among other things, promised more money for habitat management in the province and created a ministerial council to help manage future federal-provincial disputes (17 April).

However in mid-election the situation deteriorated once again, with BC cancelling a lease for the Canadian Forces Nanoose Bay testing facility in protest against continued federal inaction in negotiating a new Pacific salmon treaty with the U.S. Although the federal government eventually went to court to block the cancellation, the BC action produced immediate results as Foreign Affairs Minister Lloyd Axworthy announced the resumption of salmon talks (*Globe and Mail*, 23 and 24 May, 15 August).

The talks went nowhere, however, and a record catch by Alaskan fishers made matters much worse, prompting Premier Clark to declare a 'salmon war' on the West Coast. That move prompted Ottawa to issue a diplomatic note to Washington protesting Alaskan interceptions of Canadian fish. The entire situation worsened when BC fishers blockaded an Alaskan State ferry in the Prince Rupert harbour, leading to threats and recriminations all around (*Globe and Mail*, 17, 18, 19, 21, 22, and 23 July). The dispute dragged on throughout the rest of the year with no resolution in sight (11 September and 25 October).

Health care

The subject of a great deal of debate in previous years, health care proved to be a less salient issue in 1997. The year began with the release of a provincial report calling for a national debate on medicare. The report, *A Renewed Vision for Canada's Health System*, proposed weakening the elements of the Canada Health Act guaranteeing Canadians a single uniform national system. The federal government's own blue-chip panel of experts on the subject, however, urged the expansion of the system to include home care and prescription drugs, and called for an end to federal cuts in the area (*Globe and Mail*, 30 and 31 January, and 1 February).

The federal government took the middle road, failing to endorse a new medicare strategy, but also refusing to commit additional new funds to health care (*Globe and Mail*, 19 February). Faced with ample evidence of the popularity of the program and public dissatisfaction with federal cuts, Prime Minister Chrétien took the initiative on the first day of the federal election campaign in April to suspend proposed cuts to provincial transfers and declared this a 'health-care measure.'

Mr Chrétien said the decision not to cut the Canada Health and Social Transfer below $12.5 billion per year would result in an almost $2-billion increase in funding over the next two years and close to $6 billion over the next five. Critics were quick to point out that not carrying through on proposed cuts was not the same as providing new funds and argued that since the CHST was transferred to the provinces *en bloc*, the federal government could not guarantee that any of the money would actually be allocated to health care (*Globe and Mail*, 29 April).

The Liberals continued to press the issue during the election, announcing plans for a new pharmacare system that would coordinate the plans currently in place in many provinces. The contingent nature of the proposal, however, was quickly established when, pressed by reporters for details, the Prime Minister proved hazy on the costs and elements of the plan (*Globe and Mail*, 7 May).

Health Minister David Dingwall also joined in the electioneering, slamming a proposal to build a private health-care centre in Calgary, saying it could lead to the establishment of a two-tiered medicare system in the country. Alberta Premier Ralph Klein was quick to accuse Mr Dingwall of attempting to score political points during the election. The Western premiers fought back at the end of the month, arguing that federal cuts over the past several years had done more damage to the existing system than any provincial actions could ever do (*Globe and Mail*, 16, 17, and 31 May).

When the election was over, things got back on a more normal course, and the federal and provincial health ministers meeting in Fredericton developed a plan to establish a workable dispute resolution system in order to avoid similar blow-ups in future years (*Globe and Mail*, 11 September).

GST

Facing a general election, the federal Liberal government became wary of its published 1993 promise to abolish the federal Goods and Service Tax (GST). The government had tried to negotiate a series of agreements with various provinces to hide the tax in a new 'harmonized' federal-provincial sales tax and had succeeded in doing so with Quebec, Newfoundland, Nova Scotia, and New Brunswick.

In early 1997, however, the proposal for a new Harmonized Sales Tax (HST) with the three Atlantic provinces appeared to be in trouble when regional retailers opposed the plan (*Globe and Mail*, 17 January). The Retail Council of Canada argued that unless the plan was adopted throughout Canada, manufacturers and others would be forced to develop two separate pricing schemes: one for provinces with the GST and one for those with the HST.

Under pressure, the federal government agreed to allow retailers to advertise pre-HST prices, as long as they included a disclaimer to that effect. The House of Commons financial committee, however, called the lack of momentum towards a national HST a 'disgrace' (*Globe and Mail*, 23 January and 6 March).

DEAN F. OLIVER

Foreign affairs and defence

The Somalia inquiry came to a noisy, rancorous end in 1997, the government fighting with its own commissioners for the first six months of the year but later admitting that it had accepted 132 of the inquiry's 160 recommendations. With the promising, if controversial, tenure of Doug Young cut short by his defeat in the 1997 federal election, stewardship of the largely unwanted defence portfolio fell to Art Eggleton, who had barely arrived prior to the inquiry's final report. Amid a flurry of commissions, reports, inquiries, recommendations, and scandals, the slow recovery of the Canadian Forces from Somalia, both morally and politically, went largely unnoticed. It was eclipsed in large part by the activism, commitment, and global profile of Foreign Affairs Minister Lloyd Axworthy, whose human security agenda scored remarkable success with a global ban on anti-personnel land-mines, signed in Ottawa in December. Mr Axworthy's style and methods were not uniformly appreciated, but there could be little doubt by year's end that he had helped to place Canada at or near the forefront of several high-profile international issues. Trade remained perhaps the real engine of Canadian internationalism, as the January trade mission to the Asia-Pacific demonstrated, but Mr Axworthy's agenda at least posited, for the first time in recent memory, a well-articulated project at the heart of Canadian foreign policy and one departing somewhat from the all-but-obnoxious emphasis on trade in the government's 1995 policy paper on foreign policy.

Part of Mr Axworthy's new agenda appeared to include an injudicious questioning of U.S. foreign policy on such issues as nuclear weapons, Cuba, and the United Nations, arousing a vigorous debate in the extended foreign policy community. Part of the agenda also reflected more noble strains in Canada's international persona: humanitarianism, individual rights, and a sense of mission. The efforts were neither uniformly successful nor equally well developed, but the extent to which they approximated a genuinely holistic approach to foreign policy represented a refreshing change to recent practice and an intellectual conception worthy of some note. The long-term implications of Mr Axworthy's approach, and the equally interesting question of its originality, remained a subject of fierce debate during 1997, but its public iterations touched chords in the Canadian body politic that bode exceptionally well for its longevity. In this, at least, the articulation of foreign policy was superb in 1997, even if ruminations on its effects remained incomplete. The gravitation of non-governmental organizations from the peace movement, the development field, and other more traditionally left-leaning areas towards Mr Axworthy's ministerial circle was a source of considerable worry to more traditional foreign policy analysts, but it represented for supporters nothing less than the long-overdue democratization of the policy process.

In as much as they can ever be, Canada's international relations were relatively tranquil in 1997, marred near year's end by events at the APEC summit in Vancouver. Canada's military began to emerge from its Somalia shadow while foreign policy moved, controversially to be sure, towards a more activist and self-confident agenda set by one of the most assertive foreign ministers in Canadian history. Peacekeeping commitments were low, Bosnia was (relatively) stable under a large NATO-led military force, and the Manitoba flooding portrayed Canada's beleaguered military in a far better light than the Somalia inquiry might lead one to expect. Moreover, as both Mr Eggleton and Mr Axworthy promised during the year, improvements in government finances seemed to indicate that, budget wise, the worst cuts might be over. Trade and policy irritants with the United States, over Pacific salmon and Cuba, with NATO over nuclear weapons, and with some NGOs and political groups over Canada's still-predominantly trade-driven agenda continued, but the year ended on a high note: the December signing conference in Ottawa for a treaty banning anti-personnel land-mines, a movement that earlier in the year had netted a Nobel Peace Prize.

The breadth and possible implications of human security raised critical questions regarding resources, personnel, and intentions, none of which received satisfactory answers in official communiqués. However, the unbridled optimism generated by the land-mines crusade infused the public policy debate with a sense of righteous optimism long missing from most discussions of Canada's post–Cold War international persona. The optimism was far from universally shared, however, as even the land-mines campaign had evinced a disturbing smugness on the part of recently empowered NGOs and a cavalier approach by some policy practitioners to the new methodology of foreign policy as articulated by Mr Axworthy and his supporters. Diplomatic niceties, bilateral relations, and military strength continued to matter in a 'wired world,' the critics answered, citing but three sources of objection to the evolving new security agenda. Assurances that the new foreign policy tent was big enough for all worshippers tended to fall on deaf ears when issued more as admonishments to the heretical than as invitations to the flock.

The federal election

A federal election in 1997 returned Canada's second straight Liberal majority government, with the Reform Party becoming the Official Opposition. Foreign affairs and defence policy played a decidedly marginal role in the campaign, although the government's decision early in the year to terminate the Somalia inquiry was the source of some spirited commentary. More generally, in international security policy as elsewhere, criticisms of the Liberal record were scattered and weak, representing both a favourable commentary on the government's performance and an indictment of the Opposition's extreme ineffectiveness on either the foreign affairs or defence files.

Some of the federal parties put markers down early as to their post-election defence and foreign affairs strategies. The Progressive Conservative plan, made public in March, envisaged a rapid reaction division of 14,000 troops as the military's core capability; improvements to procurement, command and control, and civil-military relations within the department; and the appointment of a military inspector general. Liberal policy continued to echo the themes of the 1993 campaign, including human rights, trade, and the democratization of the policy process.

Foreign affairs

United States

Canada's ongoing dispute with the United States over the West Coast salmon fishery escalated in 1997, one of the few serious trade disputes in an otherwise stable and friendly relationship. British Columbia Premier Glen Clark, exasperated at the collapse of bilateral talks, announced plans in May to cancel the lease on the Nanoose Bay submarine and torpedo testing facility, used by both the Canadian and U.S. navies. (The facility itself is on federal land, but BC holds the seabed rights.) Ottawa announced the resumption of talks the following day, but the incident epitomized the complexity of both bilateral and intrastate trade policy in both countries. The resumed talks struggled on for only five days in June before collapsing again, the U.S. refusing to submit the issue to international arbitration. In the meantime, Canada challenged the legality of BC's decision in court on the grounds that it violated standing federal-provincial agreements.

The dispute escalated considerably in July with Canadian accusations, in a 'stiff' diplomatic note to Washington, that Alaskan catches of Canadian-bound sockeye violated the 1985 Pacific Salmon Treaty. The federal government's actions were not enough for many BC fishers, or for Premier Glen Clark. On 19 July, BC fishers retaliated by blockading an Alaskan ferry in Prince Rupert's harbour. Columnist Andrew Coyne referred to the incident as 'an unprincipled hostage-taking' (*Ottawa Citizen*, 22 July). On 20 July a federal court ordered BC fishing boats not to delay ferries, but the blockade continued for another twenty-four hours. Federal and provincial officials still worked to develop alternative plans to retaliate against Alaskan fishers and, despite almost universal media condemnation, the dramatic seizure at least helped precipitate talks between senior Canadian and U.S. officials.* Mr Clark's actions were not endorsed by a meeting of provincial and territorial leaders in August, many of whom, in fact, criticized BC's tactics, especially its threat to close Nanoose Bay. Brian Tobin, the Newfoundland premier and former federal fisheries minister who had opposed both the United States and Europe in high-profile fisheries disputes in the North Atlantic, was a notable critic. Mr Tobin reportedly warned Mr Clark that his tactics played into Washington's hands and that his own international confrontations had proceeded on the basis of a unified federal-provincial front.

With Premier Clark's office claiming character assassination by federal officials and federal Fisheries Minister David Anderson warning the province not to sabotage the bilateral negotiating process, the talks seemed imperilled as much by personality as by policy or environmental concerns. David Strangway, the retiring president of the University of British Columbia, and William Ruckelshaus, head of the U.S. Environmental Protection Agency, assigned to reinvigorate the process, thus began their work during a considerably stormy internal Canadian debate. On 14 August, Ottawa filed suit in the BC Supreme Court to

*For a good assessment of the salmon dispute, see Julian Beltrame and Ian Haysom, 'The Salmon Wars,' *Ottawa Citizen*, 9 August 1997.

prevent the province from cancelling the Nanoose Bay lease and closing the facility, threatening a court injunction if BC decided to proceed
(*Globe and Mail*, 15 August). On 8 September, BC filed suit as well,
this one aimed at the U.S. government for failing to curb overfishing
by Alaska and other states in the Pacific Northwest. U.S. officials
called the BC effort 'terribly counterproductive' (8 September). Premier Clark also accused the federal government of trespassing on the
Nanoose Bay site, noting that they had been doing so since BC's
22 August eviction notice. In the middle of this contretemps between
all parties involved in the dispute, Canadian treaty commissioner
Robin Wright, a member of the U.S.-Canadian commission since 1985,
resigned in disgust. He criticized all parties in the dispute, including
the BC government, for inflaming relations with Washington in order
to boost the premier's local popularity, and the federal Department of
Fisheries and Oceans for badly mismanaging stocks.

Canada's relations with Cuba, a perennial irritant in the bilateral
relationship, again cropped up in January as Foreign Minister Axworthy visited Cuba to sign agreements on trade and investment and to talk
about human rights with Fidel Castro. It was the highest-ranking Canadian delegation to visit Cuba since former prime minister Pierre
Trudeau visited in 1976. Initial U.S. reaction saw the visit as 'rewarding a dictator,' but the comment was retracted later in the day, both
countries resuming their agreement to disagree. Still, some Canadian
press accounts pilloried the minister for according Cuba legitimacy
through the diplomatic approach. Mr Axworthy's visit came in the
wake of continuing disagreement over Washington's Helms-Burton
law, which levied sanctions against foreign businesses accused of prof-
iting from expropriated U.S. property in Cuba. It also highlighted the
long rift between Canada and the United States over engagement ver-
sus isolation. Prime Minister Chrétien, speaking on the issue during a
state visit to France, joined French officials in chiding Washington
over its Cuban policy, adding negative comments on U.S. cultural policy in an intervention that again stirred the waters initially riled by Mr
Axworthy's arrival in Havana.

In the face of Mr Chrétien's untimely comments, U.S. President
Clinton also expressed official scepticism over the effects of Canada's
mission, prompting several additional days of press comment on the
visit and Canada's Cuban policy. Minister Axworthy perhaps had the
best quip of the exchange, commenting that Canada had achieved more
in five hours of talks than the U.S. had in thirty years of embargo
(*Ottawa Citizen*, 27 January). Canadian officials spoke to the Cuban

issue with some confidence as poll results from March 1996 had indicated that 71 per cent of Canadians thought Helms-Burton should be ignored. Another poll pegged that number at roughly 60 per cent, but both indicated very strong support for Ottawa's Cuban trade policy.

The Helms-Burton law was a source of controversy during the year, but also an inspiration for comedy. Liberal MPs Peter Milliken and John Godfrey, speaking at a conference in Washington, explained a plan, similar to Helms-Burton, to reward Loyalists who had fled the United States during the American Revolution for any properties seized by the victorious revolutionaries. Mr Godfrey said he wanted Carter's Grove mansion on the James River near Williamsburg, Virginia. Though light-hearted, the performance also reflected growing Canadian and international disgust with the U.S. legislation. In mid-March, the U.S. State Department prevented four executives of Sherritt International Corp. from entering the United States on the grounds that the company's Cuban investments violated Helms-Burton, echoing a similar decision against seven Sherritt employees in July 1996. In response, International Trade Minister Eggleton called the decision an 'all-time low.' Canada, said Mr Eggleton, was still not prepared to challenge the law under NAFTA but, instead, would await the result of a World Trade Organization (WTO) challenge launched by the European Union, with support from dozens of other countries. The situation was aggravated further by news that the U.S. Treasury Department intended to pursue an investigation into the sale of Cuban-made pajamas by Wal-Mart Canada.

Central and South America

The United Nations peacekeeping mission to Haiti continued in 1997. An *Ottawa Citizen* article on 23 February noted that in three years Haiti had cost Canada's defence budget $430 million. With some 750 soldiers (approximately 50 per cent of the mission) and more than 100 police officers in the country, Canadian policymakers continued to pay special attention to Haiti, especially in the face of widespread reports that lawlessness, corruption, and human-rights violations endangered both the overall mission and the safety of Canadian personnel. Foreign Affairs Minister Axworthy visited in March, announcing that Canadian forces would remain until year's end to help in the transition to full democracy.

In July, the UN extended the Haitian mission but reduced the troop complement. At the mission's termination on 30 November, a civilian police mission of some 300 officers, including twenty-four Canadians, took its place.

Canada sent a small team of unarmed military observers to Guatemala in February for a three-month deployment. Part of a small, sixteen-country truce supervisory force, the Canadians would help monitor the December 1996 cease-fire agreement in Guatemala's decades' old civil war. The fifteen Canadians returned in May.

United Nations

New UN Secretary-General Kofi Annan selected Canadian Maurice Strong to lead a reform of the international organization and, later in the year, announced plans to cut UN spending significantly and to reduce staff. A proposal by the president of the General Assembly, Ismail Rizali, to expand Security Council membership by nine, met a cool response in most Western capitals, but other reform efforts moved quietly forward. In July, Mr Annan announced several organizational changes, including the creation of a deputy secretary-general. Canada opposed the addition of permanent seats on the Security Council, preferring instead the addition of non-permanent seats.

Canadian participation in UN activities in 1997 occurred against the backdrop of impending elections in 1999 for two seats on the UN Security Council among the 'Western Europe and Other' group. Canada would be competing against Greece and the Netherlands. Canada's candidature did not prevent it from developing vigorous positions on human security and land-mines, and from considering a possible ban on small arms. Nor did it prohibit the articulation (yet again) of Canada's displeasure with Washington's failure to meet its financial obligations to the international organization.

Trade and culture

Canada lost an important battle over the protection of its magazine industry early in 1997. A World Trade Organization (WTO) panel made an interim ruling that Canada's efforts to prevent *Sports Illustrated* magazine from publishing a Canadian edition with mostly U.S. content violated world trade rules. The decision struck down preferential postal rates, a tariff restriction, and a tax on split-run magazines, all part of previous efforts to protect Canada's magazine industry from foreign, especially U.S., competition. The U.S. representative to the WTO had filed the case. The ruling left many observers contemplating a cultural 'assault' by the United States on Canadian cultural industries even as Heritage Minister Sheila Copps vowed to appeal the decision. Reports soon circulated that Washington's new trade representative, Charlene Barshefsky, would push the advantage confirmed by the WTO ruling, which prompted further warnings from Canadian magazine and book publishers and other groups.

Canadian prickliness on the cultural trade front stood in marked contrast to its earnest free trade proclivities in other venues. At the World Economic Forum in February, for example, International Trade Minister Art Eggleton said Canada would push for free trade throughout North and South America by 2005. Also in February, Mr Eggleton commented in a speech at Osgoode Hall Law School that it was 'worth asking whether these instruments [Canadian content regulations and foreign investment restrictions] continue to be useful,' which sparked debate on whether or not the government was contemplating the dismantling of Canadian cultural protections. Other commentators suggested that the WTO interim ruling merely provided a welcome opportunity to modernize Canadian trade practices in this area, pointing out, for example, that nothing prohibited Ottawa from funding cultural institutions like museums, theatres, or the Canada Council.

Canada announced its intention to appeal the WTO ruling on 14 March on the grounds that Canada's protectionist measures were aimed at a service (namely, advertising) and not the sale of magazines, a critical distinction as the WTO did not govern the movement or trade of services. The WTO not only rejected the appeal but also ruled that $50 million per year in federal postal subsidies to Canadian magazines was unacceptable. Dave Robinson of the Council of Canadians, a nationalist lobby group, laid blame for the ruling on Ottawa's negotiating position, which, he claimed, had been weakened by accepting the proposition that culture was the same as any other commodity. He called the WTO decision 'a body blow to Canadian culture' (*Ottawa Citizen*, 28 August). The one possible option left open to the federal government, direct subsidies for Canadian magazines, would be extremely expensive.

Europe

Canada's relations with Europe were largely trouble-free in 1997, at least in comparison to the fish wars and boundary disputes of recent years, but the stability of Europe's southern flank still generated international concern. In March, the civil unrest in Albania, which erupted after the collapse of high-risk investment schemes, forced several international organizations to revisit the criteria under which they might proffer assistance and, if so, in what form. After considerable dithering by the European Union and the Western European Union, Italy, facing growing numbers of Albanian refugees, offered to lead a multinational military intervention to stem the flow and to protect humanitarian aid convoys, an offer later accepted by the United Nations. The vanguard of the six-nation force arrived in mid-April. The last troops left on 12 August.

NATO's Stabilization Force (SFOR) continued in Bosnia in 1997 and was not cut during the year as originally planned due to lingering interethnic tensions. Canada approved an extension of its military commitment until June 1998, clearing the way for another battle group rotation in January, pending a review of the force's mandate. The House of Commons Standing Committee on Defence visited Bosnia in November.

The North Atlantic Treaty Organization

Canada and the other members of the North Atlantic Treaty Organization (NATO) wrestled with the subject of enlargement in 1997, including Russian objections to the potential inclusion of former Warsaw Pact states, but in July invitations were issued to Poland, Hungary, and the Czech Republic to enter the alliance. NATO leaders rejected Moscow's call for a virtual veto power over the enlargement process and the Kremlin's interpretation of the degree of influence bestowed on Moscow by the Moscow-NATO Charter, offering instead the possibility of greater flexibility on arms control arrangements, economic assistance, and special consultative status in NATO counsels. In February, U.S. Secretary of State Madeleine Albright proposed a freeze on NATO force levels in Central Europe; the following month, the alliance committed to fulfill its defence mission in new member states by interoperability, integration, and the provision of sufficient reinforcement capability instead of stationing additional permanent forces on new members' territories. NATO also pledged not to deploy nuclear weapons into new member states. Following a March meeting between Russian President Boris Yeltsin and U.S. President Bill Clinton, the West offered Russia full political and economic participation in June's G7 Summit (now the G8) in exchange for dropping its vigorous opposition to the enlargement project.

The gesture was only partially successful. Russian leaders continued

to express profound pessimism over what they perceived as the unnec-
essary aggrandizement of an unreconstructed Cold War–era alliance
and predicted a severe deterioration in East-West relations if the process
moved forward without due consideration of its own position. Their
apparent intransigence, coupled with evidence that Russia's under-
funded military was coming to rely increasingly on nuclear weapons in
its military doctrine, played into an important debate throughout the
West over the future of the alliance. The furore, which included duelling
assessments of the enlargement's anticipated costs, represented one of
the more serious debates in NATO's history leading up to the July summit in Madrid at which invitations to potential new member states
would be offered. Cost estimates of the enlargement project varied
wildly. A U.S. study in February placed costs at roughly $10–13 billion
U.S. for armed forces restructuring, $8–10 billion U.S. to improve exist-
ing NATO forces' ability to deploy into new member states, and $9–12
billion U.S. in 'direct enlargement costs.' The study drew criticism,
especially in the United States, for lowballing the costs in an attempt to
smooth the passage of any actual invitation through the U.S. Senate.

As the Madrid summit approached, NATO leaders redoubled their
efforts to ease Russian concerns over enlargement. A cooperative
agreement in May, framed around a NATO-Russia Permanent Joint
Council, led to competing interpretations of the extent of Russian influence on the alliance. Moscow again claimed – largely for domestic
political reasons – that it possessed a virtual veto over critical NATO
decisions. The Founding Act on Mutual Relations, Co-operation and
Security between NATO and Russia was signed on 27 May in Paris.
Prime Minister Chrétien, busy with the federal election campaign, was
the only NATO leader who did not attend.

Prime Minister Chrétien made Canada's position plain during a state
visit to Ottawa by Czech Prime Minister Vaclav Klaus in late February,
by supporting not only widely touted applicants Poland, Hungary, and
the Czech Republic but also Slovakia, Slovenia, and Romania. The
widely cast net of Canadian endorsements appeared designed at least
as much to appease domestic political constituencies as to establish a
firm foundation for post–Cold War Canadian foreign policy in the
region. Moreover, Mr Chrétien's public commitments came in the
absence of parliamentary debate or a full explanation of the reasons for
Canada's pro-enlargement position. Canadian policy echoed that of
France, Germany, and other members on a broader expansion project,
and not that of the United States, which wanted enlargement limited to
the Poles, Czechs, and Hungarians. Polish President Lech Walesa

pushed for Canada's support during a visit to Ottawa in March. NATO Secretary General Javier Solana visited in April to discuss enlargement with government officials and parliamentarians.

At the Madrid summit in July, NATO issued invitations to Poland, Hungary, and the Czech Republic, as U.S. officials had insisted all along. Other states, including Romania, Slovenia, and the Baltic republics, received plaudits for their progress on democratization and the promise of a future open-door policy, but no invitation. The alliance also decided not to use its forces to hunt down war criminals in Bosnia. The summit also led to a special partnership agreement with Ukraine. A new Euro-Atlantic Partnership Council included all NATO members plus twenty-eight partner states.

Canada's military commitments to the alliance remained small but not inconsequential, including the deployment of HMCS *Fredericton* with NATO's Standing Naval Force Atlantic (STANAVFORLANT) in January for a five-month tour. HMCS *Winnipeg* replaced *Fredericton* in June; HMCS *St John's* replaced it in August. Its political and financial commitments, on the other hand, remained in doubt as the February budget cut Canada's contribution to NATO programs for the fourth consecutive year, down to $145 million per year from $181 in 1993. NATO officials visiting Ottawa in April expressed concerns over Canada's continued commitment to the alliance, even as the NATO Flying Training Program (NFTC) took flight with Doug Young's announcement that Denmark, Norway, and the United Kingdom would participate. A twenty-year, $2.85-billion contract with Bombardier followed in November.

In June, Canada sent six CF-18 aircraft and 125 personnel to participate in NATO's Stabilization Force in Bosnia. They returned in November, having flown 261 missions over that country.

The Middle East

A crisis in Iraq over the UN weapons inspection process, which had been imposed on it after the Gulf War, escalated in the fall. When Baghdad barred U.S. team members from inspections (claiming they were spies), the United States retaliated with sanctions; Iraq then ordered several U.S. inspectors to leave, and the UN evacuated its personnel. U.S. and British military forces prepared for action in the Gulf in support of what was evidently a tottering international inspection regime. Inspections resumed on 22 November, only to have personnel barred from presidential palaces and other politically sensitive sites where, in the past, chemical, biological, and nuclear weapons research and production had been sheltered. Canada expressed support for the UN sanctions against Iraq and the weapons inspection process, but demonstrated far greater reluctance on the possibility of military retaliation in the face of Iraqi intransigence.

Asia-Pacific

Prime Minister Chrétien kicked off Canada's Year of the Asia-Pacific in January with a two-week trade mission to the Pacific, declaring that 'Canadians now realize the Pacific is the future.' It was the clearest indication yet of the declining role of Europe relative to that of Asia in Canadian international trade policy. As *The Globe and Mail* noted on 17 February, 'Asia has come to dominate the Western consciousness. Whether it is economics or ideology, it is hard to think of the future – our future – without thinking of the impact of Asia ... If the 20th century was the American Century, the 21st will be the Asian.' The trip, including nine of the ten Canadian premiers, both territorial leaders, and more than 400 business representatives, was the largest trade mission in Canadian history. It was Mr Chrétien's third mission to the region in two years. The Prime Minister spoke in Vancouver to a gathering of Asia-Pacific parliamentarians and noted that in a competitive global market, the size and profile of the group would have an impact. He also said he expected to see the establishment of a free trade zone among member countries of the Asia Pacific Economic Cooperation forum (APEC) by 2010. In addressing the potential conflict between trade policy and concern for local social and economic conditions, the Prime Minister simply noted that expanding trade was the best route to improving living standards.

The mission's arrival in South Korea drew attention because of Mr Chrétien's refusal to address that country's labour laws, which were the focus of widespread strikes and protests before and during the trade mission. Amnesty International and the Canada-Asia Working Group, a coalition of Canadian churches, were among those criticizing Canada's stand that the disputes were an internal matter. The Prime Minister, the premiers, and South Korean Prime Minister Lee Soo Sung later discussed in private the labour disputes, but labour activists viewed the move as mere sophistry. Roy Culpeper, president of the North-South Institute, accused the government of selling out its own foreign policy principles in elevating trade and jobs to the top of its agenda. The Canadians signed over $200 million worth of contracts and nearly

$400 million worth of memoranda of understanding on the first day of the South Korean visit, a resounding success, said Mr Chrétien. The entire two-week visit witnessed $2 billion in contracts and future undertakings. Between 1986 and 1995, according to a report by the Asia Pacific Foundation of Canada, the value of Canadian exports to Asia increased from $10 billion to $28 billion, representing 9.2 per cent of total exports.

The trip also showcased the contest between federal officials and the province of Quebec over international diplomacy and the benefits of federalism. Ottawa sought to portray the mission's success as support for the benefits of Quebec in the larger federation, while Quebec Premier Lucien Bouchard argued that the mission demonstrated the success of the province's own independent international posture. Such varying interpretations of 'partnership' were more important for domestic consumption. As Mr Chrétien quipped during a ceremony in Seoul, 'Let's sign the contracts, make the money and all of us will collect the taxes' (*Ottawa Citizen*, 11 January).

The trade mission encountered further controversy in the Philippines, where a protest over the adherence by Canadian companies to lower environmental standards in Asia than in Canada greeted the group. As in South Korea, Canadian officials claimed that business environmental standards in the Philippines were not for Canada to decide, but the controversy again pointed to the potential pitfalls of trade liberalization in developing states. As critics of the Canadian stand argued, the environment and trade were intimately related – the push to be competitive globally was adversely affecting environmental protections at home, making it irresponsible (and disingenuous) for world leaders to push the former without acknowledging the problems likely to be created as a result.

Canada placed trade restrictions on the military government of Burma (Myanmar) in July in an effort to force that country to respect basic democratic and human rights. Relations had generally deteriorated throughout the year with the arrest of hundreds of dissidents and the continued house arrest of Nobel Peace Prize laureate Aung San Suu Kyi. Ottawa's largely symbolic gesture affected only $16 million in bilateral trade but represented an important gesture for critics of Ottawa's human-rights record in Asia.

November saw the fifth meeting of APEC leaders in Vancouver, an event that began generating controversy in February with news that Canadian officials had been unsuccessful in adding human-rights issues to the agenda. John Klassen, director-general for APEC in the

Department of Foreign Affairs, said that discussion of human-rights issues 'is certainly not going to happen' (*Globe and Mail*, 17 February). Given its decidedly mixed records on human rights, Canada's trade relations with Asian states was a simmering dispute throughout the year. The summit provided an ideal opportunity for domestic activists and trade critics to publicize the alleged hypocrisy of Canada's doing business with dictators while preaching democracy and human rights. Although the meeting discussed financial developments in the region and APEC members agreed to strengthen international cooperation and move towards multilateral tariff reductions, the real story of the summit was the treatment by RCMP officers of anti-summit protestors. After an incident in which officers pepper-sprayed several protesters, a furious media debate began over both the propriety of Canada's hosting world leaders with questionable human-rights records, and the degree to which the Prime Minister's Office had been involved in orchestrating security precautions to protect them.

Lloyd Axworthy visited India in January, following up a 1996 visit by the Prime Minister. Mr Axworthy discussed mostly trade and investment issues, including a telecommunications joint venture and a large hydroelectric dam project. As development reporter John Stackhouse noted, the visit by Mr Axworthy epitomized the advent of economic diplomacy and the infusion, even for an avowed human-rights campaigner like Mr Axworthy, of trade into all other diplomatic realms. Unlike British Prime Minister John Major, who had spoken in Calcutta to 3,000 listeners the day before, Mr Axworthy addressed only 200 in the same venue.

Mr Axworthy's visit also highlighted the growing importance of 'human security' in Canadian international policy, the foreign minister noting that development policy would be increasingly guided by human-security concerns. In the Third World context, these would include training local journalists, promoting distance education, making development-related radio and television broadcasts available, and using the Internet to link human-rights organizations and local rural agencies. Such themes echoed the findings of a 1996 task force, chaired by Maurice Strong, that Canada's strategic advantage is most likely to lie in its potential as a 'knowledge broker' to the world. Mr Axworthy promised that the four-year, 28 per cent cut in the development-aid budget was the end of the cuts, though he committed to no increases. Sounding a theme to which he would return frequently in the coming months, Mr Axworthy argued that 'the [end of] the Cold War has really liberated us. We're now freer to establish a broader range of contacts. People see us as much less part of a broader American agenda.' 'We're shifting,' Mr Axworthy argued, 'from larger-scale projects into ones that are more supportive of environmental issues, children's issues, governance issues – ones that have a direct impact on individuals. It means projects that are much smaller and tend to be very much in the realm of soft power projects. They don't have the big ribbon-cutting attachments to them' (*Globe and Mail*, 15 January).

Africa

A Belgian inquiry into events in Rwanda in 1994 questioned the leadership of the UN's mission commander, Canadian Major General Romeo Dallaire, and the UN's own senior military adviser, Canadian General Maurice Baril. Though its criticisms of Mr Dallaire made headlines in Canada, prompting several responses by Canadian historians and defence analysts, the Belgian inquiry was more broadly critical of the structure and organization of the UN contingent, its basing arrangements and armaments, its confusing rules of engagement, and the indifference from the international community.

A report on Canada's failed effort to mobilize international support for a Zaire peacekeeping mission, released by the Department of National Defence in August, noted that Canada was 'in a weak military and political position' to orchestrate the mission successfully. The report noted a range of problems, including inadequate forces, poor command and control, lack of international support, and faulty or nonexistent intelligence. It also highlighted problems in liaising with other countries, especially the United States and other potential troop-contributing countries, and with non-governmental organizations. The report fell short of advising against leadership by small countries in such efforts, but highlighted both the difficulty of their leading at all, and the necessity of firm military commitments from supporting states, especially the United States. The report was released at a high-level conference held in Halifax and co-sponsored by the department of foreign affairs, Dalhousie University, and Oxford University.

Canadian-Nigerian relations deteriorated early in the year when Canada withdrew its high commissioner and closed its mission in Lagos in response to what Ottawa viewed as inadequate security guarantees for its staff. The move was also part of Canada's criticism of Nigeria's military government and its treatment of Nigerian dissidents.

Defence

Arms control

Canada continued to play a key role in the global effort to ban the use, production, transfer, and stockpiling of anti-personnel land-mines in 1997. In January, the United States rejected Canada's argument that a ban should proceed through an international conference outside the aegis of the United Nations Conference on Disarmament (CD). Canada and several other countries and non-governmental organizations had complained at the pace and commitment of the larger agency. The United States supported the Conference on Disarmament as the best means of bringing recalcitrant states like China and Russia into the process. Canadian officials, however, noted that because the CD operated on a consensual basis, even one of its sixty-one members could stall the process, now identified as a major Canadian policy initiative. Because of the global 'crisis' over land-mines, in other words, ban supporters professed themselves increasingly willing to skirt or avoid existing multilateral channels in favour of new arrangements.

By mid-February, Canadian predictions of the CD's ineffectiveness appeared incontrovertible, even the United States branded the CD's agenda 'a disgrace.' Outside the CD, in the 'Ottawa process,' however, 111 states sent representatives to a February meeting in Austria. Britain's new Labour government provided an important boost to the campaign by coming onside in May; France signed on shortly thereafter. Following another conference in Brussels in June, ninety-five countries agreed to meet in Ottawa in early December to sign a comprehensive ban. The United States, Russia, and China remained outside the 'Ottawa process,' but the speed and effectiveness with which the campaign unfolded during the year represented a stunning success for ban advocates. UN support for the fast-track approach appeared to legitimize the process, undercutting U.S. support for the lethargic Conference on Disarmament.

At a final conference in Oslo in September, attended by ninety countries, the United States participated but proved unable to wrest key concessions, like a longer phase-in period, from hard-line ban advocates. Events in Oslo were notable both for the role of non-governmental organizations in orchestrating opposition to Washington's last-minute attempts at a compromise on its own terms, and for the personal telephone diplomacy between Mr Clinton and Mr Chrétien that sought to pave the way for a reckoning with U.S. concerns.

The Oslo meeting laid out the terms for the ban treaty and set the stage for the Ottawa conference in December. Treaty signatories would ban the use, production, transfer, and stockpiling of anti-personnel land-mines; destroy existing stockpiles over a four-year period; and clear existing minefields over a ten-year period. After Oslo, the 'Ottawa process' moved from success to success in the fall leading up to the signing conference, including a Nobel Peace Prize for U.S. activist Jody Williams and the International Campaign to Ban Landmines (Lloyd Axworthy earned a nomination for the 1997 prize but was unsuccessful). Canada's Prime Minister and other senior ministers and departmental officials pushed the project at every opportunity. Japan agreed to join, as did Australia, while Russia, though remaining out, agreed to a permanent ban on exports.

The December signing ceremony in Ottawa was widely viewed as a triumph for Canadian diplomacy and an important advancement for international human security as 122 nations signed the ban treaty. Minister Axworthy encouraged signatories to ratify the agreement as soon as possible – it would only become operational after forty signatories ratified it. Canada became the first country to ratify the agreement and announced $100 million for mine clearance and victim assistance. An important forum on the land-mines crisis accompanied the signing conference and Canada agreed to host another international gathering in March to discuss coordination, resource use, and the implementation of mine-related programs. The treaty and its speedy, successful negotiation sparked debate on the role of NGOs in the policy process and questioned whether the diplomatic means used to fast-track the agreement had been worth the price, including the confrontational approach Canada sometimes used in its relations with the United States. It also raised questions over whether or not circumstances were likely to permit the process being used again to resolve other issues, like child soldiers or small arms.

Nuclear arms control between the United States and Russia continued to fade from public prominence in 1997, a function of declining East-West tensions, despite Russia's failure to ratify START II. In March, Russian President Boris Yeltsin and U.S. President Bill Clinton discussed a third Strategic Arms Reduction Treaty at Helsinki, one that might reduce their respective nuclear arsenals to 2,000–2,500 long-range weapons each. With Russia's financial situation affecting its ability to comply with the terms of START II, Washington offered Russia extra time to destroy warheads and missile silos. Some analysts cautioned that NATO's enlargement made it impossible for Russia's parliament to approve START II, but U.S. officials insisted that no additional arms-control progress was possible without its ratification.

The House of Commons Standing Committee on Foreign Affairs and International Trade (SCFAIT) agreed to review Canadian policy on nuclear weapons, at the request of the foreign minister, but the committee's current workload precluded a full review in the spring. The committee received a confidential briefing on existing policy from foreign affairs and defence officials in early March prior to its first hearing with anti-nuclear groups later in the month.

Defence policy

Defence Minister Doug Young announced a major initiative on defence policy in January, undertaking a multifront analysis of the management and leadership of the Canadian Forces and the Department of National Defence prior to making a report to the Prime Minister in March. As one important part of the review, Mr Young asked four well-respected academics to examine the Canadian Forces and report to him by mid-March with their findings. Desmond Morton (McGill Institute for the Study of Canada), J.L. Granatstein (York University), David Bercuson (University of Calgary), and Albert Legault (Laval University) received instructions to comment on the management and control of the armed forces; military ethos and discipline; the officer corps (including officer selection, promotion, and leadership); the role of civilians in the defence department; accountability; and the role of the minister. *The Globe and Mail* dismissed the initiative, complaining that a report on management did little to address fundamental policy problems, like a Cold War organization and structure that still plagued the department. Other commentators welcomed the initiative as innovative and likely to result in better commentary than yet another formal inquiry or policy consultation process. Mr Young outlined his own objectives in an interview with *Maclean's* magazine's Peter C. Newman in February. 'My whole objective here is not just to rebuild the department, but to end up with an organization that has a realistic and meaningful mandate.' He pleased many military analysts by saying that 'we must field a military that's respected and respectable,' but raised concerns that sweeping policy changes might also be planned when he noted that 'the present peaceful environment contradicts many defence policies still in place that are really geared to war-making.'

Mr Young also appointed a three-person Special Advisory Group on Military Justice and Military Police Investigative Services, chaired by

The Right Honourable Brian Dickson, to review the Code of Service Discipline and the future role of the military police. Retired Lieutenant General Charles Belzile and Mr J.W. Bud Bird, assisted by retired RCMP Assistant Commissioner Lowell Thomas for the review of military police services, completed the panel.

The minister began receiving documents and reports in mid-March and submitted a consolidated report, along with the several commissioned studies, later in the month. In addition to the four academics' reports and the report on military justice by Mr Dickson, the review included documents on leadership and management, authority and accountability, and ethics and values. It also included comparative assessments of Canada and several other countries, plus a distillation of opinions on defence from within the Canadian defence community. From these, Mr Young gleaned 100 recommendations on everything from military discipline to command and rank structure, to conditions of service to public relations.

While the minister found no reason to revisit the basic principles upon which the CF and current policy were based or the basic structure of the military, he did suggest on 16 March that 60,000 regulars, 30,000 reservists, and a $10-billion budget, coupled with more discerning choices over military deployments, must in the future be the cornerstones of Canadian policy. Moreover, he accepted important recommendations on a broad range of topics, including making a university degree a requirement for commissioning as an officer (except for promotion from the ranks); the extension of courses and training at all levels on ethics, leadership, and accountability; and major changes to the system of military justice. (Mr Young accepted all thirty-five of the Special Advisory Group's recommendations.) The latter included the creation of a military ombudsman reporting directly to the minister.

The government and defence department wrestled with the implications of Mr Young's recommendations in the spring amidst preparations for the 2 June federal election. Somewhat surprisingly, perhaps, defence and foreign policy issues played a small role in a campaign that returned a Liberal majority government, if not all of its senior ministers. Doug Young lost his New Brunswick seat and was replaced by Toronto-area MP Art Eggleton, formerly the minister of international trade.

Defence budget, military equipment, and training

February's federal budget showed just under $9.92 billion for defence in 1997–8, compared with $10.7 billion in 1994–5, $9.9 billion in

1995–6, and \$9.6 billion in 1996–7. Roughly \$2.1 billion in 1997–8 would be capital expenditures. Art Eggleton, appointed minister of national defence after the June election, stated that the era of budget cuts was over and that restoring morale and moving forward on several equipment purchases were his top priorities.

DND awarded a \$552-million contract to General Motors of Canada for 240 armoured personnel carriers, with options for an additional 411. Announced in August 1995, the contract would see the first vehicles delivered in January 1998. Canada's fleet of maritime coastal defence vessels (MCDVs) grew during the year. HMCS *Edmonton* sailed from Halifax to its new port, Esquimalt, British Columbia, in April, where it was commissioned on 21 June. It was the fourth of a projected twelve MCDVs. By September, eight of the vessels had been launched, with keels laid for numbers nine and ten.

Four companies submitted bids for new search and rescue helicopters in May, including the Westland-Augusta consortium with a variant of the Cormorant helicopter, an order for which was cancelled by the Liberal government with some fanfare in 1993. The other competitors included Boeing (with the Chinook helicopter), Eurocopter (the Cougar), and Sikorsky (a Blackhawk variant). By fall, the selection process had stalled amid allegations by several bidders that the process had been unfairly skewed in favour of the Cormorant.

Canada made no decisions on acquiring British Upholder class submarines in 1997, despite comments by Defence Minister Doug Young in May that the decision would be made by year's end. Art Eggleton, Doug Young's successor, made similar assurances after the June election and in the wake of a poll showing 63 per cent public support for the purchase. The new minister visited Britain in July to 'kick the tires' on the submarines, amid reports that London was prepared to improve the deal, but still no decision appeared close.

Somalia inquiry

Changes in the defence team in late 1996, including a new defence minister and chief of defence staff, signalled the beginning of the end of government patience with the long-running and expensive (\$23.8 million through March 1997) Somalia inquiry. While the government did grant the inquiry a third extension to its original mandate, this time extending it to the end of March 1997, it also determined that this would be the last modification and that the final report must be submitted by 30 June. The commissioners themselves had asked for far more generous terms, including at least an extension to the end of the year. According to documents released in early March, defence department officials had recommended that the minister end the inquiry, but cabinet had made the final decision.*

The decision announced 10 January to terminate the Inquiry was almost as controversial as the events in Somalia in March 1993, which had led to its creation two years later. The chair of the inquiry, Mr Justice Gilles Letourneau, led the commissioners' criticism of the government's decision, claiming that it would now be 'impossible' for the investigation 'to comprehensively address the question of the accountability of the upper ranks' of the Canadian Forces and the defence department (*Toronto Star*, 14 January). This, the commissioners had apparently concluded, was likely the real source of the trouble. Truncating the investigation now, they argued, would protect political reputations and senior military officials but do little to get to the bottom of the crisis. Moreover, claimed the commissioners, the inquiry had not been delayed by its own indifference or inefficiency, but in large part by defence department delays in the release of official documents and by a four-month document-tampering scandal. Justice Letourneau himself went further, claiming that raw political calculations – the Liberal government's fear of bad press and damaging revelations in the run-up to a federal election – might have affected the decision. He later described the decision simply as 'political interference' (*Maclean's*, 24 February). While the inquiry had started out as a Liberal investigation into the misdeeds of an outgoing Progressive Conservative government whose prime minister, Kim Campbell, had been defence minister during the critical period in the spring of 1993, it had now blossomed, critics claimed, into something else entirely. At issue now, it seemed, was the Liberal government's handling of the post-deployment phase and subsequent events, including its response to media and public criticism between 1993 and March 1995, when the inquiry was authorized.

The commissioners, in acceding reluctantly to the government's unprecedented decision, did future researchers and the broader public a great service by releasing thousands of pages of documents brought forth during the months of testimony. Mr Young, however, in one of the investigation's more memorable phrases, bluntly dismissed the need for further analysis: 'We know who pulled the trigger. They know who beat the young man tied to a chair to death,' he noted in reference to Somali teenager Shidane Arone. Mr Young also dismissed sugges-

Ottawa Citizen, 8 March 1997, cited in *Defence Newsletter* 16/3 (March 1997), 9.

tions of an official cover-up and vowed to proceed to fix the Canadian Forces and defence department instead of wasting more time on a fruitless, expensive inquiry. Mr Young's abruptness appeared to overlook completely the complicated set of circumstances that had given rise to the inquiry in the first place, and painted cynics and doubters in a distinctly unflattering and unjust light. The Prime Minister supported his embattled colleague: 'There is a time when the minister has to face his responsibility and he cannot postpone solutions to the very difficult problems [while] waiting for a report' (*Ottawa Citizen*, 14 January). An opinion poll conducted in late January indicated that Canadians supported the government's decisiveness, with 57 per cent of respondents agreeing that the inquiry had gone on long enough. (Another poll, taken in February, found that 48 per cent of Canadians believed the early termination would prevent full disclosure of the truth, but that 43 per cent nevertheless supported the decision.)

The decision itself, and the near-venomous exchange of public comments between Doug Young, Justice Letourneau, and other principals in the days that followed, sparked renewed public debate over the inquiry, its mandate, and the scandal itself. Some commentators applauded the government's bloody-minded decisiveness and blamed the commission itself for foot-dragging. Others bemoaned what they took to be self-serving expediency and the near-useless conclusions likely to arise from a prematurely terminated investigation. As *The Globe and Mail* noted on 17 January, 'What use is half an inquiry?' In addition, the termination, and the fact that the inquiry could no longer hear all the evidence it believed necessary to conclude its original mission, helped prompt several senior officials, including former Chief of Defence Staff Jean Boyle, to file court motions barring the inquiry from reaching findings of discredit against them. (A Federal Court judge later rejected the claims.)

Federal Court judge Justice Sandra Simpson ruled in March that the government had acted illegally in terminating the inquiry before it could complete its original mandate, a transgression leaving Ottawa with few options other than to resume the inquiry or to rewrite the terms of its mandate. The government appealed the ruling but nevertheless modified the inquiry's mandate to report only on what happened prior to the December 1993 deployment, leaving to the commissioners' discretion whether or not to pass judgment on events in Somalia in early 1993.

The Senate offered to continue the inquiry's investigation, a move the federal government at one point seemed prepared to support, but the first discussions in April on how to proceed ended in rancour with little accomplished. By October, as the government tabled its detailed response to the inquiry's findings, the minister of national defence signalled his view that, while the Senate was of course free to do what it wished, the government had all the information it needed and saw no further need for an additional public inquiry. The Senate stood down.

Debate over the inquiry's termination occurred simultaneously with the investigation itself and a series of related events. Retired Colonel Geoff Haswell was found not guilty in January of two counts of ordering Somalia-related documents destroyed in September 1995 after a civilian clerk had testified that she had been asked to get rid of them. In inquiry hearings, former Airborne Regiment Captain Michel Rainville denied charges that he had promised beer in exchange for shooting Somalis, but did acknowledge setting a trap for prospective looters. He also raised a sensitive point by suggesting that former Chief of Defence Staff Admiral John Anderson had warned the troops in the theatre not to do anything that would likely harm the chances of Minister Kim Campbell becoming leader of the Progressive Conservative Party.

The possibility that Somalia had been handled badly because of concerns within DND over the effects that the potentially embarrassing revelations might have on Ms Campbell's political career surfaced several times throughout the year, including in a memorandum dated 1 March 1993 in which then deputy minister Robert Fowler urged the department to 'take as low a profile as possible' (*Ottawa Citizen*, 30 January). Ms Campbell and her political staff responded vigorously to the damaging implications in this line of inquiry, arguing – convincingly, for the most part – that she and her staff had been kept poorly informed by the defence department. One staff member, John Dixon, even claimed in an affidavit to the inquiry that senior defence officials had destroyed copies of a letter warning Ms Campbell not to participate in the legal and administrative work on the Shidane Arone murder, ostensibly to avoid the perception of meddling in a formal investigation.

The roughly five-week delay in sending a military police team to Somalia was a source of ongoing debate. Acting Chief of Defence Staff Vice Admiral Larry Murray, who was then Deputy Chief, denied having refused three requests to send investigators, claiming he was simply waiting on an incident report from the unit's commanding officer. Admiral Murray claimed at the time to be especially interested in clearing up any problems with the rules of engagement that may already have been partly responsible for the shooting of two Somalia looters. Both Admiral Murray and the officer that had complained of the long delay, retired Colonel Al Wells, offered to take lie detector tests to support their claims. A military police officer later claimed that the delay in handling promptly the 4 March shooting of another Somali, which Major Barry Armstrong, a military doctor, claimed was an 'execution style' killing, may have contributed to the overly permissive environment in which Shidane Arone was later executed.

Admiral Murray's testimony led to a fiery exchange with commission counsel Simon Noel and Justice Letourneau, in which the Acting Chief of Defence Staff expressed his disgust at the way former witnesses had been treated and insisted his own testimony not be handled similarly.* Admiral Murray's claim that the commission 'consistently demonstrated a total lack of understanding of the dimensions, the magnitude and the responsibilities of the people involved in running the department of natural defence,' precipitated a short delay in the proceedings after which Justice Letourneau admonished him for 'approaching the line of contempt' (*Toronto Star*, 29 January). The televised incident received blanket media coverage and, in the opinion of many analysts, ruined Admiral Murray's chance of ever succeeding to the office of Chief of Defence Staff. In standing up to what many observers had also come to see as a pushy, unnecessarily confrontational process, however, Admiral Murray garnered praise for protecting his officers and the military itself against what, at times, appeared to be a kangaroo court.

Admiral Murray completed his testimony in early February with decidedly less fanfare. He acknowledged that mistakes had been made in responding to the crisis, but maintained that there had been no cover-up. The Canadian Forces, on the whole, he concluded, had done 'remarkable work' in Somalia but had returned as the 'Vietnam vets' of their country.

Colonel Serge Labbe, the former mission commander, also took the stand in February, claiming that the Shidane Arone incident was the only thing to mar the six-month deployment. Testimony by another senior officer, retired Lieutenant Colonel Carole Mathieu, seemed

---

*A Federal Court judge, Justice Douglas Campbell, ruled in February that Justice Letourneau displayed bias against one of the officers involved in the Somalia affair, Brigadier General Ernest Beno, and barred him from participating in commission deliberations over the general's conduct. The ruling inadvertently echoed Admiral Murray's opinion over the professionalism and detachment of the inquiry's chair. Justice Letourneau announced his intention to appeal in late March. In May, the Federal Court of Appeal vindicated Justice Letourneau, commenting that it was 'a gross error for the judge to conclude that the ... chairman was not impartial' (*Toronto Star*, 3 May).

designed to discredit the warnings of Major Armstrong, whose concerns had been instrumental in revealing the crisis to the public, but Lt. Col. Mathieu wilted under questioning, admitting that Major Armstrong, far from being a 'loose cannon,' had indeed warned him of his suspicion of murder by members of the Airborne Regiment. The doctor's testimony in March represented a damning perspective on the Somalia operation. Having pressed for an investigation of the 4 March killing, Major Armstrong had first been assigned bodyguards to protect him from the troops, and was later sent home from the theatre entirely. Senior military officials appeared to have attempted to question Major Armstrong's character by probing whether Major Armstrong had sold drugs on the Somali black market, but Justice Letourneau cut off that line of inquiry as an unwarranted personal attack. After hearing final witnesses on 19 March, the inquiry adjourned until 7 April to hear final summations, finally adjourning to write its report on 11 April.

The inquiry finally presented its voluminous report to the government on 30 June, incensed that the government-imposed deadline appeared designed to ensure little press coverage on the Canada Day vacation of 1 July. In some ways, the report was anticlimactic, coming after a spring of fierce public debate over the inquiry, its mandate, and its cancellation. *Dishonoured Legacy: The Lessons of the Somalia Affair* was a 1,700-page indictment of military inefficiency, mismanagement, poor command, and weak leadership.* In essence, it argued that poor leadership and a subsequent cover-up had taken the criminal actions of troops – in a poorly prepared and unsuitable unit and on a difficult and thankless mission – and elevated them to the ranks of high scandal. It rejected categorically the 'few bad apples' theory initially advanced by the defence department in 1993, blaming instead, in the words of Justice Letourneau, 'systemic, organizational and leadership failures.'

The troubles were legion and stunning and, given the many revelations since March 1993, including the troubling series of videos and brutal hazing incidents, scarcely surprising. The Airborne Regiment had been unready for the mission. 'Political expediency and a desire to be visible on the world stage overrode all practical logistical concerns' in planning, dispatching, and basing the mission. Public affairs officers conspired to alter or destroy critical documents. Some senior officials

---

*The core report consisted of five volumes plus an executive summary. There were an additional ten studies on subjects ranging from racial prejudice to peacekeeper training and the organization of defence headquarters.

lied to the inquiry. The report criticized eleven senior officials for having failed in their duty, including Generals de Chastelain, Reay, Beno,
MacKenzie, and Boyle. Two commissioners also took the extraordi-
nary step of voicing the personal opinion that Vice Admiral Murray
was not fit to inherit the position of Chief of Defence Staff. The
inquiry's list of recommendations ran to 160, including parliamentary
guidelines for participation in future peacekeeping operations, major
reforms to the system of military justice, a civilian inspector general,
and the re-creation of merit as the primary criterion for senior officer
promotion.

The government's initial reply to the report came forty-eight hours
after its presentation. Mr Eggleton, after just one month as minister,
responded forcefully – and critically – to the charges. He dismissed
outright the charges of cover-up and lying by senior officials and railed
against the title of the report, its excessively critical tone, and the
unbalanced judgments it contained. The Prime Minister expressed similar views. Indeed, as senior officials quickly noted, many of the recommendations proposed by the inquiry had already been highlighted in
Doug Young's March 1997 report to the Prime Minister on the leadership and management of the Canadian Forces and were therefore in the
process of being fixed. (Mr Chrétien said 70 per cent fell into this category.) Thus, concluded Mr Eggleton, in a not-entirely-convincing argument, many of the problems were already being fixed and the Somalia
recommendations, if anything, merely confirmed that the department
was on the right track.

The explanation pleased almost no one. While opinion within the
defence community and, according to some opinion polls, in the public
at large, had been running against the inquiry for some time, expert and
public reaction to the comments of both Mr Eggleton and the Prime
Minister were, on balance, extraordinarily harsh. Even media outlets
that had been supportive of the government's decision to terminate the
inquiry, viewed the defence minister's breezy and dismissive response
as arrogant and appalling. Major presses like the *Ottawa Citizen*, *The
Globe and Mail*, and *The Gazette* (Montreal) echoed a chorus of complaints against Liberal arrogance and abuse of power. Others, less
shocked by the government's caustic response, were nevertheless disappointed by the government's tone and severity. *The Globe and Mail*
was especially scathing: 'As a neophyte, Mr Eggleton gave a breath-
taking performance on Wednesday, as a sycophantic agent of both the
Prime Minister, whose hardball fingerprints are all over this case, and
of the military brass at bay' (4 July).

If substantially critical, however, the spate of press reactions to Mr Eggleton's wildly unsuccessful press conference soon dissipated. As the Halifax-based *Defence Newsletter* noted, 'After the initial flood of articles on the Somalia report when it was published on 2 July, media and public interest had slowed to a trickle the following week, and had virtually disappeared by mid-July. It appears that Prime Minister Chrétien correctly judged the attention span of the Canadian public.'* A gag order issued by Vice Admiral Murray later in the month to have all departmental media statements cleared through his office appeared to confirm the truth of some of the inquiry's charges, but this story too faded quickly from the headlines. Admiral Murray himself soon departed as well, passed over in promotion to CDS for General Maurice Baril, an officer not deemed to have been tainted by Somalia. It was widely assumed, and frequently lamented, that his testy exchange with Justice Letourneau, and the publicity it generated, had ended his military career. Within months, he retired; not long afterwards, he appeared in the senior ranks of the civil service, first in the Department of Fisheries and Oceans, and later at Veterans Affairs Canada.

The combativeness of the government's initial reaction to the inquiry's findings was followed in October by a more detailed, formal response from the department. In a 112-page report entitled *A Commitment to Change*, presented by Mr Eggleton, the department said that it had accepted all or a part of 132 of the inquiry's 160 recommendations. The most notable among the twenty-eight rejected or, in the minister's opinion, being dealt with on other fronts, was the establishment of the position of inspector general. The department instead opted for a military ombudsman who would answer directly to the minister's office; for reforms to military justice and the system of military policing (having accepted all thirty-five recommendations of the Dickson Report from March 1993); for a new national investigation service; and for a revised grievance procedure for civilian and military staff.[†] Mr Eggleton also announced changes to the manner in which various military and departmental units reported to the minister, and announced the formation of a civilian monitoring committee, chaired by a former supreme court justice, that would report biannually for two years on the department's implementation of the changes. Former inquiry commis-

---

Defence Newsletter, 16/7–8 (July–August 1997), 16.

†The government introduced a raft of changes to the National Defence Act later in the year, including reforms to military justice and discipline and the abolition of the death penalty.

sioner Peter Desbarats dismissed the reforms as creating the 'illusion of accountability.'

Other scandals

The army released several thousand pages of documents in January after a lengthy investigation of events at Bosnia's Bakovici hospital in 1993–4. The documents accused fifty-seven soldiers, most from the Royal Twenty-second Regiment and ten of whom had since left the military, of drunkenness, sexual misconduct, and abuse of patients during the mission. Those who had not left could not face courts martial because the military's three-year statute of limitations had already expired, but army commander Lieutenant General Maurice Baril asked the Chief of Defence Staff to convene a special career review for each individual. Moreover, Lieutenant General Baril noted on 17 January, several of the infractions were exceedingly minor (like alcohol consumption) and the soldiers had already suffered public embarrassment. He also reminded Canadians, in remarks that appeared callous and insensitive to much of the national press corps, that because the conditions faced by those on dangerous overseas deployments induced high stress, similar incidents were bound to recur. The documents also noted that rules on alcohol consumption had been disregarded by officers and that previous investigations of the Bakovici incidents had been insufficient and untimely, even though the army found no evidence of a cover-up. Not all charges were cleared up by the January release of documents; in at least one case, the troops were exonerated on the charge that soldiers had sold a heavy machine gun on the local black market, although the report noted that the weapon had been inadequately guarded.

The Bakovici incidents appeared to offer dramatic support for those claiming that the problems in Canada's military went far beyond the misdeeds of a few individuals. Both Lieutenant General Baril and Mr Young expressed outrage at the findings that came just as Mr Young launched into a multifront assessment of departmental management, justice, and administration. Former RCMP assistant commissioner Lowell Thomas cleared the army's chain of command of cover-up but also criticized the two-year delay in initiating a serious investigation. He also recommended that the military police be removed from the military's formal chain of command to protect their independence and freedom of action.

Simultaneous with the release of the Bakovici documents, the army released a report on the alleged abuse of former Captain Sandra Perron during an April 1992 training exercise and her later decision to leave the military. A capable officer, well liked by the troops, the report found that Ms Perron had faced both subtle and overt forms of sexual harassment throughout her military career, including her two peacekeeping tours in the former Yugoslavia. On the night of the incident in Gagetown, New Brunswick, Ms Perron was tied to a tree and interrogated for four hours during a snowstorm. Her interrogator, former Captain Michel Rainville (the same Rainville involved in the shooting of Somali looters in early 1993), meted out harsher treatment to her than to male soldiers 'captured' on the same mission. Again, as in the Bakovici case, the military's statute of limitations on courts martial had expired.

The Perron case fed into a broader debate on the role of women in the military. Purists argued that military standards were being lowered to facilitate gender integration in the combat arms; critics cited Ms Perron as evidence of continuing widespread harassment and sexism in a male-dominated institution. Some, including retired Major General Lewis MacKenzie, complained that the incident had been blown out of proportion by reporters unaware of and unsympathetic to the necessity of tough, realistic military training.

Public anger and scepticism greeted the news in early January that the department spent over $100,000 on a one-week leadership seminar in Cornwall, Ontario, for seventy-five employees. The seminar, which included a session in which employees painted their thoughts and emotions as a cathartic exercise, received attention and highly unfavourable media coverage at a time when the department remained mired in controversy.

Organization and personnel

The House of Commons Standing Committee on National Defence and Veterans Affairs (SCONDVA) began important hearings in February on the social and economic challenges facing members of the Canadian Forces. As Minister Young said in his appearance before the committee on 12 February, 'the 'people problems and needs [of the CF] ... impact on the future of the organization.' The morale of military personnel and their families is an important social responsibility of the government, he argued, doubly so in that such factors affect everything from institutional structure to operational effectiveness. 'The time has come to sort out the source of these problems and to recommend the changes needed to improve morale.'

Admiral Murray, who testified that a five-year pay freeze (to end 1 April) had left military personnel well underpaid by civil-service standards, nevertheless maintained that low morale in the CF was not only the result of poor pay but also of lack of public recognition. Press coverage of Admiral Murray's comments appeared on the same day as a DND-commissioned study, prepared by Ottawa's Martial Research, claimed that military personnel perceived their leaders as out-of-touch with reality and the needs of the troops. Many witnesses before the committee echoed such sentiments, sounding an almost incessant note of criticism over pay, benefits, working conditions, and family services. Army commander Lieutenant General Maurice Baril admitted, in response to an exposé series by the *Ottawa Citizen's* David Pugliese, that 'we have failed miserably to provide support for those who have lost their health in the service of our country and for families who have lost a loved one' (*Ottawa Citizen*, 27 March).

Domestic emergencies

Canadian Forces personnel, helicopters, and transport planes rescued some 300 anglers from the ice on Lake Simcoe, Ontario, in January after a crack in the ice had separated them from shore. The expensive rescue mission raised questions about whether or not military search-and-rescue missions should be remunerated in part by fees from hunters, anglers, and, especially, adventure travellers like those who attempt to row or sail across the North Atlantic.

Massive floods along Manitoba's Red River in April and May led to the declaration of a state of emergency and the deployment of some 8,000 troops to provide aid to the civil power. The soldiers assisted with sandbagging, dike construction, search-and-rescue operations, evacuations, and provided medical assistance and other local services. In yet another year marked by controversy and scandal, Operation Assistance provided a badly needed publicity boost for the Canadian Forces. The operation began to wind down on 8 May.

The provincial perspectives

The provincial perspectives

Ontario ROBERT DRUMMOND

The Conservative government of Premier Mike Harris entered the third year of its mandate during 1997, and the Thirty-sixth Legislature likewise began the third year of its first session. The Assembly was called to resume sitting on 13 January and remained in session until 6 March; it recessed until 1 April and then continued, with occasional short breaks, until 3 July. It sat again from 18 August to 9 October, and from 17 November to 18 December. The Legislature passed forty-six public bills (and nineteen private bills) in that period, including several large and complicated pieces of legislation. The pace at which the government pursued its restructuring of the Ontario public sector seemed to be accelerating, and in the course of the year, some unease began to emerge, even among the government's supporters, that they might be going too far and too fast.

The focus of attention for an Ontario government in the modern era has to include the health-care system and public education, but emphasis on one or another of these important areas may vary over time. In 1997, the weight of the government's attention was clearly on education. It introduced and passed a highly controversial piece of legislation aimed at reforming many elements of school organization; restructured tax and expenditure responsibilities for schools; promised and began revision of the elementary and secondary curriculum; and reduced local school boards in number, size, remuneration, and influence. The reaction from elementary and secondary school teachers was expressed in a two-week, province-wide withdrawal of services, which the government called an illegal strike and which the teachers called a political protest. Teachers received considerable support from parents and the media, and the government took considerable bad publicity for a while. In the end, however, the legislation passed with little change, and it was not clear that any further protest from the teachers could muster the same level of support.

On the health-care front, the government successfully concluded negotiations on a fee schedule for physicians, though speculation about other forms of payment continued to come up in public discourse. As the year wore on, questions were raised about the other areas of the system, such as nursing care, that might have suffered as a result of the deal made with the doctors. Considerable attention was directed to the Health Services Restructuring Commission, an arm's-length body created by the government to make recommendations on the reorganization of (mainly) hospital facilities in the province. The government was subjected to pressure from many quarters to intervene and reject some recommendations of the commission – pressure they were able to resist. The commission recommended hospital closures and mergers in several areas, and by year end, many of the recommendations were in the early stages of implementation. It was still too soon to tell whether the dire predictions of critics would be borne out, and too soon to know whether the commission's insistence that hospital closings be accompanied by expansion of the home-care system would be honoured.

A somewhat unusual aspect of the provincial government's activity in 1997 was the extent of its concentration on several elements of provincial-municipal relations. The government had embarked in the previous year on a program of study to determine how the tax, expenditure, and legislative authority of municipal governments might be reorganized so as to maximize efficiency and save money. In addition, based on the reform of the education system, the government was intent to centralize at the provincial level those responsibilities for education that had ordinarily been left to municipal school boards. As a result of this intention to have the province take over responsibility for education taxes and education spending, it became necessary to move some provincial responsibilities to the municipal level in order to make the shift of education 'revenue-neutral.' The changes to taxation and expenditure were the subject of debate for much of the year, with many municipal politicians and interest groups insisting that the balance would not be revenue-neutral and that the wrong services were being moved. Some changes in the government's original plan were made before final passage of the legislation, but not all municipal authorities or interest groups were satisfied. In addition to this 'downloading' controversy, were changes to the province's rent-review legislation, the proposal to amalgamate all municipalities of Metropolitan Toronto into one city, and the introduction of a property-tax reform labelled 'current value assessment.'

The reduction of school boards, the amalgamation of municipalities (especially but not exclusively in Toronto), the reorganization of municipal services, and the closures and mergers of hospitals all created the need for complicated transition plans involving personnel and labour relations. The province's attempt to order, and to some extent simplify, the transition ran into opposition from affected workers and their unions, and in the end the government was forced to make some concessions from its original position. A further complication was created in some areas by the province's attempt to proceed with its 'workfare' scheme in a way that forced reluctant municipal governments to participate.

Finally, this was a year in which there was significant attention paid to legal matters. The provincial government sought to turn public attention to matters of crime and corrections through the activity of a backbench investigatory group, and by the creation of a young offenders 'boot camp' in the Barrie area. It passed bills concerning police services, community safety, and road safety. In other areas of the law, the courts ruled that the government's revision to the pay equity rules was unconstitutional and that the province's insurance law discriminated unlawfully against gays.

Despite the suggestion in some quarters that the government was endangering its popularity by the pace and breadth of its agenda for change, it ended the year in a favourable position in the opinion polls, well ahead of the NDP and neck-and-neck with the Liberals. The Premier had stayed aloof from the federal election campaign in the spring, though several of his cabinet colleagues had taken part in support of Conservative or Reform candidates. When the election was over, and the Liberals had taken all but two of Ontario's 103 seats, the Premier called for a merger of the federal Conservative and Reform Parties so as not to continue splitting votes on the right. The call was quickly rejected by federal Conservative leader Jean Charest. In July, the Premier announced that by-elections would be held on 4 September to fill three vacancies in the Assembly. The opposition parties retained all three seats – the Liberals held on to Oriole (in suburban Toronto) and Ottawa West, while the NDP kept Windsor-Riverside. It remained to be seen whether the Conservatives would seek to soften their image and slow the pace of change in the run-up to a provincial election expected in 1998 or 1999.

Education

Towards the end of January, the government announced the creation of a seven-member, semi-autonomous commission to implement reform of public education. (The government had already signalled its belief in the need for such reform.) Additionally the commission would oversee the planned reduction in school boards throughout the province. Perhaps the government hoped to insulate itself from criticism of the reform agenda by the appointment of such a commission, but in the end it was compelled to proceed by legislation to achieve the most significant of its reforms, and the Opposition was thus directed at the government rather than at the commission. Labelled the Education Improvement Commission, the body was co-chaired by David Cooke, former minister of education in the NDP government of Bob Rae, and Ann Vanstone, former chair of the City of Toronto Board of Education and widely regarded as a conservative voice in education matters.

In April, in the hope of opening up more jobs for newly graduated teachers, the government announced a plan to provide early retirement incentives to teachers approaching eligibility for full pension. A fund of between $320 million and $350 million was to be created from a combination of provincial revenues and surplus money in the teachers' pension fund. The money would be used to offer relief from the actuarial reduction in the pension to teachers who were aged fifty-five or older. To be eligible, they would need a combination of age and years of service that reached eighty-five or more, but was less than ninety – at ninety points (age and service) they would ordinarily be eligible for full pension. Earlier challenges by the teachers' unions, concerning ownership of the pension surplus, had led to an agreement to halve the actuarial reduction, but teachers still lost 2.5 per cent of their pension for each point below ninety. The incentive fund would wipe out that reduction for teachers who qualified. It was assumed that some local school boards might also create early retirement plans, perhaps for teachers who had attained eighty-five points but who had not yet become fifty-five. The government estimated that 5,000 teachers might take advantage of the scheme. Sceptics, aware of the government's cost-cutting efforts in its first two years in office, wondered how many of the retiring teachers would actually be replaced by new graduates.

In June, the Ministry of Education announced the general outline of its plans for curriculum revision. The main elements of the changes proposed were the reintroduction of streaming by ability in Grade 9, the phasing out of Grade 13, and the introduction of a literacy test as a requirement of high-school graduation. Destreaming had been instituted by the NDP government in 1993, in recognition of the fact that children from working-class backgrounds seemed to be concentrated in the 'basic' stream. They suspected that such placement was a result of bias and would have detrimental, long-term effects on those children's career prospects. The return to streaming was welcomed in some quarters, since in principle it would permit teachers to better tailor their instruction to the abilities of their students. The end of Grade 13 had been a long-promised goal of successive Ontario governments, and indeed it had been assumed that the introduction of the Ontario Academic Credits system would have accomplished that goal. It appeared, however, that many students were still taking five years after Grade 8 to complete their high-school diplomas. The government's announcement projected that students entering Grade 9 in 1999 would graduate from high school in 2003. The announced reform preserved the requirement of thirty credits for graduation but was silent on which courses would be compulsory and which optional. Moreover, there was no discussion of the balance expected among mathematics, science, technology, English, humanities, and the arts. Clearly there would be many details to fill in before September 1999, when the new curriculum was to be in place, and the ministry promised widespread consultation with teachers and parents as they proceeded to implement the changes.

In early September, the Education Improvement Commission issued its first report, and in its recommendations were many of the elements of Bill 160, the controversial legislation which led to the teachers' political protest in October. The commission recommended that the school year be lengthened, that there be more instructional time per student during each school day, that there be no increase in average class size, and that principals be given a clearer managerial role in the administration of their schools. Some school principals and other critics asked why there was no mention in the report of money for materials needed to achieve the improvement in education that the report promised. One principal, quoted in *The Globe and Mail* (14 September), noted that there was not enough money available in his school to provide textbooks for his Grade 4 students. Lengthening the school year would not solve that problem. Some observers, including Martha Harron of the government-appointed Ontario Parent Council, wondered whether a model common in parts of Europe – longer winter and spring breaks, combined with a shorter summer break – would be a more effective way of lengthening the school year, rather than the commission's recommendation of cancelling some professional development days and starting the fall term a week before Labour Day. The commission also recommended a redefinition of teachers' work to include extracurricular activities (currently voluntary activities), meetings with parents, and remedial work with students. It was not clear whether the recommendation was aimed at requiring all teachers to undertake such activity at a uniform level, or at recognizing (and potentially rewarding) the normal work of teachers not currently treated as an essential part of the job. The controversy over Bill 160's treatment of teachers' preparation time was to some extent foreshadowed by this recommendation.

About ten days after the report was issued, Education Minister John Snobelen indicated the government would not proceed with the recommendation that the school year commence a week earlier. Although many Canadian provinces started the school year in the week before Labour Day, Mr Snobelen noted that he had received numerous representations, especially from rural constituencies, opposing the change. In an earlier era, such opposition might have been linked to the need for family farm labour, but with so small a proportion of the Ontario population engaged in agricultural production, rural concerns now seemed to be centred on the tourist industry, with as much attention to the vacationing clientele as to the teenaged labour force. Whatever the reason, Mr Snobelen reaffirmed his intention to add two weeks of instructional time to the elementary school year and three weeks to the secondary, but not by starting the term a week early.

On 22 September, the government introduced Bill 160, entitled the Education Quality Improvement Act, into the legislature. Among the changes the bill would produce were a province-wide limit on average class size (twenty-five at the elementary level and twenty-two at the secondary level), a reduction of paid preparation time for secondary school teachers (as a consequence of an increase in required in-class time), and the possibility of using non-certified teachers in some subject areas such as music and physical education. Teachers and their unions reacted negatively, and on 27 October the five teachers' unions, under the umbrella of the Ontario Teachers Federation and the leadership of its president, Eileen Lennon, withdrew their services across the province. Some 126,000 teachers were on what the government quickly labelled an illegal strike. The teachers insisted it was a political protest aimed at the provincial government and not a strike against their employers, the local school boards. On 10 October, with relations between the government and the teachers deteriorating, the Premier completed a small cabinet shuffle that removed John Snobelen from education and replaced him with David Johnson. Mr Johnson's experience in negotiating with the Ontario Public Service Employees Union during their 1996 strike was thought to be promising for a favourable resolution to the dispute with the teachers. When the teachers walked out, however, the government moved quickly to seek an injunction against their action and to petition for an order that they return to work.

On 1 November, the government placed a full-page advertisement in several Ontario newspapers, calling on public support for their agenda of education reform. Many of the changes they cited – understandable report cards, province-wide testing, a back-to-basics curriculum – were not part of Bill 160, but it was clear the government wanted the electors to see the controversial bill as one more step in a highly desirable program of educational improvement. The teachers' unions argued that the government's main aim was not improvement but merely cost-cutting, while the government reiterated its commitment not to cut funds for classroom use and promised it would reinvest any savings from other areas back into the system. The government was embarrassed just before the walkout when the opposition leaked to the press the performance goals set for Deputy Minister of Education Veronica Lacey. The document made clear the government's expectation that Ms Lacey was to find two-thirds of a billion dollars in savings in the education field; there was no mention of reinvestment. Four days before the teachers withdrew their services, the Premier acknowledged that there had been a plan to cut over $600 million from the education budget, but not, he insisted, from classroom teaching. Critics were unimpressed by the distinction, and from that point the government found it difficult to argue that the aim of Bill 160 was simply to improve the educational performance of Ontario schools.

The request for an injunction ending the walkout was heard near the end of the first week by Mr Justice James MacPherson. Because talks were resumed between the teachers and the government on the weekend of 1–2 November, Justice MacPherson reserved his judgment to allow the possibility that they would reach an agreement. When no agreement was achieved during the weekend, Justice MacPherson announced his decision. There was not yet, he declared, evidence of irreparable harm that would justify his intervention. The application was premature, since it was open to any local school board (the direct employers of the teachers), and indeed to any affected citizen, to apply to the Ontario Labour Relations Board for a declaration that the teachers were violating their contracts by undertaking an illegal strike. Sanctions could then have been applied. Since no such action had yet been taken, the application for injunctive relief was denied. Justice MacPherson was careful to point out that he was not to be read as saying that he agreed the teachers were acting in the public interest by being out of the classroom, but it would simply be some time before irreparable harm would occur. He did describe teachers as law-abiding in the main and unlikely to prolong the dispute to the point of such harm. The teachers took this judgment as something of a victory, and they also found the majority of public opinion on their side. Not surprisingly, therefore, talks with the government broke off on 4 November, though the following day there was some speculation that the teachers might call off their protest without a satisfactory resolution of their differences around Bill 160. On Friday, 7 November, three of the teachers' unions announced that they were ending the walkout and would return to their classrooms on the following Monday. On the weekend, the two hold-outs – the Ontario Secondary School Teachers Federation and the Ontario English Catholic Teachers Association – agreed that they too would go back to work on the Monday. The strike/protest was over, with most of the publicity having favoured the teachers.

The government, however, had not yielded on many of the main elements of the bill, and it was free to proceed with the bill's passage. The government agreed that uncertified personnel would not be used to replace, but only to complement, certified teachers, and ultimately agreed that class size limits would be set by legislation rather than by regulation. However, it maintained the reduction in preparation time for high-school teachers and reintroduced an item dropped earlier – the requirement that principals and vice-principals be removed from the teachers' unions. On 1 December, Bill 160 proceeded to second reading and it was passed into law on 8 December. The teachers vowed to continue their fight against the bill through its implementation and to pursue what they described as their defence of quality public education, but it was clear that the government had succeeded to a considerable extent in achieving its education goals. School boards had been reduced, a new curriculum was being developed, streaming had been reintroduced, school tax rates and budgets were to be largely the responsibility of the province, and tighter restrictions had been applied by the province to working conditions of teachers in the schools. As the year drew to a close, opponents of the government's approach were facing an uphill fight.

In the area of post-secondary education, the government maintained its long-standing hands-off approach to the internal governance of the province's universities, preferring to use control of grants and fees to influence the system indirectly. Tuition fees were again permitted to rise and the basic grant-funding was stabilized, after years of cuts. In March, full-time faculty members at York University in Toronto went on strike. As in most strikes, issues of money and working conditions were in contention, but also of importance was the university administration's decision to amend the collective agreement unilaterally, once the parties were in a strike/lockout position. The changes made related to the flexible retirement scheme then in place for faculty, which the employer described as unaffordable – a description challenged by the union. The strike ended in May with a mediator-crafted settlement; it was, at fifty-five days in length, the longest faculty strike at any English-language university in Canada's history.

Health

Towards the end of 1996, the provincial government and the Ontario Medical Association had reached a tentative agreement on a fee schedule, but ratification was delayed until January of 1997. The agreement covered the removal of salary caps and the creation of provisions to ensure service to underserviced areas, but there was no firm agreement on the fees associated with specific procedures. The OMA accepted the agreement as an interim deal on 16 January, and the parties set 28 February as a deadline for resolving outstanding issues. In the end, it took considerably longer – a new three-year deal on OHIP billing was not reached until 14 May and not ratified until 31 May.

The government's approach to health care, as with education, was to make the more difficult decisions the responsibility of an arm's-length body. In the case of health, the province had established a Health Services Restructuring Commission in 1996 under the chairmanship of Dr Duncan Sinclair, former vice-principal (health sciences) and dean of medicine at Queen's University. Referred to as the Sinclair Commission, its first task was to receive submissions from District Health Councils on the reorganization of hospital services, and then to recommend hospital closures and mergers to improve the efficiency of the health-care delivery system. It had long been recognized that Ontario had a surplus of acute-care beds and a deficit in chronic-care and rehabilitative facilities. Over several years of hospital budget cuts by governments of different partisan stripes, hundreds of beds had been closed across the province, but with few exceptions, hospitals remained opened. As well, there had been little development of community and home-care services to provide the support needed when acute-care beds were closed. Better techniques and technology might have made it possible to release people from hospital sooner, but there was still a need for monitoring and assistance when patients returned home. The commission's purpose was to provide independent judgment about the most efficient organization of hospital resources, and to make recommendations about the services that should be developed in the community to substitute for hospital care.

Between 24 and 26 February, the commission made its first series of reports on recommended hospital closures, covering five communities, including Ottawa and London. On 6 March, the commission announced its recommendations for what was still Metropolitan Toronto. Perhaps to soften these blows, Health Minister Jim Wilson announced 7 March that the government was seriously considering cancelling the last phase of planned cuts to hospital budgets. In addition, because of accounting changes, the hospitals would receive a one-time cash infusion of some $400 million – the three to four weeks of payments that had been held back annually under an accounting system put in place in the 1970s.

Throughout the year, the Sinclair Commission continued to make recommendations for hospital reorganization and for programs of reinvestment in community health services. In almost every instance, representatives of affected hospitals and interest groups made appeals to the commission for changes in its plans, and in some few cases the appeals were successful. Appeals to the government to overturn the work of the commission were much less successful, though the government did undertake in late June to establish a comprehensive approach to rural and northern hospitals, which preserved some facilities, in modified form, that were otherwise slated for closure. On 27 February, a Liberal member of the Ontario Legislature, Sandra Pupatello, brought a resolution to the floor of the House calling on the government to end the cuts to hospitals and to suspend the work of the commission. The resolution passed, with the support of six Conservative backbenchers and the tie-breaking vote of the Speaker. However, a resolution of the House has no more weight than an expression of opinion, and the government took no action to curtail the commission's work.

In Ottawa, the commission originally called for the merger of two hospitals (the Ottawa Civic and the Ottawa General) and for the closing of three small hospitals. In addition, the forensic and long-term psychiatric services of the Brockville Psychiatric Hospital (which was to be closed) were to be moved to the Royal Ottawa Hospital. Among the three small hospitals to be closed was the Hôpital Montfort, the only entirely French-language hospital in the Ottawa area. Quebec Premier Lucien Bouchard and Prime Minister Jean Chrétien were among those who petitioned the provincial government and the commission to reconsider that closing. Implicit in Premier Bouchard's intervention (at least as far as some in Ottawa were concerned) was that protection of anglophone institutions in Quebec would be more likely if the Ontario government did not shut down a major francophone institution in the nation's capital. There were some French-speaking personnel in other Ottawa hospitals, of course, but francophone critics argued they could not provide the same service as could be found at Montfort. There, they argued, francophones could be certain, when they were ill and at their most vulnerable, that they would be dealt with universally in their mother tongue. Whether because of the logic of that argument, or the sense that national unity was in the balance, Hôpital Montfort was spared in the commission's final Ottawa report. However, its budget was halved and its number of beds sharply reduced.

In Toronto, the District Health Council had itself recommended the closing of eleven hospitals, and some of the institutions affected had begun investigating mergers and reorganization strategies that would permit them to maintain an independent existence. In particular, the Wellesley Central Hospital and the Women's College Hospital in the downtown area had begun merger talks. The commission recommended the closing of ten hospitals, including six acute-care facilities, three small chronic-care hospitals, and a private addiction-treatment facility. The commission called for a decrease in acute-care beds of 28.5 per cent. The strongest opposition campaigns from among the hospitals to be closed or merged came from Women's College (which asserted the pre-eminence of its commitment to women's health issues), Branson Hospital in North York (which served a large community of seniors, living nearby and with limited mobility), and Wellesley Central (whose AIDS/HIV treatment centre was to be moved farther downtown to St Michael's Hospital). The commission also recommended that some existing hospitals be converted into ambulatory-care centres, and ultimately the solution for Branson was to accept that role in a merger with North York General. Women's College Hospital was to merge with Sunnybrook Health Sciences Centre (in the northern part of the old City of Toronto), and a lengthy round of negotiations began with the aim of preserving a separate identity for Women's College, and of ensuring in the new institution a commitment to women's health needs.

Eventually a compromise was achieved: greater weight was given to the representatives of Women's College in the decision-making bodies of the merged hospital, and the downtown site of Women's College was preserved as an out-patient facility. Spokespersons for St Michael's Hospital sought to assure those involved as patients or care-givers in the AIDS/HIV community, especially gay men, that their treatment needs would not be jeopardized in any way by the fact that St Michael's was affiliated with the Roman Catholic Church. An uneasy truce was in place by year's end, supported in part by anecdotal evidence of Roman Catholic institutions in other places with strong and supportive AIDS/HIV treatment programs. The closing of Wellesley did mean the loss of a centre for therapeutic abortions, however, and St Michael's understandably would not be filling that gap.

The government had announced plans to save $1.3 billion across the province through hospital mergers and closures but had promised to reinvest that money in long-term and community care. It was clear such reinvestment might involve regional redistribution, since in Toronto some $430 million was being extracted through hospital reorganization, but only $50 million was projected for reinvestment in community care. Among the items that the government called reinvestment was an $8–$10-million commitment for a Women's Health Council to promote a focus on women's health. Although the council might direct some money to research, it was not itself a treatment or research facility.

Dr Sinclair made clear that the commission's intention was that services might be relocated, but that the overall level of service provided in the community would not be diminished. Reporters began to seek out instances where services were unavailable, but it was never clear whether these cases resulted from hospital closures, unprecedented peaks in demand, the transfer of resources out of nursing to cover increased costs of physicians, the temporary dislocations of a transition period, or some other cause.

Savings were often described in terms of buildings being closed, and heat, light, and water costs being recouped. However, the magnitude of savings projected clearly included some job losses. Premier Harris took some flak in March, when he compared the job losses in the health-care sector to those incurred in plastics firms when the hula-hoop craze faded in the 1950s. Retraining would similarly be possible for those in the health sector, he opined, but critics felt he was denigrating the importance of health care by comparing it to a faddish toy. Projections of job losses in Toronto ranged from 'low thousands' (David McKinnon, head of the Ontario Hospital Association) to 'close to 10,000' (Sue Colley, executive director of the Health Sector Training and Adjustment Program, an agency created by unions and health-care organizations to assist laid-off workers).

When the Sinclair Commission first addressed hospitals in rural areas, it recommended the closing of twenty-five out of eighty sites, and the conversion of four others into ambulatory-care centres. In late

June, the government announced a revised plan for rural and northern hospitals that allowed most of them to remain open. The difference was that they were now to be divided into four categories with varying resources and services: the first category would provide twenty-four-hour service by registered nurses, but might not have any in-patient beds; the second would have some acute-care beds and would have physicians on call; the third category would provide acute care, including some services requiring advanced technology, as well as some specialty services (such as cardiac care or psychiatry); while the fourth category would be full-service teaching hospitals, located in Academic Health Sciences Centres, which would be linked into northern networks for purposes of referral and consultation. Residents of rural areas, including those living in quite remote locations, were pleased to learn that at least emergency care would not be moved further from their homes. Critics of the government painted this move as an attempt by the Conservatives to preserve their rural support base.

As part of the cabinet shuffle in October, Jim Wilson was replaced by Elizabeth Witmer as health minister, and in November the government proposed a review of the entire health-care system. To some, it appeared that a wholesale review of health care was already underway, through the work of the Sinclair Commission, but others felt the process had begun at the wrong end; it would have been preferable to begin with an investigation of the primary-care system. One might have begun by considering the use of nurses and nurse-practitioners to prevent hospitalization, and only then turned attention to the scope and organization of the hospital system. In late July, the commission had made some detailed recommendations about the reinvestment that should take place in long-term care and home care, and the government made promises to consider those recommendations. At year end, there was no indication what form a wholesale review of the health system might take, and the Sinclair Commission continued with its work.

Municipal affairs

The province's reform agenda for municipal affairs included a reorganization of taxing authority and policy responsibility between the province and municipalities (the so-called downloading issue), the introduction of a new system of real property assessment for municipal taxes, the loosening of rent-review restrictions, and the amalgamation of some municipalities, most notably the five cities and one borough of Metropolitan Toronto, which were to be joined into a single 'Megacity.'

In the third week of January, the government made several announcements of changes to be made in municipalities, including the reduction in the number, size, salaries, and influence of school boards. They announced the plans to amalgamate Toronto into a single city and the move to 'current value assessment' (which observers had difficulty distinguishing from the supposedly discredited 'market value assessment'). Finally, they outlined the changes in municipal responsibility that would result from the shift of education costs to the provincial level. The press dubbed the period 'Megaweek' and highlighted the pace and breadth of the task on which the government had embarked.

Opposition to the amalgamation of Toronto was beginning to crystallize even before details for the scheme were revealed. On 10 January, *The Globe and Mail* columnist John Barber quoted U.S. author and consultant Wendell Cox's opinion that the amalgamation would not save any money (presumed to be the government's aim). Larger municipal employee bargaining units would, he believed, bid up wages and benefits to the level of the best available before the merger. He cited numerous U.S. examples to support his case. On 7 January, five of the six municipalities in Metro announced their intention to hold plebiscites on amalgamation. The sixth, North York, soon agreed to hold a vote as well, but the provincial government, citing its constitutional authority over municipalities, made clear its intention to ignore the results of any such poll.

The municipalities all held their votes on 3 March, though with slightly different voting procedures among them, and in every case amalgamation was rejected by over 70 per cent of those voting. The province, which had already said it would ignore the results, nevertheless spent some time trying to argue that the votes were unrepresentative and otherwise flawed, though the turnout in most cases was comparable to that in ordinary municipal elections. The question of amalgamation was undoubtedly confused in some voters' minds with the issue of downloading and the reform of the property tax system, but so uniform a result was hard to ignore. Opposition organized around a group called Campaign for Local Democracy (abbreviated to C4LD in some publicity and reports). With its greatest concentration of support in downtown Toronto, it mounted a campaign around most of the issues addressed in 'Megaweek,' but with the main focus of attention being the planned amalgamation and the province's stated intention to ignore the results of the local plebiscites. The group mounted protests at the legislature, presented briefs when the legislation was being debated, and conducted public meetings and information sessions to raise the consciousness of Toronto citizens about the amalgamation and downloading issues. Prominent in its leadership was former city councillor and mayor of Toronto, John Sewell.

The amalgamation bill (Bill 103) came before the Legislature for approval in principal on 1 April and was sent to committee. The Opposition parties promised to delay the bill as long as possible, and the technique they used was to move over 12,500 amendments – 8,000 of which, presented by the NDP, were identical motions calling for residents of each street in Metro to be advised of any changes in regulations. Simply reading all the amendments threatened to bog down the Assembly for several days. The NDP proposed that the government withdraw the bill, or at least suspend its taking effect until after municipal elections had been held under the old boundaries in the fall. (Such a delay would have allowed campaigns for municipal office between pro- and anti-amalgamation candidates.) The Liberals, with somewhat fewer amendments, were resigned to the bill's being passed, but they wanted to delay it long enough to permit some careful attention to problems of implementation. As the days dragged on, the Conservatives sought agreement to measures that would speed up the process, but the opposition parties insisted on receiving some concession for their agreement. Given the number of amendments, it was perhaps inevitable that at some point, the government would fail to signal its vote against an amendment and it would pass on voice vote.

On 4 April, such an amendment did pass, potentially giving significant power to the residents of a small street in Etobicoke. (When the legislation eventually passed, the government withdrew the section that contained this amendment and introduced and passed a second bill to reinstitute the section in unamended form.) On 7 April, the Speaker ruled that it would not be necessary to read every amendment in full; only the street name need be read. That decision speeded up the process somewhat, but it was not until 11 April that the bill passed committee stage, and for that to occur, it was necessary that the standing votes on the amendments be conducted by groups of members in four-hour shifts. The normal locking in of members for votes was modified so that the lobbies (where food was available) and the washrooms were included in the locked-in space. The government had hoped to pass both the amalgamation bill and the fewer school boards bill within four days of 1 April. As it was, they had to wait until the Legislature resumed sitting on 21 April.

As soon as Bill 103 passed, five of the six Metro municipalities declared their intention to challenge the law under the Charter of

Rights, citing violation of the freedom of thought and association and equality before and under the law. North York, having received advice that the challenge had little hope of success, elected not to join in the court case. When the case was decided in July, the court took the traditional constitutional view that municipalities were creatures of the province and that therefore the legislation was entirely valid. Another opposition tactic considered was a petition to the governor general to ask that the bill be disallowed; more properly (but with the same low likelihood of success), the petition should have been directed to the lieutenant-governor, asking that she reserve the law for consideration of disallowance by the federal cabinet. This tactic was not pursued, and the opponents turned their attention to the process of implementation and to the elections for the new city council and mayor that would be held in the fall. C4LD remained in existence as a municipal lobby group with a somewhat broader agenda.

When the provincial government announced its plans for downloading, it called for municipal governments to pick up the full cost of public health, social housing, and homes for special care, as well as half the costs of family benefits and long-term care. In addition, municipal governments would be made to increase the proportion (going from 20 per cent to 50 per cent) they paid for general welfare, child care, and emergency hostels. They would be relieved of the costs they currently bore (20 per cent) for women's shelters. Finally, the province declared it was getting out of the business of local transit, including GO transit, and transferring full responsibility to the local level. In return, the province would take up all the costs of public elementary and secondary education. Critics of the plan observed, first, that many of the services being shifted to the local level were 'soft' services to people, rather than 'hard' services to property (like roads and sewers), and as such should not be funded by the property tax. Second, it was noted that many of these items were likely to increase in cost at times of economic downturn and should therefore not be dependent on a municipal tax levied on the value of property rather than income or consumption, especially as the effects of a recession might vary across municipal boundaries. Instead their burden should be spread across the range of taxes and the full territory of the provincial level. Third, it was suggested that the items selected would have differential cost across the province; the heaviest burden would fall on Metro Toronto, since it had a disproportionate number of persons and families requiring the services in question. The changes proposed did not entirely conform to those recommended either by the Crombie 'Who Does What?' panel, or by the Golden Commission on the Greater Toronto Area. The Association of Municipalities of Ontario mounted a vigorous campaign to lobby the government in the hope of inducing a change in the proposal, and in May the government did move to modify the plan.

In May, the government indicated that it would take only half of the education costs from the local level, though it would undertake to set province-wide rates for the portion of education funding that would remain on the property tax. In return, the province agreed to take on 80 per cent of the costs of general welfare and family benefits and a 100 per cent of the costs of long-term care. As well, it undertook to provide some transitional funding for repairs to social housing, since the cities had complained that they were being given responsibility for a stock of housing in need of considerable repair. The legislation was finally passed on 2 December and would take effect, along with a new assessment system and the coming into existence of the new City of Toronto, on 1 January 1998.

In municipal elections held for the new city, the mayoralty was contested by a long list of candidates, but the main contenders were Barbara Hall, Mayor of the of City of Toronto, and Mel Lastman, long-time Mayor of the City of North York. When the votes were counted, both candidates showed well in their home communities, but it was clear that Mr Lastman had been more successful in generating support outside North York than Ms Hall had been in doing so outside old Toronto. Accordingly he was elected the first mayor of the new Toronto.

In the January 'Megaweek,' Finance Minister Ernie Eves announced that municipal taxes would henceforth be based on a uniform assessment system throughout the province, and that the system would be based on the actual value of the property assessed. Most municipalities would be little affected by this change, since their properties had been reassessed relatively recently. In Metropolitan Toronto however, some properties had not been reassessed since 1954 (when 1940s values had been used), and it was likely that many property owners would see substantial change in their tax position as a result of the new 'current value assessment.' Since the system was to take effect in January 1998, it would be the new City of Toronto that would set tax rates for the former Metro under the new scheme. The new system afforded one further complication for the amalgamation plan.

The legislation created six classes of property, for which municipalities might set different rates, replacing the two classes that had existed before. Assessed values of properties were to be calculated on the basis of sales in an area, and the location, lot size, quality, and local amenities that contributed to the value of those sales. The likely selling price of other homes in the area would thus be determined, and then specific additions to a property (such as a swimming pool, garage, or finished basement) would be factored in. Assessments would be based initially on 1996 values, but in the long run a three-year rolling average would be used.

Municipalities were given the option of phasing in tax changes over a period of up to eight years, and to defer all or part of any tax increases for seniors and/or the disabled until the property was sold. There was widespread recognition that the existing patchwork of assessments, especially in Toronto, led to unfair tax bills, but there was also anxiety in some quarters about the effect of rapid increases in the tax burden. It was feared that rapid tax increases would drive some home-owners out of the city and weaken the residential community that was widely credited with making Toronto's downtown safer and more liveable. At one point, there was concern that some wealthy corporations would have their buildings in downtown Toronto reassessed as lower in value, which would mean that less lucrative commercial properties elsewhere in the city would be faced with higher taxes. Business fears were somewhat lessened by the fact that, in concert with the changes in property taxes, the province had opted to repeal the business occupancy tax levied on firms in addition to their regular municipal taxes. Of course the revenue previously raised by the business occupancy tax would have to be found elsewhere, or service costs cut accordingly. One side benefit promised by the system was a diminution in the number of appeals levied each year against assessments in Toronto. The appeals process was streamlined, and it was argued that a simpler, more uniform system would be more transparent and would therefore generate less opposition. The legislation was fairly quickly passed in late May, and it remained for the municipal governments (including the new Toronto) to deal with the effects of transition.

In November of 1996, the government had introduced a change in the province's rent-review legislation, creating a Rental Housing Tribunal to handle a variety of landlord-tenant disputes. The legislation was criticized by tenants organizations because it weakened the effects of rent control by exempting new tenancies from rent-review protection. Once a rental property became vacant and was rented anew, the landlord could charge whatever rent the market would bear. In other jurisdictions where this sort of provision was in place, it had resulted in a kind of sclerosis in the housing market, since people were reluctant to leave controlled premises to rent in another location. Proponents of the change argued it would remove one disincentive to the creation of new rental accommodation and might therefore improve the housing market. The new law also provided that the landlord and tenant could agree to a rent increase above that allowed by review guidelines if there was a capital improvement in the property or a new service provided. Again there was controversy about this provision, since some tenants did not believe they were in an equal position with their landlords when such 'negotiations' were taking place, while supporters of the change believed it would encourage improvements in the existing housing stock. After lengthy hearings and debate in the spring and summer, the new assessment legislation was passed in November.

The changes planned in municipalities, school boards, and hospitals would result in the merging of workforces with different union contracts. The government proposed a piece of legislation in June that was intended to make the transition smoother, but it did so by limiting or suspending rights that labour unions considered crucial. The proposed law would have created a Labour Relations Transition Commission, to address labour matters in the period of reorganization, and a Dispute Resolution Commission, to handle disagreements in areas where strikes were not permitted and to arbitrate first contracts for newly merged workplaces. Since the latter body could effectively ban strikes and impose first contracts, unions vowed a massive public sector strike if the bill was not amended. Another provision of the bill opposed by the unions was the requirement that new first contracts be drafted with an eye to what the private sector would charge for the same services and to the ability of the employer to afford the contract costs. Public-sector employers favoured the proposed law. David McKinnon of the Ontario Hospital Association was quoted as saying, 'We have to cut eleven per cent over two years. We can't do it unless we make some significant changes faster than is usual' (*Globe and Mail*, 4 June). In late August and early September, the unions lobbied the labour minister and the Premier vigorously, and before the bill was passed in early October, the government agreed to remove the most contentious elements.

Such labour peace as the concession bought was rather short-lived, as the dispute with the teachers escalated through October. At the end of November, the Ontario Federation of Labour in convention vowed to continue its battle to unseat the Harris government, including a continuation of its Days of Protest (an example of which had been held in Windsor on 17 October) and a one-day, province-wide general strike, to be held within one year of the convention. The rift with the NDP, occasioned by the Rae government's Social Contract, seemed to be on the mend, as the OFL once again endorsed the NDP as its preferred alternative to the Conservatives.

Crime and punishment

Towards the end of 1996, the government had introduced a bill entitled the Community Safety Act. The main provisions of the bill required those seeking a name change to be subject to a police records check, and permitted police and/or corrections officers to release otherwise confidential information about persons in the interests of informing victims of crime or of preserving public safety. The bill became law in October.

As part of the 'Megaweek' in January, the government proposed changes to the organization of police services in the province, including the mechanisms for reviewing police conduct. The reform was part of the general review of municipal responsibilities and required municipalities to be responsible, alone or in concert, for the provision of police services. Alternatively, they could pay the province for the services of the Ontario Provincial Police. In addition, some changes were made to the complaints review process. The Ontario Civilian Commission on Police Services was given the authority, on its own motion, to conduct inquiries into complaints against a police force, an individual officer, or a police service. They were also empowered to hear appeals from hearings held by police chiefs or local police services boards into civilian complaints. Police chiefs and deputy chiefs were made subject to many provisions of the complaints procedures, though the chiefs retained considerable authority to investigate complaints against officers under their command. They could, for example, refuse to investigate complaints found to be frivolous or vexatious, though they were required, within thirty days of a legitimate complaint, to declare whether it was against an officer or the force and to ensure it was referred to the proper person or body for handling. Public complaints against police were hereafter to be lodged only by the person directly affected by the policy or service that was the basis of the complaint.

Also in January, the Solicitor General's ministry announced the end of funding for a program that had provided supervision on bail for accused persons who did not have sufficient funds to post a surety of their own. The cost of the bail program was estimated at less than $5 per person per day (as compared with over $100 per person per day for those held in jail). However the ministry had elected this program as a means of meeting budget-cut targets because it was not a 'core business' service of the ministry, since it was not required to supervise persons awaiting trial. Criticism was widespread among defence lawyers, prosecutors, and students of the criminal justice system. Professor Gail Kellough of York University observed that about one-third of those referred to bail plans in her research had their charges withdrawn by the Crown (*Toronto Star*, 26 January). Thus, in the absence of the plan, some people would end up serving time in jail for offences of which they were innocent or could not be convicted. By March, since so many people were still on bail program release, it was administratively difficult to cancel the program. After continuing funding through a series of three-month extensions for about a year, the government agreed to the continuation of the program, with more limited funding and a shift in responsibility from the solicitor general to the attorney general's department.

In February, plans were announced for a new sort of facility for young offenders – described as a 'boot camp' – to be established near Barrie. The facility was intended to be a 'get-tough' measure to deal with violent youth, with few privileges and mandatory hard physical labour. However, it was also an institution that would continue to segregate young offenders from hardened adult criminals and aim to provide reform and development rather than simply punishment and deterrence. In late May, the government announced it had given the contract to manage the new facility to a private U.S. firm. The official opening of the camp was scheduled in late August, with Solicitor General Robert Runciman as the guest of honour. On the eve of his visit, two of the very few offenders already resident at the camp escaped, suggesting that security was not perhaps as tight as it should be. The youths were quickly recaptured, but the flagship institution, in what the government suggested might be a new direction in treatment of young offenders, was not off to a good start. The 'boot-camp' approach came under fire from some quarters early on, since the absence of 'privileges' made it difficult to instill self-discipline and there was little one could use as rewards or sanctions to reinforce or discourage behaviour. The experiment continued as the year progressed, however, and in the fall the ministry signalled its wish to extend the tough discipline of the Barrie facility into other provincial institutions where young offenders were incarcerated.

In June, the long-awaited measures aimed at improving road safety were introduced. The new law provided for the impounding of trucks (for thirty days) that showed major safety defects when inspected. In response to several incidents in which truck wheels had come loose and caused death or injury to other drivers, the law made truck firms automatically liable for the loss of a truck wheel. In addition, penalties were increased for impaired drivers – one year's driving-licence suspension on conviction for a first offence; three years' suspension and a mandatory treatment program after a second conviction; and a lifetime suspension of the right to drive for those convicted three times. The last penalty could be reduced to suspension for ten years if the offender had his/her car fitted with a device to make ignition dependent on passing a breath test, or if they paid for their own alcohol or drug treatment program. Some questions were raised about the constitutionality of the automatic liability for truck-wheel loss, and representatives of trucking firms suggested the legislation could have included more of the items recommended by a study group that had recently reported. The bill received all-party support, however, and was quickly passed in early July.

In early September, the government's reform of pay equity encountered a set-back when the courts declared the repeal of 'proxy' job comparisons (for female-dominant job classes in the public sector without a male comparator in their own workplaces) to be unconstitutional. Labour Minister Elizabeth Witmer suggested an appeal was likely, but in early October the government announced it would not appeal. Just before that announcement was made, the government met another set-back as provincial insurance laws were found to be discriminatory against gays and lesbians. Increasingly groups were turning to the courts to challenge the government's actions, and on occasion such challenges were successful. On the whole however, the courts had sustained the government's position in most of the significant cases brought before them.

In mid-November, panellists at an Ontario Law Union conference were critical of the Ontario justice system, asserting that it had become something of an assembly line. One panellist, provincial judge David Cole, was quoted by *The Globe and Mail* as saying, 'Everything is reduced to getting the numbers through' (17 November). There were calls for restoration of funding to the courts and the legal aid system. The provincial auditor added his voice to concerns about the courts later in the month, citing the considerable backlog of cases and the danger that some criminal charges would have to be dropped if they could not be processed more quickly. There were suggestions from some observers that justice and corrections might be a focus of attention for the government in the coming year, especially if such matters seemed like a promising basis for an election campaign issue.

The economy and the budget

The Ontario economy continued to perform well in 1997, with growth high and unemployment falling over the year (from 9 per cent in January to less than 8 per cent in December). In February, Finance Minister Ernie Eves suggested that most of the government's cost-cutting had been done. On 6 May, he brought down his budget, predicting a falling deficit and promising a further instalment of cutting the provincial income tax, which had figured so prominently in the Conservatives' 1995 election campaign.

The budget projected total spending of some $55 billion (including $17.8 billion in the health sector). The restructuring to take place in health would require an expenditure of some $2.7 billion over a five-year period. Mr Eves observed that the deficit in the fiscal year just concluded had been lower than predicted, and that permitted him some confidence in announcing a further reduction in the income-tax rate (apart from surtaxes), to 47 per cent of basic federal tax on 1 July, and to 45 per cent of the basic federal tax on 1 January 1998. Ontario's income-tax rate would then be the lowest in the country, matched only by that in the Northwest Territories.

The level of cuts to basic program spending that had been promised in the Common Sense Revolution had not quite been met (13 per cent promised, 10 per cent achieved), and actual expenditure on programs had been some $2.5 billion higher than projected, in large part because of short-term costs associated with 'restructuring,' such as severance or early retirement payments and office reorganization. Revenues had been higher than projected, however, so that the deficit was falling faster than predicted.

The Budget Speech was critical of the federal government for failing to cut taxes in the same manner, and for 'unfair' payments to Ontario in support of health care (through the Canada Health and Social Transfer). Tax incentives were promised for small businesses, film and television production, and publishing, and a fund of $27 million over four years was announced to combat violence against women (an area where the government had earlier cut programs), as well as $25 million to combat serial predators (presumably with the Paul Bernardo/Karla Homolka case in mind). The government also indicated it was ending the ban on school construction, and it promised a child-care tax credit to assist working parents.

Planned expenditures in health and education were apparently in accord with the wishes of the electorate, as expressed in an April survey from the Pollara polling firm. A majority of Ontario residents rated health and education higher in importance than balancing the budget or providing a tax cut.

When the provincial auditor reported in November, he was critical of the extent to which the government had failed to collect fines levied for traffic and other offences, and the failure to successfully recoup defaults and overpayments on student loans. In addition, he observed that almost half of the provincial government's expenditures were in the form of transfers to other agencies – municipalities, universities, school boards and hospitals, for example – over whose spending the government had little or no control. The auditor asked for the power to examine the books of such agencies, and the government seemed sympathetic to that desire. Nothing of that sort had emerged by year's end, however.

Another central element of the Conservatives' economic agenda had been the establishment of a program of 'workfare' as a reform of the social assistance system. An important aspect of the election campaign in 1995 had been the promise to overhaul welfare and to require the able-bodied to work for their benefits. However, Margaret Philp reported in *The Globe and Mail* (4 June) that implementation of workfare placements had been very slow. A very small proportion of welfare recipients were actually involved in 'community participation' or employment in return for their cheques, and in many cases those who were working had previously volunteered in the same capacity. The government argued that people were mistaken if they imagined the program was going to be Draconian and that the numbers of people employed would grow slowly but would never reach 100 per cent. Some observers asserted that there was little that was new in social assistance, despite the government's promises. The social-assistance reform package, introduced in the legislature on 12 June, was finally passed at the end of November, replacing the Family Benefits Act, the General Welfare Assistance Act, and the Vocational Rehabilitation Act with two new laws – the Ontario Works Act and the Ontario Disabilities Reform Act. The new laws were intended to provide income support to those who were unemployable and to require community service or education and training for those who were able-bodied, as a condition of their receiving assistance. In addition there was a commitment to try to move people from welfare to jobs. It remained to be seen how different these programs were from those they had replaced and how successful they would be in achieving the government's stated goals.

Quebec*

The year 1997 in Quebec, like 1996, was marked by the repercussions of the referendum defeat of 1995. In his second year in office, Premier Lucien Bouchard focused on the economy and relegated the promotion of sovereignty, a less and less popular option with voters, to the back burner. The federalists, on the other hand, both in Ottawa and Quebec, put more effort and energy into challenging the Parti Québécois's plans for independence politically as well as before the courts. Economically and socially, the provincial government was facing increasing dissatisfaction from a segment of the population and the emergence of an articulate, combative left wing. Finally, the year was also marked by the death of three great Quebec personalities – Gérard Pelletier, Michel Bélanger, and Pierre Péladeau – and a tragic bus accident that claimed the lives of forty-three people.

Politics

The Parti Québécois government and its leader, Premier Lucien Bouchard, grappled with some tough challenges in 1997. Public courtesy brought nationalists and federalists together at the beginning of the year, when the new lieutenant-governor of Quebec, Lise Thibault, was sworn in with great pomp in the Red Room of the National Assembly in Quebec City on 30 January. Smiling, relaxed, and friendly, Ms Thibault, a fifty-seven-year-old paraplegic with links to the Liberals, was praised by people from all political parties, in striking contrast to the treatment received by her predecessor, the actor Jean-Louis Roux. A convinced federalist, but with a harsh, brusque manner, Mr Roux lasted only a few weeks as the Queen's representative in Quebec. Following a humiliating swearing-in ceremony in September 1996, he was forced to step down in early November after it was learned that he had worn a swastika on his student's smock in 1942. The affair caused a huge controversy that extended far beyond its original cause and revealed the depth of the wounds opened up by the referendum campaign in which Mr Roux had spared no effort to discredit the separatist position. He had even said publicly that he was ready to leave Quebec if it became independent.

The Thibault effect did not last for long. Nationalists and federalists clashed again in the debate over the federal government's decision to file a reference to the Supreme Court of Canada concerning the legality

*Translated by Karen Montin.

of a unilateral declaration of secession by Quebec. In the aftermath of the 1995 referendum, which the 'no' camp had won by the slimmest of majorities (50.6 per cent of the votes), the federal government had set about trying to win back the hearts and minds of Quebecers by following a twofold strategy. Plan A was designed to spruce up Canada's image in Quebec and create a feeling of belonging to Canada among French-speaking Quebecers. Plan B, a more hard-line approach, was a sweeping political and legal initiative aimed at countering the separatist option. Ottawa was going to use every diplomatic, political, and legal means at its disposal to remind Quebecers, as well as other Canadians and foreigners, that Quebec independence was not something that could be achieved easily and that, if it did come to pass, it would be costly. In 1997, the debate focused essentially on legal questions, even though the Quebec government tried to shift it to the political arena.

On 26 September 1996, the federal government asked the Supreme Court to rule on the legality of a unilateral declaration of independence. Ottawa wanted to know whether the National Assembly or the Government of Quebec had the right to proceed unilaterally under the Canadian Constitution and under international law; and if the two contradicted one another, which should take precedence? According to the 28 February *News Release* of the Government of Canada, its decision to file the reference to the Supreme Court had been made 'as a direct result of the position repeatedly taken by the current Quebec Government – that it has a right to take Quebec out of Canada *unilaterally*, that international law sanctions such a process, and that Canadian laws and courts have no role to play in the process. The Government of Canada believes that there is no basis in Canadian or international law for this claim of the Government of Quebec' (emphasis in original). To many observers, the Supreme Court's answers to the first two questions had to be no. Quebec rejected the federal initiative, saying that it would not be a party to the legal process. For its part, the Supreme Court agreed to hear the case and gave any group, individual or government until 29 November to apply to be heard before the Court. Some fifteen parties indicated they wished to file arguments on the question.

On 28 February the federal government filed its factum with the Supreme Court. In its filing, Ottawa stated that 'since there is no other mechanism for unilateral constitutional amendments by a province, it follows that there is no right of Quebec's governing institutions to effect unilaterally the secession of Quebec from Canada under the Canadian Constitution.' With respect to international law, 'the Government of Canada believes that Quebecers, like other Canadians, exercise their right of self-determination within Canada. The right of self-determination does not imply a right to secession. While the concept of self-determination has evolved over time, it has never included a right to secede from democratic independent states.' Last, the federal government's brief argued that there could be no conflict between Canadian law and international law with respect to Quebec secession, 'as neither body of law provides a right to unilateral secession,' in the view of the Government of Canada (Centre for Research and Information Canada www.cric.ca). Intergovernmental Affairs Minister Stéphane Dion, Justice Minister Allan Rock, and even Prime Minister Jean Chrétien pointed out that Ottawa 'does not argue against the legitimacy of a consultative referendum' and agreed that 'the country will not be held together against the clear will of Quebecers' (*La Presse*, 18 June). The purpose of the reference to the Supreme Court, they said, was to clarify the situation. Secession must be carried out in an orderly fashion and with the cooperation of Canadians.

Reactions to the federal positions were not long in coming. The Quebec government responded vigorously. On 16 April, to mark the 15th anniversary of the unilateral repatriation of the Canadian Constitution, the Quebec cabinet adopted a resolution reiterating, in the name of the people and the Government of Quebec, the right of Quebec to determine 'its political status democratically and on its own.' The Quebec Liberal Party followed suit, and on 21 May had the National Assembly adopt a motion reasserting Quebec's right to self-determination. Even the federalist daily *La Presse* distanced itself from the federal initiative. In an editorial titled 'A Truncated Exercise,' *La Presse* (4 March) wrote that, while the government might be justified in wanting to clarify the path that leads to independence, it was evading a fundamental problem: 'For sovereignty to become legal, a constitutional amendment is necessary that requires the support of seven provinces having over half the population, or perhaps even – it's not too clear – the unanimous agreement of all the provinces. The process is so complex that in actual fact there is a good chance that a situation would arise in which Canada, while recognizing Quebec's right to sovereignty, would prevent it from being achieved.' However, noted the editorialist, the federal brief says nothing about 'the way to amend the constitution in order to allow sovereignty.' Since the constitutional law route seemed unachievable, 'sovereignists opted for the unilateral declaration of independence,' wrote *La Presse*.

The debate on the reference to the Supreme Court then moved to the political arena. On 27 April, Jean Chrétien called a general election for 2 June. During the election campaign, Stéphane Dion and Jean Chrétien spoke with increasing frequency about the process for attaining independence and its possible consequences. The two leaders said that the purpose of the initiative was to remind people that Quebec did not have a monopoly on defining the process and that the federal government had a duty to play a role in resolving the Quebec question. In an 18 June interview with *La Presse*, Mr Dion noted that the 'rules have to be very clear to make sure that it's really what the people want (independence) and there has to be a recognized legal framework.' He said that Ottawa wanted to take part in drafting the referendum question. Meanwhile, Jean Chrétien again stated that he would not recognize a 'yes' result based on a simple majority, even if the question was clear and dealt with the separation of Quebec. In federal government circles, there was talk of bringing in legislation to set down the conditions for secession.

The reference to the Supreme Court raised a problem that Chief Justice Antonio Lamer had mentioned when the federal government had applied to the Court in September 1996: Who was going to represent the main party concerned, the Government of Quebec? Since Quebec had announced that it would not be a party to the process, the Chief Justice had said that he could appoint an amicus curiae, a friend of the Court. But this amicus curiae did not represent any party in the debate, his sole role being to respond to arguments. The appointment of a friend of the court is a common practice that is done to respect the fundamental legal principle that for justice to be done in a case, all the parties must be heard. In spite of the Government of Quebec's opposition, the Supreme Court announced on 14 August that a lawyer with close nationalist ties, André Joli-Coeur, had been chosen to respond to the arguments of the federal government. The Quebec government responded angrily to the appointment, maintaining forcefully that Mr Joli-Coeur represented no one but himself.

The federal government would have liked to see the hearings on the reference to the Supreme Court begin as early as possible, and had even selected the date of 23 June, but was forced to back off because of the complexity of the case and because of Chief Justice Lamer's firm insistence that he would not be hurried. The Chief Justice reminded the government that the Court's agenda was not the government's agenda, and that the Court alone would decide on its calendar. Finally, on 18 September, Chief Justice Lamer set the start of the hearings for 16 February 1998. That September day, some thirty or so Bloc Québécois

MPs, led by Gilles Duceppe, gathered outside the Supreme Court building in Ottawa to denounce the legal process. Mr Duceppe cast doubt on the impartiality of the Court, noting that all its judges have been appointed by the federal government. 'A court of law can never replace the will of a people,' he said.

The friend of the Court, André Joli-Coeur, submitted his factum on 18 December. He urged the Court to refuse to hear the case, arguing that it had neither the power nor the obligation to respond to 'political,' 'theoretical,' and 'premature' questions. If, however, the Court decided that it was competent to rule on the questions, then it should conclude, said Mr Joli-Coeur, that nothing in either Canadian law or international law prohibited secession. Mr Joli-Coeur noted that the right to unilateral secession was recognized under the principle of 'effectivity,' a principle, he said, which is intrinsic to British law and which is implicitly included in the preamble of the Constitution of 1867. In Mr Joli-Coeur's view, 'the new State does not find any legal justification for its existence in the consent of the State from which it originates, but only in the simple fact that it exists and that it exercises the functions of a State effectively and peacefully, in other words, in the principle of effectivity.' Thus, argued Mr Joli-Coeur, there was no need for Ottawa to pass legislation to allow Quebec to secede. He based his argument on the fact that the independence of Canada did not result from a British law 'but rather from a political reality.' Internationally, 'secession is a fact of political life,' the lawyer noted, 'and international law contents itself with drawing the appropriate conclusions when secession results in the establishment of an effective, stable, State authority.' As for determining which of the two bodies of law takes precedence over the other, Mr Joli-Coeur concluded that the question did not arise, as each of them covers distinct, parallel legal spheres. The federal government reserved its comments on Mr Joli-Coeur's arguments for January 1998. Quebec Intergovernmental Affairs Minister Jacques Brassard issued a reminder that the Government of Quebec did not recognize the legitimacy of Mr Joli-Coeur's factum and refused to comment on it.

During the year, the debate between nationalists and federalists also saw Stéphane Dion and Quebec Deputy Premier Bernard Landry exchange some strongly worded open letters, published in newspapers, with each of them defending his position with political and legal arguments. Mr Dion accused Mr Landry of constantly 'denying the relevance of the law yet referring to it whenever it suited him,' while Mr Landry accused Mr Dion of 'turning his back on the democratic principles' on which Canadian society was based. These arguments aside, what the exchange did reveal was the total incomprehension and futility of any dialogue between the two sides. Then, towards the end of the summer, the publication of excerpts of a biography of Lucien Bouchard got some people worked up and caused a general outcry among the chattering classes and in the general population. On 23 August, the *Ottawa Citizen* published an excerpt from *The Antagonist: Lucien Bouchard and the Politics of Delusion* by Lawrence Martin. The author revealed that after the 1995 referendum, Liberal MP John Godfrey had asked an eminent psychiatrist, Dr Vivian Rakoff, for a psychological profile of the Premier. In his report, Dr Rakoff, who had never met Mr Bouchard, drew a rather unflattering portrait of the politician and cast doubt on his mental equilibrium. He concluded that the Premier of Quebec suffered from a serious 'character disorder.' In short, Lucien Bouchard was a vain and narcissistic man, with a very volatile personality, who had little awareness of the consequences of his actions.

Mr Godfrey forwarded the report to the office of Prime Minister Jean Chrétien, where it became the subject of considerable debate. The affair caused a commotion. Politicians in general dissociated themselves from the report, and the psychiatrist himself apologized. The nationalists called it a witch hunt. On 27 August, the editor of *Le Devoir*, Lise Bissonnette, took the opportunity to remind readers that for some time the federalists, and the journalists in their camp, had been waging a smear campaign against Quebec nationalists. Having run out of intelligent arguments against sovereignty, she said, federalists were using 'weapons from old colonial times that it is very difficult to defend oneself against. Instead of opinions being deformed and misrepresented, people are being decreed morally inferior. These sovereignists are crazy, they're corrupt.'

All this constitutional wrangling was, of course, good news for public-opinion pollsters. A close reading of their research results shows, however, that neither camp could lay claim to the support of a majority of Quebecers. In September, when a polling firm asked Quebecers whether they would give the government a mandate to achieve sovereignty, 34 per cent said yes, 43 per cent said no, and 23 per cent refused to give an opinion. In October, the results were 39 per cent yes and 61 per cent no. Then, in December, the firm Angus Reid asked two very different questions. First it asked Quebecers whether they would vote in favour of Quebec sovereignty if it was coupled with a partnership with the rest of Canada. The 'yes' option scored 55 per cent while the 'no' option garnered the support of 45 per cent of respondents. But when they were asked whether they would like to see Quebec become an independent country separate from Canada, support for the 'yes' option dropped to 38 per cent while the 'no' score jumped to 62 per cent. On the question of the reference to the Supreme Court and the unilateral declaration of independence, Quebecers were divided and ambivalent: 46 per cent said that Quebec has the right to separate from Canada unilaterally, whereas 42 per cent said that it does not. In another poll, 42 per cent of respondents thought that the Supreme Court should not rule on the legality of a unilateral declaration, whereas 35 per cent expressed the opposite view and 23 per cent did not have an opinion. However, in answer to another question in the same poll, 57 per cent believed that their government would have no choice but to abide by the ruling of the Court if it declared unilateral secession to be illegal.

At the same time as it was responding to the federal government's initiative to contest the legality, if not the legitimacy, of the separatist option, the Bouchard government also had to deal with the attack of the partitionist movement. Composed for the most part of English-speaking Quebecers living in western Montreal and in the Outaouais region, the movement was established in the wake of the slim victory of the 'no' side in the 1995 referendum. Its members, shocked by the referendum result, called on the federal government to defend the right of the citizens of certain towns and regions of Quebec to remain Canadian in the event of secession. The movement adopted the ideas of Stéphane Dion, who holds that if Canada is divisible, then so is Quebec. Furthermore, it succeeded in recruiting flamboyant lawyer Guy Bertrand, originally one of the most determined defenders of the separatist cause, who, in the 1990s, did an about-face and became a fervent advocate of federalism.

The partitionist movement targeted towns – the only political entities, in its view, that gave it legitimate representation since its repudiation by the Quebec Liberal Party. By the end of 1997, some fifty towns and villages in Quebec had passed 'pro-unity' resolutions, which defended the principle of keeping federalist areas of Quebec within Canada. Although the movement met with a certain degree of success, even among French-speaking Quebecers, in 1996 and early 1997, it began to lose steam when several large cities on the Island of Montreal, such as LaSalle, Verdun, and Lachine, refused to take sides during stormy, emotional debates. Moreover, while public opinion was initially sympathetic to the movement, it began to swing against it after a strong Quebec government campaign designed to convince Quebecers that the territory of Quebec was indivisible. A SOM-*L'actualité* poll conducted in mid-August indicated that six of every ten voters thought that regions of Quebec that wanted to remain in Canada in the event of sovereignty had the right to do so. Two months later, a CROP poll asked the same question. This time, the results were reversed: 56 per cent answered no, and 32 per cent answered yes. What was more embarrassing for the partitionists was that the CROP poll revealed that even a majority of federalists were opposed to partition, with 48 per cent against and 35 per cent in favour. Acknowledging the debate, Quebec Intergovernmental Affairs Minister Jacques Brassard made a public statement on 12 November, denouncing the strategy of the proponents of partition and reasserting the integrity of the territorial limits of Quebec.

On the domestic political scene, independence hard-liners remained distrustful of Lucien Bouchard, and the Parti Québécois had to face another rebellion from members who insisted on taking an uncompromising stance on the language issue. In addition, its Bloc Québécois allies suffered a major set-back in the 2 June federal election.

Called radicals and even 'language ayatollahs' by moderates and by the English media, activists from the most hard-line ridings on this issue, those in central Montreal and Ville Marie, again sought to breathe new life into the language debate and bring the party back to a more social-democratic platform. But Lucien Bouchard was on the alert and resisted their scheming. Neither party members nor the general population sympathized with the radicals, and the Premier remained very popular with most grass-roots members. In provincial government matters, Mr Bouchard went ahead with a major cabinet shuffle, as seven ministers changed portfolios and two new faces, Jean-Pierre Jolivet and Jocelyne Caron, became cabinet ministers. In the National Assembly, by-elections held in six ridings did not change the balance of power between the PQ and the Liberals, as the Parti Québécois kept two ridings and the Liberal Party four ridings.

It was quite another story for the representatives of the Quebec nationalist movement in Ottawa, the Bloc Québécois, who suffered the after-effects of the departure of its founding father, Lucien Bouchard. In 1996, the BQ was torn apart by a leadership crisis. Mr Bouchard's successor, Michel Gauthier, managed to remain head of the party for only a few months before he had to step aside for Gilles Duceppe, the first MP elected for the BQ in August 1990. But the leadership race in the winter of 1997 turned out to be a bruising contest. Gilles Duceppe was up against five other candidates, including former PQ ministers Yves Duhaime and Rodrigue Biron. The real struggle was between Mr

Duceppe and Mr Duhaime, as they represented two different camps within the separatist movement. Mr Duceppe was perceived as being Mr Bouchard's man and more moderate, whereas Mr Duhaime was seen as being more orthodox and close to the hard-line views of Jacques Parizeau; if he became leader of the Bloc in Ottawa, it would act as a counterweight to Mr Bouchard, now in power in Quebec City. After some acrimonious debates, Gilles Duceppe was elected leader on 15 March, but his victory was marred by the refusal of his main adversary to lend his support to the new leader. It took Mr Duhaime three days to get over his defeat and rally his troops to the cause. The Bloc was finally ready for the 2 June federal election. Unfortunately for the Bloc, its new leader performed disappointingly during the election campaign and he was made to look ridiculous. In contrast with Lucien Bouchard, the young Gilles Duceppe had no charisma whatsoever. He never really connected with voters. Moreover, the leader of the Conservative Party, Jean Charest, charmed the Quebec public and succeeded in winning the votes of soft nationalists. Newspaper cartoonists took a no-holds-barred attitude to Mr Duceppe, and he provided them with plenty of opportunities. During a tour of a cheese factory, the Bloc leader donned a hair net in front of photographers. The pictures made the front page from coast to coast to coast. Mr Duceppe became the laughing stock of the country.

Then came a bombshell in the midst of a fairly colourless election campaign. A book by Jacques Parizeau sparked a controversy that threw the separatist movement into confusion. On 7 May, the newspaper *Le Soleil* published excerpts from *Pour un Québec souverain*, in which Mr Parizeau seemed to say, according to the journalist Michel Vastel who interpreted the excerpts, that sovereignty would have been proclaimed in 1995, just ten days after a victory for the 'yes' side, without waiting for the results of negotiations on partnership. Lucien Bouchard and Gilles Duceppe were furious when they heard the news and denounced the former premier, who was forced to issue a retraction. Then, after rereading Mr Parizeau's statement and the offending excerpts from the book, Mr Bouchard and Mr Duceppe went back on what they had said and absolved the former separatist leader of any wrongdoing. No one knew what to think anymore. Federalists could barely hide their satisfaction, seeing the affair as proof of the illegitimacy of a question that was not limited exclusively to sovereignty.

By the end of the election campaign, despite some new controversial statements by the Chrétien-Dion duo on the process leading to the independence of Quebec, the Bloc Québécois had run out of energy.

On 2 June, the Liberals won the election, carrying twenty-six seats in Quebec compared with forty-four for the BQ, ten fewer than in 1993. Some 500,000 Quebec voters changed allegiances, with most of them giving their support to Jean Charest's Conservatives.

On the constitutional front, concerted pressure from several provinces and from federalist leaders pushed nine provincial premiers and two territorial leaders to meet in Calgary, where on 14 September they adopted a declaration regarding a framework for discussion of Canadian unity. The Calgary Declaration, while reasserting that all Canadians and all provinces are equal, recognized the 'unique character of Quebec society, including its French-speaking majority, its culture and its tradition of civil law,' and the role that the National Assembly and the Government of Quebec had in protecting this character. While Canadians outside Quebec were happy with the Declaration, Quebecers were not so enthusiastic. The Bouchard government did not even want to discuss it, whereas Daniel Johnson's Liberal Party noted its limitations.

Under attack from the federalists and with the Bloc Québécois weakened, the Parti Québécois government was not given an easy ride by its traditional allies in Quebec either. After thirty months in power, the PQ had dropped to its lowest level in the opinion polls. Cost-cutting budgets in education and health care, the reform of social assistance that affected those most in need, and the increasingly spectacular actions of various social movements had sapped the morale of the government and earned it the ire of students, the poor, unions, and intellectuals – its natural power base. From the time it took power in January 1996, the Bouchard government had set itself the objective of achieving a balanced budget by 2000. This objective was to be achieved essentially by trimming the fat from the public service and reducing spending. The education and health-care systems were the hardest hit. As many as 30,000 civil servants, including hundreds of doctors and nurses, left their jobs in 1996–7, with most of them taking early retirement. These were savage cuts that would have severe consequences. The government also launched a reform of social assistance that slammed young people, women, and single parents. The government's moves in these areas were labelled neo-liberal and were seen as being a repudiation of the social-democratic philosophy that the Parti Québécois had always advocated. To denounce the government's new initiatives, over 1,500 people gathered in Quebec City, not far from the National Assembly, on 15 November to inaugurate a Street Parliament, consisting of two trailers housing the representatives of community groups. They called for immediate action to be taken to put an end to poverty. For a month, the Street Parliament garnered the sympathy of the general public and some MNAs.

Other groups opted for more direct means than the Street Parliament. At noon on 3 December, 108 poor people and leftists staged a commando raid on the buffet of a restaurant in the Queen Elizabeth Hotel and handed out the food in the street. Four people were arrested and charged with assault. But the most worrisome development for the Parti Québécois was the founding, in the fall, of the leftist movement Rassemblement pour une Alternative Politique (RAP) by hard-line separatists, disenchanted social democrats, and leftists of all stripes. Some 600 people gathered in the auditorium of a Montreal college to lay the foundations of a movement that would soon become the subject of much discussion.

The Bouchard government found some consolation in the fact that the Quebec economy showed a sharp improvement in 1997. With GDP growth of 2.9 per cent (compared with 3.8 per cent for Canada as a whole), Quebec posted its best performance since 1994. Nevertheless, despite significant job creation, the unemployment rate remained relatively high, at 11.4 per cent, compared with a national average of 9.1 per cent. This good showing, considering Quebec's lag with respect to the other provinces, reinforced the determination of Deputy Premier and Finance Minister Bernard Landry to achieve his objective of a balanced budget by 2000. On 25 March, he tabled an austerity budget that confirmed the government's intention to erase the deficit. Mr Landry anticipated that the measures contained in the 1997–8 budget would cut the deficit from $3.2 billion in 1996 to $2.2 billion in 1997, and to $1.2 billion in 1998, with a balanced budget expected for the 1999–2000 fiscal year. To achieve this objective, a number of government departments, including education and health, had to absorb further budget cuts. In his speech to the National Assembly, Mr Landry warned: 'The coming year will be the hardest, but it is the last one that will demand such major sacrifices: afterwards we will find ourselves in calmer waters.' The budget imposed expenditure reductions totalling $2.3 billion on government departments. But while the minister cut in some areas, he invested money in others. Mr Landry presented a number of measures designed to boost employment and investment. He announced the establishment of a fund to promote the growth of private investment, the introduction of a capital tax holiday and of a complete tax holiday of five years for new small businesses, and capital spending to modernize Quebec roads and the Montreal metro system.

Lastly, he announced a 3–15 per cent cut in income tax, but an increase in the provincial sales tax to 7.5 per cent. The two measures would take effect in 1998.

Federal-provincial relations

Federal-provincial relations between Ottawa and Quebec have always had their ups and downs, times of high tension and other, calmer periods. The year 1997 was no exception to this rule. Notwithstanding the question of the reference to the Supreme Court, Ottawa and Quebec managed to reach agreement in two areas: a labour force agreement was signed and a constitutional amendment authorizing the shift to a non-confessional school system was passed. Quebec refused to discuss a plan for a social union, however. On 21 April, the two governments put an end to thirty years of discord and signed a labour training agreement. With an estimated value of $2.7 billion and a term of five years, the agreement would allow Quebec to design and manage its own labour market re-entry programs. It provided for the transfer of many federal civil servants to the Quebec public service. The labour market agreement did not spark much debate. In fact, it was completely overshadowed by the agreement reached by the two governments to ask the federal Parliament to pass a constitutional amendment authorizing the deconfessionalization of Quebec schools.

In early 1997, Education Minister Pauline Marois initiated a sweeping reform of the Quebec school system, which included completely overhauling the curriculum, involving parents in running schools, reducing the number of school boards, and replacing confessional school boards with language-based boards. After wide consultations with the players concerned, the government obtained the support of the Quebec Liberal Party and introduced legislation to give Quebec language-based school boards. The legislation was passed by the National Assembly on 15 June, but it could not be implemented without an amendment to section 93 of the Canadian Constitution, which guarantees the preservation of the confessional system in Montreal and Quebec City. The federal government announced that it was willing to amend the Constitution. On 18 November the federal Parliament passed a motion (204–59) to allow Quebec to abolish its confessional school system and set up a language-based system. The constitutional amendment was made possible by a special procedure, provided in the Constitution of 1982, that authorizes such an amendment provided there is joint consent between the provincial legislature and the federal

Parliament. Of course, federalists and nationalists took advantage of the opportunity to remind people of their respective views on Canadian federalism. Jean Chrétien noted that Canada had 'a good Constitution that works,' but he couldn't resist pointing out the irony in the fact that the separatists had asked for an amendment to a Constitution that, according to them, did not exist. 'There's something a little ridiculous in coming here to ask for an amendment to a Constitution that doesn't exist,' he said. Minister of Education Pauline Marois said, for her part, that the amendment did not, from the standpoint of her government, constitute proof that the Canadian federation can adapt to Quebec reality. 'One swallow does not make a summer,' she said without elaborating (*Le Devoir*, 19 November).

While the two governments managed to agree on those two questions, Quebec refused to join the other Canadian provinces to begin negotiations with the federal government about establishing a Canadian social union. The aim of the initiative was to provide a framework for federal-provincial relations in the areas of health care, education, and social assistance. In recent years the Chrétien government had cut federal transfers to the provinces to cover social and education expenditures, but at the same time had set up new programs that encroached on provincial jurisdictions. At the Calgary meeting on 14 September, nine premiers and the leaders of the two territories called for a federal-provincial conference on the question, which was finally held in Ottawa on 12 December, with Quebec in attendance. Premier Bouchard demanded that a stop be put to any new federal initiatives in the social sphere and an unconditional right to opt out, with full financial compensation, for a province that refused a federal initiative in a sphere of provincial jurisdiction. All the provinces agreed that Ottawa should increase its transfers of funds. At the end of the meeting, attracted by the financial offers made by Ottawa, all the provinces except Quebec agreed to discuss the establishment of a negotiating framework that could lead to the signing of an agreement on a social union.

Other significant events

Quebecers and other Canadians were deeply shaken when on 13 October a bus carrying forty-seven members of a seniors' club plunged down a ravine at the foot of the big hill at Les Éboulements, not far from Quebec City. It was the worst road accident in Canada, claiming the lives of forty-three people, most of them from the small village of

St-Bernard in the Beauce, and it caused a lot of soul-searching when the terrible details of the accident became known: a poorly maintained bus, brakes that failed, a slope that was too steep and that was supposed to have been rebuilt years ago, and entire families decimated. The facts of the tragedy caused not only sorrow but also anger at the political authorities. Expressions of sympathy came in from everywhere, and the funeral was shown on television across Canada.

Nova Scotia   ROBERT FINBOW

The trial of Westray Mine managers Gerald Phillips and Roger Parry was declared a mistrial because of inadequate disclosure of Crown evidence. The Supreme Court of Canada ordered a new trial and also ordered the province to pay the two men's legal bills. Mr Phillips filed a complaint against prosecutors for mishandling evidence. Two former Westray executives who resided in Ontario, Curragh chair Clifford Frame and president Marvin Pelley, were ordered by an Ontario court to testify at the provincial inquiry. But Justice Peter Richards issued his report without their testimony in December. The report concluded that mine owners ignored safety to maximize production. Ventilation equipment was inadequate to reduce levels of methane gas, and coal dust was allowed to build up without precautionary use of stone dust. The report accused the Department of Natural Resources of 'willful blindness' about mine hazards, and called labour department inspectors 'incompetent' (*Chronicle-Herald*, 2 December). The government agreed to implement all seventy-four recommendations of the report, fired two bureaucrats, and suspended three others. The province apologized to families of the victims but declined to offer compensation. Bankrupt Curragh was ordered to pay $1.2 million in severance pay to miners who lost their jobs after the explosion. The province promised to pay this out of proceeds from the sale of Westray assets. Lawsuits from families of deceased miners sought $30 million from the province, Ottawa, equipment manufacturers, and Curragh Inc. (*Globe and Mail*, 19 December).

Dr Nancy Morrison, a doctor at Halifax's largest hospital, was charged with first-degree murder when a colleague claimed she had euthanized a terminally ill man. Other suspicious deaths were investigated, but no further charges resulted. Hospital officials were criticized for not reporting the incident to the medical examiner. Senior administrators resigned while the investigation continued. An external report suggested that charges could have been avoided if the hospital had dealt openly with the case, but that police and prosecutors were too heavy-handed in their response. Reports of high cancer rates in Sydney prompted renewed calls for a clean-up of the toxic Tar Ponds. All three levels of government promised to spend $1.67 million on another study of the problem. Unionized construction workers in Cape Breton burned down an unfinished apartment complex to protest against the Steen Act, which reversed a court ban on non-union contractors. The building's owner agreed to rebuild with union workers.

The investigation into abuse at Nova Scotia youth detention centres spread to include 400 alleged perpetrators and 1,500 victims over a fifty-year period. Documents indicated that, despite evidence of abuse, some youth counsellors kept their jobs in the 1960s and 1970s because of political connections. But the union representing youth counsellors claimed that 90 per cent of the allegations were false and demanded compensation for those wrongly accused. A troubled school in Cole Harbor brought in guards and video cameras after racial skirmishes in which seventeen people were arrested. Black leaders demanded the dismissal of teachers accused of harassing black students. Some called for a separate black school. The school board promised to hire more minority teachers, introduce anti-racism classes, and provide training for student mediators.

Justice Michael MacDonald rejected Romania's request for extradition of six Taiwanese officers of the *Maersk Dubai*, accused of forcing Romanian stowaways overboard at sea, because the offence did not occur in Romania. The four Filipino sailors making the allegations were denied refugee status in November, despite fears for their safety if they returned home. Four CBC-TV journalists were ordered to testify in the preliminary hearing for former premier Gerald Regan, on seventeen sex-related charges. Lawyer Ed Greenspan tried to have the charges dismissed claiming they reflected harsh treatment for Mr Reagan as a political notable and applied today's standards of sexual harassment to a previous era (*Maclean's*, 27 January).

Politics

Premier Savage bowed to intense pressure and resigned in March. Unpopular policies, notably the blended sales tax, amalgamation of urban municipalities in Halifax County and Cape Breton, and hospital closures, eroded his support. Unionists angry at public-sector wage roll-backs and the law allowing non-union construction labour mounted challenges to his leadership by taking out party memberships.

And party loyalists chaffed at his reluctance to reward them with patronage appointments. Controversial MP Roseanne Skoke, noted for her stand against homosexuality, ran for the leadership. (She had been denied renomination when her federal seat was merged with a neighbouring one.) Health Minister Bernie Boudreau, former MP Russell MacLellan, and backbencher Bruce Holland also sought the post. The campaign aired divisions over health and education cuts and the wage freeze. On the first ballot, Mr MacLellan took the lead over Mr Boudreau, who was blamed for austerity measures undertaken when he was minister of finance and health. Mr Holland threw his support to Mr MacLellan, giving him a second ballot victory. Critics assailed the new Premier when he promoted supporters to cabinet posts. After lengthy criticisms, he donated his pension from his seventeen years as an MP to Cape Breton charities (*Chronicle-Herald*, 16 December).

In the June federal election, all eleven Liberal MPs were defeated, including Health Minister David Dingwall. The New Democrats, led by former provincial leader Alexa McDonough, made a historic breakthrough, electing six MPs alongside five Conservatives. Some of the defeated Liberals secured government posts, including former Halifax MP Mary Clancy, appointed as provincial representative in Boston. A June poll showed the provincial NDP holding 33 per cent of public support, compared with 28 per cent for the Tories, and 26 per cent for the Liberals. The Opposition criticized Mr MacLellan for holding four by-elections in the fall, at a cost of $500,000, when a general election was needed by May 1998. In the by-elections, the Liberals won two seats, while the NDP won one and placed second in two others. The Premier easily won his seat in Cape Breton North. Several veteran ministers announced their retirement from politics. Liberal support improved late in the year to 40 per cent versus 31 per cent for the NDP and 19 per cent for the Conservatives.

Controversy followed a decision to allow mining in Jim Campbell's Barren, a lichen-covered rock, bog, and boreal forest in Cape Breton, which had been designated as a protected site in 1995. Reports suggested that well-connected political figures played a role in lobbying to remove the protected status to allow Regal Goldfields Inc to begin exploratory work. Regal purchased shares in two smaller companies, which owned exploration rights in the area four days after the cabinet lifted protected status in November 1996, even though the decision was not made public until December. The RCMP investigated a possible leak of confidential cabinet documents. A U.S. sports fishing group threatened to boycott Nova Scotia, since the mine could threaten two key salmon rivers. Premier MacLellan restored the Barren's protected status prompting bitter criticism from Regal and the mining industry (*Globe and Mail*, 11 November).

A controversial toll highway opened in Cumberland County. A court ordered the release of the contract with private operators, which revealed that 50 per cent of the construction costs were paid by the province. Premier MacLellan backed down on his promise to scrap the tolls, opting for 'frequent driver' discounts instead. The province would have owed compensation to investors if tolls had been abolished. The NDP criticized a secret deal with ITT-Sheraton over construction of a permanent casino in Halifax. Finance Minister Bill Gillis also criticized the Nova Scotia Gaming Commission for prohibiting officials from publically discussing the pact. The head of the gaming commission decided not to release a report on casino revenues, which ITT-Sheraton said would harm its competitive position (*Chronicle-Herald*, 20 November).

The legislature

Finance Minister Gillis promised the first balanced budget in twenty-five years, with surpluses of $4 million for each of the next two years, and larger surpluses after that. It was a 'good news budget' in the run-up to the leadership race and election, with new spending of $38.8 million for health care, $13 million for education, and $14 million for road paving. The province made a $179-million payment on debt principle, the first in thirty years, using dividends from pensions, low interest rates, and the budget surplus. Mr Gillis pledged that 50 per cent of the royalties from the offshore gas project would be used to reduce the debt. The minister also promised a 3.4 per cent income-tax cut, a $13-million tax break to low-income earners, and a 30 per cent corporate tax credit for investments in manufacturing and processing. Municipalities received $50 million to compensate for increased costs from the Harmonized Sales Tax (HST).

The auditor general accused the province of using an 'inappropriate accounting adjustment' to predict a balanced budget by transferring $50 million in capital spending to a previous year. Without this adjustment, the $2.8 million surplus would become a $48-million deficit. Opposition leader John Hamm noted that the balanced budget reflected the one-time federal payment of $249 million to ease the transition to the Harmonized Sales Tax. Opponents accused the minister of using spending on highways to buy victories in rural ridings (*Globe and*

Mail, 18 April). The budget impressed bond-rating agencies sufficiently to prompt an upgrade of the province's credit outlook from negative to stable. But the balanced budget was in doubt later in the year, when a proposed reduction of the HST on oil and electricity, restoration of the 3 per cent wage cut to public employees, and high labour settlements after the wage freeze threatened to push the province back into the red.

The April Throne Speech promised more spending on education, including private construction of high-tech schools. Funds were also promised for home care and for community-based disease prevention. Doctors were offered a 10 per cent fee increase over four years, plus rebates on the HST, and increased ceilings for earnings. The government announced $20,000 bonuses plus overtime pay for nights and weekends to keep physicians in rural areas. But the Queen Elizabeth II Centre planned 500 more job cuts and 200 bed closures to meet its $292-million budget. Rural communities in northern Nova Scotia faced the prospect of sending pregnant women to New Brunswick to deliver babies, because of a lack of obstetrical care. A Glace Bay doctor declared that reduced services were killing patients. A couple sued the province for failing to pay for in-vitro fertilization. The province set aside $8 million for an interactive telemedicine video network to link rural patients to specialists, and agreed to pay for midwifery to fill gaps from health cuts. Overall, $60 million was added to the health-care budget.

The spring session was quiet, as the Liberals restricted the agenda to the Throne Speech, budget, and Sable Island gas distribution bill. The only embarrassment for outgoing Premier Savage was the auditor general's critique of his government's accounting methods. Premier MacLellan was forced by caucus dissidents to dismiss the party's House leader, Paul MacEwan, as the fall session began. In the November Throne Speech, Mr MacLellan tried to reorient the government's image in a more caring direction, to prepare for an election required by May 1998. The government pledged to spend $40 million on air ambulance services, cancer treatment, and critical care. Legislation was promised to ease student loan debt, to create a youth employment strategy and new civil service internships, to provide racially sensitive education and scholarships for black students, and to fund Mi'kmaq schools. The government also announced that it was negotiating with twenty to thirty companies connected to offshore gas development that might relocate to the province, and it promised funds for training to ensure lasting local benefits from such employment. The Opposition charged that the government had abandoned its commitment to a balanced budget in a pre-election ploy to buy votes. But the Opposition did not effectively criticize Premier MacLellan despite his failure to reduce the HST on heating oil and his return to patronage-based politics (including the appointment of his brother as communications director at $79,700 per year).

The economy

The Sable Island gas project was delayed when Gaz Metropolitaine of Montreal and TransCanada Pipelines of Calgary proposed to ship gas to the United States via Quebec through the TransQuebec and Maritimes (TQM) pipeline. Westcoast Energy of Vancouver had proposed a shorter pipeline to New England through New Brunswick (the Maritimes and Northeast Pipeline or M&NP), and claimed the rival proposal would cause unacceptable delays. The federal-provincial review panel approved the M&NP project and declined to consider the TQM proposal. The National Energy Board and federal cabinet approved the decisions and the Federal Appeal Court rejected a challenge from TQM. But TransCanada Pipelines sued the province for $18 million, claiming it had a deal with Nova Scotia Resources Ltd (a Crown corporation) to transmit the gas. The review panel criticized Nova Scotia for its inaction on training and development plans to maximize benefits and job creation from gas development. The project was approved on condition that Nova Scotia companies making competitive bids be given first chance at contracts (*Globe and Mail*, 28 October and 31 December). Environmentalists worried about potential damage to the Gully, a sensitive marine canyon, but their attempts to delay the project were rejected. The environment minister was criticized for keeping the environmental review secret.

New Brunswick insisted that a lateral pipeline be built to serve Saint John and that gas prices be equivalent to those in Nova Scotia, before it would approve construction across its territory. But Nova Scotia Power proposed to buy 13 per cent of the gas produced if Nova Scotia received preferential rates. The two provinces agreed to a higher break (8 per cent vs. 4 per cent) on pipeline fees for Nova Scotia for eight years. But after he was chosen, Premier MacLellan reneged on this in favour of a permanent 20 per cent break for Nova Scotians, even though experts questioned whether the pipeline would be viable with such extensive discounts. Late in the year the government announced an improved royalty deal for Sable Island gas worth another $20 million over ten years, with $20 million in rebates to consumers. Nova Scotia power purchased 12.5 per cent of the pipeline project. Critics noted that the province received little for the 50 per cent stake it gave up in the 1980s (*Globe and Mail*, 11 December). A review panel began considering the socio-economic and environmental impacts of oil and gas exploration on the rich fishing grounds of George's Bank off southwestern Nova Scotia. While a moratorium on exploration was in effect until 2000, seismic surveys had shown high potential for fuel deposits.

Sydney Steel was again up for sale, after accumulating another $30 million in losses, which were covered by taxpayers, when rail shipments to CN and China Railways were rejected because of quality problems. In December a sale was announced to Grupo Acerero Del Norte of Mexico for $26 million. Devco miners faced hardship when a cave-in in October closed the Phalen mine; Nova Scotia Power also purchased some coal abroad, limiting markets for Devco production. Stora Forest industries was allowed to reopen its pulp plant in August, after a brief closure because of sulphur-dioxide leaks. Cape Breton experienced significant employment growth with Stora's expansion and new or relocated high-tech firms leading the way. Cape Breton was also promoted as a retirement haven for former residents and interested foreign senior citizens, in a bid to attract economic benefits from pension spending. Unemployment decreased by 10 per cent in that hardpressed region, but remained well over 13 per cent. Commercial office space in Halifax was again in demand from new call-centre, information technology, and offshore energy companies.

Independent foresters warned of overcutting in Nova Scotia's forests. They predicted the shutdown of processing mills and related industries if reforestation was not increased. The government promised to control harvesting and provided $4 million to promote reforestation. New Democrat John Holm demanded regulations to prevent large oil firms from selling gas at their own retail outlets for less than they charged wholesale to independent stations, which forced independents to charge higher prices. Scallop fishers in the Bay of Fundy agreed to reduce quotas since stocks had declined 66 per cent since 1989. Increased exports of unconventional species such as sea urchins, crabs, periwinkles, bill fish, razor clams, and starfish to Asia offset depleted stocks. Dry weather hurt agricultural output, reducing the largest crop, blueberries, by 25 per cent.

Tourism receipts topped $1 billion for the first time. The number of tourists was up 18 per cent. Lunenburg shipbuilders were employed to refit an old trawler, the *Picton Castle*, into a tall ship; it was hoped that this would lead to future projects. The proposed blood fractionation plant, slated for construction near Halifax, laid off most of its staff because of an inability to raise sufficient funds for the project. AT&T Canada announced plans for a call centre in Halifax, which would create 1,000 jobs, after receiving a controversial $12 million in government assistance for training and recruitment. The province gave Michelin Tires $2 million for training and forgave a $25-million loan. Michelin pledged to create 80 new jobs and to invest $150 million to upgrade its plants. The Sharjah Oil Refining Co. received $25 million from the federal Export Development Bank to dismantle the Ultramar Oil Refinery in Eastern Passage and move it to the United Arab Emirates. Provincial tax concessions allowing producers to claim up to 30 per cent of wages paid to Nova Scotians attracted more television and movie production to the province. Orenda Aerospace was given $17.7 million in government loans to set up an airplane manufacturing plant at the Debert Airport near Truro. NDP leader Robert Chisholm was critical of government writing off loans and taxes to profitable firms like the Autoport and Seafreez. The government countered that interprovincial competition made such concessions necessary.

Overall, employment grew by 2.8 per cent (over 9,500 new jobs) above the national average, but trailed New Brunswick and Newfoundland. Resource industries remained weak, and exports declined by 1.8 per cent, because of poor prices for lumber and breakdowns on off-shore gas facilities. Increased prices and high demand for pulp and paper from larger U.S. papers fuelled expansion at the Bowater and Minas Basin paper mills, and prompted Stora's upgrade to produce speciality papers. But the Kimberley Clark mill was up for sale (*Atlantic Report*, Winter 1998). A strike at IMP aerospace threatened to delay vital military maintenance contracts, but it was settled in October. Labour troubles loomed for the Trenton rail car plant, where management wanted greater flexibility for contracting out to meet stiff competition. Halifax shipyards were busy with refit work on oil platforms and fisheries patrol vessels.

Software producers scored important innovations in Internet-related programs – for example, MT&T pioneered the MPowered, using asymmetric digital subscriber lines and Novell NetWare servers, to provide fast access to the Internet plus a software and database library, while Inland technologies of Truro gained more customers for its fuel and chemical fluid recycling systems. DynaTek, which produced and distributed mass storage and memory products, laid off half its workers, despite receiving $17.5 million in government assistance when it moved from Toronto in 1993. Construction projects included private partnerships to renovate schools or to build new ones; building a hospital replacement in Amherst; building a $97-million Sheraton Casino for the Halifax waterfront; and constructing a highway twinning in Pictou and Antigonish counties (*Atlantic Report*, Fall 1997).

Intergovernmental affairs

The HST generated conflict with Ottawa and other provinces. The tax came into effect on 1 April, replacing the 7 per cent GST and 11 per cent provincial sales tax with a 15 per cent levy on a wider range of goods and services. Costs for haircuts and necessities like heating oil, electricity, and inexpensive clothing increased, while prices for restaurant meals, cable TV, furniture, and appliances decreased. Provincial and commons finance committees refused to hold local hearings, but a Senate finance committee meeting in Halifax heard numerous complaints about the HST's impact on essential goods and services for those on fixed incomes. Some argued that a family would have to spend $10,000 on luxury or big-ticket items to offset the $500 increase for essentials (*Chronicle-Herald*, 21 June). Ottawa abandoned plans to require tax-included pricing, after business complained that the public should know how much the HST added to the price. Despite a commitment during the leadership race, Premier MacLellan failed to reduce the levy on necessities like fuel oil and electricity. Talks with federal Finance Minister Paul Martin were not resolved by year's end. Quebec was upset with federal payments to the Atlantic provinces for blending the taxes, claiming that its partial blending also merited compensation.

Premier MacLellan took part in a meeting in Calgary, which produced a Declaration recognizing Quebec's 'unique character.' He joined the other premiers in resisting changes to the Calgary Declaration to accommodate aboriginal groups. An all-party legislative committee was set up to tour the province to hear views on the Declaration, which also affirmed the equality of provinces and the diversity of Canada's regions and citizens. The pre-election federal budget brought less bad news than in recent years. The restoration of $2 million to twelve centres aiding children on welfare was welcomed. But the province criticized the lack of initiatives to address regional development and unemployment. Universities welcomed the Canadian Foundation for Innovation, designed to modernize research facilities and health-care centres. But this did not offset $80 million in cuts to the Canadian Health and Social Transfer. Mr MacLellan demanded that a generous share of any federal budget surplus be sent to the have-not provinces. Nova Scotia joined with eight other provinces agreeing to reform the Canada Pension Plan, with increased premiums. But the provinces were upset with Ottawa's inflexibility on how provinces could spend health transfers. Mr Chrétien and the premiers agreed to work on joint rules for social spending. The province took control over social and cooperative housing from Ottawa in December.

Ottawa declined to help IMP of Halifax recover $22 million owed by its partners in a Russian hotel project, because it was a business and not a diplomatic matter. Ottawa and Nova Scotia opened a trade and investment centre to integrate the services of the provincial Department of Economic Development and Tourism with the federal Departments of Industry, Foreign Affairs, and Agriculture and Agri-foods. In the wake of the Westray Mine report, the province asked the federal minister of justice to amend the criminal code to make corporate officials more responsible for such tragedies. Ottawa and the province also considered integration of mining regulations and a federal role in inspections of mines and other workplaces.

A federal audit queried whether money in The Atlantic Groundfish Strategy (TAGS) program, dispersed by ACOA to regional development boards in Nova Scotia, was being used as intended for those displaced by fisheries closures. The province joined shippers in attacking new coast guard fees, which forced ships in coastal ports like Halifax to pay more per tonne for docking than inland ports on the Saint Lawrence Seaway. The fees were subsequently reduced from 17.5 cents to 9.5 cents per tonne. Federal and provincial governments pledged $1.7 million to support three sound stages for the film industry. Local officers predicted that Halifax would see an increase in port-related crime when Ottawa abolished its Ports Police Force. The regional municipality was expected to absorb the extra costs of policing the waterfront. Municipal leaders feared that local tax rates would increase dramatically to fund education under a new formula proposed by the province. But a deal was reached to turn over administration for all social welfare programs to local government, including general welfare, single-parent and disabled support, with no increase in local contributions for at least four years. Premier MacLellan pledged to give a year's notice of future changes to provincial-municipal revenue sharing, and to establish a committee to study sources of tension between the province and local governments.

New Brunswick
RICHARD WILBUR

Shortly after he led his Liberal Party to power a decade ago, sweeping all before him, Frank McKenna said publicly that ten years was 'long enough' for any politician to be premier. In April he denied rumours that he would leave, but come 10 October, ten years to the day after his 1987 triumph over Richard Hatfield, he did just that. Few New Brunswick premiers had tried as hard to turn the old province away from its have-not image and lessen its economic dependency on the resource sector. While his policies did not significantly reduce the unemployment rate, Mr McKenna nevertheless stuck to his resolve amid mounting criticism, much of it because of his administration's leaner and sometimes meaner approach to social programs, school closures, and municipal amalgamation. Undeterred, Mr McKenna continued to dip into public funds to lure more call centres and information technology firms to the province. In the end, one thing seemed certain: the ten years from 1987–97 would be known to history as the McKenna Era.

Public-private partnerships

On 2 January when he released his annual report, Auditor General Ralph Black expressed dissatisfaction with the province's accounting methods, especially those relating to regional hospital corporations and public-private partnerships. Referring to the deal between the Department of Human Resources (HRD) and Andersen Consulting, he noted that although the U.S. firm 'is supposed to be paid out of the savings it finds for the department ... it has come to our attention that HRD has signed a supplementary agreement on fees, which saw payment to the consultant of $937,550 for services prior to 31 March 1996. We would have thought the cost of these services would have been included in the original contract.' He also predicted that the agreement's revised completion date, April 1997 instead of the original September 1996, 'will add to the final cost of the project.'

In August, the acting auditor general (Mr Black had resigned with one year remaining in his five-year contract) announced that his staff would be conducting a review into reasons for the collapse of another deal Andersen Consulting had signed with the justice department. When it was first announced in 1994, it was billed as an '$8 million high-technology overhaul for an aging court system.' This figure later grew to $60 million, and when the acting justice minister Bernard Richard announced the cancellation on 10 April, he estimated the final costs would have been about $144 million. The Andersen plan had called for sixty reforms, including fewer cases before the courts, and more treatment and less jail time for criminals. Mr Richard said, 'We were looking at a reduced scope of integrated justice and we felt it was so reduced that it wasn't integrated justice anymore and we could do a lot of it ourselves.' Despite earlier rumours, the cancellation produced no law suits but, in the end, the government agreed to pay Andersen Consulting $2.7 million in compensation.

The auditor general's annual report criticized another even more controversial partnership deal. Mr Black estimated that involvement with the private sector in video gambling had cost the government $35 million in lost revenues over the past two years, including $19 million in 1996. These figures were challenged both by Finance Minister Edmond Blanchard and the NB Coin Machine Operators Association. At the same time, Mr Blanchard refused a legislature request by Tory opposition leader Bernard Valcourt for a public inquiry into video gambling because of alleged illegal activities by gaming machine operators. Two weeks later, the RCMP said it would conduct such an investigation based on Mr Valcourt's information and on information handed to them by Solicitor General Jane Barry. The government refused to react directly to a report by the National Council on Welfare showing that New Brunswick had Canada's second-lowest recovery rate from problem and pathological gambling. Instead, it conducted its own review and, as a result, Minister of Health and Community Services Dr King announced that his department would spend $750,000 for treatment and other measures, while the finance department would allocate $750,000 to hire and equip more inspectors. At the same time, Mr Blanchard said the government would negotiate for a larger share of video lottery revenues. On 25 November, the government acknowledged public concern over video lottery terminals (VLTs): it would gradually remove VLTs from non-licensed sites. In 1996, total revenue from VLTs was over $116 million, 70 per cent of which came from machines in corner stores.

Before the year had ended, two more deals with the private sector had been terminated. On 26 September, in a hastily called press conference, Dr Russell King, the health minister, announced the government was ending its contract with a group of companies led by Blue Cross. Under the terms of the original 1994 contract, Blue Cross would supervise the development of a new data base, the Medicare Administration and Technological System (MATS). The government would pay out $2.5 million to develop the software, but this quickly increased to $8.4

million. The consortium would pay about $53 million over seven years to run the new medical billing and information system. In his announcement, Dr King said Blue Cross was taking too long and he felt they would not complete it within the budget. However, according to Tim Porter, a columnist for Fredericton's *The Daily Gleaner*, another issue was the ownership of the new system. He speculated that Blue Cross wanted a cut of future sales, and when this was refused, the government issued a ninety-day cancellation notice (7 October).

On 2 December, it was IBM's turn. Under an agreement signed with the McKenna government in 1995, IBM would design a computer network that would improve the administration of the provincial sales tax. The IBM-led consortium would contribute as much as $20 million, which the government would pay for from future savings in administration costs. A year into the project, Ottawa indicated its willingness to administer New Brunswick's sales-tax system, and the IBM project was quietly shut down in October 1996. The government paid out nearly $10 million for cutting short the agreement. According to a finance department official, 'We were paying them for services rendered. Had we not harmonized the sales tax, they would have continued on with their work.' He added that a call centre developed during the project had collected $6.1 million in bad debts over the last two years (*Telegraph Journal*, 3 December). Meanwhile, the auditor general's office announced that the Revenue Management Systems project would be under review, along with other public-private partnerships; the findings would be contained in its next annual report.

The spring legislative session

Increasingly over the course of Premier McKenna's ten-year rule, decisions and especially political announcements were made outside the Legislature, causing some to wonder about the relevance of this old institution. Its image was further clouded in 1997 when the spring sitting was merely a carry-over from the unprorogued fall session. As a result, there was no formal spring opening with the traditional Throne Speech and budget address; these came when the Fifty-fourth Assembly began in November. Although the spring session was merely an extension, veteran Canadian Press reporter Chris Morris accurately described it as being 'unusually turbulent,' with almost daily demonstrations protesting higher taxes, high unemployment, and still more cuts to health care, education, and municipal funding (*Times & Transcript*, 1–2 March).

Early in the session, the Official Opposition, represented by six Progressive Conservative MLAs, joined the NDP leader and its only MLA, Elizabeth Weir, in a two-week filibuster against the passage of the new 15 per cent Harmonized Sales Tax. While lowering what consumers would pay on some items, it increased the levy on basics such as clothing and home heating. The Chrétien government had little difficulty getting Commons approval of the federal version on 11 February, but it was another two weeks before Premier McKenna got the New Brunswick version passed, and only after the government had voted down a Tory-NDP proposal allowing non-profit cultural performances to maintain exemptions permitted under the old GST. The revenue that would be lost when the current 11 per cent provincial sales tax dropped to 8 per cent would be offset by $30 million from a new tax on paid-up corporate capital.

An NDP labour bill giving unions the option of seeking third-party arbitration if negotiations on a bargaining unit's first contract stalled was also supported by the six PC members. Bolstering the government's decision to defeat the measure was a massive letter-writing campaign from almost every business group (the Irving group was a conspicuous exception). They feared spreading unionization, especially in traditionally low-paid sectors like the hospitality industry. According to Roland MacIntyre, Minister of Advanced Education and Labour, the lobbying was 'probably the largest reaction that we've had' to an initiative (*The Daily Gleaner*, 15 January). The 148 letters he and the Premier had received convinced them to allow changes in the Industrial Relations Act that would guarantee workers involved in legal strikes the right to return to their jobs, but first-contract legislation was delayed indefinitely. This set-back did not deter provincial members of the Canadian Union of Public Employees as they renewed efforts to organize workers in call centres, fast-food chains, and part-time workers in other large companies.

Another familiar sign was the McKenna government, and especially the health minister, defending further cuts. Throughout the winter, Dr King had been severely criticized for proposed changes to the Long-Term Care Program, which would force 1,800 adults living in residential homes to shift to nursing homes. On 10 January, Dr King gave in to a vigorous protest led by the New Brunswick Association for Community Living: mentally handicapped adults would not have to move, although those entering the system after 1 April would be judged 'by new criteria.' After several meetings, he refused to allow more than a modest increase in grants to 800 for-profit operators of homes for the disabled. The two opposition parties took up the issue once the Legislature got underway and their views were endorsed by the Anglican Church, whose bishop, Dr George Lemmon, in a letter to Premier McKenna, called the government policy 'a disgrace.' During the tabling of the health department estimates, criticism came from within party ranks. Carolle de Ste-Croix (L-Dalhousie-Restigouche) accused Dr King of breaking his 1992 promise to maintain surgical services at the Dalhousie hospital. She said she would not have run as a Liberal if she had known about the cuts, but rather than vote against the health department budget, she chose to stay away the day the House voted. Dr King said he would not hold a grudge, and in May, two months after the house had risen, he announced a special $12 million 'lifeline' to help the eight hospital boards cover $9 million in health-care deficits.

Mounting problems for NB Power

The McKenna government had more difficulty dealing with the actions and views of another colleague, Albert Doucet, the Minister of State for Mines and Energy, and the one responsible for the Crown-owned NB Power. His political problems became apparent the first week of January when he appeared before the Crown Corporations Committee. Under close questioning by NDP leader Elizabeth Weir, Mr Doucet admitted he knew nothing about a design flaw detected near the reactor core at the Point Lepreau Nuclear Plant, which produces nearly one-third of New Brunswick's electricity. According to Iain Lee, the on-site inspector for the Atomic Energy Control Board, the flaw, discovered as well at the reactor in Gentilly, Quebec, could be endemic to all of Canada's twenty-two Candu reactors. He predicted that within four years, NB Power would have to make one of two hard choices: spend several million to repair the problem, or mothball the plant. Built at a cost of $1.4 billion, the thirteen-year old Lepreau facility had not reached the halfway mark of its projected thirty-year operating life. In mid-January a leak in the reactor core forced yet another shut-down, and staff later found that one of the 360 feeder pipes had been left unlocked. This human error, the third since 1995, forced the facility to shut down for seventy-five days for a cost of $40 million in repairs and $35 million (about $450,000 a day) to purchase power from Quebec.

On 5 February, Mr Doucet, who represented the northern and largely francophone riding of Nigadoo-Chaleur, resigned from the cabinet, ostensibly because of illness. Two weeks later, in an exclusive interview in *L'Acadie Nouvelle*, he said the stress of trying to deal with the

NB Power situation had prompted his resignation. 'I didn't get into politics to play hide and seek with the truth. The people have the right to know the real financial situation of NB Power ... I was their messenger. I couldn't question the information.' He also challenged the corporation's profit figure of $8 million for 1996, supporting critics' view that it had actually lost $118 million (*Telegraph Journal*, 27 February). Even more damaging in the political sense was his statement that for every dollar spent by the province in northern New Brunswick, five were spent in the south. Premier McKenna strongly denied the latter allegation, pointing to the fact that the largest expenditure his government had made was on the $1-billion power plant at Belledune, in Mr Doucet's riding. On 17 March, after refusing to resign from the party, he was suspended indefinitely and was assigned a seat in the back row.

Mr Doucet's criticisms did not end the NB Power controversy. A study of its finances, commissioned by the Atlantic Institute for Market Studies and conducted by Tom Adams of the Toronto-based Energy Probe, described NB Power's $3.4-billion debt as a 'mess.' It implied that its senior executives had been less than forthright to the public about the Point Lepreau plant. When NB Power filed a defamation claim, the Institute apologized and the action was dropped. On 18 September, NB Power announced that effective 1 October, residential rates would increase 3.4 per cent while industrial and wholesale rates would increase 2.9 per cent.

The politics of education

Evidence that the proposed Education Act would be in for a rough passage surfaced in mid-January during public hearings of the Law Amendments Committee. Parents, teachers, and the federal Commissioner of Official Languages criticized the government's white paper outlining the proposed changes. Commissioner Victor Goldbloom stated flatly that they were unconstitutional because they took decision-making powers from parents and infringed on francophone rights. His views were supported by Michel Doucet, law dean at the Université de Moncton, and Ronald Brun, president of the Acadian Society of New Brunswick.

Mr Brun feared the changes would empower the minister to close schools in small rural communities, where 80 per cent of francophones lived. When Minister James Lockyer introduced the measure on 18 February, he told the Legislature that consultation had been going on for a year. He also said he would not seek a court ruling on the bill's constitutionality, because 'we need to get on with it.' He pointed to changes made after the public hearings, including giving the English and French school boards decision-making authority on spending and education plans as well as the power to appoint directors of education and superintendents. They would also have veto power over proposed school closures. In 1996, the department closed fifteen schools, thirteen of them francophone, and on 26 March, Mr Lockyer announced that twenty-five more would go at the end of the school year because of declining enrolment, especially in French-speaking districts. On 3 May, parents of students attending three doomed schools in the Acadian peninsula blocked a highway with burning tires and debris and, after two nights of rioting, a special RCMP unit was called in. Using batons and tear gas, they broke up the rock-throwing crowds, arresting fifteen. Premier McKenna later raised a storm of criticism when he said people in northern New Brunswick 'have a history of protesting when they don't get what they want' (*L'Acadie Nouvelle*, 8 May; *Telegraph Journal*, 12 May). On 26 June, the parents won a temporary injunction against immediate closure of the schools. On 24 July, just days before the court was to decide on a permanent injunction, Premier McKenna and a new education minister, Bernard Richard, announced in Caraquet that the three schools would remain open. The charges against the protesters were later withdrawn.

Fighting amalgamation and changes to policing

The government also reversed itself on another controversial issue: municipal amalgamation for the greater Saint John area. The 'supercity' concept had been recommended in February by a government-appointed commission, but after strong protests from seven municipalities, Minister of Municipal Services Ann Breault announced on 22 April that only a partial amalgamation would take place. When another was proposed for Edmundston and its three smaller neighbours, the Madawaska group won a court decision that declared uniting their communities was illegal because it dissolved an existing incorporated community without its consent. Ms Breault corrected this oversight in the dying days of the fall session when she introduced a bill aimed at forestalling legal challenges not just from the Edmundston area. It would apply to scores of amalgamations, name changes, and municipal boundary revisions approved by a cabinet order as far back as 1966, when an earlier Liberal government began a massive centralization process under its Program of Equal Opportunity.

An even angrier struggle ensued when Solicitor General Jane Barry decided to end a four-year debate over how to lower the cost of police services in the greater Moncton area. On 17 April, she told municipal leaders that the RCMP would take over policing duties, using 127 officers rather than the current 177 employed in Moncton, Riverview, and Dieppe. At the next meeting of the Moncton City Council on 21 April, a crowd of 2,000, including wives and children of local police, cheered and waved placards when council voted unanimously to reject Ms Barry's proposal. On 10 June, the council for the predominantly francophone community of Dieppe indicated it favoured shifting to the RCMP because of the cost savings. In late August, Ms Barry disagreed with a Moncton council document that the government could not impose the RCMP on the city if it did not sign a contract. 'If the city doesn't sign on the dotted line, it doesn't matter ... It will still go forward,' she said (*Telegraph Journal*, 27 August). And it did, despite a last-minute but unsuccessful legal challenge by the Moncton Police Association. On 19 December, the Legislature gave final reading to the Moncton Police bill, after a vigorous debate sparked by both the NDP leader and the Tory Opposition.

Changing political leaders ... and members

After such a tumultuous year filled with growing criticism of his policies, it was perhaps understandable that Frank McKenna would decide to step down, as he did on 10 October. His long-time colleague and former rival for the job, Ray Frenette, was picked by the caucus to replace him until a leadership convention was held early in the new year. It was a different scenario for Progressive Conservative leader Bernard Valcourt. On 7 January he called a special news conference to deny rumours he would resign. On 29 March, Senator Jean-Maurice Simard, for over a decade the 'French lieutenant' in the Hatfield government, wrote in a half-page column in the *Telegraph Journal* that Mr Valcourt was a victim of an anti-French lobby within the Progressive Conservative Party. He argued that recent polls showing Mr Valcourt was less popular than his party were not a good indication of his strength as a leader. At the party's annual meeting held 12 April, 37.5 per cent of the 1,100 delegates, in response to a questionnaire, favoured a leadership convention within six months. On 15 May, after a three-week stay in Florida to consider his future, Mr Valcourt returned to his home in Edmundston and issued a brief statement, saying he would resign as leader but would continue as a member. He cited the level of approval he received at the annual convention and 'the subsequent non-support of half the caucus.' On 18 October another leadership convention, the party's fifth since 1988, was held in Fredericton. A thirty-two-year-old Moncton lawyer, Bernard Lord captured 56 per cent of the support on the second ballot. Until he gained a seat, the party's house leader would be Ely Robichaud, member for Tracadie-Sheila in the Acadian peninsula.

The results of the federal election on 2 June provided more evidence of a restive electorate. New Brunswick's Acadians in two ridings long held by Liberals broke ranks by making a historic shift to the NDP. The region's senior federal cabinet minister, Doug Young, who had won the seat last time by a massive 15,000 votes, lost his Acadie-Bathurst riding to labour organizer Yvon Godin. In Beausejour-Petitcodiac, Angela Vautour, who had led the fight against sweeping changes in the federal UI program, became New Brunswick's second NDP member. Tories won in five other ridings, leaving the Liberals with just two MPs, compared with the nine they had prior to the election. The voters' disenchantment with the Liberals continued on 17 November, when the Tories won a by-election in Tantramar, raising their MLA contingent to seven.

The general economic picture

Based on new or additional call centres and the latest returns from tourism, New Brunswick's economy was booming, especially in the south. The ICT Canadian Group, a U.S.-based firm which already had 210 employees at its Saint John centre, would expand into Moncton with another 100 jobs. Premier McKenna revealed that $2 million in additional funds would be spent over the next twelve months to create 500 information technology professionals. Northern Telecom planned to move thirty-two jobs from Dallas to Saint John, where it already employed 118 at its call centre. On 30 July, after months of lobbying, Mr McKenna and Economics Development and Tourism Minister Camille Theriault signed a memorandum of understanding with Amdahl Corp. of California, the world's third largest software developer. Public funding would enable upwards of forty IT companies currently in the province to use Amdahl software. On 25 September, the cabinet passed an order-in-council approving a $1.5-million forgivable loan to Keltic Technologies Group of Halifax to establish 150 jobs in Fredericton. A negative note was sounded 29 October when the German owners of a potash mine near Sussex admitted their failure to stem underground flooding; the permanent closure would throw 500 people out of work.

It was a record year for tourism in 1997, thanks in part to the Fixed

Link, which attracted thousands to its official opening in June. All told, 1.3 million visitors created $790 million in revenues for tourism-related activities. In releasing the figures in mid-November, Tourism Minister Camille Theriault said revenues had more than doubled since 1987 and that New Brunswick led all of Canada in terms of increased numbers of U.S. visitors. Figures could be even better in 1998, especially for the Moncton area when it hosted the eighth summit of the world's francophone nations. The New Brunswick government planned to spend $14 million on the affair, but predicted a return of $35 million for the general economy.

The fact that much of this activity was occurring in the more prosperous southern half of the province emphasized the historic have-not status of the north. On 7 April, Premier McKenna and Minister Theriault were in Campbellton to announce that $1.5 million would be spent to help small businesses create jobs in the area. June brought a flurry of 'good news' announcements for the region. A grant and a forgivable loan persuaded a Mississauga sports textile firm to establish a plant at Atholville, near Campbellton, where it planned to hire 100 people. Another 120 jobs were promised by a Bathurst-based textile plant after it had won a subcontract with a New York–based company. On 19 June, Premier McKenna worked out a deal with crab processing plants in the Acadian peninsula that enabled part-timers to work additional hours in order to qualify for Employment Insurance benefits. The $2.5 million required to cover the cost would come in part from a fund established by the snow crab industry, with 30 per cent coming from provincial coffers.

The north-south tug-of-war surfaced as well when two groups began competing for the right to build a pipeline to carry Sable Island gas through the province. The first application of the proposal by Maritimes and Northeast Pipelines Ltd won initial approval from the National Energy Board and was backed by both the McKenna government and the powerful Irving interests. The pipeline would take the shortest route through southern New Brunswick to reach New England markets; the application indicated little interest in feeder lines to the north. The second application, filed eighteen months later by TransMaritime Pipeline, would cut diagonally across the province, exiting at Edmundston and providing more lines to northern communities.

The fall legislative session

The Throne Speech opening the Third Session of the Fifty-third Legislative Assembly on 25 November was viewed as a shift to the left with promises of tax cuts, financial relief for hard-up students, no further reductions to the health-care program, and no new VLTs in corner stores. The new premier, Ray Frenette, called it 'reaping the benefits of restraint.' No mention was made of a historic court decision handed down a month earlier, when Judge John Turnbull of the Court of Queen's Bench ruled that New Brunswick Native people had the first right to Crown land and everything that grew on it. While the government prepared an appeal, Native people began reaping immediate benefits by cutting and selling trees in tracts nearest their reserves. The decision, if upheld, could have profound implications for a cash-strapped government. Finance Minister Edmond Blanchard acknowledged that a planned $25 million surplus forecast a year ago had dropped to $4.3 million as a result of losses in tax and royalty revenues and a $90-million decrease in federal equalization payments. In his budget, Mr Blanchard's decision to spend another $196 million on roads, in addition to the $160 million earmarked for the four-lane highway between Fredericton and Moncton, angered the president of the NB Nurses Union, who noted that the $196 million was nineteen times the amount allocated for health care. The government had already suggested that the private consortium chosen to build and operate the Fredericton-Moncton route would be exacting tolls. When it was revealed that the winning group, Maritime Road Development Corporation, was headed by defeated Liberal cabinet minister Doug Young, the Tory Opposition threatened to use a filibuster to delay the necessary legislation. They relented when the government promised to make public the details of the agreement after it was signed.

Manitoba   GEOFFREY LAMBERT

The major event in the province in 1997 was undoubtedly the flooding that took place in much of the Red River Valley in April and May. The provincial economy continued to expand and, while the Progressive Conservative government suffered from a few slings and arrows, it seemed reasonably entrenched. The Liberal Party in Manitoba, however, seemed bent on self-immolation.

The economy

Most economic statistics were encouraging. The economy, by most indicators, grew at least as fast as the national average. There were some less impressive aspects, however. Population increased by only about 4,000, to 1.142 million. For the first time in a number of years, the province lost ground as a result of interprovincial migration. As has happened so often in the last thirty years, large numbers of young people packed their bags and moved to the two westernmost provinces. There was a partial offset in the fact that the province gained more than it lost in the movement of people from five of the six provinces to the East.

Data from the 1996 census revealed that the Manitoba population was becoming more diverse. The largest immigrant groups in the preceding decade were from South-East Asia, principally from the Philippines and Hong Kong. Proposed changes to the family unification category by the federal government, a move designed to appease the concerns of Ontario, encountered a great deal of opposition in the province, since Philippinos had become such an important source of new blood. The fastest growing group in the population at large, however, were the aboriginal peoples of the province. This fact was felt to have significance for future public policy. Manitoba and Saskatchewan were home to the largest populations (measured as a percentage of the total population) of First Nations people in Canada.

There was one discomfiting aspect of the province's economic performance in 1997 – the rate of inflation was greater than the average wage increase. The Consumer Price Index (CPI) increased by about 2.2 per cent (for Winnipeg), while the average pay settlement increased wages by half that. And, while the employment picture continued to be encouraging, since most new jobs were apparently full time, the fact was that a great many of the new jobs were so-called McJobs, found in the growing call-centre industry. Manitoba's labour force reached 576.4 thousand in 1997, about 1 per cent higher than the year before, and just over 2 per cent higher than in 1995. The unemployment rate was 6.6 per cent, below the levels of many previous years. As elsewhere, youth unemployment (particularly among aboriginal youth) continued to cause concern.

Every major sector of the economy grew: farm cash receipts (by 9.9 per cent); manufacturing shipments (by 11.5 per cent); mineral production (by 12.6 per cent); electric power sales exports (by 12.5 per cent); housing starts (by 12.7 per cent); and retail trade (by 6.5 per cent). Foreign exports increased by 13.6 per cent, and those to the U.S. by 19.3 per cent. The declining dollar improved tourism somewhat. Investment rose strongly – the 14.8 per cent improvement being well above the national average. The provincial GDP reached a nominal level of $28.43 billion, or $21.76 billion in real dollars.

Manitoba's economy, therefore, continued to do well, mirroring the national picture. In addition, several major initiatives were announced. Acrylon Plastics, a major custom plastics manufacturer, completed a $2.5-million expansion in Winkler. MCI announced plans to build a call centre dedicated to outsourced services. Winnipeg was chosen as the first such centre outside the United States, and the company was expected to create at least 200 new jobs. The Royal Bank's telephone and PC banking service, Royal Direct, announced plans to invest $10 million in a new Winnipeg call centre. Scheduled to open in 1998, it was expected to employ 300 people by the year 2000. Springhill Farms announced its intention of expanding its hog processing plant at Neepawa. And Winpak announced a $33.8-million expansion intended to create 'a new generation of flexible packaging products for export to world markets.' Most of these announcements were in keeping with the objectives of Manitoba's government and private sector to take advantage of the province's central location and develop the transport and telecommunications fields.

However, the most exciting and potentially most controversial announcement was that Maple Leaf Foods was to build a $112-million plant in the Brandon area. The plant was expected to create 2,250 jobs, an expansion of enormous significance to the city of 40,000 people. Following in the wake of Maple Leaf's plant closures and labour strife elsewhere, some saw the announcement as a mixed blessing. Some worried about environmental impact. Others were concerned about the possible strain on the city's resources and the impact this would have on its pleasant and comfortable way of life. Most, however, saw clear gains and a more prosperous future for Brandon.

Whatever the concerns about the type of job being created, and the blow to the provincial pride represented by the outflow of young Manitobans to other provinces, the government could safely take pride in its record of economic management. This sense of accomplishment was reinforced by a number of encouraging statements and forecasts from major financial institutions.

Politics and political parties

Both the Progressive Conservatives and the New Democrats held conferences in the course of the year; neither was memorable, both were predictable. Nonetheless, the Tory conference was an important reminder of Gary Filmon's dominance over the political life of the province and over the party, which he had now led for fourteen years.

During the federal election held in June, Mr Filmon strongly endorsed the campaign of federal leader Jean Charest. The PCs had hoped to win three seats in the House of Commons from Manitoba, but had to be content with one. They were successful in Brandon, though more because of the popularity of the local candidate, Mayor Rick Borotsik, than any other cause. One of Mr Filmon's cabinet ministers, Brian Palliser from Portage la Prairie, resigned to (unsuccessfully) campaign for election to the House of Commons in the rural Lisgar Marquette constituency.

Mr Filmon's endorsement of Mr Charest outraged Reformers, who threatened (without the sanction of their national leader) to form a provincial party. When a by-election took place in Portage la Prairie, Reformers backed an Independent candidate. The Tories won and the candidate who had Reform backing came fourth, though with a respectable share of the votes. The situation demonstrated the ongoing tension between the federal and provincial wings of the Tories, as it was well known that many provincial PC supporters (and party members) were federal Reformers. So, Mr Filmon had to tread delicately.

The Liberals provided some cheap laughs during the year. Party leader Ginny Hasselfield seemed to have the knack for alienating her three-member caucus. One of the members, Gary Kowalski, who represented the North West Winnipeg riding of The Maples, resigned from the caucus in the spring, citing policy differences and expressing a clear dislike for Ms Hasselfield. Months later, her rival for party leadership the year before, Kevin Lamoureux (from Inkster, also in North West Winnipeg), also announced a parting of the ways. He said that although he would not leave the party, he would not caucus with the Liberals (there was only one other caucus member left by that time). Furthermore, he did not intend to stay in the House beyond the next election. Again, personal dislikes and internal party dynamics seemed to play a larger role than honest differences of opinion about issues of high principle. It was reported by some that Reg Alcock (MP for Winnipeg South) was somehow an evil genius, tempting Ms Hasselfield into all manner of shocking things. Likewise, it was claimed that the North Winnipeg–South Winnipeg divide was a major source of party tension.

The issue of Ms Hasselfield's continuance as party leader naturally arose. She was criticised for many things, including her decision not to contest the Portage la Prairie by-election. When the issue was put to the party executive late in the year, a vote favoured a leadership review. Somehow, organizers got the figures upside down and announced the

vote as being against a review. An embarrassed, but under the circumstances cool, Ms Hasslefield, announced her intention of running
again. Mr Lamoureux said he was not interested (he had lost on two
previous occasions), and pressure was put on federal MP Reis Paghtakhan, a native of the Philippines, who eventually declined.

The 'flood of the century'

The major event of the year was the so-called flood of the century. The
heavy snowfalls of a cold (even by Manitoba standards) winter gave
cause for concern. Concern turned to alarm when the southern parts of
the province were battered by a blizzard in early April. It was apparent
that the Red River (and its tributaries) and the sections of the Assiniboine River connecting to it (namely, its easternmost section, which
converges with the Red at the Forks in Winnipeg) were going to over-
flow their banks.

The terrible damage inflicted on U.S. communities to the south, such
as Grand Forks, North Dakota, by floading waters there provided a
chilling reminder of the power of nature. Manitobans made the most of
the time they had available to meet the onslaught. Rural communities
and small towns, such as Emerson, did what they could to build dykes
to protect their property. There was a large-scale movement of people,
livestock, and possessions to higher ground. Close to 17,000 people
were evacuated as the crest approached. In spite of all these efforts, the
flood exacted an enormous economic and psychological toll.

The affected parts of the province resembled a medieval city girded
against attack by an invading foreign force. Winnipegers felt isolated
as news came that Emerson had been 'saved' but St Agathe had been
swallowed by the 'Red Sea.' St Norbert, a suburb on the southern out-
skirts of the city, was evacuated. The provincial capital's crucial line of
defence, however, was the Floodway, a large ditch affectionately nick-
named Duff's Ditch after Duff Roblin (premier in the 1960s when it
was built), which could divert the flow and lower the water levels of
the Red within the city. Inside Winnipeg, several thousand troops
played a key role in fortifying the shoreline defences, and thousands of
volunteers helped sandbag threatened neighbourhoods. Assisted by
substantial help from other parts of Canada, the basic needs of those
evacuated from the rural areas and those within city limits forced from
their homes were met. Working against the clock, major dyke construction at Brunkild, southwest of the city, prevented the city from falling
victim to a 'backdoor' rising of the Red by way of one of its tributaries.

The flooding occurred just before the calling of the 1997 federal election. The fact that the call was made at all seemed to many Manitobans to confirm the long-standing belief that Ottawa was indifferent to the needs of the West. The day before the election call, Prime Minister Chrétien paid a brief visit to Winnipeg. He was afterwards remembered for being handed a single sandbag and asking, 'What shall I do with it?' However, despite this unpromising start, his government proved generous in the provisions it made for those worst affected by the flood, and certainly a crucial element in the province's ability to withstand the ravages of the flood were the military personnel dispatched by the federal government.

There was some suggestion that the election in some of the Manitoba ridings should be postponed, since it was clearly impossible to conduct an orthodox campaign under such circumstances. The Chief Electoral Officer for Canada, Mr J-P Kingsley, visited the province and determined that there was no need for a postponement. Whether the early negative response to the Chrétien government's election call affected election results is difficult to say; however, the Liberals fell from twelve MPs in 1993 to six in 1997.

The Red River crested in Winnipeg on 3 May at 7.7 metres (25.3 feet). This level was lower than had been either feared or anticipated. Nonetheless, the flood destroyed thousands of homes and had a major economic impact on rural Manitoba. When it was over, there was general rejoicing and a sense of pride that the people of the province had pulled together so magnificently. However, there was the major issue of compensation to be dealt with and the desperate struggle to rebuild both homes and lives. Some felt that the needs of the city of Winnipeg had been allowed to dictate the agenda, and that some suburban and rural areas had been sacrificed in order to keep water out of the capital. The Filmon government seemed uncharacteristically clumsy in refusing to change the provincial regulations concerning compensation, namely, that the province would pay only 80 per cent of the costs. Public sentiment seemed to demand more. And although the Premier's statement that those living outside the protection of the Floodway should be prepared to accept some responsibility, since they were well aware of the risk they were taking when they built or bought homes in locations vulnerable to flooding, had some truth in it, to some his comment lacked compassion.

The flood was widely referred to as 'the flood of the century.' It was estimated that not since 1826 had water levels reached so high. Even the famous flood of 1950, which had a devastating effect on the provincial capital, was nothing like this one. Still, the Floodway proved its worth and advanced to legendary status the political reputation of Duff Roblin, whose eightieth birthday on 17 June was a cause for celebration. The quality of the emergency relief personnel in the provincial and municipal governments stood out, and the armed forces, whose reputation had been suffering from the debilitating impact of the Somalia inquiry, gained many new friends in Manitoba.

The legislative session

The Legislature resumed its sitting in March and was almost immediately presented with a budget. This was the first budget of the 'post-balanced budget legislation' era. The session continued until June, and then adjourned until the late fall.

The budget continued the Filmon government's policy of prudent fiscal management. There were no significant tax increases (none at all in the category of major taxes), and a tight check was kept on public spending. The revenue situation was good (in spite of concerns about the reductions in transfer payments from Ottawa), but the government still preferred caution. Its political situation seemed to justify this posture, although many feared the consequences of several years restraint on the functioning of major social services, such as health and education, or programs for children and abused women.

The government's legislative agenda was not an ambitious one, and much of it was designed to fine-tune previous legislation. The Opposition NDP maintained its feistiness, and seemed more effective than it had been in previous sessions. However, some thought that NDP leader, Gary Doer, lacked energy and wondered whether if, after almost a decade in his position, it wasn't time to turn elsewhere for a leader that would take the New Democrats back into office. Although there was no open or widespread mutiny, some caucus members were known to be whispering the names of Reverend Tim Sale (Crescentwood), a former social worker and activist, and Dr Jean Friesen (Wolseley), a history professor at the University of Manitoba and the party's deputy leader, as potential replacements.

The NDP caucus picked a number of targets. Health care, predictably, was one. Over the years in Manitoba, the party had developed a solid reputation as a 'protector' of public health care. Another target was the consequence of the province's sale of the Manitoba Telephone System (MTS), approved amid great and intense controversy in 1996. It appeared that ownership (and, hence, control) of the utility was passing out of the hands of Manitobans. Moreover, now that it was a private enterprise and oriented to profit, MTS raised rates up and laid off staff. The NDP exploited the situation skilfully and went after Speaker Louise Daquay (Seine River), accusing her of partiality and incompetence. However, she was able to weather the storm, which blew itself out relatively early in the session.

The Filmon government came under fire from many organized groups, but nowhere was the opposition more fierce than from health-care workers. As in every other province, demographics posed a problem for the government. An aging population demanded more and more health-care services, which were becoming more and more expensive. Faced with a fiscal crisis, the government tried to reduce costs and to direct more resources to prevention and to treatment and care outside hospitals. On the face of it, these were reasonable strategies, and Health Minister Darren Praznik (Lac du Bonnet) frequently reminded audiences that the amount of the provincial budget spent on health care was, as a proportion, about the highest in the country. However, the crisis in emergency wards, the closing of hospital beds, the failure to deliver on a promise of more personal-care homes, and the deteriorating morale among health-care professionals tended to diminish the impact of Mr Praznik's claims. Even Mr Praznik admitted that the government's earlier decision to privatize much of the home-care services had not produced the results he had expected, and that therefore the government had decided to reverse itself. This pronouncement was taken by some as a sign of the Health Minister's common sense and of the government's willingness to bend, and by others as an admission of incompetence and failure.

The province's post-secondary institutions were likewise alienated. Enrolment in community colleges and universities in Manitoba was low by national standards. Funding was about average, on a per capita basis. As in other provinces, funding had been reduced in absolute and real terms over a number of years. The Filmon administration wanted to increase its profile in the setting of policy and wanted more accountability from the universities, as there was some questioning of the universities' priorities. There was concern about the province's major university, the University of Manitoba (in Winnipeg), repeatedly taking last place in the annual *Maclean's* ranking of graduate/medical universities. No doubt the criteria and the weightings used by the weekly magazine were imperfect, a point stressed by the administration of the University of Manitoba, but a central problem was the level of financial support provided to the university through the province's 'buffer agency,' the Council on Post-Secondary Education (COPSE). The universities did not feel any better than before, either, when the government announced its approval of the establishment of a new Mennonite university, to be located in an elegant area of South Winnipeg, just below Assiniboine Park. A large number of people questioned the necessity for such a facility, especially at a time when the older universities were feeling the financial pinch.

The situation confronting universities' operating costs was exacerbated by declining student numbers (a function of both demographics and a vigorous economy), and by the attempt to induce senior faculty members to retire. The inducements offered were expensive, whatever the almost-immediate benefits. As a result, the increase in student fees was higher than when the provincial government had imposed a cap. Particularly in the professional schools, the proportion of the cost of education assumed by students reached unprecedented levels.

What universities (like most other public institutions) grieved most about, however, was the small amount of money allocated to them for maintenance and renovation. All the campuses in Manitoba had enjoyed building booms in the 1950s and 1960s, but by the 1990s, many of the buildings were in dangerous condition. Admittedly, the upcoming 1999 Pan American Games had important spin-offs for the universities (particularly the University of Manitoba), but this was a drop in the bucket compared with the existing needs of the campuses.

The citizens of Manitoba were concerned about personal safety, and law and order this year. Reports of home invasions, increased violent crime, and stories of gang members roaming the streets of the province naturally alarmed many. It is paradoxical, therefore, that the statistics suggested a decline in most categories of crime. The provincial justice minister, Mr Vic Toews (Rossmere), always talked tough on the issue, but there was great concern that the province was underfunding the policing and legal institutions of the province. As a result, a degree of friction emerged between Mr Toews and his colleagues against the members of the judiciary.

British Columbia   CAREY HILL

Asian horoscopes named 1997 as the year of the bull. For British Columbians, however, it was the year of the fish – the year of the Pacific salmon. International and federal-provincial relations seemed to swirl around discussions and disagreements about fish, fishing regulations, and resource protection. It was a year in which Premier Glen

Clark went from being a minnow on the national and international stages to being a changeling who was sometimes a fierce shark, and at other times a helpless seal. The federal government, Pacific Rim states, and even the U.S. president appeared to wonder at which moment the shark would strike.

The year was one of self-assertion abroad and self-importance at home. Americans became familiar with the province as it initiated a fish stand-off with their government and welcomed the world to the November meeting for Asia-Pacific Economic Cooperation (APEC). Canadians, and particularly the premiers of the other provinces, became increasingly wary of the bold position of Premier Clark in relations with the federal government. Mr Clark's special constitutional adviser, Gordon Wilson, exacerbated these concerns with his report on British Columbia's disaffected place in Confederation. The year also marked the beginning of consultations for the newly proposed Calgary Declaration. British Columbians involved themselves in an assortment of issues including the recall of two MLAs, a court challenge to the previous year's provincial election, and the rescue of Canadian Airlines International.

Nationally, 1997 was the year of the federal election, an election marked by an effort on the part of the parties, especially the Liberals, to court British Columbia voters. Outsiders, including the federal government, stood up and took notice of BC while local media called the year 'unfocused ... lacking any truly memorable occasions or over-arching themes' (*Vancouver Sun,* 29 December). For the province's premier, the year was one of infamous celebrity in which he was prominent on the local, national, and international stages. As the year closed, the NDP government's support shrank to its lowest since the 1996 election. Its part in the failure to achieve a renewal of the Pacific salmon treaty was on everyone's mind. Onlookers were left wondering how long Mr Clark would be able to keep the NDP afloat.

Pacific salmon treaty

The Pacific salmon treaty was the issue of the year. While the Mifflin plan of 1996 plunged some of British Columbia's fishers into a desperate situation, the lack of a Pacific salmon treaty became a hot button for residents, province wide. Fish were an important part of West Coast life, livelihood, and pride. In 1997, British Columbians proved that they would not stand idly by while 'their' salmon were in danger of extinction by foreign hands.

The Pacific salmon treaty governs catch allocations of species that range across international boundaries. It is a bilateral agreement involving the states of Alaska, Washington, and Oregon and the province of British Columbia. For the past three years, Canadians and Americans had been unable to agree on how to share salmon according to the terms of the 1985 treaty. The treaty's equity principle states that countries have primary interest in and responsibility for stocks that spawn in their rivers, lakes, and streams yet swim into foreign waters while at sea feeding and maturing. Canadians claimed that the Pacific salmon that spawn in British Columbia but swim to Alaska, Oregon, and Washington were 'their fish,' and they wanted to regulate related catches. Americans stated that they have never understood the equity principle in the way Canadians understood it. Alternate commissioner on the Pacific Salmon Commission, Alaskan Jev Shelton, explained, 'To the United States, and especially to Alaska, the Canadian equity viewpoint is and always has been completely unacceptable. All who participated in the treaty negotiations understood clearly that the [equity] wording ... did not accomplish an agreement on a theoretical level' (*Vancouver Sun*, 15 November).

To exacerbate matters, 1997 proved to be the peak of the Fraser River sockeye's four-year cycle, meaning that fish were abundant with fishers on both sides of the border demanding extra catches. On the Canadian side, fishers were forced to stop fishing or significantly decrease their catch. The Canadians claimed that if they, too, followed the lead of the Americans, the Pacific salmon could be wiped out. Glen Clark explained, 'In the absence of a functioning treaty, the Americans are conducting an all-out harvest of our runs' (*Toronto Star*, 17 July).

The fish story did not stop at the treaty, as the controversy surrounding it developed whale-like proportions. During the year, British Columbians, led by their premier, became increasingly disillusioned and disappointed by what they perceived as the failure of the national government to protect their interests. Their frustration propelled them to take matters into their own hands. In February, Mr Clark implored the Canadian government to live up to its obligations to British Columbians: 'I say the treaty is between Canada and the United States and not between Alaska and British Columbia, Oregon or Washington. Canada has an obligation to try to enforce that treaty and work with the American government to do so' (*CTV-News*, 16 February).

By April, and just prior to calling a federal election, the Chrétien government reached a much-lauded but rather ill-fated agreement with the province. The agreement stated that ultimate responsibility for the

Pacific salmon negotiations would lie with the federal government. A new BC-Canada group of councils and committees that would be made up of federal and provincial fisheries ministers was also proposed (*Province*, 17 April).

Jointly, the federal and British Columbia governments decided to enforce the 'hail-in and stow laws' that had been on the books for many years but seemed optional by convention. The hail-in and stow laws require U.S. fishing vessels to store fish gear and make radio contact with the coast guard when they enter Canadian waters (*Vancouver Sun*, 29 May). In mid-May, four skippers were fined $300 each for failing to abide by these laws. As a result, Frank Murkowski, an Alaskan senator, requested that the U.S. coast guard consider escorting U.S. fishboats through the Inside Passage to protect them from seizure. In response, Premier Clark said, 'It's almost a little bit comical that this horrendous action by the Canadian government is to enforce existing regulations. This is hardly a radical step. It's also in keeping with what the U.S. does to Canadian fish boats' (29 May).

During the weeks leading up to the federal election, in his typical grandstanding fashion, Mr Clark made a second and more controversial announcement. He stated that if the Pacific salmon dispute was not expeditiously and adequately resolved he would cancel the seabed lease at the Canada-U.S. torpedo test range at Nanoose Bay on Vancouver Island. The federal government quickly put pressure on Mr Clark to retract his ultimatum. He refused to do so. He met with Defence Minister Art Eggleton and Fisheries Minister David Anderson and warned them that a federal government decision to override him would have serious negative effects on federal-provincial relations: 'I'd be very, very angry. It's hard for me to believe Ottawa would side with the United States against British Columbia. It would be a very dangerous move' (*Vancouver Sun*, 29 May). Both ministers cautioned Mr Clark that his actions risked retaliation from the Americans.

Premier Clark's threat was sustained throughout the year. In July, Fisheries Minister David Anderson explained that the threat could cause major testing problems for the Canadian navy, which would have to rent space in a U.S. range at a cost of more than $15 million annually (*Ottawa Citizen*, July 22). Federal officials met with Mr Clark again in August and discussed the 'awkward situation' in which he had put them. Under the thirty-two-year-old Nanoose treaty, Ottawa was required to give a twelve-month notice before termination. The BC government was only required to give ninety days according to a 1989 Department of National Defence agreement (*Vancouver Sun*, 7 August).

While the threat of the Nanoose Bay closure was an unexpected surprise attack by Mr Clark on both the federal government and the Americans, unilateral action by some fishers eclipsed it. On 29 May, in what papers called the 'peak of the fish war,' Prince Rupert fishers blockaded the Alaskan ferry *Malaspina*. The U.S. State Department labelled the blockade an 'unfriendly act' and demanded that federal and provincial officials enforce a court injunction halting it (*Vancouver Sun*, 29 May). Soon after the incident, Alaska claimed the blockade cost it $3 million U.S. In addition, Alaska sued the fishers for $4.6 million in damages, and BC sued Washington and Alaska for $325 million in lost fish (24 November). The blockade of the *Malaspina* was not the only illegal citizen action during the fish wars. In August, British Columbians again took matters into their own hands when forty gillnetters illegally dropped their nets into waters just off Prince Rupert. Officials watched them closely, but no arrests were made (*CTV-News*, 4 August).

By year's end, there was no resolution to the dispute. Nevertheless, negotiators for both sides were hopeful as new talks took place on 18 and 19 December. The negotiators, special envoys of the U.S. president and Canadian prime minister, were to make recommendations that would eventually be made public. The provincial government formally participated in the talks in Seattle between the envoys, Canadian David Strangway and American William Ruckelshaus. Sources close to the talks said the envoys were attempting to resurrect the stakeholder process that had failed in recent years (*Vancouver Sun*, 9 and 20 December).

APEC

While the Pacific salmon war gave Glen Clark some notoriety in North America, the success of the APEC meetings brought him dignity internationally and at home. Problems with APEC, such as the pepper-spray scandal, were not Mr Clark's problems. The federal government and the RCMP were seen to be responsible. The meetings coincided with Mr Clark's birthday and, as one reporter put it, Mr Clark got the best 'present he could hope for – U.S. President Bill Clinton's personal attention on the salmon treaty and the world's attention on BC.' Mr Clark explained, 'As far as the promotion of British Columbia, it has exceeded my expectations – 500 million viewers watching Vancouver.' The U.S. president's attention extended to the Premier as he was presented with champagne, wished well, and promised that Mr Clinton would give the salmon dispute his attention. 'I must confess to being speechless,' Mr Clark told reporters. 'Before I could say "Welcome to

British Columbia," he said, "Happy birthday, Mr Premier"' (*Vancouver Sun*, 25 November).

In a year that could be described as alienating for BC, the Asia-Pacific Economic Cooperation forum that aims to accelerate trade between eighteen Asia-Pacific nations promised to be a 'political winner' for Prime Minister Jean Chrétien and his Liberal government. However, promises turned sour as a scandal erupted over the Vancouver police department and the RCMP's use of pepper spray to contain APEC protesters demonstrating on the UBC campus, where the APEC meeting was held. The young people carried signs with words such as 'Free Speech,' 'democracy,' and 'human rights.' More than four dozen protesters were arrested. The Prime Minister said the protesters' attempts to jump the fence contravened the law (*Vancouver Sun*, 12 and 19 December; *Montreal Gazette*, 28 November). The president of the BC Civil Liberties Association, Kay Stockholder, stated, 'If the security arrangements necessary for these leaders is such that they deprive Canadian citizens of their civil rights, these leaders ought not to be our guests' (*Vancouver Sun*, 12 December). The RCMP began conducting an internal review of police behaviour, and the RCMP's Public Complaints Commission started an investigation of complaints about excessive use of force and oppressive conduct by police (19 December).

Federal-provincial relations

APEC gave British Columbians just another reason not to trust the federal Liberal government or the RCMP. Federal-provincial relations were already marred by the failure to renew the Pacific salmon treaty. 'To British Columbians, the federal government's handling of the salmon issue had become a metaphor for national failure' (*Toronto Star*, 12 September). The Premier's view of the year in federal-provincial relations was bleak: 'Like most New Democrats, when I got elected I had a pretty strong – I always had a strong BC-first attitude – but I had a pretty strong sympathy for central government. You know national, even federal, intervention ... Its only in dealing with the federal government that you become more radical in your approach, because you see their arrogance and the way in which they treat BC' (12 September).

The fish controversy was not the year's only event of federal-provincial discord. In February, another row erupted between the province and the federal government over Canadian Airlines International. The year prior, the airline appeared to be on the brink of collapse but was saved through an $800-million rescue plan that included owners, employees, and creditors agreeing to wage roll-backs, loan deferments, and cuts to service fees and overhead costs. This plan was combined with fuel-tax concessions from the governments of British Columbia, Alberta, and the federal government. In February, Finance Minister Paul Martin demanded major tax concessions from the airline in return for a $20-million tax break on fuel each year for four years. David Anderson, then federal transport minister, asked for better terms for the airline. Premier Glen Clark blamed the federal government for 'foot-dragging' and said it was jeopardizing the restructuring plan. Days later, Mr Martin agreed to better terms so that Canadian would give up $15 million in future tax-loss claims for every $1 million in federal aid (*Vancouver Sun*, 6 March).

Canada Pension Plan talks, led by Mr Martin, also succeeded in raising the ire of the BC Premier and reinforced the shaky relations between the Finance Minister and BC, especially when BC was left out of February's CPP agreement. Premier Clark noted that BC had proposed a plan that imposed a modest increase in premiums and that would move some of the Employment Insurance surplus over to the CPP. He said, 'Instead what [Mr Martin has] done, it looks like, is increase premiums more for the poor than for the well off, cut benefits for everybody and cut benefits for the disabled. Very regressive and I think it's not necessary' (*CTV-News*, 16 February).

In October, the Finance Minister and the House of Commons Finance Committee visited British Columbia to try to 'highlight Ottawa's respect for BC' and, perhaps, to foster better relations between the department of finance and the province. This third attempt failed in its aim when Paul Martin struck out in BC. Mr Martin referred to BC as 'this great province ... the gateway to the Asia-Pacific, the gateway to an important part of our future' (*Vancouver Sun*, 16 October). BC Finance Minister Andrew Petter responded to Mr Martin's visit by emphasizing that for every dollar BC provided to the have-not provinces, Ottawa provided only 94 cents in social program funding for BC. Mr Petter noted, 'British Columbians are being treated like 94-cent Canadians ... Unfortunately the federal government seems to be of the view that coming out to BC for a couple of days and making a statement constitutes consultation and listening' (16 October).

National unity

In what might be called a year of surprises, the provincial government, in June, through its special constitutional adviser, provided the country with what *The Globe and Mail* called a 'West Coast perspective on the national unity situation.' The Wilson Report was presented to the government and the public by Glen Clark's special constitutional adviser, MLA for Powell-River-Sunshine Coast and sole Progressive Democratic Alliance member, Gordon Wilson. The report, reminiscent of Mr Clark's leadership, marked a 'dramatic departure' from BC's courtship of Quebec during the Meech Lake and Charlottetown Accords (*Vancouver Sun*, 1 May). The report was the primary deliverable of a $100,000 project begun in 1996. Gordon Wilson explained, 'There are a number of ways the government can act immediately to try to build a renewed Canada in advance of constitutional amendments. However, we also recognize the reality of the potential for a "yes" vote in Quebec and we recommend the government, concurrently while working in building the country, put in place a contingency plan in the event of that reality ... My personal opinion is that BC is not likely to simply acquiesce to a rest-of-Canada model including BC.' *Le Devoir* referred to the report with this headline: 'A separatist advises Victoria on Canada's future,' and argued that the report provided some legitimation for Quebec separatism (ibid.).

The Wilson Report consisted of three papers: (1) 'Renewing Confederation: Options for BC' by Gordon Gibson; (2) 'BC in Confederation: PMs and Premiers, 1864–1987, An Historical Brief' by John Munro; (3) 'Four Avenues to Renewal' by Gordon Wilson. The third paper focused on tax reform, aboriginal issues, globalization, and governance in British Columbia as well as federal-provincial relations. The report also expressed a sense of alienation: 'When British Columbians witness Ottawa taking $19.32 billion in taxes from the province each year, which is roughly equal to the entire provincial budget for the year, we have to ask ourselves whether or not the current tax system is equitable. Three million British Columbians currently pay $11.08 billion per year in personal income tax to the federal government. Corporations pay $1.77 billion. Add to this $3.97 billion in indirect taxes such as GST one wonders why only $2.63 billion per year is returned to BC via transfer payments.' Moreover, the report seemed to follow the centre-periphery view of Canadian development: 'Just as the Dominion of Canada served as an outpost for wealth extraction for the British, many westerners feel that the provinces of British Columbia and Alberta in the latter part of the twentieth century serve as a source of tax revenue for central Canada.' Regarding First Nations, the report acknowledged that the province needed to establish that residual title on treaties rested with it rather than with the federal government.

At times, the report went out of its way to be critical of Ottawa. For example, Mr Wilson wrote, 'The federal budgets of 1994, 1995, 1996, and 1997 were written more for the American investment community than for the Canadian people,' and, 'British Columbians have always had to fight and fight hard to make sure that Ottawa understood the concerns of the West.' Perhaps the most controversial section was the paper written by Gordon Gibson, which addressed possible scenarios that could occur after Quebec's separation. It recommended that if Quebec were to separate, 'BC would need a position on what that renegotiated Canada should look like.'

The Wilson Report was an attempt to identify BC's position on national unity. However, in September, the premiers of Canada's English-speaking provinces met to solidify their position on national unity through a declaration of their vision of the country based on a seven-point framework. The Calgary Declaration was the result of that weekend meeting. Premier Glen Clark returned to BC and announced that extensive citizen consultations, including opinion polling, would take place in order to ask British Columbians their views. If a consensus was achieved, the Legislature could pass a resolution, 'which would be a broad statement of values and principles and, hopefully, a contribution to the national unity debate.' At the heart of the Declaration was recognition of Quebec's 'unique nature' – a phrase that 'aim[ed] to sidestep the contentious designation of distinct society' (*Vancouver Sun*, 17 September).

On 25 October, Premier Clark appointed twelve citizens and ten elected officials to the BC Unity Panel. They were given a mandate to consult with British Columbians on BC's place within Canada, using the Calgary framework as a starting point. A report is expected in February 1998. The BC Unity Panel, co-chaired by John Kerr and Alice McQuade was charged with undertaking public meetings, focus groups in key centres, distribution of a questionnaire to all households, and establishment of a toll-free phone line and Web site. The media, along with special constitutional adviser Mr Wilson, quickly criticized the appointments of Mr Kerr and Ms McQuade. Mr Wilson unsuccessfully attempted to persuade Mr Clark to allow the panel to elect its own co-chairs (*Province*, 4 November).

Late in the year, the public remarks of Paul DeVillers, the parliamentary secretary for Intergovernmental Affairs Minister Stéphane Dion, and of BC Senator Pat Carney seemed to echo the pessimism of the Wilson Report rather than the optimism of the Calgary Declaration. Senator Carney stated, 'Ottawa is clueless about BC's concerns' (*Gazette*, 1 October). She also noted that separation was an option for BC. Ms Carney's disillusionment with Ottawa was the result of frustration with its handling of the fisheries. She claimed that Ottawa's imposition of the Mifflin plan was 'insensitive' and had created '3,000 Mifflin refugees' – fishers who had left the industry and for whom there was no plan in place to pay for training and support programs to help them. Ms Carney's inflammatory remarks led other Canadians such as Hugh Segal to speculate on her motives: 'In this circumstance, my sense is [Senator Carney's] public reflection on a separatist option for British Columbians only gives vent to a long-established view here that Ottawa is, at best, self-absorbed and irrelevant, and, at worst, focused on central Canada at the expense of places like BC that contribute to equalization, pay their taxes and ask for little' (*Financial Post*, 4 October).

Parliamentary Secretary Paul DeVillers observed similar sentiments in his meetings with unity groups, on radio open-line shows, and at public meetings. One observation he made was that 'BC wants a bigger voice, more say in decisions that affect the federation. And they're still expressing the same sense of "we want in. We want to be involved in the decision-making process."' At a Vancouver Board of Trade meeting, he was told that the distinct society clause is 'as dead as the cha cha.' Mr DeVillers noted that British Columbians say they don't want to talk about national unity, but then 'they'll spend three hours talking about it' (*Vancouver Sun*, 23 August).

In December, the Privy Council Office released a 318-page report on BC-Ottawa relations over a six-month period between January and June 1996. They completely censored seventy of those pages, since their release would be 'injurious' to BC-Ottawa relations. Other pages were partially whited-out. The PCO official who provided the documents to the media said, 'BC and Quebec are the provinces that receive more thought and attention than other provinces, when it comes to looking at how to manage issues and ensure decisions are made thoughtfully and sensitively' (*Halifax Daily News*, 20 December).

Federal election

Federal-provincial relations suffered several blows in 1997 but the real fallout for Chrétien's Liberals was their failure to achieve the expected breakthrough in BC during the country's thirty-fourth general election. Local and national newspapers forecasted great prospects for the party in British Columbia. As UBC political scientist Phil Resnick underscored, '[W]ithout trying to predict the outcome, the Liberals are in a stronger position at this point than they were back in '93' (*CBC-TV*, 20

May). Just as Liberal hopes for political gains in BC would be shattered later in the year amid the APEC scandal, their effort to win federal seats proved 'mediocre' (*Vancouver Sun*, 22 May).

During the campaign, Mr Chrétien visited the province three times, but to no political gain. The Liberals did not win any additional seats as the Reform Party swept the province. The 2 June election outcome resulted in Reform becoming the Official Opposition, with 40 per cent of their seats in BC. The Reform Party's strength in BC was recognized by both the Liberal and Tory Parties during the election campaign. Jean Chrétien accused Reform of using 'hot buttons' and 'code words' to get Western votes while PC leader Jean Charest attacked Preston Manning for his party's BC-only ad, which read 'Leaders of both old-line parties say don't worry about national unity. Distinct society for Quebec is the answer. They think all Canadians are not equal' (*Vancouver Sun*, 8 May).

For her part, NDP leader Alexa McDonough attempted to capitalize on the strong position taken by Premier Clark on the national and international scene. She said his leadership provided an example of why voters should send more NDP members to Ottawa (*Vancouver Sun*, 28 May). When asked if he would be assisting the federal NDP in winning seats in his province, Premier Clark stated, 'My first priority is to the people of BC. I'm the Premier of BC. That comes first above any partisan politics.' These comments were made after Mr Clark signed a job-training agreement with the Liberal government. He did say that he would help in his own constituency (*Vancouver Sun*, 27 April).

Besides their poor showing, the Liberal Party also raised some controversy in the Vancouver-Kingsway riding. Controversy surrounded the appointment of Sophia Leung as the Liberal candidate. The Prime Minister appointed female candidates in several ridings across the country as a signal of the party's commitment to supporting women in politics. Ms Leung was a questionable candidate as some regarded her a 'tad highbrow' for the working-class riding. When a reporter asked her how much it cost to ride the bus, she said she did not know. Her main competitor, Victor Wong, even furnished her with a bus ticket (*Vancouver Sun*, 22 May). In the end, Ms Leung won the safe Liberal seat with 40.6 per cent of the vote.

Following the federal election, the Prime Minister appointed all but two of the BC Liberals to cabinet. David Anderson (Victoria) replaced Fred Mifflin in the fisheries portfolio. Herb Dhaliwal (Vancouver South–Burnaby) was named to revenue in place of Ontarian Jane Stewart. Raymond Chan (Richmond) and Hedy Fry (Vancouver Centre) retained their positions as Secretaries of State for Asia-Pacific and the Status of Women and Multiculturalism, respectively.

TABLE 1
1997 Federal election results – British Columbia

Party	Seats – National (popular vote)	Seats – British Columbia (popular vote)
Liberal	155 (38%)	6 (17.7%)
Reform	61 (19%)	25 (73.5%)
BQ	44 (11%)	0
NDP	20 (11%)	3 (8.8%)
PC	20 (19%)	0
Other	1 (2%)	0
Total	301	34

British Columbians held an election of their own in the provincial riding of Surrey–White Rock. The September by-election was held to replace Liberal MLA Wilf Hurd who resigned to run unsuccessfully in June's federal election. At the time of Mr Hurd's resignation, Liberal leader Gordon Campbell had approached BC's Reform Party president, David Secord, to run as the Liberal candidate. Mr Secord was unwilling to do so and eventually ran under the Reform banner.

The story of the by-election was the comeback of the Liberals and their candidate Gordon Hogg. The former White Rock mayor had left municipal politics in 1993 to run unsuccessfully in the federal election. In 1996, he also failed to be re-elected to his mayoral post. A decision he made as director of Willingdon Youth Detention Centre in 1993 had affected his reputation in the community. Mr Hogg had recommended that an inmate, Danny Perrault, be transferred to an open-custody facility in New Haven. Mr Perrault escaped from the New Haven facility and raped a woman at knifepoint. A public inquiry into the case led to a six-month cut in pay for Mr Hogg and damage to his reputation, which he considered a reason for his loss of the mayoral bid. In the contest for the legislature, however, Mr Hogg was successful, garnering 52 per cent of the vote. His next closest competitor, Reformer David Secord, received half as many votes at 26 per cent. The NDP received only 17 per cent of the vote, and Glen Clark refused to make an election night response to the media (*Vancouver Sun*, 8 and 17 September).

In Gordon Hogg's victory speech, he offered his sentiments about the race: 'The media were right – this was all about leadership.' Mr Hogg's message for Premier Clark was clear, 'You've had it, buddy. You're going down' (*Vancouver Sun*, 17 September). Liberal House Leader Gary Farrell-Collins explained, 'If there was any question about who the free-enterprise alternative was in BC, now we know. It's the BC Liberals, and people who want the NDP out had better get behind us' (*Vancouver Province*, 16 September).

Court challenge and recall

Other election-related news involved the previous year's provincial election outcome. In February, Mr Justice Bryan Williams of British Columbia's Supreme Court ruled that British Columbia voters could sue the New Democrats for allegedly lying to them during the 1996 provincial election. Three voters brought the case as members of HELP BC (Help Us Eliminate Lying Politicians in British Columbia), a group organized by David Stockell to launch the Court challenge under the Election Act (*Financial Post*, March 13; *Calgary Herald*, March 6; *CAR 1996*). If successful, they could force Premier Clark out of office, because, under the BC Election Act, the use of fraud to win votes is illegal and can nullify the outcome (*Financial Post*, 13 March). The outcome of the Court challenge will not be known until 1998.

Another event whose outcome will wait until next year is the recall of two MLAs. In the days leading up to the coming into force of recall legislation, the NDP government continued to tweak it under the direction of Attorney General Ujjal Dosanjh (*Vancouver Sun*, November 14). The recall procedure was endorsed by BC voters in a 1991 referendum; the recall legislation finally took effect on 28 November 1997. Attempts to recall two MLAs began almost immediately. Residents of Prince George North began collecting signatures to unseat Education Minister Paul Ramsey, while residents of Skeena geared up to unseat Helmut Giesbrecht. The recall legislation required 40 per cent of eligible voters to agree to the recall and imposed a deadline of 3 February 1998 for the 1996 general election. For example, the recall group in Prince George North, Active Citizens in BC, had to sign up 8,909 eligible voters by 3 February in order to force a by-election. In response to the recall attempt, supporters of Education Minister Paul Ramsey announced that they would launch a counter-recall campaign against the forces trying to kick Mr Ramsey out of office (*Province*, 4 November and 14 December).

The economy

Much like federal-provincial relations, the BC economy performed poorly in 1997. It grew by a dismal 1 per cent. Statistics Canada reported that the BC economy had lost 9,300 jobs between January and June, although the number of jobs in June was 33,400 higher than the previous year. In June, the unemployment rate was 8.5 per cent. The Bank of Montreal downgraded its forecast for the province, pointing to a 'temporary halt' in job creation due to reductions in the size of public administration and downsizing in the pulp and paper, retail, and financial-services industries. In BC, the Credit Union Central's chief economist said the bank's forecast was 'too optimistic.' The province's tax-supported debt as a share of GDP almost doubled since the beginning of the 1990s, rising to 20.3 per cent in 1996–7 (*Vancouver Sun*, 8 August).

The forestry sector had a particularly difficult year. Price Waterhouse determined that the forest industry suffered a net loss of $132 million in 1997. This was the second consecutive year of losses; the industry suffered losses of $290 million in 1996. Forest industry shipments during 1997 totalled $16.8 billion, unchanged from 1996. This was 49 per cent of the value of all shipments by manufacturing industries in BC. Forest product exports in 1997 totalled $14.8 billion and accounted for 55 per cent of provincial exports. Direct forest employment, according to Statistics Canada, averaged 86,600 hours in 1997, down from 88,100 in 1996. The Price Waterhouse report cited lower commodity prices, lower wood chip prices, a strike involving Fletcher Challenge Canada Limited, and higher costs for logs as factors in the results.

Economists pointed to the downturn in Asian markets as one reason for the decline of BC's economy. Economist Leo De Bever noted, 'BC's a very open economy. It's much more of a trading economy than either Canada or the U.S. as a whole. So it will feel the brunt given that it's most directly exposed to southeast Asia.' Thirty-five per cent of BC exports go to Asia annually. In 1996, lumber shipments to Japan were down precipitating the close of coastal mills and Asian demand for fish was off while the price of coal was under pressure (*CBC-TV*, 18 November).

In November, Finance Minister Andrew Petter reported that BC would end the fiscal year with a $185-million deficit. The drop in forest revenues was offset by higher revenue growth in areas such as retail sales and oil and gas (*Vancouver Sun*, 28 November). Opposition leader Gordon Campbell greeted Mr Petter's projections with scepticism, stating, 'I don't trust Petter's projections and I don't trust his books. We're losing jobs but this is a government that believes in big debt, big taxes and playing games with the books to hide the facts' (*Province*, 28 November).

Dismal economic projections were emphasized as the year closed and the Vancouver Board of Trade released the findings of its member survey. The survey, conducted by Angus Reid and sent to all 2,000 members of the Vancouver Board of Trade, had a response rate of 10.6 per cent. Seventy-five per cent of respondents felt that the province's overall business climate was not supportive of business, while 70 per cent felt that the government's economic policies were preventing their business from prospering. The Board of Trade chair, Bob Fairweather, noted, 'The most telling finding is that 24 per cent of respondents intend moving or relocating some of their BC operations outside the province – mainly into Alberta – in the next two years' (*Province*, 10 December).

Prince Edward Island   PETER E. BUKER

The year 1997 in Prince Edward Island saw a relatively slow-growing economy, a huge celebration associated with the opening of the Confederation Bridge, and legislative sessions that showed that political patronage was the single biggest domestic political problem for the Binns administration. The economy was affected by the ending of construction on the Confederation Bridge and the changes the bridge made in transportation to and from the Island. It was the first year of the Conservative government's mandate and the provincial legislature was fraught with raucous debate.

The economy

Predictions early in the year for PEI's economy were that the province would be an economic 'laggard' as the Confederation Bridge megaproject between PEI and New Brunswick came to an end. Indeed, the Conference Board of Canada predicted in May that PEI would have the lowest economic growth among all Canadian provinces due to the loss of construction jobs and related activity when the building of the bridge was completed. In November, the Conference Board's provincial growth estimate still placed PEI with the worst provincial growth rate in Canada. Still, PEI's GDP at market prices in 1997 was $2,943 million, which was an increase of 1.2 per cent over 1996 in constant dollars.

While the PEI economy was affected by the completion of the 12.9 kilometre bridge, which connected Borden-Carleton, PEI, to Cape Jourimain, New Brunswick, tourism was also given a boost after it was officially opened on 1 June. Not only did the bridge provide better transportation access to PEI, but it became a tourist draw in its own right. The Confederation Bridge was the longest of its kind in the world, and in the winter the longest bridge to cross ice-covered waters. The total cost of construction was $840 million, including $120 million in financing costs. On average, 70 per cent of the construction costs were incurred in PEI.

The population, measured by Statistics Canada, was 137,100 as of 1 July. Employment grew by only 0.7 per cent over the previous year, with a total of 60,500 people employed in 1997. This was the lowest growth rate in the country, and the annual unemployment rate rose to 14.9 per cent from 14.5 per cent in 1996. Payments in Employment Insurance increased after three years of decline. The total benefit payments were $175.2 million, which was an increase of 4.8 per cent compared with a national decrease of 8.2 per cent. The average number of beneficiaries fell slightly to 11,806, compared with 11,993 in 1996.

In agriculture, total farm cash receipts were $270.4 million. Of these, cash receipts for potatoes, which were PEI's largest single agricultural product representing 46.3 per cent of total farm receipts, were $125 million. This was down from $138 million in 1996, although the total volume of potato production was 1.35 million imperial tons, an increase from 1.29 million tons the previous year. There were potential problems due to a wet spring, but a warm, dry autumn in the end gave top yields with a late harvest. The decline in cash receipts and rise in production reflected the structural change in the potato industry as growers increased production to supply french-fry processing plants, which had expanded throughout the previous years. PEI's 1997 potato production was one-third of the total Canadian volume of 4.1 million tons.

In other agriculture, crops as a group had decreased receipts of $146.5 million, compared with $162.3 in 1996. The only crops that had increased in receipts were wheat (excluding durum), which increased by 5.8 per cent, and soybeans, which increased by 23 per cent. Livestock receipts were $116.4 million, with dairy products contributing $47.1 million, hogs $29.4 million, and cattle also $29.4 million. Receipts from livestock sales were up by 1.1 per cent compared with 1996. Dairy, cattle, and poultry all increased, while all other livestock receipts decreased.

In 1997 the fishing industry had its highest volume of landings since 1991, at 125.1 million pounds, an increase of almost 10 per cent over 1996. The value of the catch was $113.7 million, which was an increase of 15 per cent. The volume of lobsters increased by about 2 per cent, but the value increased by almost 11 per cent. Lobster value accounted for 64 per cent of the total value of the PEI fisheries. The value of the snow-crab fishery was up by 4.4 per cent. Cod sales and volumes rose by 150 per cent. Mackerel sales rose by 74 per cent, and rock-crab values rose over 110 per cent to $1.6 million. Aquaculture continued to grow for the seventh consecutive year in both volume and value. Annual sales were up 11.4 per cent to $16.1 million, and annual volumes increased by 8.9 per cent to 25.4 million pounds. Cultured mussels represent 75.2 per cent of total aquaculture values, while cultured oyster production decreased by 15 per cent, and finfish remained unchanged.

Total annual forestry production decreased slightly due to reduced production of fuel wood and wood chips, while industrial wood production increased by 9 per cent. Total production was 601,000 cubic metres with a total value of $25.1 million.

Manufacturing increased by 17 per cent to $877 million, which was mostly due to increased french-fry output at Cavendish Farms. About 71 per cent of PEI's manufacturing is related to food and fish products industries. Of the total food industries, fish products accounted for 26 per cent. In July, Canadian/Dutch AgraWest Investments announced they would build a $30-million state-of-the-art potato dehydration plant in the Souris Food Park. In the fall, there was a $3.5-million expansion to Irving-owned East Isle Shipyard in Georgetown, which created the most modern shipyard for small and mid-sized vessels on the Atlantic coast, with a modular shop that employed over 100 Islanders.

The value of international exports grew by about 24 per cent; PEI exported $424 million worth of goods, over two and half times the 1990 level. In 1990, primary resource exports accounted for 92 per cent of exports, while in 1997 they were three-quarters of exports. The United States was the destination for 80 per cent of exports in 1997, compared with 77 per cent in 1996, and 63 per cent in 1995.

Because of the completion of the Confederation Bridge, total capital expenditure on new construction decreased by 6.2 per cent to $345.7 million, compared with 1996. The number of housing starts fell by 15 per cent to 470 units, compared with a boom year in 1996. Of housing types, semi-detached houses and duplexes experienced a slight increase.

The value of PEI's retail trade rose 7.5 per cent to $996.2 million, which was the highest growth since 1988. This reflected a country-wide trend of strong retail growth. Interestingly, retail growth surpassed employment growth and personal disposable income in the province, especially in the summer season, making it likely that retail growth was partly due to tourist spending. The number of new motor vehicles sold increased by 14 per cent to 4,717, and the value increased by 20.7 per cent, compared with 1996.

The economy of PEI was predicted to change somewhat given that the ferry service between Borden-Carleton and Cape Tormentine, New Brunswick, ended 31 May. Up to that time, Marine Atlantic Services had 561,834 passengers and 82,000 commercial vehicle crossings, an increase of 4 per cent for passengers and a decrease of 7 per cent commercial vehicle crossings compared with the same five months in 1996. Of note, in 1997 the number of passengers using the ferry service between Wood Islands, PEI, and Caribou, Nova Scotia, which serves a different part of the Island and goes to a different destination, decreased by 19.3 per cent compared with 1996. On 26 February it was announced that there would be a $3-million expansion project to upgrade the loading ramps at both Wood Islands and Caribou. The expansion would convert the docking to accommodate a used double-decker ferry from the Marine Atlantic service. There was poor information about the true effects of the Confederation Bridge, as Strait Crossing International, the company that operates the bridge, did not release information regarding the traffic crossings. That being said, Enterprise PEI estimated that the number of tourist parties visiting by automobile rose by 34 per cent, mostly due to the opening of the Confederation Bridge. Visitor expenditures were estimated to be $245.9 million, an increase of 63 per cent or almost $100 million compared with 1996. However, an accommodations survey showed that while more tourists came to PEI because of the Confederation Bridge, they did not stay on the Island as long.

In the public sector, as the year's average, 5,700 people were employed in all levels of government administration, which was a decrease of about 3 per cent. Another 5,700 worked in the health and social-service sectors, an increase of 9 per cent over 1996, and 4,500 worked in education and related services, a decrease of about 2 per cent. Federal employment increased in 1997 but did not reach its peak level of 1994; there was an annual average of 3,141 federal government employees, an increase of 1.8 per cent from 1996.

Fiscal events

In the fiscal year ending 31 March 1997, the Province of PEI received a total revenue of $800.1 million, up 1.4 per cent compared with the previous fiscal year. Total provincial government expenditures increased 2.4 per cent in the fiscal year ending in 1997, reaching $811.9 million.

The deficit for the 1996–7 fiscal year was $3.6 million after pension adjustment, compared with a surplus of 4.1 million in the 1995–6 fiscal year. As of March 1997, the net provincial debt was $990 million, up 0.4 per cent from the previous year.

On 8 April, provincial treasurer Pat Mella delivered her first budget. Ms Mella maintained that the $776.9 million budget reduced both the cost and size of government. Her Conservative government said the province would run a $17.1-million deficit in 1997–8 fiscal year, considerably less than the $55 million she predicted after her Conservative government was elected in the fall of 1996. The budget was delivered after a build-up of public hearings threatening huge cuts in government spending, and so was a 'good news' budget following government efforts to create expectations for the worst. The budget raised the gas and diesel tax by one cent a litre, increased vehicle license and registration fees, and expanded the personal-income-tax base. High-income earners and big business were taxed more, while people on social assistance got a break through reinstatement of GST rebates. The threshold for the high-income surtax was reduced to $60,000 a year, so that about 3,700 Islanders would pay the surtax. The corporate-income-tax rate rose to 16 per cent from 15, while operating expenditures dropped by $21 million, mostly through measures already planned or instituted. The provincial tax credit for investors in labour-sponsored venture capital funds was removed. Spending on education, health, and social services was reduced by a combined 0.3 per cent, which was far less than many Islanders feared. Spending in other areas dropped 8.4 per cent, without resorting to a civil-service wage-freeze.

On the social front, an 8 September Statistics Canada report was released using data from the 1994 International Adult Literacy Survey, which showed that the literacy of PEI youth aged 16–25 was about one-year of schooling below the national average, along with Ontario, New Brunswick, and Newfoundland. Information from the survey associated poor literacy with higher rates of unemployment, more dependence on social assistance, and poorer long-term health. On 25 February, Statistics Canada reported that Newfoundland and PEI had the fewest number of police officers per capita; and on 27 November, Statistics Canada reported that Manitoba and PEI had the highest proportion of people who claimed the donations they made to charities.

The legislature and politics

In the federal election of 2 June, all four seats in PEI went to the Liberals. The four members were George Proud in the Hillsborough riding;

Wayne Easter in the Malpeque riding; Joe McGuire in the Egmont riding; and Lawrence MacAulay who won by a very slim margin (97 votes) in the Cardigan riding. A provincial by-election for the provincial district of Charlottetown–Kings Square was held 17 November; the seat became vacant when Liberal Wayne Cheverie stepped down to take an appointment with the Island Regulatory and Appeals Commission (IRAC), and was won by Liberal Richard Brown, a veteran Charlottetown councillor. Mr Brown took almost 43 per cent of the votes cast compared with his opponents, second place Conservative Brian McKenna and New Democrat Leo Broderick who ran third.

In the provincial Throne Speech of 6 March, read by Lieutenant-Governor Gilbert Clements, the government promised to shore up health care, provide longer-term funding for education, put television cameras in the Legislature, and put the audio portion of the proceedings on the Internet. It also warned of tough times because of cuts in federal government spending and programs, although Premier Pat Binns vowed he would not close Island hospitals because of their contribution to community identity and development. Mr Binns also promised to provide multi-year funding to post-secondary schools to help them with longer-term plans and boasted that his government's decision not to blend its retail sales tax with the federal goods and services tax gave PEI a business edge when combined with the opening of the bridge to the mainland. On 19 November, the PEI government gave a tax break to some retailers by eliminating the provincial sales tax on clothing and footwear.

The spring legislative session ended 29 May, after a boisterous two months of debate spurred on by opposition MLAs who occupied one-third of the Island's twenty-seven seats. There were fifty-four bills passed in that session, and there was an autumn sitting for the first time ever. Among the legislation passed were Medical Act amendments that toughened sanctions against doctors who sexually abuse their patients and changes to the Health and Community Services Act that would place most of the authority over the health system in the minister's office.

In April's provincial budget, it was projected that the government's share of profits for video lottery terminals (VLTs) would increase from 50 per cent to 55 per cent, increasing revenue by $900,000. However, in the Charlottetown municipal election of 4 November, in a question included on the ballot asking if the government should shut down PEI's $9-million video gambling industry, Charlottetown voters overwhelmingly said 'yes' – 10,921 voted to ban video lottery terminals, while 2,991 voted against the ban. In response, the Binn government announced that VLTs would be banned from all non-licensed establishments on PEI.

The issue of patronage was prominent in the fall session. On 25 November, PEI's Conservative government agreed to pay $750,000 to 314 seasonal workers who claimed they were fired because of their Liberal Party affiliations after the 1996 provincial election. This settlement was made by the government ostensibly to avoid time-consuming and costly human-rights actions. Premier Binns stated that these Islanders were paid for the 'hurt and humiliation' of losing their jobs, rather than for lost wages. The government had rejected about 140 other complainants for not having a case. Critics said that the successful claimants were pressured to accept the settlement of $2,000 a person under the threat of legislation that would destroy their legal claim. The patronage issue was not new. The government also agreed to a settlement in March 1997 of an eleven-year political discrimination battle between the former Liberal government and St Peter's resident Mickey Burge. Mr Burge was paid $197,588 in compensation after losing his government trucking contract with the Liquor Control Commission when the Liberals took power in 1986. The government did table new human-rights legislation on 26 November that would, among other things, give the cabinet power to limit or prohibit payments of settlements in political discrimination cases.

This led to a two-week deadlock in the Legislature as the opposition Liberals and the one NDP member sought changes to the human-rights legislation; in the end, Attorney General Mitch Murphy amended the bill to eliminate cabinet control of discrimination settlements and incorporated a formula for determining those settlements in law. Members of the Legislative Assembly sat for a few minutes Christmas Eve to pass the bill amending the Human Rights Act by making changes that would remove cabinet from the process of putting human-rights claims to public inquiry. Also on 26 November, Premier Pat Binns announced that the government had asked the provincial Staffing and Classification Board to review seasonal hiring practices in light of the Island's strong tradition of handing out government jobs according to political affiliation. At the time, this was seen as a shift in Island political culture away from government patronage.

In another ongoing issue, on 18 September, the Supreme Court of Canada ruled in a 6–1 decision that provincial governments have the right to reduce or freeze judges' salaries if they set up impartial tribunals to oversee judges' salaries. This was because of an appeal of legislation in PEI, Manitoba, and Alberta; PEI had previously cut judges salaries by 7.5 per cent under the Callbeck government. The Court issued a stern warning to judges and their associations to cease engaging in any form of salary negotiations with government officials, saying 'the expectations of give and take and of threat and counterthreat are fundamentally at odds with judicial independence.'*

Controversy also plagued the government over a proposed eighteen-hole extension to the government-owned golf course at Brudenell by a development consortium, Golf PEI Inc., which consisted of prominent Tories. In 1996, while in opposition, the Conservative government was against government-funded golf courses; in 1997, they maintained that golf-course development was important to the Island's economic development and an appropriate project for government subsidies. The extension required that the government agree to transfer hundreds of acres of prime Crown real estate next to the Brudenell course to the development group, free of charge. The land at Brudenell was given to the province in perpetual trust by the late Robert L. Cotton in 1961. In the end, the Binns government approved that 450 acres be given to the corporation.

In significant legal decisions, Chief Provincial Judge Ralph Thompson reduced the sentences given to impaired drivers from the benchmark of three days to a new one-day standard sentence for first-time offenders, reflecting the trend of fewer incidents of drinking and driving on PEI. There were 550 impaired driving convictions in 1997, compared with 1,700 recorded several years earlier. PEI led Canada by sending 74 per cent of impaired drivers to jail, compared with 16 per cent in most other Canadian jurisdictions studied. PEI also imposed the highest fines for impaired driving.

Two new judges were appointed to provincial courts, Linda Katherine Webber, a Charlottetown lawyer and the former chair of IRAC, was appointed to sit on the trial division of the provincial Supreme Court replacing the late Joe Ghiz. John Douglas, another Charlottetown lawyer, was appointed as judge of the provincial court. On 24 September, Prime Minister Jean Chrétien appointed former PEI premier Catherine Callbeck to the Senate.

Other events

The Confederation Bridge linking PEI and New Brunswick was opened with events and ceremonies at the end of May. The bridge was

---

Canadian News Facts (MPL Communications Inc., 1997), 5559.

touted as representing 'the cooperative spirit of Confederation' by Premier Pat Binns. The Calgary-based consortium Strait Crossing Development Incorporated (SCDI) began construction of the two-lane bridge in 1993. It financed, designed, and built the bridge and took over operations upon completion. The federal government undertook a thirty-five-year deal of buying the bridge at the rate of $42 million a year. The bridge replaced the ferry service over the Northumberland Strait and decreased travelling time by over 30 minutes; it also featured state-of-the art video surveillance, emergency call boxes, a weather monitoring station, changeable message signs at each end, and an automatic debit-card system to pay the toll. The tolls were set at $35 per car after much controversy. SCDI wanted to charge more than the federal government allowed in order to cover alleged cost overruns of over $200 million.

The biggest event on PEI in 1997, and perhaps of the decade, was Bridgefest, the festival surrounding the official opening of the Confederation Bridge. The event attracted huge media attention, with more than 600 media accreditations given status at the event. Bridgefest began 29 May with the unveiling of a monument dedicated to the more than 6,000 women and men who had some part in building the bridge. The monument was made of clay bricks that were inscribed with the names of those workers who built the bridge, and a plaque was unveiled that honoured the three men who died during the bridge's construction. Close to 2,500 runners from all over North America ran and jogged across the bridge starting at 8 a.m. on 30 May; by noon that same day the line-up to participate in the bridge-walk was stretched back 20 kilometres from the festival gates. The bridge opened to traffic 31 May, and more than 20,000 vehicles crossed in the first four days. In the first two days, many cars drove across the bridge and returned immediately. On 31 May, there was a gala concert attended by 3,000 people, and a concert the night before attracted 11,000 people.

A two-hour ceremony was broadcast live on national television on 31 May at the official opening. Over 150,000 people took part in the Bridgefest activities, and the bridge was featured on a new PEI vehicle licence plate. Traffic was lined up for 10 kilometres down the Trans-Canada Highway on 1 June, the day after the bridge opened to traffic. That same weekend people said goodbye to the ferry service; the *Abegweit* was the last vessel to dock at Borden-Carleton just after the bridge opened to traffic at 5 p.m. on 31 May, and made a sunset sail on 1 June. SCDI held a two-day auction of 3,200 pieces of equipment used in the construction, bringing in $6 million.

In the fall, problems developed due to high winds and the bridge closed on several occasions to all but passenger cars. High-sided vehicles were deemed unsafe to cross, which spurred a debate over a proposal to allow them to cross single-file while the bridge was closed to other traffic. Overall, traffic to the Island was estimated to be up 30 per cent from 1996, and the bridge became both a tourist draw and a normal part of life for Islanders.

On 23 May, a fire badly damaged the interior of Green Gables, the house made famous by Lucy Maude Montgomery's 1908 classic *Anne of Green Gables*. Green Gables is a Parks Canada site and one of PEI's most notable landmarks and most lucrative draw for tourism. Each tourist season, approximately $600,000 is brought in through tour fees and concession sales. In the summer of 1996, 741,000 tourists visited PEI, with one-third of those visiting Green Gables. Because the opening of the Confederation Bridge was expected to bring in record numbers of visitors to Green Gables, Parks Canada rushed to reopen the site for Canada Day, 1 July. The cause of the fire was undetermined. Another tourist site got a rather unique addition. In September, the town of O'Leary unveiled a statue of a potato that was 63 metres tall and 31 metres wide. The $7,500 potato was put in front of the Prince Edward Island Potato Museum.

Another high-profile news item was the sentencing of Roger Charles Bell, a former chemistry teacher. Mr Bell was sentenced on 30 June in Charlottetown to ten years in jail after he pleaded guilty to four counts of planting an explosive device. Mr Bell had planted pipe bombs that went off in three places: at the PEI Supreme Court in 1988, in a garbage can at a Halifax park in 1994, and at the PEI Legislature in 1995. A bomb he set at a Charlottetown propane station in 1996 was found and detonated by police. Mr Bell's notoriety was partly created by his letters that claimed his work was by a group called Loki 7. In his letters he criticized police, politicians, and the courts, and he called provincial judges 'political hacks who sit in judgment of their betters.' Mr Bell's actual motives for the bombings remained a mystery.

In an act of protest, on 12 August, 500 people blocked a government crane from tearing down Basin Head's famous bridge. The Department of Fisheries and Oceans and the East Kings Development Corporation in charge of the operation called off the crane later in the day because of the protest. In sports, Dave MacEachern of Charlottetown and Pierre Lueders of Edmonton won the two-man Corel Cup bobsledding title on 22 February in Nagano, Japan. Islander LGPA Golfer Lorie Kane was named Canadian Press Athlete of the year in 1997.

Saskatchewan

JOSEPH GARCEA

In Saskatchewan, 1997 was an eventful year in politics and public affairs. There were major developments on the political front at the local, provincial, and federal levels. The provincial government continued to govern in ways that made it an interesting case study in progressive neo-conservatism as it tried to balance its socialist roots with the conservative demands of current political winds. Its ability to do so was facilitated by gods who continued to smile on the province by providing it with the fundamentals for an expanding economy. An indication of this was that the economy could still sustain the 'Pride of Saskatchewan,' the Roughriders football club, which managed to stave off a financial crisis when the public responded quite well to a fundraising drive that included what must surely be a Canadian first, a ticket-selling telethon by a sports club (*StarPhoenix*, 17 March).

The legislature and government

The theme of the Throne Speech – investing in people – foreshadowed the thrust of the provincial government's budget and major policy initiatives for the session. In Saskatchewan, as in Alberta, a special effort was being made to create the impression that the sacrifices of previous years had paid dividends which would now be distributed to deal with various program needs as well as the ongoing fight to reduce the debt. Thus, the Speech marked a reorientation in this session from one of fiscal rationality and downsizing to one of building for and investing in the future. In keeping with that reorientation, the Speech promised policy and funding changes in the fields of health care, education, transportation, and welfare.

In the welfare field it promised that while waiting for the implementation of the National Child Benefit Program, the government would strengthen its Action Plan for Children by introducing amendments to the Saskatchewan Assistance Act to accommodate a Saskatchewan Employment Supplement designed to provide an incentive to parents to increase their earnings and pursue child maintenance; introduce a Youth Futures program to help young people complete their education and make the transition into the workforce; and provide a Provincial Training Allowance to help low-income individuals enrolled in adult education programs. The government also promised to introduce a statute to strengthen provisions to collect child support from parents defaulting on their payments.

Although the bulk of the Speech was designed to send a message that the government would be adopting a more progressive agenda than in past sessions, it also contained the promise that the government's fiscal restraint program would not be abandoned completely because 'responsible public finance and the orderly reduction of the debt' was important for good governance and democracy.

The second session of the Twenty-third Legislature was an eventful one. The Progressive Conservative Party, despite the fact that it only had four members in the Legislature and was not the Official Opposition, managed to make this a very uncomfortable session for the government. In the words of one columnist, largely due to the efforts of its leaders, analysts could well look back on this session and say: 'That's when the chinks in the NDP armour started to appear' (*StarPhoenix*, 22 May). What may have saved the government from greater discomfort during this session was the lacklustre performance of the Liberal Official Opposition, which still found itself without a leader at the opening of the session.

There were several controversial issues related to the Crown sector, ranging from accounting practices to losses on some major investments, to secrecy surrounding various ventures, including SaskPower's bid to purchase the Guyana Power Corporation. As well, several sensitive issues emerged in the field in which the government continued to be vulnerable − health care. Opposition parties and health activists forced the government to defend itself on a number of issues: decisions made by some health districts related to the closure of hospitals and beds (*StarPhoenix*, 19 June); the level of pay for doctors and its effect on attracting and retaining doctors in rural areas (*StarPhoenix*, 20 August); the delays in decisions to approve certain drugs under the provincial drug plan for people suffering from MS (*StarPhoenix*, 6 December); and the restructuring of the health-sector unions as recommended by the Health Labour Relations Reorganization Commission (the Dorsey Commission) to reduce the number of bargaining units from 538 to 45, an issue which resulted in both a legal challenge on whether the Commission had overstepped its mandate and a threat of a wild-cat strike (*StarPhoenix*, 16 January and 20 February). Even the decision to legalize midwifery met with some political sensitivity for the provincial government (*StarPhoenix*, 22 March).

Other controversies faced by the provincial government included the salaries for in-house babysitters. After a protracted controversy, the provincial government repealed a law that required parents to pay in-house babysitters minimum wage, overtime, and employment benefits, and eventually also reimbursed those who had paid such costs while the law was in force (*StarPhoenix*, 29 January and 22 October).

The most significant development in the legislature was when the newly created Saskatchewan Party supplanted the Liberal Party as Official Opposition. This happened in August, when the Conservative caucus and four members of the Liberal caucus joined forces under the banner of the Saskatchewan Party. At the same time, the decision of Liberal MLA Arlene Jule to join former Liberal leader Lynda Haverstock as an independent member gave the Saskatchewan Party a two-seat advantage over the Liberals. After reviewing the submissions of the various parties, and some precedents in Manitoba and Alberta when changes in status of Official Opposition were considered between elections, the Speaker decided to recognize the Saskatchewan Party as the Official Opposition (*StarPhoenix*, 22 August).

When the legislative session ended, Premier Romanow made a significant cabinet shuffle. Notable changes included the transfer of Minister of Finance Janice MacKinnon, who had charted the relatively successful course on deficit and debt reduction, to Economic Development replacing Dwain Lingenfelter, who was given responsibility as the sole minister responsible for the Crown corporation sector. Eric Cline was promoted from Minister of Health to Minister of Finance; Bernie Wiens was appointed minister responsible for the new Intergovernmental and Aboriginal Affairs Secretariat, and Social Services Minister Lorne Calvert was given the additional responsibility of the newly created Disabilities Directorate (*StarPhoenix*, 28 June). The cabinet shuffle was accompanied by the shuffling of some prominent deputy ministers, the most notable of which was Duane Adams, who was moved out of his position as deputy minister of health after implementing the controversial restructuring of the health-care system, which entailed the creation of thirty-two health districts (*StarPhoenix*, 25 June).

Parties and elections

It was a historic year in the evolution of Saskatchewan's party system, as each of the existing provincial parties faced major challenges both from within and without. This was the year of the rise and demise of parties.

Although the New Democratic Party continued to benefit politically from the scandals surrounding the dying Conservative Party and the internal dissension that continued to plague the Liberals, it was not entirely free of its own internal dissension. The leftists in the party continued to express their displeasure with what they perceived as the right-wing drift of the Romanow government. Some disenchanted members, including former MLAs, formed 'The New Left,' which held at least one formal meeting in Saskatoon in February to establish a new party (*StarPhoenix*, 10 February). The Romanow government faced a scandal of its own when its former clerk of the executive council was charged, but ultimately not convicted, of committing indecent assault (25 February). In the spring, a cabinet minister was forced to resign for allegedly making inappropriate remarks to a female patron in a Regina restaurant (3 May).

For the Progressive Conservative Party, 1997 began much the same way as 1996; some former MLAs were sentenced and charges were laid against others for their part in the alleged diversion of caucus funds either for party or personal use. The party faced what seemed interminable political scandal and another charge was laid against a caucus member for buying sex from a minor (*StarPhoenix*, 6 May), all of which made more headlines than anything else that the Progressive Conservative Party did. By June, the decision was made to transform the party into a new entity, which, as discussed below, produced the Saskatchewan Party. After the four caucus members defected to form the new party, the major issue facing the Conservative Party was whether it would be dissolved. Ultimately, despite efforts by the outgoing caucus members to dissolve it, a convention of party members decided to 'mothball' it by 'rendering it inactive' for at least two elections and leaving the management of its financial resources to a board of trustees (*StarPhoenix*, 10 November).

For the Liberal Party, 1997 began as a year of rebuilding after the debacle in which its former leader, Lynda Haverstock, felt compelled to resign. Her successor, James Melenchuk, who did not have a seat in the Legislature, appointed Ken Krawetz as leader of Her Majesty's Official Opposition. By the middle of the year, the Liberal Party was faced with the most daunting challenge since it lost power in 1971. The problems stemming from the internecine battles that persisted after Ms Haverstock resigned were compounded by disenchantment among some caucus members with the management style of their new leader. The ensuing struggles resulted in the loss of five members, four of whom joined members of the Conservative caucus to form the Saskatchewan Party and one who decided to sit as an independent. Furthermore, the loss of these caucus members and the formation of the new party meant that the Liberals lost Official Opposition status. The only positive aspects of the loss of these members were that factionalism was reduced, though not eliminated, and the party escaped collapse. In an obvious move to avoid further factionalism and turmoil, within a week of the defection by five of his caucus members the Liberal leader was given a vote of confidence both by the party executive and the Saskatchewan Liberal council (*StarPhoenix*, 18 August). Later in the year, in an effort to position themselves more liberal and compassionate than the Saskatchewan Party, the Liberal Party engaged in developing what it characterized as a left-leaning policy agenda (18 August and 24 November).

The creation of the Saskatchewan Party was the most surprising development to the party system in 1997. It was the product of a 'unite-the-right' initiative by members of the Conservative and Liberal caucuses designed to increase the prospects of defeating the NDP government. It is unclear who made the first overture. In the early days it was denied that negotiations were taking place either for a merger or at least a strategic electoral alliance, the object of which was for one of the two parties not to contest constituencies because doing so could have a negative effect on the other's prospect of winning. Nonetheless, in July the process that ultimately led to the creation of the party had commenced, and within a month the Saskatchewan Party was formed. In the interim, the Progressive Conservative Party caucus, desperate to save itself from a very bleak future in the face of a mounting grass-roots initiative by Reform Party supporters to create a provincial party, began making overtures for a PC-Reform alliance or merger. On 8 August, the Saskatchewan Party emerged consisting of the four members of the Conservative caucus and four defectors from the Liberal Party (Bob Bjornerud, Rod Gantefoer, Ken Krawetz, and June Draude) (*StarPhoenix*, 6 and 9 August). The decision of another Liberal MLA to join former Liberal leader to sit as an independent shifted the balance of power on the Opposition benches, and the newly formed Saskatchewan Party displaced the Liberals as official Opposition. Media reports indicate that the Liberal caucus members who defected decided to do so after a closed-door meeting in which they were disenchanted by the continuance of interpersonal conflicts (9 August).

Within three days of its creation, the Saskatchewan Party caucus chose Ken Krawetz as its interim leader (*StarPhoenix*, 12 August). While caucus members were busy convincing the Speaker to recognize them as the Official Opposition, members of the other parties were calling on them to resign their seats and face the electorate in by-elections to see if they had the voters' confidence (14 August). Although the Saskatchewan Party's drive to produce sufficient membership to gain party status did not progress very quickly and its public meetings were not as well attended as organizers had hoped, a poll indicated that its level of support was approximately the same as the Liberals, but nearly 20 per cent behind the NDP (28 August, 4 and 12 September).

At its founding convention in November, the Saskatchewan Party adopted a constitution that, like the Reform Party's, rendered the general assembly as the supreme governing body whose decisions would be binding on the leader and caucus members. It also adopted a policy platform that echoed Reform in the areas of fiscal, social, and justice policy, and called for changes to the electoral system that would reform the recall of MLAs. In keeping with the spirit of the policy position, all eight caucus members indicated that they were willing to see a by-election held in their constituency if 51 per cent of all eligible voters indicated that they favoured holding one either to endorse or oppose them. The new party did not enjoy much of a honeymoon period with either the Liberals or New Democrats who accused them of being opportunistic turncoats intent on polarizing the electorate and the public on key issues of public policy where there was a need to build understanding and even consensus (*StarPhoenix*, 17 and 24 November). The thrust of their critique was most cogently captured by former Liberal leader Ralph Goodale, who spoke of the 'self-righteous rightwingdness of the Saskatchewan Party' (14 November).

In 1997 the Saskatchewan-based Reform Party members considered the creation of a provincial wing. Initially, there was strong grass-roots support for such an initiative; however, interest in that option waned after the Saskatchewan Party was formed. A mail-in ballot, returned by approximately 20 per cent of Reform Party members in the province, indicated that 53 per cent were in favour of the option, with 34 per cent indicating that party members should support the fledgling Saskatchewan Party (*StarPhoenix*, 4 September). The extent to which those who called for and supported the creation of a provincial Reform Party were genuinely interested in such a development or were merely posturing to create a stronger impetus for the merger of the Conservative and Liberal Parties is moot. In the fall of 1997, three dozen Reform Party members established what they termed 'a provisional Reform Party' and hoped to raise the issue of establishing the Party on a permanent basis at a regional party conference before submitting it for final approval at the 1998 national Reform Assembly (19 September). Although those Reform Party members were not successful in their bid to create a provincial wing, some of the federal Reform MPs were quite actively involved in the formation of the Saskatchewan Party. Their participation made the Saskatchewan Party a coalition of Conservative, Liberal, and Reform Party members.

All provincial parties found themselves under scrutiny regarding the way they dealt with donations when the chief electoral officer launched an investigation into the fundraising practices of the provincial parties. In his nine-page report, he concluded that there had not been full compliance with the statutory provisions on, among other things, the full disclosure of money that the parties received from anonymous contributors (such as their constituency associations and the federal wings of their parties). He concurred with the Department of Justice prosecutors not to lay charges against the official agents of the parties because ambiguity in the rules meant there was no reasonable probability of obtaining a conviction. The process, therefore, would not be in the public interest either in terms of the expenditure of resources or the effect it would have on the diminishing trust and confidence in political institutions (*StarPhoenix*, 4 June). The provincial auditor argued in his fall report that all parties should at least be required to turn over anonymous donations to the provincial treasury (2 December).

In 1997, Saskatchewan voters were given the opportunity to participate in federal and local elections. The federal election engendered considerable controversy in strongly contested races, but this did not translate into high voter turnout on election day. The average voter turnout in Saskatchewan was 66 per cent (ranging from 59 per cent to 73 per cent in various ridings), down from 73 per cent in the 1993 election and the 76 per cent average for elections in recent decades (*StarPhoenix*, 4 June). The federal election produced some interesting results in Saskatchewan. The New Democratic Party had hoped that it could win ten of the fourteen seats as it had done in 1988, and the Liberals hoped that they could hold on to all four of their seats. Both their hopes were dashed, however, when voters took a right-wing turn and supported the Reform Party to a much greater extent than had been predicted.

Although the NDP did not win as many seats as it had hoped in the federal election, there was cause for some satisfaction and optimism as all of its candidates except two finished either in first or second place in their contests. The Reform Party took seats away from both the NDP and Liberal Parties. The final count was Reform 8, NDP 5, and Liberal 1. All candidates for these parties, including those who lost, managed to garner more than 15 per cent of the vote qualifying them for a return of their deposit and reimbursement of 50 per cent of their campaign expenditures. The Progressive Conservative Party failed to capture one seat. In all fourteen constituencies, the level of support for the Conservatives was less than 15 per cent. The level of support for the major parties was approximately PC 8 per cent; Liberal 25 per cent; NDP 31 per cent; and Reform 36 per cent. The Canadian Action Party and Natural Law Party received approximately 1 per cent of the vote in the constituencies in which they fielded candidates. All five Canadian Action Party candidates and all three Natural Law Party candidates lost their deposit, as did the lone independent candidate who ran in the Saskatoon-area constituency of Wanuskewin. The election produced some very close contests, none more so than in the Saskatoon-Humboldt constituency in which the Reform candidate beat the NDP candidate by 221 votes (*StarPhoenix*, 4 June). The NDP lost the seat that had been held by Simon deJong, who decided not to run after a long career that included his interesting but unsuccessful bid for the party's leadership. Although it lost DeJong, the NDP regained Lorne Nystrom who, after a short stint outside Parliament, ran in the election and won his seat.

The key financial issues in the election were the federal government's fiscal management strategies that impinged on the level of taxation, the level of federal transfers to the provinces for various social programs, and the level of unemployment. In addition to these issues, the most pronounced issue in the election was the federal government's gun control legislation, which had been a controversial issue in the province for some time. Indeed, this issue cost the Liberal Party dearly in the election as it lost three of the four seats that it had won in 1993. Two of the seats lost were in the Saskatoon area and one was in the Prince Albert area. Ralph Goodale retained his seat in the Regina area; he was later appointed minister responsible for natural resources with the additional responsibility for the Canadian Wheat Board.

In 1997, elections were held for urban municipalities and school boards as well as for rural municipal wards and health-district wards. One common element in all of these elections was the low level of candidacy and the low level of voter turnout. Many positions on municipal, school board, and health-district governing bodies were filled by acclamation, and the level of voter turnout was generally in the 20–40 per cent range. The low level of participation in the local elections raised questions among various participants and observers about what this meant for the efficacy of democracy in local governance. A survey of local government elections revealed that 46 per cent of the 365 municipalities that responded had acclaimed both the mayor and the council. Even more astounding was that seven of the twenty-nine health districts filled all of their seats by acclamation; overall 61 per cent of health-district wards were filled by acclamation (*StarPhoenix*,

24 October). Thus another major common element in these elections was the traditionally high rate of success for incumbents.

One of the most surprising aspects of the local elections was that the implementation and imposition of the new property assessment system for the province was not more of an issue. Part of the reason for this was that major decisions regarding the general nature of the system were made long before the elections and those who were displeased with the effect that the new system would have on their assessment were told that the Saskatchewan Assessment Management Agency was to blame and not the municipal councils. In a plebiscite that attested to the strong preference for the ward system for all types of local elections, the Saskatoon Public School Division supporters voted in favour of such a system for electing their trustees in the future.

The budget and economy

The Budget Speech of 20 March reflected continued confidence on the part of the government to meet its fiscal targets in terms of a balanced budget, the chipping away at the debt, tax reductions on the revenue side of the ledger, and increased resources for various programs on the expenditure side of the ledger.

The major budget highlights were as follows. First, in the case of the balance sheet, there was to be a $369 million surplus for 1996–7, and a projected $24 million surplus for 1997–8; and the debt would be reduced from $14.1 billion in 1996–7 to $12.8 billion for 1997–8, to $12.6 billion for 1998–9, and to $10.9 billion by the first year of the new millennium. Second, there was to be a 2 per cent cut in sales tax and an increase in taxes on cigarettes to offset the sales-tax cut. Third, there was to be an additional $18-million spent in the health-care sector and the purchase of an MRI machine for Regina; a $10-million expenditure in welfare to increase the wages for child-care workers for the next three years; and more than $40 million in operating and capital funds in the primary and secondary educational sector over two years. In the post-secondary education sector, the budget included an additional $3 million to improve resource sharing between the universities; a doubling of capital grants to $14 million; a guarantee that global operating funding for universities would be $163 million both for 1997–8 and 1998–9; and a guarantee to SIAST and Regional Colleges that any shortfall resulting from a reduction in federal transfers would be covered. In the transportation sector, an additional $26 million was granted for highway improvements as well as a commitment for a

$2.5-billion expenditure over the next ten years, starting with a $200 million expenditure in 1997–8. Finally, the budget included the 25 per cent cut in municipal revenue sharing as had been foreshadowed in the previous year's budget (*StarPhoenix*, 21 March).

The Minister of Finance pointed out that, since 1993, the government had made some progress on improving the debt to GDP ratio from 70 per cent to 49 per cent with a target figure of 36 per cent for 2001, and that if it continued to meet that target it would reduce its debt servicing by $200 million from the 1995 levels. The government's ability to meet its fiscal targets for 1996–7, including the reduction of the debt from $14 billion, was substantially aided by its $365-million dividend from its Crown Investment Corporation, the holding company for its Crown corporations; the $515-million return from the sale of Cameco shares during the 1996–7 fiscal year; as well as a $400-million withdrawal from its Fiscal Stabilization Fund, consisting of revenues from gambling and liquor revenues (*Globe and Mail*, 21 March).

In designing the budget the provincial government took its cue from a poll conducted a few months earlier, which indicated that although there was substantial support for reducing the debt before cutting income taxes, there was also support for cutting the sales tax before the elimination of the debt (*StarPhoenix*, 8 January). The poll was undoubtedly a factor in the government's decision not to eliminate the deficit-fighting surtax that it had imposed in 1993 (*Globe and Mail*, 21 March). Predictably, the budget received the usual critique from the opposition parties for not cutting taxes enough and for not spending enough in certain sectors. The only vote of support from the opposition parties came from the PC leader who supported the 2 per cent cut in the sales tax. A week after the budget speech and after selling it politically within the province, the Premier headed to Toronto and New York to sell it to the bond-rating agencies. On his return to Saskatchewan, he had to deal with a controversy sparked by the provincial auditor's critique of the accounting practices related to the way SaskPower raised $14 million from a new capital reconstruction levy (*StarPhoenix*, 1 and 19 April).

The provincial government's progress on balancing the budget and reducing the debt in 1997 was made possible by a strong economy in 1996 that was driven by bumper crops, a boom in the natural resources sector, and high returns from gambling. In 1996, crop production was 25 per cent higher than the previous year; royalties from the oil patch alone were more than double what the government had predicted; and revenues from gambling were $247 million, $16 million more than the government had predicted (*Globe and Mail*, 21 March). The provincial government hoped that the good economic climate of 1996 – which saw business investment increase by 18 per cent; manufacturing shipments by 10 per cent; retail sales by 8 per cent; and housing starts by 40 per cent – would continue in 1997. Quite early in the year, however, the vulnerability of the provincial economy to the weather and the transportation system was again in evidence as the cold temperatures created massive delays and backlogs in the grain transportation system. The resulting problems created considerable political controversy for the railways and the minister of agriculture, who also continued to face considerable hostility from farmers who wanted to see an end to the Wheat Board monopoly (*StarPhoenix*, 13 and 15 February, and 8 July). The problems of a very cold winter were compounded by those that emerged in the summer when hot weather in July damaged new crops (27 August).

This was the year that dispute ended between the farmers and the provincial government over the government's unilateral decision to change the GRIP crop insurance program in 1992 – the judiciary ruled that the government was well within its purview to change the program. The farmers may have found the judgment somewhat more palatable in light of the recent reduction of approximately 23 per cent in premium payments for most farmers (*StarPhoenix*, 16 January and 15 July). Evidence of the provincial government's continuing efforts to diversify the agricultural sector emerged in its decision to provide various types of financial and non-financial supports to assist the pork industry in the province (8 February and 10 October).

A key indicator of how well Saskatchewan's economy was doing was that by the end of the year it began to appear as if Saskatchewan was on the verge of becoming a 'have province' that would no longer qualify for federal equalization payments. Indeed, for the 1997–8 fiscal year, it received only $36.1 million in equalization payments compared with $540 million only three years earlier. The growing strength of the Saskatchewan economy led the Reform Party to suggest that it should be one of three provinces that should not be receiving equalization payments (*StarPhoenix*, 17 May and 7 November). Other indicators of a relatively good economy in 1997 were the highest employment rates in a decade during the first six months of the year, the lowest unemployment rates in Canada, which government critics attributed more to outmigration from the province than to increased job opportunities, and a drop in the overall poverty rate. Despite the drop in the overall poverty rate, however, the child poverty rate remained above the Canadian average. This explained in large part the undertaking by the provincial government to develop a provincial and national program aimed at reducing the incidence of child poverty (*StarPhoenix*, 8 March, 2 and 18 April, and 9 August).

The solid economic and fiscal performance of the provincial government was in no small part due to record operating profits in the Crown corporations' sector. Despite a few losses in some ventures, the various Crown corporations recorded a total profit of approximately $741 million, which included $515 million from the sale of its Cameco shares (*StarPhoenix*, 15 April). This was also an interesting and important year for the Crown corporation sector as it began to experience the effects of globalization. Sasktel was busy warding off the challenge from international long-distance competitors such as ITT and Sprint, shutting down a U.S.-based subsidiary that installed fibre-optic cable in the American Midwest – a venture through which the provincial government lost $16 million over three years – and looking for investment opportunities abroad (17 January, 9 April, and 12 December). SaskPower ventured into the global market by offering to pay the Guyanese government $31 million to become equal partners in Guyana Electricity Corporation (1 February). The political instability in that country led the provincial government to adopt a cautious approach in pursuing that purchase. The provincial government also contemplated selling the Saskatchewan Transportation Corporation to any interested buyer, including Greyhound, but before the year was over had decided to retain and subsidize it because of its valuable role in providing province-wide bus service (17 June).

In 1997 the provincial government completed its 'Talking About Saskatchewan Crowns' consultation and review process. Launched in February 1996 and costing $3.4 million, the review was designed to produce a report on the structures, functions, value, and accountability of Crown corporations. The major change in the governance of Crowns that resulted from the review was the elimination of ministers from the boards of individual corporations, even though one minister would continue to be responsible for the Crown Investments Corporation, the holding company for all such corporations. Rather than applauding the distancing of partisan political cabinet ministers from Crown corporations, the opposition parties criticized what they viewed as a loss of political oversight and accountability to the legislature. In a predictable fight for the right-wing vote, opposition parties were advocating the privatization of all Crowns. In response to that position, the provincial government argued that a substantial number of those who participated in its 'Talking About Crowns Review' and other government polling indicated that privatization was not a preferred option (*StarPhoenix*, 26 June).

There were other initiatives and controversies in the Crown corporations sector in 1997 revolving around rate increases and the sale of a petroleum company. All the major utilities as well as the insurance company (Saskatchewan Government Insurance) implemented rate increases during the year. These increases led to a call for a more effective rate-review agency and process (*StarPhoenix*, 1 and 29 December). Another major controversy revolved around the sale of Channel Lake Petroleum, a subsidiary of SaskPower. The sale created a furore in the legislative spring session because the government sold it without a public tender. Later that year the sale was subjected to more criticism when the provincial auditor's report released in the fall revealed that Channel Lake had lost approximately $8 million during the previous fiscal year. The Opposition criticized the minister for not notifying the legislature's Crown Corporations Committee either of the sale or the financial losses prior to the sale. The new minister responsible for Crown Corporations, Dwaine Lingenfelter, replied that the rules did not require him to report to the Committee the sale of any asset that was less than 1 per cent of the the total assets of the Crown Investment Corporation (17 December).

The Calgary Declaration

The provincial government continued to criticize the federal government for reducing fiscal transfers and for not making more progress on developing certain social programs such as the Child Benefit Program and for the plan to increase CPP premiums over the next several years (*StarPhoenix*, 15 and 18 February). Nevertheless, the provincial government, and particularly Premier Romanow, continued to occupy a central role in the so-called Canadian unity initiative. This was the year that he brokered the consensus on the Calgary Declaration that provided some principles on future constitutional reform and federal-provincial relations. Following the Premiers' Conference, the provincial government established a consultation process on the Calgary Declaration in every constituency with the intent of drafting a resolution in the legislature to endorse it. The consultations were co-chaired by an MLA and someone selected from the constituency. The provincial government also established an Internet site, an e-mail address, and a toll-free phone number for people to express their views (21 August and 2 October).

At the end of the six-week consultation process, Saskatchewan became the first province to affirm public support for the Declaration and to give formal and unanimous legislative support from all parties shortly thereafter. In the weeks leading up to the legislative support for the Declaration, Premier Romanow had indicated that in dealing with the unity issue it was better to use a combination of Plan A and Plan B and not dwell on Plan C, proffered by Alan Cairns in a C. D. Howe publication (*StarPhoenix*, 1 October, 1 and 4 December). Plan A focused on renewal of the federation to preclude Quebec separation, and Plan B focused both on a 'tough' approach in responding to demands and threats from Quebec secessionists and 'clarity' in setting out the rules for secession. Plan C focused on developing a strategy on political arrangements for the 'rest of Canada' in the wake of Quebec secession.

Aboriginal affairs

The Federation of Saskatchewan Indian Nations (FSIN) held an election for the position of grand chief in which the incumbent, Blaine Favel, easily defeated his opponent by a vote of 643–46. Major accomplishments during his first term included the maintenance of unity in the FSIN and progress on some major issues such as the elimination of the FSIN's deficit; establishing a framework for achieving fiscal equity for First Nations in the province; the reorganization of the FSIN executive and commissions; the signing of a memorandum of understanding with the federal and provincial governments that touched on several matters of mutual interest; and the creation of the First Nations Bank in a special partnership with the Toronto-Dominion Bank and the Yellow Quill First Nation. The First Nation community continued to acquire land both in rural and urban areas pursuant to the Treaty Land Entitlement process (*Free Press*, 19 October).

The election of Blaine Favel as FSIN grand chief proved to have significant implications not only for the provincial Native organizations but also for the national Assembly of First Nations (AFN). Philosophical differences between Mr Favel and the AFN national chief, Ovide Mercredi, contributed to the decision of the majority of chiefs in Saskatchewan to support Phil Fontaine in his successful bid to replace Mr Mercredi (*StarPhoenix*, 16 July and 1 August). That philosophical difference emerged in many areas, none so clearly perhaps as on the 'Native Day of Action' organized by the AFN, which was not well supported by the FSIN or its membership because in Mr Flavel's words:

'Every day in Saskatchewan is a day of action for the FSIN ... We are busy working every day' (18 April).

Although the aboriginal vote may not have been very significant in many federal constituencies, Blaine Favel and the FSIN made it clear that they did not consider the Reform Party friendly to aboriginal peoples or its success in the federal election as beneficial in advancing their interests (*StarPhoenix*, 6 June).

The FSIN sent out a strong and clear message to the people of the province in 1997 regarding the current and future political and economic clout of aboriginal peoples. It did so by commissioning two studies that were published and widely distributed as a monograph entitled *Saskatchewan and Aboriginal Peoples in the 21st Century: Social, Economic and Political Changes and Challenges,* which on the cover was described as 'An essential Resource and Guide for government and business planning.' The economic analysis in the study indicated that over the next fifty years the aboriginal population of Saskatchewan would constitute one-third of the province's population. It noted that unless something was done soon to improve aboriginal participation in the labour force, the unemployment rate would skyrocket, as would related social problems. The political analysis in the study indicated that the projected growth of the aboriginal population, together with more active and strategic participation by the aboriginal population in the political process, could have a significant effect on federal, provincial, and local elections in the future (*StarPhoenix*, 9 September).

The aboriginal communities in the northern part of the province began to lay claims to some of the financial benefits from resource development as they entered into negotiations with the provincial government for some form of royalty revenue-sharing. Although the provincial government rejected the royalty revenue-sharing option recommended by the panel looking into environmental impacts of northern development, it agreed to examine other options as part of a 'northern strategy' for ensuring that northern communities benefited from future resource exploitation (*StarPhoenix*, 6, 10 and 13 May, and 25 November). The aboriginal people living in northern communities also acquired some say in the creation of the two health boards for their area. The province agreed that it would appoint half of those boards from nominees submitted by various major Native organizations in the north, such as the Prince Albert Grand Council and the Peter Ballantyne Cree Nation (*StarPhoenix*, 22 August).

The ongoing saga of Native land entitlement continued in the province as various First Nations either took or threatened court action to compel the federal government to recognize and respond to their land claims. At the same time the Saskatchewan Association of Rural Municipalities decided that it would take legal action against the federal government to recover $12 million in lost property taxes resulting from the conversion of municipal lands to reserve status (*StarPhoenix*, 6 May, 7 August, and 9 September).

Taxation issues continued to be an irritant in the relations between Native organizations on the one hand and the provincial government, SARM, and the Saskatchewan Party on the other. The provincial government wanted some bands to turnover sales tax from the sale of liquor at bars on reserves (*StarPhoenix*, 18 March and 23 April). The Premier continued to express his optimism that if both sides negotiate and collaborate in good faith in serving the needs of aboriginal people in the province, some day First Nations would opt to forgo certain tax exemptions. The FSIN criticized the Saskatchewan Party when, at its founding convention, it decided to adopt a policy to make Natives pay PST off-reserve (19 and 20 November).

The Report of the Royal Commission on Aboriginal Peoples received mixed reaction from aboriginals in the province. While some were outright critical of the timing, length, and thrust of the report, the FSIN was more circumspect in its reaction. Although the extent to which the FSIN endorsed some of the philosophical underpinnings, some of its officials indicated that the organization was committed to pressing the federal government to implement the Report (*StarPhoenix*, 27 January).

The issue of hunting rights made news in Saskatchewan as some Native and Métis leaders began asserting what they deemed to be their traditional hunting rights, including night hunting, in the face of opposition from non-aboriginal hunters and the Saskatchewan Party (*StarPhoenix*, 15, 19, and 22 November).

Justice sector

In 1997, the justice sector continued to generate its usual share of intrigue and controversy in the province. The government was able to settle some outstanding controversial issues that had proven politically problematic for some time. The first of these was the issue of what constituted fair compensation for David Milgaard, whose claim to innocence was corroborated by the results of a DNA test of material left at the scene of the crime for which he was jailed (*StarPhoenix*, 19 July and 25 August). The second was a settlement in the salaries of judges as the government decided to give them a 19 per cent increase as an out-of-court settlement to end the bitter dispute (19 June). The government also released the independent review of the province's Crown prosecution division that recommended some changes to preclude certain problems that had emerged in the past in various legal cases (27 March).

Alberta
HAROLD JANSEN

It would be difficult to identify a period in recent memory where Alberta politics went through more upheaval than between 1993 and 1996. After cutbacks, layoffs, hospital closures, and protests, residents of Alberta emerged in 1997 with surplus budgets, a rapidly diminishing debt, some modest restoration of funding cut from the province's education and health-care systems, and a provincial economy that was growing at levels not seen since the oil boom of the 1970s and early 1980s. This was a year of reflection, of taking stock of what the province had been through, and the beginning of a debate over the future direction of the provincial government.

The provincial election

A provincial election on 11 March provided a formal opportunity for this reflection. Prior to the 'Klein revolution' of spending cuts and fiscal restraint, conventional wisdom held that a government could not follow those policies and still be re-elected. This logic would be put to the test in Alberta, as this election was the first opportunity voters had to pass judgment on the Klein government's performance after four years of government retrenchment.

Even leading up to the election, however, there were clear signs that the conventional wisdom was flawed, at least in Alberta. Both the government and the Premier's approval ratings were very high, and neither Liberal leader Grant Mitchell nor New Democrat Pam Barrett posed a serious threat to the Premier. Indeed, Mr Klein's approval rating (65 per cent) almost exceeded Mr Mitchell's (35) and Ms Barrett's (32) *combined*. That the Progressive Conservatives would win the election was never questioned. In fact, pre-election polls showed that the Klein government was headed for a landslide victory; with the support of 63 per cent of decided voters compared with 24 per cent for the Liberals and 11 per cent for the NDP, some pundits mused publicly that the Conservatives might sweep all 83 seats in the legislature.

The March election was not a well-kept secret. By late January and

early February, it was clear that the government was planning on calling an election a few months shy of the four-year mark. The signs were
especially apparent the week before the election call. The Conservative
Party, not the government, paid for Premier Klein's traditional television address to the public. This was to deflect any criticism that taxpayer money was being used for campaign purposes. Mr Klein's
speech was an indication of the campaign to come. He made no specific promises or policy pronouncements, but instead chose to list successes from the previous four years. The only promise for the future
was that job creation would be a government priority. Mr Klein called
on Albertans to devote themselves to the task of creating employment
with the same energy and dedication that they had used to eliminate the
deficit. The Premier also indicated that health care and education
would be important priorities for 'reinvestment' (the government's
word for spending increases), but warned Albertans not to expect a
return to the past. While the Premier's speech was arguably short on
substantive policy, it did put a more moderate face on the government.

This kinder, gentler image was reinforced by a week of announcements following Mr Klein's speech. In keeping with the emphasis on
job creation, the government announced a new job skills plan. MLA
Heather Forsyth's task force on child prostitution reported and recommended several measures to give police and child welfare officials
greater latitude in dealing with child prostitutes. Finally, the province
signed an agreement with the federal government to extend the federal
infrastructure program for another year. The language of deficit cutting
and debt payments was notably absent in the run-up to the election.

The Conservatives were not alone in getting an early start on the
campaign trail. The provincial Liberals took advantage of their position
as Official Opposition to use $100,000 of their legislature funding to
finance full-page newspaper ads and the production and distribution of
brochures to the province's households. The Liberals' use of taxpayer
money for this advertising campaign so close to the election call
attracted criticism, particularly from the Conservatives. Certainly, the
contrast with the Conservatives' decision to pay for the Premier's
address themselves did little to deflect the criticism.

The Klein government opened the legislature on 10 February with a
Speech from the Throne that parallelled the Premier's television
address: it made no dramatic announcements and dwelled on the government's past accomplishments. On 11 February, Jim Dinning brought
down his final budget as provincial treasurer. The government projected a $144-million surplus for the upcoming fiscal year, potentially

as high as $800 million if resource revenues were relatively buoyant. With no new taxes or tax increases, the government was counting on strong economic growth to finance a 1.2 per cent increase in spending, particularly in health care and education. This budget served as little more than a campaign document as it was followed by the dissolution of the legislature and an election call for 11 March.

As the election campaign formally got underway, polls revealed that health care was the issue that concerned most Albertans. Surprisingly, however, there was relatively little debate about the health-care issue during the campaign. The parties' stances were virtually indistinguishable on this issue; they all promised various levels of new spending within the confines of the Canada Health Act. Other issues sparked more serious disagreements. In particular, the issue of video lottery terminals (VLTs) divided the parties. The Liberals were promising to phase out VLTs over three years; the NDP promised to restrict the machines to casinos; the Conservatives wanted to leave it up to municipalities; and Social Credit wanted to ban the machines altogether.

The Conservatives could not avoid the health-care issue altogether, though. In the end, the opposition parties were not the ones to force the issue; rather, it was the province's registered nurses. RNs were negotiating a new contract with regional health authorities during the provincial election. Mr Klein promised to intervene to prevent a strike. Retroactive pay and staffing issues proved to be the most serious stumbling blocks in the negotiations. Negotiations broke down and the nurses decided on a strike vote for 4 March, which would lead to an illegal strike during the provincial election. The strike was averted when a settlement was reached on the eve of the strike vote (which was 85 per cent in favour of a walk-out).

The nurses brought what little drama there was to a Conservative campaign otherwise devoid of excitement. In late 1996, Ralph Klein had promised that the 1997 election would be boring; that was a promise he clearly kept. Indeed, keeping promises was the theme of the entire Conservative campaign. Most telling were the campaign posters with pictures of Mr Klein and the slogan 'He kept his word.' Premier Klein and the Conservatives ran on their record, and little else. Their message to the electorate was that they had promised to restore the province's finances in 1993 and delivered on that promise; for this, they deserved to be re-elected. This campaign strategy left the Conservatives vulnerable to the charge that they were short on ideas for the future. They did little to spell out a vision for government now that the budget was balanced and the debt was being paid down. Indeed, a vague promise to subject future new taxes and tax increases to provincial referendums was the only apparent plan.

On the other hand, the Conservative campaign strategy proved remarkably effective against the opposition parties. It was difficult to dispute the Conservative claim that they had kept their word to balance the budget. The Liberals emphasized an alternative future for the provincial government that saw the government paying down the debt more slowly and reinvesting money into health care, education, and social services more aggressively. To that end, Grant Mitchell announced plans in the first week of the campaign to spend more on health care and long-term care, to hire 1,000 more teachers, and to increase spending on social assistance. This left the party open to charges that they would return the province to the free-spending past, a point the Conservatives were happy to hammer home. This Tory tactic backfired on them when it was revealed that the Conservatives had asked treasury department bureaucrats to examine and cost out Liberal campaign promises. The use of government resources for campaign purposes had come full circle. The Liberals launched a complaint with Ethics Commissioner Bob Clark (who later exonerated the Tories). The New Democrats did not even pretend that they were trying to form a government. Their campaign centred on the claim that they would be a more effective opposition to the Klein government than the Liberals had been. The NDP focused on a handful of Edmonton constituencies in which the party was competitive, particularly Edmonton Highlands, where leader Pam Barrett was running.

While the Liberals and NDP threatened to split the anti-Conservative vote, the re-emergence of Social Credit as a small but vociferous force in electoral politics raised the possibility of a split on the right. Social Credit was exploiting two rifts among Conservative supporters. One rift was between fiscal and social conservatives, who agreed on the need for fiscal restraint. Many social conservatives felt abandoned by the Klein government on issues like public funding for abortions and VLTs. The other rift was between supporters of the federal Conservatives and Reform Party. Mr Klein was clearly a federal Tory; Social Credit unabashedly claimed to be the provincial version of Reform. While the Social Credit campaign was amateur at times, party leader Randy Thorsteinson proved to be a surprisingly articulate and effective critic of Mr Klein.

In the end, the real battleground in the provincial election was the City of Edmonton. Edmonton had been hostile territory for the Conservatives since 1986 and the party was determined to win there. The campaign seemed to matter little; polls showed little movement among voters during the election. Fluctuations in party support were within the polls' margins of error. The Tories were consistently ahead in all regions – including Edmonton – and enjoyed the support of about 60 per cent of the decided voters.

On election night, every party could point to successes and failures. Ralph Klein and the Conservatives emerged as the big winners, taking just over 51 per cent of the vote and winning a large majority government with sixty-three of the legislature's eighty-three seats. Both popular vote and seats were up substantially from 1993. This victory was the best the Conservatives had done since the retirement of Premier Peter Lougheed. Yet there was a palpable sense of disappointment among Conservatives on election night. For one thing, the popular vote was considerably lower than the polls had been predicting; while the party did well, it had not met expectations. The other problem was that the City of Edmonton once again eluded Mr Klein and the Conservatives' grasp. While the Conservatives won two seats – retaining Liberal defector Julius Yankowsky's seat in Edmonton-Beverly-Clairview and winning Edmonton Whitemud (formerly held by retiring Liberal finance critic Mike Percy) – this was much less than the party had hoped for and expected. The high standing in the polls may have hurt the Conservatives in two ways. Voter turnout was down to 54 per cent; and complacency among Conservative supporters combined with an election-day snowstorm may have depressed voter turnout. In addition, there was something of a 'send an opposition' mood among Edmonton voters. Some voters were clearly nervous about returning the Klein government to office without a reasonably sizeable opposition.

Expectations were also important in the evaluation of the Liberals' performance. By no means could the Liberal campaign be described as a success; the party dropped 7 per cent in the popular vote to 33 per cent and won only 18 seats, losing almost half of their 1993 total. Calgary Conservatives had made defeating Frank Bruseker, who had been instrumental in criticizing Ralph Klein in the Multi-Corp scandal over the past two years, a priority. They were successful, leaving Gary Dickson as the sole Liberal MLA for Calgary. The Liberals were reduced to their Edmonton base, with Mr Dickson and Lethbridge-East MLA Ken Nicol the only Liberal MLAs outside the Edmonton area. Grant Mitchell took full responsibility for the party's losses. Still, the Liberals were not entirely devastated in the 1997 election, as many polls had predicted. While the losses were real and significant, the Liberals had lived to fight another day, with a large enough caucus to form a credible opposition.

The NDP achieved its primary objective: the election of Pam Barrett to the legislature. Ms Barrett re-took the Edmonton Highlands seat she previously represented. As a bonus, the party also elected Raj Pannu as an MLA in a very close three-way race in Edmonton Strathcona. Those successes aside, there was not much good news for the NDP on election night. Their share of the popular vote had declined from 11 per cent to under 9 per cent between 1993 and 1997. While that aggregate decline was not troublesome in and of itself, the NDP did not reassert itself as the primary opposition to the PCs. The NDP came in second in only two constituencies. In the majority of the constituencies in which the party ran candidates, it finished fourth, behind the Conservatives, Liberals, and Social Credit.

Social Credit's much hoped for breakthrough did not materialize. While winning just under 7 per cent of the vote, the party did not elect a single MLA. The party did show surprising strength in rural Alberta, however, finishing second to the Conservatives in seven constituencies. In four constituencies, Social Credit earned over 20 per cent of the vote. While this was a reasonable start upon which to build, the party's poor showing in Edmonton and Calgary indicated that its growth potential might be somewhat limited.

The end result of four weeks of campaigning was a Conservative government elected with a renewed and strengthened mandate but without having revealed a clear blueprint for the future. They would face an opposition with fewer seats and one divided between the Liberals and the New Democrats.

Sorting out the future

The lack of a clear vision for the future meant that the composition of Mr Klein's cabinet was eagerly anticipated for what it would reveal about the government's priorities. Here, too, the government sent a mixed message. There were a number of openings after several senior cabinet ministers had decided not to seek re-election in 1997. On 26 March, the new look for the Klein cabinet was unveiled. The biggest promotion went to Stockwell Day, who took over as treasurer and deputy premier. Mr Day also became chair of the Treasury Board, where he was joined by other fiscal hardliners, such as Steve West and Lorne Taylor. Through this, Mr Klein seemed to be setting up a powerful enough board to say no to future spending requests. On the other hand, cabinet moderates Gary Mar and Halvar Johnson remained in the education and health portfolios, respectively. Another large promotion went to Jon Havelock, who became the minister of justice, attorney general, and government House leader. Mr Havelock was viewed with suspicion by social conservatives, who believed him to be sympathetic to legal protection for the rights of gays and lesbians. With a Supreme Court decision on the *Vriend* case regarding the inclusion of sexual orientation in Alberta's Human Rights Code expected in 1998, this was seen as an indication that Mr Klein was not going to resist a ruling against the government. Mr Havelock's appointment was balanced by the surprise addition of Lorne Taylor to the cabinet as science minister. Some analysts speculated that this was a tactic to muzzle the outspoken MLA, who had caused the government some headaches in the previous term with his opposition to publicly funded abortions and gay rights. Even though Edmonton did not embrace the Conservatives with large numbers in the election, the city was rewarded with a cabinet post when newly elected Edmonton Whitemud MLA Dave Hancock was appointed to the federal and intergovernmental affairs portfolio. Steve West and Pat Black traded their portfolios, with Mr West taking on the important energy portfolio and Mr Black becoming minister for economic development. Mr Black had not made much progress in deregulating the province's electricity industry. Mr West's fondness for privatization indicated that the government intended to move in this direction more vigorously.

Despite a new mandate and a new cabinet, the ghosts of past decisions continued to haunt the Conservative government. In the spring, the government wrote off a number of failed loan guarantees worth millions of dollars. The province was clearly having trouble extracting itself from the 'business of being in business.' Nowhere was this clearer than in the government-owned Alberta Treasury Branch. While other banks were posting record profits, the ATB was posting a loss due to questionable loans. The provincial government granted the ATB permission to expand into new areas, such as mutual funds, if it cleaned up its loan practices. The ATB wrote off several bad loans in an attempt to restore credibility to its operations, a move widely seen as a precursor to privatization. By the end of 1997, however, talk of privatization had subsided. It seemed odd that a government committed to deregulation and privatization continued to own a financial institution. However, many rural Albertans – the most loyal Conservative supporters – opposed any sale of the ATB because it would likely mean the closure of rural branches.

Despite the losses on past loan guarantees, the province's finances were in very good shape. In late June, Mr Day updated the province's fiscal situation, announcing a $2.9-billion surplus for the fiscal year ending in March. This was largely created by a windfall from higher than expected energy revenues (a common occurrence over the past few years). While this made the job of the Alberta treasurer easy in one sense, it also made it difficult to refuse demands for increased spending. To that end, the provincial government was increasingly talking about tax cuts. Mr Day mused publicly on various occasions about ideas such as a one-time fiscal dividend to be paid to Alberta taxpayers, the possible adoption of a flat tax, levying Alberta's taxes directly on income rather than as a percentage of federal tax, and setting up a separate Alberta pension plan. Tax cuts were clearly a direction in which he wished to travel.

Albertans, however, did not seem to have their minds made up as decisively as the treasurer. This became clear at the government-sponsored Growth Summit, held at the end of September in Edmonton. The Growth Summit – attended by delegates from different economic sectors, including business, energy, agriculture, government, the social economy, and other public sector institutions – was intended to be a consultation exercise about the province's post-debt future. While the first three sectors called for tax cuts and deregulation, delegates from the other sectors called for an increased minimum wage, a publicly funded day-care program, and a home-maker's pension. If the ideas of delegates to the summit were any indication, Albertans were unclear about the role of government.

With the lack of an overriding focus, non-fiscal issues dominated the political agenda. VLTs became the most contentious issue in Alberta politics. The issue leapt onto the agenda late in 1996, when the Rocky Mountain House ministerial council began to circulate a petition to remove VLTs from the town. The petition received enough signatures to force a referendum on the issue and the citizens of Rocky Mountain House voted to remove the machines. There was some legal manoeuvring by the owners of the machines, who generated substantial revenues from VLTs, but in the end, Rocky Mountain House became VLT-free. Buoyed by the town's success, VLT opponents in other municipalities began petitions of their own. The VLT opponents were an interesting cross-section of Alberta public opinion, including religious leaders, community activists, and anti-poverty organizations. This was an issue that cut across traditional left-right distinctions.

The provincial government seemed somewhat at a loss as to how to respond to the increasingly vociferous opposition to VLTs. Alberta had permitted VLTs in 1991, and their numbers had quietly swelled to over

5,600, primarily located in bars. The machines were huge revenue generators for the provincial government, putting over half a billion dollars into provincial coffers each year. At the same time, many of the opponents to VLTs were otherwise supporters of the government. In the past, the Tories had dismissed their opponents as whiners and complainers; clearly that option was not available this time. In fact, the public statements of many MLAs indicated that several in the government caucus were uneasy about the social toll of VLTs on Alberta's communities. Torn between the revenues and the concerns of opponents, the government's response often seemed incoherent and constructed on the fly. Initially, Steve West, the minister responsible for lotteries before the provincial election, indicated that any community voting to remove its VLTs would have to forego its share of provincial revenues generated from VLTs. After accusations of blackmail were levelled at the government, the Tories recanted. Then, after communities voted to remove the machines, the province seemed to drag its feet on removing them. With petition drives organizing across Alberta, including in Edmonton and Calgary, this dispute seemed likely to continue well into 1998.

VLTs were not the only conflict in Alberta politics. After a period of dormancy, environmental issues re-emerged on the agenda. Many of the disputes involved Alberta's beautiful mountain parks. One major dispute was over a proposed coal mine on the boundary of Jasper National Park. A coalition of environmental groups opposed the Cheviot mine proposal, arguing that the coal mine would impede wildlife movement and damage an ecologically sensitive area. The mining company and unions argued that the mine would prevent job losses, as a nearby existing mine was almost depleted. The environmental hearings were acrimonious, but in the end, the mine was approved. The Banff town council sparked another conflict when it unveiled a development plan for the town that proposed an expansion of the town's commercial base, much to the chagrin of those concerned over the impact of increasing tourism on the park. Environmentalists won a victory in the battle over development in the Rockies when the provincial government announced a freeze on commercial development in the Kananaskis region.

While environmental issues caused debates within Alberta, they promised to be a source of conflict between the federal and provincial governments as well. Late in 1997, the federal government signed an international agreement to reduce greenhouse gas emissions at a conference in Kyoto, Japan. As home for many of the industries that generate greenhouse gases – oil, gas, and coal – Alberta was very concerned over the potential impact of the Kyoto Agreement on its economy.

Ralph Klein's role in federal politics increasingly became the subject of public discussion. Mr Klein was seen to be sympathetic to Quebec's demands to be recognized as a distinct society. This put him decidedly at odds with the Reform Party and Preston Manning. While this contro- versy divided the two, both were singing from the same page in their support of the Calgary Declaration that tried to square the circle by simultaneously supporting provincial equality and recognition of the unique position of the province of Quebec.

In December, an important member of the Klein government team announced his resignation from provincial politics. Rod Love had served as Ralph Klein's right hand throughout his seventeen-year polit- ical career. Mr Love was known for his fierce loyalty to his boss, his tough tactics, and well-honed political instincts. With the Conserva- tives safely through another election, his boss approaching an 80 per cent approval rating in the polls, Mr Love felt it was safe to resign to spend more time with his family. Mr Klein appointed Peter Elzinga, a former Conservative MP and MLA, to be Mr Love's successor.

The legislature

While 1997 had its share of vigorous debate and conflict, the year will not go down in history as an example of the influence and importance of the legislature in Alberta politics. While the legislature passed a lot of legislation in a short period of time, most of it was routine. The leg- islature did meet for two days in February, but was dissolved before anything could be accomplished. Prior to the new legislature sitting in April, the government announced that it would not renew its agreement with the opposition that provided for two sessions of the legislature a year. The government indicated that it might not hold a fall session, arguing that the September Growth Summit would provide for public consultation. In the end, the ratification of the Calgary Declaration necessitated a brief December session, but for all intents and purpose, the legislature sat for only one session in 1997.

The legislature certainly got off to an interesting start with a surprise outcome in the election of the Speaker. Three Conservatives – Ken Kowalski, Dan Tannas, and Glen Clegg – put their names forward as candidates. Mr Clegg was the favoured candidate and the apparent choice of the Premier and cabinet. There was a noticeable look of shock on the faces of the cabinet when Mr Kowalski defeated Mr Clegg on the second ballot by a 44–39 margin. Considering there were only twenty opposition MLAs, a majority of Mr Kowalski's support had actually come from Conservative benches. Mr Kowalski's political stock had fallen after an extended and bitter run-in with Mr Klein during the previous legislature that saw Mr Kowalski demoted to the backbenches. This was a surprise for the Premier, especially coming after Mr Kowalski publicly criticized the government's decision not to hold a fall session of the legislature.

Jon Havelock, the government's House leader, promised a legislature with 'no glitz, no pizzazz,' and the Speech from the Throne on 15 April seemed to deliver. While more substantive than the pre-election Throne speech, there were few major initiatives in this address. Among the most notable announcements was a proposed No Tax Increase Act, as promised during the election. This legislation was to freeze provincial income taxes at current or lower levels unless Albertans voted in a referendum to increase them. The government's proposed framework of performance goals for the health-care system also attracted some attention.

The central event of the spring session of the legislature is usually the provincial budget. In this case, however, the content of Treasurer Stockwell Day's inaugural budget was essentially the same as that of Mr Dinning's February pre-election budget. There were some minor changes necessitated by changing economic forecasts. Lower than expected interest rates reduced the government's debt servicing costs; this was offset by a reduction in the projected oil price to $18.50, down 50 cents from the February budget. The net effect was a projected $10-million increase in the surplus to $154 million. Mr Day also announced an additional $20 million in health-care funding to be shared between Calgary and Edmonton. Spending cuts in other areas offset modest spending increases in education and advanced education and career development. The net result was that provincial spending was increasing by 1 per cent.

Besides the provincial budget, the legislature passed twenty-nine bills during the thirty-six day session. Among the bills passed were changes to freedom of information and privacy protection legislation. Bill 1 expanded the reach of the legislation to municipalities, school boards, and regional health authorities. Ethics Commissioner Bob Clark had called without success for the addition of a lobbyists' registration to the legislation. The government ended up using closure to get the bill passed. The Liberals were objecting to the bill, not because of its contents, which were generally seen as an improvement, but because the legislation did not provide any dates for implementation. Other legislation passed included a crackdown on tobacco smuggling, amendments to the Child Welfare Act targeting child prostitution, and legislation that would let shopping-centre owners charge 'mall rats' with loitering.

This meagre list of accomplishments at the end of the session was a reflection of the fact that the high profile legislation was beset with opposition both within the government caucus and from opponents outside. The proposed legislation subjecting future tax increases to provincial referendums encountered opposition within the government caucus. Many MLAs worried that it would reduce the government's financial flexibility, particularly a concern in a volatile economy like that of Alberta. When the legislation finally materialized in June, it had been weakened substantially, applying only to personal-income-tax increases. Even that watered down legislation was not seriously debated. The government made it clear that this was a 'trial balloon' bill, intended to get public reaction. The bill died on the order-paper at the end of the session.

A similar fate met the health-care charter. The government bill proposed to protect patient records from being used by hospitals and regional health authorities for fund-raising or marketing purposes. Furthermore, it proposed to allow patients to shield parts of their medical records from some medical providers. The legislation would establish an office of the health commissioner who would be in charge of enforcing this health-care bill of rights. This trial balloon also died at the end of the session.

Arguably, the most controversial bill of the session was not one introduced by the government, but a private member's bill. Carol Haley, the MLA for Airdrie–Rocky View, introduced Bill 209, legislation that would substantially increase government support for independent schools. This bill was controversial, not because of the debate it created in the legislature, but because of the rift it opened in the Conservative caucus and cabinet. Bill 209 pitted Education Minister Gary Mar, who opposed the bill, against Treasurer Day, who supported it. Mr Klein dealt with the problem through a compromise. The bill would die, but Mr Klein struck a task force to study the issue, moving out of the realm of legislative debate. The public hearings provided a forum for all sides in the debate, but were not entirely successful in defusing the debate within the Conservative Party. In their fall policy convention, Conservative Party delegates not only voted against increased funding for independent schools, but also narrowly voted to eliminate funding to them altogether. The government had not acted on the resolution or moved to increase independent school funding by the end of the year.

The lack of a substantive legislative agenda provided little fodder for the Opposition. The most effective government critic was Pam Barrett, who effectively challenged the government on a number of points, including the revelation that people who were late in paying their Alberta Health premiums were being charged 19.5 per cent interest. Ms Barrett also forced the province to allow welfare recipients to cash their food vouchers at grocery stores other than Safeway, which was involved in a protracted and bitter labour dispute. The NDP leader's best moment came when she forced the province to admit it had lost $2.5 billion in selling off social housing and other real estate ventures in its privatization efforts.

Ms Barrett's feisty efforts in the spring session contrasted with a lacklustre and demoralized effort by the Liberal caucus, who spent much of their energy in the session unsuccessfully opposing applications by the NDP to get research funding and guaranteed questions in question period. Right after the session prorogued, Grant Mitchell announced his resignation as party leader, giving the Liberals until the end of 1998 to find a leader. The party opted for a leadership vote in April 1998. MLAs Linda Sloan and Ken Nicol announced their candidacies as did defeated MLA Frank Bruseker. The most intriguing development was the candidacy of former Conservative cabinet minister and leadership aspirant Nancy MacBeth (formerly Betkowski). Ralph Klein had defeated Ms Betkowski for the leadership of the Conservative Party in 1992. In December, Ms MacBeth announced her intention to seek the leadership of the Alberta Liberals.

The legislature met briefly in December. The three-day session had only one agenda item – the ratification of the Calgary Declaration. The Declaration passed with unanimous support.

Despite some occasional opposition successes, the legislature was not the central forum for Alberta politics. Premier Ralph Klein demonstrated this best by his extended absences from the legislature. In thirty-six days in the spring session, Mr Klein managed to attend only seventeen Question Periods. While his absences often had good explanations – his tour to promote Calgary's bid to host the 2005 World Fair, attendance at the annual premiers' conference, and recovering from rib fractures after a fall – it is an indication of the lowly status of the Alberta Legislature in 1997.

The federal election in Alberta

The ink was barely dry on the provincial election results when Albertans were summoned to the polls once again, this time for a federal election on 2 June. Alberta was not a major battleground in this election. Most of the province's twenty-six seats were firmly in the hands of Reform Party MPs and would be difficult for others to take. Still, the Liberals were hoping to hold and possibly increase their seat totals in Edmonton, as well as to establish a toe-hold in Calgary. Of particular interest was Calgary West, which was open after Reform MP Stephen Harper decided to leave federal politics to take on a position as the head of the National Citizens' Coalition. Reform had nominated Rob Anders, a relatively young and unknown candidate; the Liberals countered with Dave Bronconnier, a Calgary city councillor.

While Reform was primarily focused on an Ontario breakthrough in 1997, there were a few gains to be realized in Alberta. The Liberals held four Edmonton seats and Reform had designs on all of them. The highest profile target was Liberal Natural Resources Minister Anne McLellan who won her Edmonton West seat by only a few votes in 1993. Ms McLellan had become the senior and most influential Liberal MP from Alberta.

The most interesting aspect of the federal election was the way it intersected with Alberta's provincial politics. Given the regionalized character of the federal campaign, it was not surprising to see the major contenders playing regions off against each other. While the Reform Party's controversial television advertisement questioning the dominance of federal politics by Quebec politicians drew most of the attention, federal Health Minister David Dingwall chose the Alberta government's health-care policies as an example of the creeping health-care privatization that the federal government intended to stop. While polls showed that Albertans were unsure about the provincial government's direction in health policy, federal Liberal stigmatization of Alberta likely did little to help the party's fortunes in the province.

The federal election brought questions about Ralph Klein's federal role to the fore. Mr Klein was in a difficult position because a majority of his caucus supported the federal Reform Party. This limited his ability to campaign for the federal Conservatives. Federal leader Jean Charest and Mr Klein's friendship went back to the time when they were the federal and provincial environment ministers, respectively. Mr Klein drew the wrath of Reformers when he introduced Mr Charest at a campaign stop in Calgary. In a clear shot at Reform, Mr Klein endorsed Mr Charest as the only leader who could appeal to all Canadians. Speculation was rampant that Mr Klein was considering making the jump into federal politics, possibly succeeding Mr Charest should the Conservatives not do well in the federal campaign.

After the votes were counted on 2 June, Reform had tightened its stranglehold over the province by taking twenty-four of Alberta's twenty-six seats. The Liberals failed to win a seat in Calgary. Reform took Edmonton North (where the party's first MP, Deborah Grey, successfully relocated after her constituency was eliminated in a seat redistribution) and Edmonton East (where Peter Goldring defeated former Edmonton city councillor and incumbent MP Judy Bethel) from the Liberals. Ms McLellan hung on to her seat, increasing her margin of victory to a comfortable 1,500 votes. Liberal MP David Kilgour held his Edmonton Southeast seat by a similar margin. Liberal losses to Reform in western Canada enhanced Ms McLellan's position in the cabinet as a regional spokesperson for Alberta and for the West.

The economy

In 1997, Alberta was basking in the glow of an economic boom not seen since the early 1980s. While Canada as a whole posted strong economic growth, Alberta's real GDP grew by a staggering 5.5 per cent. This growth was driven by strong domestic demand rather than exports. Indeed, domestic demand increased more quickly than exports for the first time in the 1990s. Residential construction was very strong, with a 42 per cent increase in housing starts. Retail sales increased by an incredible 13 per cent.

This booming economy fuelled strong job growth. Alberta's unemployment rate averaged 6 per cent throughout the year and reached a low of 5.6 per cent by December. There was a 3.1 per cent increase in the number of jobs in 1997. Not surprisingly, this had a dramatic impact on interprovincial migration. The number of migrants to Alberta reached its highest level since 1981, with British Columbia and Newfoundland supplying a disproportionate share of the new residents. This combination of high levels of employment and net migration tightened the rental market. The province's vacancy rate dropped from 7 per cent in 1995 to 2.9 per cent in 1997. The housing crunch was felt particularly in Grand Prairie (0 per cent vacancy rate) and Fort McMurray and Calgary (both at 0.5 per cent).

The oil and gas sector continued to expand, with a 30 per cent increase in drilling activity. More oil rigs were drilling in 1997 than at any point since 1980. Oil prices averaged around $20 a barrel, but there was considerable volatility in the price throughout the year. Overall, Alberta's oil output increased by about 2 per cent for the year, but non-conventional oil (primarily from the tar sands) accounted for all of the increase;

conventional oil production actually decreased in 1997. Similar volatility was seen in natural gas prices through 1997. Natural gas sales increased in Alberta, as did exports to the United States. An unusually warm winter in central Canada decreased demand there, leaving the province with an overall 1.5 per cent increase in natural gas sales.

In agriculture, Alberta's farmers enjoyed what could best be described as an average year: lower wheat prices were offset by higher livestock prices, particularly for pork. Alberta's hog industry expanded in response to these high prices, driven by strong demand in Asia. The Fletcher's hog processing plant in Red Deer doubled its capacity. A number of hog megaprojects were in development. The City of Lethbridge rezoned some industrial land to allow a Taiwanese corporation to build a huge hog processing plant. In the summer, construction began in Fairview on a huge farrowing barn. These projects created community backlash, as residents in both communities expressed concern over air and water quality.

The business story of the year in Canada, and one of special concern to Albertans, was the saga of Calgary based Bre-X Minerals. Bre-X had catapulted to fame when it claimed to have discovered an incredibly rich gold vein in the Busang jungle in Indonesia. The company's stock sky-rocketed and, after some difficulty with the Indonesian government in late 1996 and early 1997, Bre-X reached an agreement with a U.S. company to develop the mine on 16 February. On 26 March, Bre-X announced than an independent review of the company's claims had found that the company overstated the amount of gold in Busang. Shortly after this bombshell, Bre-X's U.S. partner revealed that its seven test holes had found insignificant amounts of gold. Subsequent analysis revealed that the original Bre-X samples had been salted with outside gold; there was no proof of any gold in Busang. Bre-X stock suddenly became worthless, devastating many small investors and leaving the company in ruins.

With spring came a bitter labour dispute that affected most people in Alberta, as workers in the province's Safeway grocery stores went on strike for seventy-five days. Safeway had asked its employees to take a pay cut in 1993, when the chain claimed to be losing money and market share to stores such as the Real Canadian Superstore. After Safeway's parent company posted a $700-million profit, workers wanted to recoup those lost wages. Talks broke down and the workers walked off the job. Safeway hired replacement workers to keep its stores operational. As the strike dragged on, several strikers crossed the picket lines and returned to work. In the end, it was hard to find any winners in the strike. The final settlement saw a guarantee of twelve hours for part-time employees and the removal of a wage cap for new full-time employees, modest wage gains for some employees, but actual wage reductions for others. Although Safeway workers voted to accept the offer, they were not happy with the settlement, after the sacrifices of the strike. Although Safeway appeared to have won the conflict, the chain lost an estimated $24 million during the strike and the chain was subject to a consumer boycott that continued to affect the chain well after the strike had ended.

Miscellaneous

The booming provincial economy led both Edmonton and Calgary to consider stepping out onto the world stage by hosting major international events. Throughout the first half of 1997, Calgary pursued a bid to bring the 2005 World's Fair to the city. Calgary spent $5.5 million – all raised through private donations – in pursuit of the fair. Everyone was expecting a close vote on 12 June, but Calgary was shocked when it lost 52–27 to Nagoya, Japan. The result left a sour taste in the mouths of Calgarians, who were outspent and, apparently, out-organized in the bid for the fair.

After Atlanta held the summer Olympics in 1996, Edmonton mayor Bill Smith had floated the idea of the Alberta capital putting together an Olympic bid. The mayor's critics saw that dream as incredibly unrealistic; in early 1997, the mayor and city council formally decided to abandon it. Instead, Edmonton turned its attention to bidding for the 2001 World Championship in Athletics, an event that had previously been held only in Europe.

The story of the once-mighty National Hockey League Edmonton Oilers took a couple of strange turns in 1997. Early in the year, owner Peter Pocklington announced that he would be taking the team public, selling shares in the team. Mr Pocklington announced that he would retain majority ownership and control of the franchise. In the spring, Mr Pocklington announced that he was selling the team outright, in a sale supervised by Alberta Treasury Branches, to whom Mr Pocklington was heavily indebted. Fears that the team would be moved to the United States proved well founded when Houston millionaire Les Alexander was negotiating to buy the team and move it to Texas. A team of local investors was also negotiating to buy the team. By the end of 1997, the team's future in Edmonton was still not clear.

Newfoundland and Labrador   RAYMOND B. BLAKE

In 1997, Newfoundland celebrated its history and welcomed new begin-
nings. The province marked the 500th anniversary of John Cabot's landing in the New World, and Queen Elizabeth II and Prince Philip were on
hand at Bonavista on 24 June to greet a replica of Cabot's ship *The Mat-
thew*, which had set out from Bristol, England, in May to recreate the historic voyage of 1497, when England laid claim to Newfoundland. Not
surprisingly, it was a good year for tourism. It was also, finally, a year for
the promoters of the Hibernia project to celebrate, as the long wait for oil
production came to a happy end. On 17 November, a full month ahead
of schedule, Newfoundland became an oil-producing province as the
first barrels of oil began flowing from the Hibernia reserve on the Grand
Banks. Despite other economic problems, some people in the province
started to whisper about a brighter future.

The budget and the economy

When Finance Minister Paul Dicks delivered his budget in the House
of Assembly on 20 March, he again reduced spending as the government continued its difficult march towards a balanced budget, now
expected by 1999–2000. As the government had promised earlier in the
Speech from the Throne, Newfoundlanders had to accept a 'leaner'
government, though Premier Brian Tobin promised bold new measures
to help welfare recipients. The province provided refundable sales-tax
credits of $40 per adult and $60 per child for those with family
incomes less than $15,000, but the promised overhaul of social welfare
would have to wait until the following year. The government continued
to slash its payroll, cutting the number of public servants by a further
1,100 over the next three years; another 486 teaching positions were
eliminated, bringing the total loss to 1,700 since 1990. To deal with a
1.8 per cent reduction in revenue, the government cut operating grants
to municipalities, increased numerous service charges, including motor
vehicle registrations, and raised the tobacco tax. However, $37 million
was injected into health care and education, suggestion that fiscal
restraint might be coming to an end.

On 1 April, Newfoundland joined with Nova Scotia and New Brunswick to blend its provincial sales tax with the federal Goods and Services Tax (GST) to create the Harmonized Sales Tax (HST). The new
tax rate, set at 15 per cent, broadened the tax base considerably to

include many services and a few goods, which had previously been exempt from the provincial sales tax. Under the arrangement, the federal government continued to collect its 7 per cent GST. Although the tax base for the province was broadened, its revenues declined as the 12 per cent PST was replaced with an 8 per cent tax. However, Ottawa provided a one-time $961 million transfer to be divided among the three provinces as compensation. Newfoundland had not yet announced how it hoped to recoup those losses once the federal compensation had expired, but New Brunswick and Nova Scotia intended to institute a corporate capital tax. All three provinces believed that the HST would improve the economic climate and stimulate growth and thus improve revenue from other sources, especially as the cost of doing business in the three provinces would decrease with the new tax regime.

In fact, Newfoundland might lead all other provinces in economic growth for 1998 if the Canadian Imperial Bank of Commerce's annual economic forecast is accurate. The Conference Board of Canada also predicted that the province would surge ahead by 4.5 per cent in 1998, once Hibernia oil started to flow. While the province was buoyed by prospects of future growth, much of 1997 remained grim; the provincial unemployment rate fell to 17 per cent, but some regions of the province, especially the south coast, had an unemployment rate of 25 per cent, the highest in the country.

The Inco Ltd. development at Voisey's Bay continued slowly throughout 1997. The $1.4-billion project was to begin production in 1999, but negotiations between the company and the province were painfully slow as the two sides failed to agree on a benefits package. Moreover, Native groups obtained a court injunction from the Newfoundland Court of Appeal in August, forcing Inco to cease construction on a temporary road and airstrip and overturning a lower court ruling that because the construction was related to exploration, it was not subject to a joint environmental assessment panel on which the Natives had representation. The Court of Appeal ruled that the proposed temporary road and airstrip must undergo a full environmental assessment. Just three days prior to the court's ruling, Inco announced that it had postponed the start-up date of the project to at least 2000 because of the slow environmental review process and protracted negotiations with the Native groups. It also warned that further delays might have a profound impact on Voisey's Bay as increased competition from other companies, the discovery of a large nickel deposit in the South Pacific, and a precipitous drop in commodity prices might make development of the site less attractive. The price of nickel had dropped from $4.50/lb in 1995 to $2.70 in 1997, prompting Inco to review its whole operation and focus on lower cost production. It subsequently announced the closure of four mines in Ontario, and hinted that it was examining the size of the proposed smelter for Newfoundland. However, the provincial government warned that if Inco did not proceed with the smelter as intended there would be no development at Voisey's Bay. Inco had paid $4.3 billon U.S. to acquire the Labrador deposit and was expected to spend another $20 million in each of the next five years to explore the region, but the enthusiasm initially associated with the project started to wane through the year.

There was some good news for the project in November, however, when the Newfoundland government reached a land deal with the Labrador Inuit in what the two parties called a negotiator's text. They hoped to have a land-claims agreement in principle early in 1998. In the deal, the Inuit were given 5 per cent of Labrador, some 15,700 square kilometres, as well as co-management with the province of a further 56,000 square kilometres to be known as the Labrador Settlement Area. Nearly 8,000 square kilometres were set aside for the proposed Torngat Mountains National Park. Under the agreement, the Inuit will receive 25 per cent of the province's revenue from mining, oil, and gas production, including 3 per cent of its take from the Voisey's Bay nickel deposit and up to $255 million in cash transfers, but under a proposed cap, provincial royalty payments will be cut off once the per capita annual income of the Inuit reaches the Canadian average of $17,000. The Inuit will receive additional payments from so-called impact benefits' agreements to be worked out with Inco Ltd as Voisey's Bay is developed.

After years of controversy, the Hibernia offshore oil megaproject produced its first barrel of oil on 17 November, one month ahead of schedule and under its $5.8-billion pre-production budget. The various components were moved to the Gravity Base Structure at Bull Arm and assembled in early May but Newfoundlanders were unable to see Prime Minister Jean Chrétien christen the Hibernia platform as protestors prevented a media bus from reaching a site during the spring federal election. Even so, nine of the world's largest tugs began towing the 660,000 tonne, 224-metre high platform to its destination some 315 kilometres out on the Grand Banks in mid-May.

Oil had been discovered on the continental shelf in 1979 and development had started in the late 1980s. The project almost grinded to a halt on several occasions, particularly in 1992 when Gulf Canada Resources pulled out. However, the other partners, Mobil Oil Canada,

Chevron Canada Resources, Petro-Canada, Murphy Oil, and Norsk Hydro, as well as the federal government, remained committed to its development. By December, Hibernia had set a pumping record by producing between 40,000 and 45,000 barrels a day, nearly double the rate of any well in Canadian oil production history. It hopes to increase production levels to 180,000 barrels per day by 1999, lowering the break-even price for production from $12.95 U.S. per barrel to $11.50 U.S. per barrel. Mobil Oil, the lead partner in the project, revised its estimate of the recoverable reserves from 615 million barrels to 750 million.

In December, the federal Natural Resources Minister Ralph Goodale and Environment Minister Christine Stewart approved the Terra Nova offshore oilfield project, which also promises to bring tremendous economic benefits to the province. Contracts have already been awarded for drilling units for the Terra Nova fields, and prospects in the oil sector in the waters off Newfoundland continue to show promise as Petro-Canada, Mobil, Chevron, Norsk Hydro, and several other firms have bid more than $100 million for seven new parcels of land. Moreover, Husky Oil and Norsk Hydro, two of the major players in the Newfoundland offshore, announced plans to open offices in Newfoundland. The Hibernia project currently employs 280 people with plans to add an additional 400 at full production levels; another 400 will be employed at the Terra Nova site when production begins in 2001. Premier Brian Tobin said he expects the province to earn more than $10 million in revenue over the next few years; the federal government, which owns an 8.5 per cent equity share in Hibernia and provided more than $2.6 billion in grants and loan guarantees, will also see a return on its investment. It is estimated that royalties from Hibernia alone will be $1.5 billion over the next eighteen years. With the spin-off activities, the affects on employment and income from oil and gas will be enormous.

Even so, the provincial government terminated its support for two industries that it had kept afloat for years: shipbuilding and chicken processing. The Marystown shipyard was sold and the Integrated Poultry Ltd, a consortium of twenty chicken producers, purchased the provincially run Newfoundland Farm Products Corporation. A U.S. firm, Friede Goldman International Inc., bought the Crown-owned Marystown shipyard and steel fabrication facility for $1, with the promise to provide work for 600 people a year for five years. RIGCO North America signed a tentative contract to construct a deep water oil rig for the Grand Banks. Even as the government cut support for some industries, it offered support to others to compete with the other Atlantic provinces to attract call centres, two of which were set up in St John's in 1997, employing about 500 people.

The fishery

There was little hope for the groundfish fishery throughout 1997 as the stocks showed few signs of recovery. In April, Fisheries Minister Fred Mifflin announced that a limited fishery would open 19 May, following the recommendations of the Fisheries Resource Conservation Council. The Department of Fisheries and Ocean set a quota of 10,000 tonnes along the south coast of Newfoundland and 6,000 tonnes for the northern Gulf of St Lawrence. Before the moratorium was imposed in 1992, the quota for the south coast region had been 57,000 tonnes. However, Mr Mifflin noted that even the limited fishery was worth $10 million to Newfoundland fishers and would provide some relief for some of the 40,000 fishery-related workers in the region. Even so, Mr Mifflin's decision to reopen the fishery just prior to an impending election was severely criticized by many who saw it as a political move. The fishery was opened only for five days as fishers filled the quota quickly. Still, fisheries scientists say that the catch was of juvenile cod that must be allowed to reproduce so that stocks can recover. A report from the Northwest Atlantic Fisheries Organization in 1997 suggested that there was practically no fish off Labrador and the northern tip of Newfoundland, the fishing grounds for the once lucrative northern cod. Fisheries Minister David Anderson subsequently banned a food fishery along Newfoundland's north and northeast coasts, but decided to permit a limited one along the south and west coast as well as in parts of Quebec in mid-September.

In late July, the Fisheries Resource Conservation Council warned in its report that the fishing power of the Atlantic fleet remained two to three times larger than was necessary even if the stock recovered fully. Fred Woodman, chair of the advisory council, said that Ottawa and the provinces had not done enough during the moratorium to address the causes of the 1992 cod collapse, as there were still too many vessels using high-tech gear, an inadequate resource management regime remained in place, and there was insufficient scientific information about the stocks. Although Ottawa had spent more than $300 million to retrain fisheries workers, retire fishing licences, and offer early retirement packages under The Atlantic Groundfish Strategy (TAGS), only about 14,000 of more than 40,000 had left the industry. The Council called upon Ottawa to work with the provinces to immediately reduce the capacity of the fleet and to enforce strict measures in the fishery, including closing the fishery during spawning season and restricting the types of gear fishers use.

What little good news there was for out-of-work fishers came during the 1997 federal election when Mr Mifflin announced that after the election people cut off TAGS would have to work just 420 hours or earn $2,500 to qualify for Employment Insurance. They had previously been treated as new entrants and had to work at least 910 hours or earn $5,500 to qualify. The change affected as many as 15,000 fishers and plant workers. The move was designed to appease workers who had protested being cut off of TAGS. The move did little, however, to end the uncertainty over the income-support program for fishers. Because the fishery had not recovered, many were worried about what would happen to fishery workers after TAGS. Ottawa was clearly concerned about the cost overruns associated with the $1.9-billon program and had warned that the program might be terminated a year early because of the costs involved. After Auditor General Denis Desautels offered a scathing review of the program in his 1997 report for failing to achieve any of its objectives, including ensuring a sustainable fishery and helping fisheries workers make the transition to other sectors of the economy, the Prime Minister's Office cast doubts on a future bail-out for fisheries workers. Even though Fisheries Minister David Anderson defended the program, he admitted that too many people clung tenaciously to the fishery. Still, by October he had promised that Ottawa would not abandon those in the fishery, though he intimated that income support may not necessarily be part of the post-TAGS scenario. Human Resource Minister Pierre Pettigrew announced on 3 October that his department would consult with various groups in Atlantic Canada and report by the end of the year. At year's end, he announced that TAGS would be extended to 31 August 1998.

Although the Newfoundland fishery employed only a mere fraction of what it had in the pre-moratorium days, the value of the fishery to the provincial economy had recovered significantly from its collapse in the early 1990s. Landed values of fish increased to $300 million in 1997, as species such as crab and shrimp became increasingly important. In 1997, eighty-five new vessels were licensed for shrimp, which had been previously harvested by foreign factory vessels. The shrimp stocks appeared to be doing well, and jobs in the shrimp sector were expected to double from 750 to 1,500 by 1998. Shrimp had become the most valuable specie in the province's fishery, but there were now more than forty different species caught and processed in Newfoundland, as the fishery continued to move in new directions away from a reliance on groundfish. The province continued to promote aquaculture, providing an additional $4.5 million for three new facilities in 1997; the sector contributes about $10 million to the provincial economy. However, the Sea Forest Plantation cod hatchery at Jerseyside was destroyed by fire on 21 May, killing more than twenty million eggs and three million small cod.

The continued crisis in the fishery was largely responsible for people leaving the province in record numbers. Between 1991 and 1996, the population of the province declined by 2.9 per cent, it was reported in 1997, the only province to show a decline in population. During that period more than 20,000 people left the province than moved in. What was most disturbing about the trend was that most of those who left were under thirty-five years of age, and nearly three-quarters of them had some form of post-secondary training.

For the second year in succession, the International Fund for Animal Welfare (IFAW) captured on videotape images showing cruel and illegal acts by Canadian sealers. In 1996, four Newfoundlanders were convicted of violating sealing rules after the IFAW presented a gruesome sealing video. The 1997 version was treated with scepticism by the Department of Fisheries and Oceans as the IFAW continued its efforts to discredit the seal fishery; as Tina Fagan, the executive director of the Canadian Sealers Association, commented, 'Killing is not pretty anywhere, whether it is on the ice ... or in an abattoir' (*Toronto Star*, 11 February). Later, in October a group of well-known Canadians, including actors Margot Kidder and William Shatner and authors Farley Mowat and Michael Ondaatje, criticized the seal hunt as David Anderson began to consider expanding the quota. The group, founded by lawyer Clayton Ruby, called the seal industry 'archaic and immoral' and said that it should not be supported by governments (Canada Press Newswire, 9 October). The group had released a study claiming that the hunt provided 120 full-time jobs in Newfoundland, each one costing taxpayers nearly $30,000 in subsidies. Fishery ministers from the East and West Coasts continued to support the seal hunt however, and Mr Anderson said that the seal hunt was a legitimate occupation and one that he supported. Many in Newfoundland saw the rapidly expanding herds as a threat to the recovery of the cod stocks and an economic opportunity as new markets for seal products opened up.

Politics

Premier Brian Tobin showed himself in 1997 once again to be a shrewd politician. Amid what many commentators saw as a potential health-care crisis in the province, he shuffled his cabinet and moved Joan Marie Alyward, a former nurses' union president, into the health portfolio on 8 May. The former health minister, Lloyd Matthews, was moved to the Department of Works, Service and Transportation. Julie Bettney was moved from transportation to Ms Alyward's old portfolio of human resources. Within two months, Mr Tobin had shuffled his cabinet again, this time moving Chuck Furey to mines and energy, replacing Rex Gibbons who had resigned but failed to win a seat in the federal Parliament. Judy Foote was promoted to industry, trade and technology; Beaton Tulk to development and rural renewal; Kevin Alyward to forest resources and agriculture; and Oliver Langdon, a former Conservative MHA, was named environment and labour minister.

In the 1997 federal election, the Premier of Newfoundland and his Liberal counterparts in New Brunswick and Nova Scotia criticized the Conservative's policy on health care, but it did the party little good. In a joint statement released on 26 May, they claimed that the Tory plan to convert transfer payments into equalization tax points would cost the region $100 million a year and harm the health-care system. Jean Charest responded that the Atlantic premiers were 'the three stooges of Liberal politics' and that they had deliberately omitted a key part of the tax-point plan that had promised a stabilization fund that would assist the poorer provinces. Mr Charest also encountered severe criticism for his proposal to merge the Department of Fisheries and Oceans into one huge federal department (Canada Press Newswire, 27 May).

The Liberals were re-elected but their dominance in Atlantic Canada was sharply diminished. In 1993 the Liberals had swept all seven seats in Newfoundland, but three were lost to the Conservatives in the 1997 election. Long-serving Liberal Roger Simmons was defeated by Bill Matthews, a former cabinet minister in the government of Brian Peckford, as were Charlie Power and Norm Doyle who also won seats for the Conservatives. Liberals Lawrence O'Brien, Gerry Byrne, George Baker, and Fred Mifflin were all returned, though Mr Mifflin with only a 570-vote margin over NDP candidate Fraser March. Still, the Liberals fared better in Newfoundland and Labrador than they did throughout the rest of Atlantic Canada. They now held only eleven of the thirty-two seats in the region; before the election they had held thirty-one. Following the election, Mr Mifflin was removed from the fisheries portfolio to veterans affairs and Secretary of State for the Atlantic Canada Opportunities Agency. David Anderson, an MP from British Columbia, became the new minister of fisheries and oceans.

In a mid-summer by-election to replace Rex Gibbons, who had

resigned his position as Minister of Mines and Energy in Mr Tobin's government to run unsuccessfully for the Liberal in the federal election, Sheila Osborne won the St John's seat for the Conservatives, bringing their number in the House of Assembly to nine. The Liberals held thirty-six seats, the NDP a single seat, and an independent held a single seat. Loyola Sullivan stepped down as leader of the provincial Conservative Party on 29 December.

In 1997, Newfoundland politician Jack Pickersgill died in Ottawa on 14 November. He was ninety-two. Although he was born in Manitoba and lived much of his life in Ottawa, he played a key role in New-foundland politics and history. He was involved in the negotiations leading to union with Canada and was subsequently elected Liberal MP for Bonavista-Twillingate in 1953, and became Newfoundland's cabinet representative in the governments of Louis St Laurent and Lester B. Pearson. The other notable political news was the appoint-ment of Dr Maxwell House, a professor at Memorial University and a pioneer in telemedicine, as the lieutenant-governor of Newfoundland and Labrador on 5 February.

Education and social issues

The province's plan to reform and streamline its educational system was thrown into turmoil on 8 July, when Mr Justice Leo Barry of the Supreme Court of Newfoundland granted Pentecostal and Catholic par-ents an injunction against the province's educational reforms, prevent-ing school boards from closing any undenominational school which operated in 1996–7 without the consent of the Roman Catholic or Pen-tecostal denominational committees. Following a constitutional amend-ment in 1996, which limited the role of the churches, the government had introduced reforms to the denominational education system, but some parents charged that the process whereby the government declared some schools interdenominational and unidenomination was flawed and unconstitutional. Even though the province had merged various school boards and closed schools, the ruling forced the government to put resources and teachers back into schools that had been closed. Premier Tobin said the decision would cost the province as much as $20 million, but instead of appealing the ruling, he took the matter directly to the peo-ple when he called a second referendum on the issue for 2 September, rather than wait for the courts to settle the matter. In a televised address to the province, Mr Tobin stated the issue clearly when he said, 'What we're proposing quite simply is that parents, not church, have the ultimate right and responsibility to direct their children's education.' Voters were asked to terminate the current denominational-based education system in favour of one where all children regardless of religious affiliation would attend the same schools. In an effort to appease the religious groups, he said that religion would remain a part of the curriculum, but it would not be based on any one denomination. Historically, Newfoundland had a system of education that was state-funded but managed by various councils representing seven religious denominations.

Voters overwhelmingly approved of the government's plan to abandon the church-run education system in favour of a nondenominational one. More than 73 per cent of Newfoundlanders voted in the referendum to radically reform the education system. Premier Tobin said the vote 'has given government the clear result that we needed in order to bring about a new vision for the education system of Newfoundland and Labrador' (Canada Press Newswire, 2 September). Three days later, the legislature passed a resolution asking Ottawa to amend the Constitution once again to allow reform of the provincial school system. Despite the popular support for reform, Catholic and Pentecostal churches, the most prominent of the seven denominations that had traditionally run the school system, vowed to continue to fight the Tobin government on the issue. Supreme Court Justice Gerald Land dismissed an application by representatives of the Roman Catholic Church to prevent Governor General Romeo LeBlanc from proclaiming the new Term 17 into law. The House of Commons passed the constitutional amendment on 9 December, bringing the process that had begun in 1995 to an end. A similar amendment aimed at reorganizing the school system in Quebec along linguistic rather than religious lines was passed a few days later.

Newfoundland joined the growing list of provinces in 1997 to include sexual orientation in its human rights code. Alberta and Prince Edward Island are the only provinces that do not extend protection to gays and lesbians. When the House of Assembly amended the human rights code in December, it prohibited discrimination against gays in areas such as employment, housing, literature, and access to establishments and services. However, some pension plans were excluded from the legislation to conform with the federal Income Tax Act, which continues to define a spouse as a person of the opposite sex.

The problems continued at Davis Inlet in 1997. The Innu community had attracted national attention four years earlier when a group of youths was discovered high and suicidal in a freezing shack after sniffing gasoline and solvents. Despite treatment and community programs to help control the problem, many of the young people returned to the isolated community from treatment and detention centres to find their parents of little help – many parents themselves had turned to substance abuse to deal with unemployment and hopelessness, leaving the children to fend for themselves. On New Year's Day, seventeen young people in the community destroyed the school and were arrested by the RCMP. The federal and Newfoundland governments had reached an agreement in July 1996 to relocate the community to a better inland site, but there do not seem to be easy solutions to the problems that confront the isolated Native community.

Even with its economic problems, particularly in the fishery, and its embarrassingly high rate of unemployment, the province of Newfoundland and Labrador celebrated 500 years of history in 1997. The province remains proud and looks confidently forward. The future looks bright for those parts of the province that do not depend on cod and other groundfish that so excited John Cabot and his Bristol backers five centuries ago. The future now lies with other species of fish and with those other promising resources that the Grand Banks has to offer – oil and gas.

Yukon and the Northwest Territories   JAMES B. LAWSON

The territories in Confederation and the world

Territorial decentralization, devolution, and aboriginal land settlements had been interlocked forces in the North over decades of negotiations. In 1997, while Yukon politics were dominated by a new government and the closure of its leading mine, NWT politics were dominated by pending division and the maturation of a new diamond sector.

The Yukon government had promised in 1996 to assume more province-like powers from Ottawa and to complete final aboriginal land settlements. Both goals were at the centre of NWT politics. For its part, Ottawa maintained the controversial trend of cuts to First Nations and the transfer-dependent territories, while devolving authority to them. In February, it offered to devolve oil and gas powers to the Yukon. On 5 December, it announced plans to negotiate the transfer of aboriginal health care to local Inuit groups.

Both territories won intervenor status in court cases on Quebec's constitutional rights and on federal gun control legislation, principally because of the impact of these issues on aboriginal rights. On 1 October, the NWT Legislature and cabinet established a special committee on national unity, and on 2 December, passed a resolution, demanding formal territorial and aboriginal participation at any future constitutional talks. In April, the CBC reported on a controversial 1996 Canada-U.S. deal, in which $100 million in U.S. military equipment purchases compensated Canada for toxic waste clean-up costs at former northern NORAD radar bases. The Canadian government defended the controversial deal. The Yukon government worked towards binational repairs to the Alaska Highway, and continued protection of the cross-border Porcupine caribou herd along the oil-rich Arctic shore.

Key new figures entered the federal scene. In June, Jane Stewart became Minister for Indian Affairs and Northern Development. In September, the Inuit Tapirisat elected Okalik Eegesiak to a three-year presidential term. In the June federal elections, newcomer Nancy Karetak-Lindell beat Okalik Eegeesiak (PC), keeping Nunavut for the Liberals, and Louise Hardy retained Yukon for the NDP. In the Western Arctic, federal secretary of state Ethel Blondin-Andrew (Liberal) won again.

World resource markets were crucial to the economies of both territories. London gold dropped to $457.84 an ounce, and lead dropped 17 per cent to 87 cents/kg. Silver was also off (−1.1 per cent), but by less. Zinc rose 29 per cent to $1.82 per kg, and copper held its own. Finally, improved fur sales in both territories coincided with a controversial European Union decision on 22 July to continue Canadian fur imports. In return, Canada agreed to phase out steel-jawed leghold traps. But these world trends were not perfect indicators of territorial performance. First, there was the new role of NWT diamonds. But also, gold production in Yukon actually rose nearly 28 per cent to $98.2 million, against the price trends. Natural gas production declines were offset by price increases for a near-20 per cent sales rise. And as in NWT, Yukon mining exploration advanced, reaching a ten-year high at $57.9 million.

Finally, the federal presence was evident in the reregulation of telecommunications. This sector was critical to territorial plans for decentralization, devolution, and distance education. In presentations to the CRTC in early April, Northwestel proposed increased basic residential and commercial rates, 35 per cent and 14 per cent respectively, to offset its long-distance costs. This provoked considerable protest. In May, the CRTC ordered competition in these services.

Yukon

In 1997, the Yukon population rose to 33,519, growing much more slowly than in 1996. GDP for 1997 measured $944.1 million ($1992), down 9.4 per cent. These were linked to the December 1996 closure of the Anvil Range lead-zinc mine at Faro. This was the territory's largest, accounting for almost 20 per cent of Yukon GDP, and remained closed most of the year. Amid entrenched left-right animosities in the legislature about how to handle this crisis, the third-party Liberals revitalized their leadership.

Yukon: Economy

Silver, lead, and zinc production plummeted in 1997, halving total metal production to $200.6 million. Unemployment reached 13.4 per cent, a level not seen since 1993. Employment Insurance claims and payments rose to 2,428 (+12.9 per cent) and $28.3 million (+11 per cent). Capital spending rose 3 per cent, but at $208 million remained low, and repair spending fell 11 per cent to $79 million. Electricity production was off nearly 25 per cent; domestic petroleum product sales, by 17.3 per cent. Restaurant receipts, $28.5 million, were in decline. Retail sales grew more slowly; wholesale sales were flat. The few personal bankruptcies rose sharply (from 27 in 1996 to 37), and bankruptcies as a whole were more debt-laden. Average weekly earnings in construction, transportation, and utilities all sank. Vehicle registrations also declined about 8 per cent, and Yukoners travelled abroad less. But outside travellers were more numerous, especially other North Americans. Air travel in and out of the Whitehorse Airport was up. Air Canada affiliate NWT Air was sold to its major competitor, reducing competition.

But not all economic indicators were down. Yukon experienced rising but still modest inflation (2.3 per cent in Whitehorse) and lowering interest rates (7.07 per cent for five-year mortgages). Median rents in Whitehorse were stable, and vacancies a historically moderate 7.2 per cent. Whitehorse conducted almost $89 million of real estate business; the whole territory, $111 million. The capital's building permits came to 884, or $30 million. New residential permits were few (131) – eighty-eight commercial permits came to $7.4 million, and forty institutional permits to $4.1 million – but were worth some $18.1 million. Retail sales still rose to $309.6 million, with vehicle sales leading; overall average weekly earnings rose to $706.74 from $695.14.

In the Faro closure, world lead prices played a key role, down 17 per cent from 1996 highs. Rising public administration jobs, and good or indifferent news in other sectors, probably explained some of the moderating figures. Public administrators came second in weekly earnings ($813.36, or +1.7 per cent); at 43 per cent of the workforce, their numbers grew 6 per cent. Even relatively weak pay for the trade sector (only $512.71 a week) grew 3.6 per cent. Service jobs (11,742) outstripped those in goods production (2,192), and the remaining goods workers retained high and stable weekly earnings ($944.67). Municipal (368) and territorial (3,208) public services grew 16.5 per cent apiece. Total public sector payrolls increased more slowly than their sheer numbers, to $248.8 million (+3.5 per cent); but again, territorial and municipal gains led the way. In renewable resources, the strong upward secular trend in timber production, checked in 1996–7, grew again in 1997–8. Fur sales were still half those of the late 1980s, but rallied to half a million dollars.

Yukon: Government policy and politics

This was the first full year of NDP administration, and of more government activism. With Ottawa, the government was committed to further devolution; but it had also highlighted its domestic priorities with cabinet commissions for forest management, preferential local hiring, energy, and development assessment. The philosophical transition from a conservative to a social-democratic governing party posed potential staffing problems, most controversially in numerous arm's-length boards and commissions like the land-claims secretariat. Yukon's Workers' Compensation Health and Safety Board changed both the board chair and president by August. The NDP also had set the stage for some payroll gains in December 1996, repealing the Public Sector Compensation Restraint Act.

The first session of the Twenty-ninth Territorial Legislature resumed on 24 March and ended on 13 May. On 2 April, debate resumed on the 1997–8 budget. A $10-million deficit was projected on a budget of $452.4 million. The accumulated surplus was drawn down by $10 million. Personal income taxes rose by 9 per cent. Electricity rates and provision had already been a major NDP concern, when the Faro collapse forced rates up 20 per cent. The government quickly promised rate relief. On 30 October, key Whitehorse generating facilities burned down, creating further complications. On 1 April, a five-year agreement reorganized the public Yukon Energy Corporation and Alberta Power Corporation's Yukon Electrical Company. The deal sold and reinvested some Yukon Energy assets, and enhanced its management role.

To respond to the economic problems, the government stressed its export development strategy, an oil and gas act, and funding for community development. In late December, it also increased the minimum wage to $7.20 an hour. By contrast, the Yukon Party stressed targeted capital spending, and in various ways questioned the government's integrity. In the spring, for instance, it pursued media allegations that a negotiator for the Yukon First Nations had taken confidential documents from a federal official during devolution talks. The accused negotiator had worked as a deputy minister and an NDP adviser.

The spring session also resolved a simmering dispute from the September general elections, in which New Democrat Robert Bruce and the Yukon Party's Esau Shafer had tied at sixty-eight votes in Vuntut Gwichin. Mr Bruce had been selected by a draw, and entered the Legislature as Speaker. On 24 February, after a court case, the election was voided and a by-election called, while Doug Livingston became Speaker. On 2 April, Mr Bruce beat Mr Shafer by 88–62, and resumed the Speaker's chair.*

In other elections, incumbent Whitehorse Mayor Kathy Watson won re-election on 16 October, against a solid challenge from former mayor Don Branigan. And in territorial politics, Pat Duncan succeeded mentor Ken Taylor as Liberal Party leader, winning by acclamation.

The fall sitting began on 30 October. In November, the government revealed that health-care costs would raise the budget to $476 million and the deficit to $22.6 million, further encroaching on the accumulated surplus. In mid-November, the Faro mine briefly reopened, after intense talks between government and industry and a $20-million infusion from Cominco Ltd. The fall sitting ended in a marathon session with a loaded agenda on 15 December; it ended in partisan rancour after 6:00 a.m. on 16 May.

Yukon: Aboriginal affairs and constitutional development

Two First Nations signed agreements in 1997, but no new agreements were reached. Devolution of province-like federal powers continued (see below), and talks on oil and gas transfers would continue into 1998. On 1 April, Yukon Department of Health and Social Services gained control over five more universal medical programs, phase two of a multiyear devolution. But federal health and social transfer cuts were disappointing devolution advocates. On 2 April, the legislature denounced the cuts. Amid this austerity, the Whitehorse General Hospital experienced staffing problems, and on 6 August, 130 workers

---

*In a surprising final twist, Mr Bruce admitted to a drinking problem in May after several days' absence. He began treatment in the fall.

went on strike over pay and compensation for lay-offs. Union negotiators were split over how to end the seventeen-day strike.

Yukon: Society

Substance abuse and youth crime were part of a panoply of important social problems in Yukon. On 2 April, the government and the RCMP announced a 1997 vision statement for policing, which emphasized community partnerships and public participation. That vision was tested by a string of youth crimes in the capital. Most were property crimes and burglaries, though in May, a teen-on-teen murder occurred. An August meeting drew 130 residents to discuss youth crime, and organizers strategized afterwards with members of the cabinet. The 1995 killing of Susan Klassen of Lake Laberge became a celebrated cause. Her husband Ralph's five-year manslaughter sentence in January was confirmed in December, but through the year provoked appeals, petitions, and protests. Questions also re-emerged about the funding of safety reforms at the Whitehorse Correctional Institute. In late December, the government assumed responsibility for the closing of a noted program at the Whitehorse Alcohol Treatment Centre. It also announced a promised homeless shelter. Two group homes were scrutinized, under criticism from opposition MLAs and aboriginal leaders.

Northwest Territories

NWT residents decreased marginally to about 67,300 during 1997. Alongside a net out-migration of about 920, natural increase remained high at 1,215. The birth rate was nearly double and the death rate almost half those of all Canadians. The NWT economy was generally healthier than the Yukon's, but significant exceptions and a harsh government budget complicated the pattern. These contrasting pressures intensified the lead up to territorial division in 1999.

NWT: Economy

Territorial GDP stood at $2.9 billion: a modest increase that contrasted with Yukon's decline. Corporate registries rose 4.7 per cent; prices were nearly stable. Above all, capital spending grew 61.6 per cent to $613 million. Spikes in private spending were especially strong, notably in mining, quarrying, and oil, construction, and real estate. Annual social assistance was down slightly, though monthly numbers continued a ten-year rise. In a workforce of twenty-five thousand, EI payments fell to $32.1 million for 1,503 recipients.

Retail trade was up to $507.5 million (+7.3 per cent); as in Yukon, vehicle sales led the way, but wholesale trade was also up, at $175.1 million (+13 per cent). Vehicle registration was also slightly higher. Restaurant receipts and especially other prepared food sales continued to increase, reaching nearly $27.9 million (+1 per cent) and $21.3 million (over 11 per cent). Average weekly earnings, like those in the Yukon, reflected high costs of living: $726, up marginally at 0.6 per cent. But in NWT, public administration earnings declined (to $799, or –2 per cent), along with finance, insurance, and real estate ($782, or –3.6 per cent). Generally, goods producers experienced income growth ($967, or +2.8 per cent); the service sector, income decline ($675, or –0.7 per cent).

New mineral potential, particularly in diamonds, was central to this relatively good news. Fewer exploration licenses were issued, but at $178.8 million, exploration was still nearly six times higher than it was earlier in the decade. In January, World Wildlife Fund Canada removed its last legal challenges to Canada's first diamond mine, the $750-million BHP project, and expressed its satisfaction with a strategy to protect nearby wildlife areas. On 25 September and again on 18 November, MLAs pressed Ottawa and Yellowknife to keep diamond benefits in the territory.

But all was not well economically. Petroleum product and electricity sales were down 11.4 per cent to 523.3 thousand m3, and 2.7 per cent to 816,061 MWh. Other private and public sector capital expenditures also fell, and repairs fell nearly one-quarter to $155 million. Manufacturing shipments declined sharply to $18.9 million (–44 per cent). Natural gas and zinc sales (shipments of nearly $309.7 million, or +26 per cent) kept mineral shipments up 1 per cent, at over $788 million. But gold, silver, and lead all declined, and virtually all shipment *volumes* were in decline. Moreover, mineral development was hardly problem-free. In October, Royal Oak Mines' Colomac property leaked tailings into a nearby lake, an accident that would provoke extensive investigations and charges.

Fossil fuel figures were mixed. In production, natural gas and crude oil were both off at 169.4 million m3 and 1.6 million m3 respectively. Pipeline movements rose to 1.67 million m3. In sales, however, crude petroleum was down to $235.5 million (–7.5 per cent), while natural gas was up to $10.1 million. Commercial renewable resource sales were relatively small, though socially and economically important, and their results were also mixed. Fur production and revenues in 1996–7 recovered from the mid-1990s, at $1.5 million and 46,801 total pelts. But at nearly 1,268 tonnes, fish landings for 1997–8 were at ten-year lows. In some respects, the government sought to stimulate the relatively small tourist sector. In July, for example, Parks Canada expanded its staff in three Nunavut national parks. But air traffic was generally at a six-year low at only 180.4 thousand arrivals and departures, and these figures also reflected the maturation of both the Nunavut process and diamond exploration.

NWT housing was a long-term policy problem, and typically was heavily subsidized and organized by government. In 1997, such investments fell to just under $57 million. Residential building permits were around half their 1996 levels in both the west and Nunavut ($6.8 million and $2.8 million respectively). In June, a government study pronounced housing in crisis. Some 4,000 new units were needed; over one-quarter of the residents were inadequatedly housed.

Building permit declines were slight in the west (to $35.1 million), and increases considerable in Nunavut (from $10.5 to $11.7 million). This was possible because of non-residential permit growth in both subregions, especially in the private sector ($28.4 million or +24 per cent, and nearly $9 million or +140 per cent). The importance of private building in Nunavut was more surprising, but it likely reflects the diamond boom, as well as the deliberate use of build and lease-back arrangements to provide a new government infrastructure. In March, Ottawa announced that the prestigious contracts to build the legislature in Iqaluit would be left to incoming Nunavut authorities. In July, the Nunavut Corporation received permission to construct three new government buildings there.

These special arrangements in Nunavut were intended to build-up locally owned Inuit business, but they were not without problems. They had the potential to divide the public and private Inuit leadership, which were closely intertwined. In September, the Baffin Regional Health Board denied the Inuit-owned Qikiqtaaluk Corporation the right to build and lease back Iqaluit's new hospital, citing the defence of public health care. In November, a similar internal divide led Isuma Productions to protest the tendering of $10 million in Inuktitut-language broadcasting.

This incident shows Nunavut business was not confined to construction work. Spin-offs from resource projects were increasingly common. And in Nunavut, plans for decentralization and domestic educational and job opportunities after division put broadcasting and telecommuni-

cations at the forefront. Ongoing work on a high-speed digital communications network met with numerous barriers.

NWT: Government policy and politics

The legislature resumed on 20 January, rising in early March. Finance
Minister John Todd delivered a painful $1.16-billion budget with no
new taxes and minor social spending and business aid initiatives. It cut
$100 million, hundreds of employees, and minimized public capital
spending. It intended a surplus of $8.9 million, and a reduced accumu-
lated deficit of $57 million. The Aurora Fund targeted immigrant
investors.

Mr Todd argued federal cuts were harming the NWT, but only a
tough budget would open Ottawa's ears. In October, a report would
warn that federal cuts also affected territorial division, and another $135
million was needed. The government had also argued that private sector
and community action would have to compensate for government cuts.
In related news, the GNWT founded a reform group to streamline the
regulatory burden. Other issues during the spring session included the
issue of gender representation in the new Nunavut Legislature, the
widely criticized Plan 2000 housing proposals, the compliance of the
legislature's parking lot with Yellowknife by-laws, and $325 million in
computer equipment for multilevel distance education in Nunavut.

Many objected to the budget, and NWT teachers had already rejected
wage cuts in December. Public servant discontent stemmed from labour
relations provisions in the 1995 Public Service Act amendments, and as
tensions grew in the public service, questions arose about the wisdom of
the amendments. In late August, in another costly labour issue, the
Supreme Court of Canada confirmed a Human Rights Commission
gender-bias ruling, leaving the GNWT liable to female employees for
tens of millions of dollars. Here, too, some MLAs called for a compromise arrangement to reduce the heavy costs. When Charles Dent, Minister of Education, formed a task force into educational funding, MLAs
protested, fearing more cuts.*

In May, the NWT Supreme Court confirmed Thebacha MLA Michael
Miltenberger's 1995 election, and in August, it ordered the fifty-eight
petitioners and Canada's chief electoral officer to share some of his court
costs. When the fifth session of the Thirteenth Legislative Assembly

---

*Special individual funding for NWT students had long reduced the North's high costs of travel,
accommodation, and board.

opened on 21 October, the cabinet faced regular review by the Assembly, during which the Aurora Fund came under particular question.

Finally, annual supply shipments from southern ports and resource export shipments were always both vital and lucrative, especially in Nunavut. When federal cuts to ice-breaking services threatened export lines, private firms offered their own subsidies in February. And when Kit Resources of Toronto announced it would develop the dormant Izok Lake copper/lead site, it depended on co-financing a deep-sea port in Bathurst Inlet.

Fuel resupply contracts in Keewatin were in open dispute in 1997. This contributed to the discomfort of interim Nunavut commissioner Jack Anawak, and to an NWT cabinet shuffle. Rankin Inlet lost its right to be the resupply base in January, and in November, cabinet moved instead to link several communities by pipeline. This angered area Inuit and the Nunavut Tunngavik Inc. Under personal criticism, Goo Arlooktoo, Minister for Public Works and Services, moved to postpone the decision. But on 5 December, Premier Don Morin reassigned him to Justice, and Jim Antoine assumed Public Works.

NWT: Aboriginal affairs and constitutional development

In 1999, the NWT would be divided into a western NWT and an eastern Nunavut. In 1997, preparations intensified. In April, two-term Liberal MP for Nunatsiaq, Jack Anawak, resigned to become Nunavut's interim commissioner. In June, he received his official orders and a $10-million transitional budget. On 10 November, future elections were turned over to territorial bodies. On 2 December, the legislature's clerk, David Hamilton, was named the future NWT's chief electoral officer.

In January, the GNWT responded to the Nunavut Implementation Committee's interim report revising constitutional structures, *Footprints 2*. While accepting some affirmative action for resident Inuit, the GNWT called for more guarantees for existing employees and future outside applicants. It also questioned Nunavut's plans to centralize health and education boards.

Long a goal of the Inuit-dominated east, division had been less popular in the west, and ethnic and regional tensions had delayed preparations there. On 14 October, the minister for transition planning in the west and the western caucus announced an action plan. Many Inuit saw vigorous affirmative action, decentralization, and training as core rationales for division. But many in the west worried about the likely impact of these changes on territorial public servants and on the west's future fiscal liability for severance packages. To allay these pressures, Mr Anawak assured public servants in July that they would be welcome.

Mr Anawak's appointment rankled some federal MPs, opposed to his support for federal gun control legislation. As interim commissioner, Inuit leaders criticized him more for poor oversight of their interests in Yellowknife, including supply and health-care controversies. In October, the Nunavut Tunngavik Inc.* even established its own shadow cabinet in the capital. Some observers saw this $100,000 move as incipient partisan politics, a potentially significant constitutional change. In December, Inuit leaders announced there would be a closed-door meeting with Mr Anawak in January.

Division, devolution, and aboriginal land settlements had combined over time to put novel institutions in place in the North. Many new resource management and government arrangements guaranteed a new and unique role for aboriginal people and traditions. Some of these provisions came under criticism in 1997. First, former GNWT employee Frances Widdowson and Albert Howard gained notoriety for an article questioning traditional aboriginal resource knowledge. Second, the complexity of these negotiations constantly impinged on mundane policy matters. For instance, Yellowknife area plans for two new arenas came up against Dene land claims in the area in late summer.

Third, proposals for institutionalized gender parity in Nunavut's Legislature were intended to reflect the key political role of Inuit women. In December 1996, the Nunavut Implementation Committee had recommended dual-member, dual-gender constituencies. This provoked much controversy, and the Legislature postponed a decision. On 7 March, the commissioner formed a three-member commission for public consultations. On 26 May, a referendum was also held. It showed 57 per cent opposed, but also a low 39 per cent turnout. On 18 July, the commission proposed three models: eleven dual-member districts, twenty single-member districts, and seventeen single-member ones. It recommended the third, a relatively new option, and on 8 October, MLAs agreed.

NWT: Society

Alcohol sales were down in both price and volume; reported crimes rose in 1997, but not to the highs of the early 1990s. As in the Yukon, interlocking social pathologies stood behind such figures, including

*Nunavut Tunngavik Inc. is a 'birthright corporation' responsible for much of the Inuit community assets won under the Nunavut final land settlement.

high rates of substance abuse, prostitution, and prior sexual abuse. Treatment and recreational facilities were common responses, especially for youth. For this reason, the government's proposed extension of liquor-store hours provoked protests. Inuvik in particular had emphasized alcohol control, and was angered by the closure of its alcohol treatment centre. Eventually, its protests won a reduced schedule. In June, it hosted a conference on aboriginal justice.

In Nunavut, the Baffin and Keewatin regional health boards were in severe difficulty, and in October, the GNWT health minister ordered a review. The Baffin leadership was reorganized over November. Proposals to reallocate health-board funding to such underserviced boards threatened to impinge on relatively well-funded western boards. After years of general cuts, western MLAs called for a stay of major transfers. By late September, the GNWT announced some $4 million for the poorest boards.

Obituaries

ADDY, GEORGE (4 August, age 81): former judge who sat on the Federal Court of Canada and the Supreme Court of Ontario.

ADDY, GEORGE (4 August, age 81): former judge who sat on the Federal Court of Canada and the Supreme Court of Ontario.

BAINS, HARDIAL (24 August, age 58): national leader of the Communist Party of Canada (Marxist-Leninist).

BAILLARGEON-CÔTÉ, HÉLÈNE (25 September, age 81): host of the popular CBC children's television show *Chez Hélène* from 1959 to 1973, member of the Order of Canada.

BELANGER, MICHEL (1 December, age 68): former head of the National Bank, prominent federalist voice in Quebec politics.

BOWES, JIM (12 March, age 73): publisher, co-founder of Bowes Publishers Ltd.

BRAGG, ROSS (31 March, age 40): former Nova Scotia cabinet minister, forced by failing health to give up his seat in Premier John Savage's government in 1995.

BRYCE, ROBERT (30 July, age 87): former clerk of the Privy Council who held a variety of senior posts in the federal bureaucracy before serving as executive director of the International Monetary Fund.

COLE, JACK (22 January, age late-70s): founder of Coles Books and the World's Biggest Bookstore.

COLLISTER, RON (6 June, age 69): noted print and electronic journalist, television talk-show host, recipient of the Order of Canada.

COOKE, JACK KENT (6 April, age 84): tycoon who made his fortune in real estate and print and electronic media, owner of several professional sports franchises in the United States.

DION, LEON (20 August, age 74): political scientist, constitutional expert who served as adviser to then Quebec premier Robert Bourassa

DUMONT, FERNAND (1 May, age 69): sociologist, a central figure in Quebec's Quiet Revolution, deputy minister of cultural development in first Parti Québécois government, helped draft Bill 101.

FERGUSSON, MURIEL M. (11 April, age 97): Liberal senator, appointed first woman Speaker of the Senate in 1972, officer of the Order of Canada.

FRASER, ALISTAIR (1 September, age 74): former clerk of the House of Commons.

FRASER, MURRAY (12 March, age 59): academic, former president of the University of Calgary.

GALE, GEORGE ALEXANDER (25 July, age 91): former chief justice of Ontario, served as vice-chair of the Ontario Law Reform Commission, companion of the Order of Canada.

GILMOUR, CLYDE (7 November, age 85): popular radio personality and host of CBC Radio's *Gilmour's Albums*.

GOODMAN, ALLAN (9 August, age 76): former judge of the Ontario Court of Appeal.

GOODRIDGE, NOEL (12 December, age 67): former Newfoundland chief justice.

GROSSMAN, LARRY (22 June, age 53): former leader of the Ontario Conservative Party, served in a variety of cabinet posts in the government of Bill Davis, member of the Order of Ontario.

HARDY, HAGOOD (1 January, age 59): musician, winner of three Junos, awarded the Order of Canada.

HORNER, HUGH (25 March, age 72): doctor, former Conservative MP, later held several provincial cabinet posts and served as deputy premier in Alberta.

IANNI, RON (6 September, age 62): president of the University of Windsor, former vice-president of the Canadian Civil Liberties Association, member of the Order of Canada.

JORDAN, PAT (25 February, age 66): former British Columbia cabinet minister in the Social Credit governments of W.A.C. Bennett and Bill Bennett.

JOUBIN, FRANCIS (25 February, age 85): geologist who discovered one of the world's largest uranium deposits, member of the Order of Canada and the Order of Ontario.

KELLAND, JIM (25 February, age 63): former Newfoundland environment minister in the Liberal government of Clyde Wells.

KNEBLI, JOHN (4 March, age 93): businessman, maker of custom skates for leading Canadian figure skaters.

KNOWLES, STANLEY (7 June, age 88): parliamentarian, prominent member of the Co-operative Commonwealth Federation and the New Democratic Party, member of the Privy Council and the Order of Canada.

LANG, DANIEL (28 November, age 78): former Liberal senator who chose to sit as an Independent before his retirement in 1994.

MACDONALD, JOHN M. (20 June, age 91): Conservative senator appointed by John Diefenbaker in 1960, last senator to be appointed for life.

MALOUF, ALBERT (8 April, age 80): judge, headed the inquiry into Montreal's 1976 Olympics cost overruns.

MCCAIN, FRED (12 October, age 79): New Brunswick politician whose career in the provincial legislature was followed by sixteen years in the House of Commons.

MCCAIN, PETER (4 February, age 39): president of McCain Foods International.

NEMETZ, NATHAN (21 October, age 84): former British Columbia chief justice, former chancellor of the University of British Columbia.

NEWMAN, SIDNEY (30 October, age 80): television producer whose career included work for the CBC and the National Film Board, officer of the Order of Canada.

PELADEAU, PIERRE (24 December, age 72): publisher, founder of Quebecor Inc., committed Quebec separatist.

PELLETIER, GERARD (22 June, age 78): secretary of state and communications minister in the Liberal government of Pierre Trudeau, served as Canada's ambassador to France from 1975 to 1980.

PICKERSGILL, JACK (14 November, age 92): former clerk of the Privy Council, elected to the Commons in 1953, held a variety of cabinet posts in the Liberal governments of Louis St Laurent and Lester Pearson.

RIZZUTO, PIETRO (3 August, age 63): senator, leading Liberal Party organizer.

SCRIVENER, MARGARET (11 September, age 75): Ontario cabinet minister in the provincial government of Bill Davis.

SOLOMON, ART (29 June, age 83): Native spiritual leader, former director of the Union of Ontario Indians, recipient of the National Aboriginal Achievement Award.

SOPINKA, JOHN (24 November, age 64): justice of the Supreme Court of Canada who once played in the Canadian Football League.

STRINGER, ALF (12 March, age 75): pioneer of Canada's helicopter industry.

TAYLOR, CHARLES (8 July, age 62): author, journalist who served in a number of foreign correspondent posts for *The Globe and Mail*, prominent on the Canadian horse racing scene through his family's Windfields Farm.

THOMPSON, ROBERT (16 November, age 83): former national leader of the Social Credit Party who later joined the Conservatives.

TWINN, WALTER (30 October, age 63): controversial Conservative senator, former chief of the Sawridge Cree Band.

ZEIDLER, MARGARET (19 May, age 81): businesswoman, ran Zeidler Forest Industries, prominent supporter of the arts in Edmonton, member of the Order of Canada.

ZIMMERMAN, PAUL (6 August, age 77): former publishing executive who made his career at *Reader's Digest* and Torstar Corporation.

Index of names

Adams, Tom: NB Power problems 151
Adams, Duane: and deputy minister shuffle (Saskatchewan) 190
Addy, George: death of 243
Albright, Madeleine: on NATO enlargement 75
Alcock, Reg: and Manitoba Liberal leadership of Hasselfield 159
Alexander, Les: and Edmonton Oilers 220
Alfred, Jean: and BQ leadership race 17
Allmond, Warren: becomes head of International Centre for Human Rights and Development 16
Alyward, Joan Marie: cabinet position of (Newfoundland) 228
Alyward, Kevin: cabinet position of (Newfoundland) 228
Anawak, Jack: appointment of as commissioner (Nunavut) 16, 240–1; and fuel resupply contracts (NWT) 240
Anders, Rob: nomination of as Reform candidate 217
Anderson, David: cabinet appointment of 29, 174, 228; and Canadian Airlines 170; and Clark's threat to close torpedo test range 167; and cod quota 43; and food fishery ban (Newfoundland) 225; and Pacific salmon treaty xxii, 70; and seal hunt (Newfoundland) 227; on TAGS program xxviii, 226
Anderson, John: and Somalia inquiry 89
Annan, Kofi: and United Nations reform 73
Antoine, Jim: cabinet position of (NWT) 240
Arbour, Louise: and Supreme Court 34

Arlooktoo, Goo: and fuel resupply contracts (NWT) 240
Armstrong, Barry: and Somalia inquiry 90–1
Arone, Shidane: and Somalia inquiry xvi, 49, 87, 89–90
Aung San Suu Kyi: and house arrest of 79
Axworthy, Lloyd: and anti-personnel land-mines ban xxvi, 6, 83; cabinet appointment of 28; development-aid budget 80–1; foreign policy of 67–9; and Haitian mission 72; on Israeli agents and Canadian travel documents xxviii; meeting with Castro xiii; nomination of for Nobel Peace Prize 7, 83; and Pacific salmon treaty 64; visit of to Cuba 71; visit of to India 80

Baillargeon-Côté, Hélène: death of 243
Bains, Hardial: death of 243
Baker, George: re-election of in Newfoundland 228
Barber, John 112
Baril, Maurice: named CDS xxvi, 93; on problems in the CF 96; and scandal at Bosnia's Bakovici Hospital 94; and UN's Rwanda mission 81
Barrett, Pam: election campaign (Alberta) 204, 207; role of as NDP critic 216; wins seat in election (Alberta) 209
Barry, Jane: police services (New Brunswick) 153; and video gambling issues 147
Barry, Leo: and educational reform (Newfoundland) 229
Barshefsky, Charlene: on split-run magazines 74

Barth, Marisa Ferretti: Senate appointment of 33

Bastarache, Michel: appointment of to Supreme Court xxvii, 34

Bedard, André: and influence-peddling charge against Corbeil 53

Bélanger, Michel: death of 123, 243

Bell, Roger Charles: sentencing of 187

Belzile, Charles: report of on military police services 85

Beno, Ernest: and Somalia inquiry 90n, 92

Bercuson, David: report of on Canadian Forces 84

Bernardo, Paul 121; charges against former lawyers of xiii

Bernier, Gilles: does not seek re-election 21

Berntson, Eric: and allegations of misuse of caucus funds 53; resignation of xiii

Bertrand, Guy: referendum/sovereignty issues 129; Supreme Court reference 37–8, 56–7

Bethel, Judy: loses seat in election 218

Betkowski, Nancy. See MacBeth, Nancy

Bettney, Julie: cabinet position of (Newfoundland) 228

Bhaduria, Jag: and election campaign 22

Binns, Pat: announces compensation to seasonal workers xxx; Confederation Bridge opening 186; legislative session of 183–4; and patronage issue 184

Bird, J.W. Bud: report of on military police services 85

Biron, Rodrique: and BQ leadership race 17, 130–1

Bissonnette, Lise 128

Bjornerud, Bob: joins Saskatchewan Party 192

Black, Pat: cabinet appointment of (Alberta) 210

Black, Ralph: resignation of as auditor general (New Brunswick) 146–7

Blanchard, Edmund: budget of 156; and revenue from video gambling 147

Blondin-Andrew, Ethel: cabinet appointment of 30; re-election of 232

Borotsik, Rick: wins seat in election 159

Bouchard, Lucien: accuses McKenna of interference in Quebec's affairs 58; cabinet shuffle of (Quebec) 130; Calgary Declaration and 37, 135; campaign and referendum/sovereignty issue 131; challenges of 123; on closing of Hôpital Montfort (Ontario) 108–9; on federal-provincial transfers 62; and first ministers' meeting 59–60; and psychiatric assessment by Rakoff xxv, 128; referendum/sovereignty issues xxii, xxxii, 4, 38, 59–60; on social union agreement 32; and support of France for Quebec xxvii; and 'Team Canada' trade mission 54, 79

Boudreau, Bernie: and Nova Scotia Liberal leadership race 138

Boudria, Don: cabinet appointment of 29

Bowes, Jim: death of 243

Boyle, Jean: and Somalia inquiry 50, 88, 92

Bragg, Ross: death of 243

Branigan, Don: loses election for mayor of Whitehorse 235

Branscombe, Nancy: campaign debates 23

Brassard, Jacques: on Calgary Declaration 59; on partition of Quebec 130; and Supreme Court reference 127

Breault, Ann: municipal amalgamation issue (New Brunswick) 152

Broadbent, Ed 16

Broderick, Leo: loses PEI by-election 183

Bronconnier, Dave: nomination of as Liberal candidate 217

Brown, Jan: does not seek Reform re-election 19; joins PC Party 21; loses election 21

Brown, Richard: wins PEI by-election 183

Bruce, Robert: and election tie in Vuntut Gwichin (Yukon) 235

Brun, Ronald: education and francophone rights 151

Bruseker, Frank: and Alberta Liberal leadership race 216; loses seat in election (Alberta) 208

Bryce, Robert: death of 243

Burge, Mickey: political discrimination battle of 184

Butts, May Alice: Senate appointment of 33

Byrne, Gerry: re-election of in Newfoundland 228

Cairns, Alan: Plan C 201

Callbeck, Catherine: Senate appointment of 33, 185

Calvert, Lorne: cabinet position of (Saskatchewan) 190

Cameron, Donald: and Westray Mine xxxi

Campbell, Douglas: and Somalia inquiry 90n

Campbell, Gordon: and BC by-election 175; on Petter's economic projections 177

Campbell, Kim: and Somalia inquiry 87, 89

Caplan, Elinor: bypassed for cabinet 28; runs for election 16

Carney, Pat: and BC secession threat xxvii; on BC separatist option 172–3; on Wilson Report 172

Caron, André: death of 18

Caron, Jocelyne: cabinet appointment of (Quebec) 130

Castro, Fidel: meeting with Axworthy in Cuba xiii, 71

Cauchon, Martin: cabinet appointment of 30

Chalifoux, Thelma: Senate appointment of xxx, 33

Chan, Raymond: cabinet appointment of 30; cabinet position of 174

Charest, Jean: on Calgary Declaration 59; on election call 14; election campaign 21, 25, 174; endorsement of by Filmon 159; endorsement of by Klein 217; and federal election issues in Atlantic provinces 228; leader debates 23; as leader of PC Party 13, 20, 131; and united-right alternative 27, 101; wins election debate 3

Cheverie, Wayne: resignation of (PEI) 183

Chirac, Jacques: on support of France for Quebec xxvii

Chisolm, Robert: on writing off loans and taxes 143

Chrétien, Jean: Airbus affair 52; announces scholarship fund for post-secondary students xxvii; anti-personnel land-mines ban and 82; cabinet shuffle of 28; Calgary Declaration and 35–6, 59; calls election 3, 13–15, 126; and Clinton xxiii; Clinton and anti-personnel land-mines ban xxii; on closing of Hôpital Montfort (Ontario) 108; declines to meet with aboriginal leaders xix; election campaign 22, 60–1, 65, 174; on federalism 55; first ministers' conference 31; on halt to Somalia inquiry 88; and helicopter purchase 45; leader debates 23; on NATO enlargement 76; and Pacific salmon treaty 64; and pepper spray use by RCMP at APEC 169; popularity of 13; protestors and Hibernia christening 223; Red River flooding and election call 5, 14, 161; re-election of 3; referendum/sovereignty issues xxxi, 38; and report of Somalia inquiry 51; and retirement rumours xxix, 27; selection of women as Liberal candidates xvi, 16; Senate appointments of xxx, 32–3, 185; and Somalia inquiry 92–3; Supreme Court appointment of 34; and Supreme Court reference 125–6; 'Team Canada' trade mission 40, 78–9; and unilateral secession issue 57; on U.S. Cuban policy 71; on U.S. withholding of UN dues xviii

Clancy, Mary: appointment of as provincial representative in Boston 138; loses seat in election 25

Clark, Bob: election campaign (Alberta) 207; and lobbyists' registration bill 214

Clark, Glen: on BC by-election 175; Calgary Declaration and 36; and Canadian Airlines 170; and child poverty issue 62; and federal-provincial relations 165, 169, 170; and 'hail and stow' laws 167; on national unity 172; and Pacific salmon treaty xxiii, xxvi, 6, 44–5, 64, 69–71, 166; threat of to close torpedo test range at Nanoose Bay xxiii, xxiv–xxv, 167–8; on tobacco companies and health-care costs xxii

Clark, Joe: on Plan B 57

Clegg, Glen: loses election for Speaker (Alberta) 213–14

Clements, Gilbert: reads PEI Throne Speech 183

Cline, Eric: cabinet position of (Saskatchewan) 190

Clinton, Bill: anti-personnel land-mines ban and 82; and Canada's Cuban policy 71; and Chrétien's remarks about xxiii; Clark's birthday and 168–9; and nuclear-arms control 83–4; Russia and G7 participation 75–6

Cole, David: on Ontario justice system 120

Cole, Jack: death of 243

Collenette, David: cabinet appointment of 28

Colley, Sue: on health-care job losses (Ontario) 110

Collister, Ron: death of 243

Cooke, David: co-chair of Ontario Education Improvement Commission 102

Cooke, Jack Kent: death of 243

Cools, Anne: child-support payments issue 43

Copps, Sheila: cabinet appointment of 29; on split-run magazines 74

Corbeil, Pierre: influence-peddling charge against xxviii, 52–3

Cotton, Robert L.: land at Brudenell (in trust) 185

Cox, Wendell: on amalgamation 112

Coyne, Andrew 70

Culpeper, Roy 78

Dallaire, Romeo: and UN's Rwanda mission 81

Daquay, Louise: role of as Manitoba Speaker and MTS 163

Day, Stockwell: announces legislature will sit for one session per year xxiii; budget of (Alberta) 214; and budget surplus (Alberta) 210–11; cabinet appointment of (Alberta) 209; and education bill 215

De Bever, Leo: on decline of BC's economy 177

de Chastelain, John: and Somalia inquiry 50, 92

DeJong, Simon: resignation of 195

Dent, Charles: and educational funding (NWT) 239

Desautels, Denis: auditor general's reports of 34–5, 226; health care and aboriginal population 35; on immigration process 35; on TAGS program 35, 226; and toxic waste 35

Desbarats, Peter 94

de Ste-Croix, Carolle: on health-care cuts 150

DeVillers, Paul: on Wilson Report 172–3

Dhaliwal, Herb: cabinet appointment of 29, 174

Dicks, Paul: budget of (Newfoundland) 221

Dickson, Brian: report of on military police services 85

Dickson, Gary: re-election of in Alberta 208

Dingwall, David: election campaign 65, 217; loses seat in election 25, 138; on privatization of health care in Alberta xx; and tobacco company sponsorships 45

Dinning, Jim: budget of (Alberta) xiv, 205, 214

Dion, Leon: death of 243

Dion, Stéphane: blasts Bouchard over issue of Quebec's borders 58; cabinet appointment of 28; referendum/sovereignty issues 127, 129; and Supreme Court reference 125–6

Dixon, John: and Somalia inquiry 89

Doer, Gary: Manitoba NDP leadership of 162

Dosanjh, Ujjal: and BC recall legislation 176; and closing of courthouses (BC) xiv

Doucet, Albert: NB Power problems 150–1; resignation of from cabinet (New Brunswick) 150–1

Doucet, Michel: education and francophone rights 151

Douglas, John: appointment of as judge (PEI) 185

Doyle, Norm: wins seat in election 228

Draude, June: joins Saskatchewan Party 192

Duceppe, Gilles: and election campaign 22, 24; as leader of BQ 3, 12; questions Supreme Court appointment 34; and role of BQ 27; and Supreme Court reference 126, 127; wins BQ leadership race xvii, 17–18, 130–1

Duhaime, Yves: and BQ leadership race 17, 130–1; runs for election 18

Duhamel, Ronald J.: cabinet appointment of 30

Dumont, Fernand: death of 243

Duncan, Pat: acclamation of as Liberal leader (Yukon) 235

Easter, Wayne: wins seat in election 183

Edmondson, Warren: and CUPW labour problems 46

Eegesiak, Okalik: election of as president Inuit Tapirisat 232; loses federal election 232

Eggleton, Art: announces CF will remain in Bosnia for six months xxxi; cabinet appointment of 29, 67, 85–6; and Clark's threat to close torpedo test range 167; on free trade 74; on Helms-Burton law (U.S.) 72; and Somalia inquiry xxviii, 51, 92–3

Elizabeth II: on celebration of 500th anniversary of Cabot's landing 221

Elzinga, Peter: appointment of as successor to Love 213

English, John: pulls out of campaign 16

Estey, Willard: and Canadian Wheat Board 47; and Somalia inquiry 51

Eves, Ernie: budget of (Ontario) 121; on municipal taxes (Ontario) 115

Fagan, Tina: on Newfoundland seal hunt 227

Fairweather, Bob: on decline of BC's economy 178

Farrell-Collins, Gary: on BC by-election 175–6

Favel, Blaine: wins re-election as grand chief of FSIN 201–2

Fergusson, Muriel M.: death of 244

Fiengerwald, Fraser: Airbus affair 52

Filmon, Gary: leadership of (Manitoba) 158–9; and Red River flooding 161

Fontaine, Phil: on national unity discussions xxvi; sworn in as AFN national chief xxiv; wins leadership of AFN 201

Foote, Judy: cabinet position of (Newfoundland) 228

Forsyth, Heather: election campaign (Alberta) 205

Fowler, Robert: and Somalia inquiry 89

Frame, Clifford: Westray Mine inquiry and 136

Fraser, Alistair: death of 244

Fraser, Murray: death of 244

Frenette, Ray: leadership change in New Brunswick 153, 156

Friesen, Jean: and Manitoba NDP leadership 162

Fry, Hedy: cabinet appointment of 30; cabinet position of 174

Furey, Chuck: cabinet position of (Newfoundland) 228

Gagliano, Alfonso: cabinet appointment of 29; and CUPW labour problems 46; on funding arrangements with provinces 61

Gale, George Alexander: death of 244

Galganov, Howard: announces dissolution of Quebec Political Action Committee xi

Galloway, Roger: and bill to ban negative option billing 14–15; loses election for Speaker 30

Gantefoer, Rod: joins Saskatchewan Party 192

Gauthier, Michel: resignation of as BQ leader 17, 130

George, Dudley: calls for public inquiry into shooting of xxiii; OPP officer found guilty in death of xix

Gerrard, Jon: loses seat in election 25

Gibbons, Rex: resignation of 228–9

Giesbrecht, Helmut: and BC recall legislation 176

Gillespie, Alisdar: cabinet appointment of 28

Gillis, Bill: budget of (Nova Scotia) 139; budget surplus projection of (Nova Scotia) xix; and casino in Halifax 139

Gilmour, Clyde: death of 244
Godfrey, John: on Helms-Burton law
 (U.S.) 72; and psychiatric assessment
 of Bouchard 128
Godin, Yvon: wins seat in election 154
Goldbloom, Victor: education and fran-
 cophone rights 151
Goldring, Peter: wins seat in election 218
Goodale, Ralph: approval of Terra Nova
 project by 224; cabinet appointment of
 29, 195; Canadian Wheat Board and
 46–7; critique of Saskatchewan Party
 by 193
Goodman, Allan: death of 244
Goodridge, Noel: death of 244
Graham, Alasdair: cabinet appointment
 of 29
Granatstein, J.L.: report of on Canadian
 Forces 84
Gray, Herb: Airbus affair 52; cabinet
 appointment of 29
Greenspan, Ed: and sex-related charges
 against Regan 137
Grey, Deborah: wins seat in election 218
Grossman, Larry: death of 244
Grubel, Herb: does not seek Reform re-
 election 19

Haley, Carol: and education bill 215
Hall, Barbara: loses Toronto mayoralty
 race 115
Hamilton, David: as chief electoral
 officer (NWT) 240
Hamm, John: on Nova Scotia budget
 139–40
Hancock, Dave: cabinet appointment of
 (Alberta) 210
Hardy, Hagood: death of 244
Hardy, Louise: re-election of 232
Harnick, Charles: announces compensa-
 tion to Morin xiii; and treatment of
 Dionne quintuplets xxxi
Harper, Ed: does not seek Reform re-
 election 19
Harper, Stephen: and National Citizens'
 Coalition xii, 217; resignation of xii,
 18–19
Harris, Mike: cabinet shuffle of (Ontario)
 104; calls Ontario by-elections 101;

and education cuts (Ontario) 105; on
 health-care job losses (Ontario) 110;
 and national unity issue 58; public sector restructuring of 99; and united-right
 alternative 27, 101
Harron, Martha: of Ontario Parent Council 103
Hasselfield, Ginny: alienates Manitoba
 Liberal caucus 159–60; and Manitoba
 leadership review 159–60
Haswell, Geoff: and Somalia inquiry xii,
 89
Hatfield, Richard 146
Havelock, Jon: and Alberta legislature
 214; cabinet appointment of (Alberta)
 210
Haverstock, Lynda: quits Saskatchewan
 Liberal Party and sits as an indepen-
 dent 190; resignation of as
 Saskatchewan Liberal leader 191
Hellyer, Paul: and Canadian Action Party
 xii, 21
Hogg, Gordon: wins BC by-election
 175
Holland, Bruce: and Nova Scotia Liberal
 leadership race 138
Holm, John: on oil and gas sector regula-
 tion 142
Homolka, Karla 121; testimony of and
 video tapes xiii
Horner, Hugh: death of 244
House, Maxwell: appointment of as lieu-
 tenant-governor (Newfoundland) 229
Howard, Albert: and aboriginal land set-
 tlements 241
Hurd, Wilf: resignation of 175

Ianni, Ron: death of 244
Ignace, William Jones (Wolverine):
 found guilty of mischief in Gustafsen
 Lake stand-off xx–xxi
Irwin, Ron: does not seek Liberal re-
 election 16

Jessop, Christine xiii
Johnson, Daniel: on Calgary Declaration
 132
Johnson, David: replaces Snobelen as
 Ontario health minister 104

Johnson, Halvar: cabinet appointment of (Alberta) 209

Joli-Coeur, André: amicus curiae for absent Quebec government 58; and Supreme Court reference 37, 126, 127

Jolivet, Jean-Pierre: cabinet appointment of (Quebec) 130

Jordan, Pat: death of 244

Joubin, Francis: death of 244

Joyal, Serge: Senate appointment of xxx, 33

Jule, Arlene: quits Saskatchewan Liberal Party and sits as an independent 190

Kane, Lorie: named Canadian Press Athlete of the year 187

Karetak-Lindell, Nancy: wins seat in election 232

Kelland, Jim: death of 244

Kellough, Gail: on bail program (Ontario) 119

Kerr, John: co-chair of BC Unity Panel 172

Kidder, Margot: on Newfoundland seal hunt 227

Kilgour, David: cabinet appointment of 30; re-election of 218

King, Russell: and Blue Cross contract 147–8; health-care cuts 149–50

Kingsley, Jean-Pierre: Red River flooding and election call 14, 161

Klassen, John: on human-rights issues at APEC 79–80

Klassen, Susan: murder of 236

Klaus, Vaclav: visit of to Ottawa 76

Klein, Ralph: absences of from legislature 216; cabinet shuffle of 209–10; Calgary Declaration and 36; and education bill 215; election campaign (Alberta) 204–5, 206, 207; election campaign (federal) 65, 217; on Kyoto 31–2; and Multi-Corp scandal 208; re-election of in Alberta 5, 208; role of in federal politics 213; support of for elected Senate 33

Knebli, John: death of 244

Knowles, Stanley: death of 53, 244

Kowalski, Gary: resignation of from Manitoba Liberal caucus 159; wins election for Speaker (Alberta) 213–14

Krawetz, Ken: appointment of as leader of Saskatchewan Liberal Party 191; defection of from Liberal Party to Saskatchewan Party 192; Saskatchewan Party leadership of 192

Krever, Horace: tainted blood report of 47–9

Labbe, Serge: and Somalia inquiry 90

Lacey, Veronica: performance goals of and Ontario education budget 105

La Forest, Gerard: resignation of from Supreme Court 33–4, 57

Lalonde, Francine: and BQ leadership race 17

Lamarche, Claire: as moderator of French-language debate 23

Lamer, Antonio: and Supreme Court reference 57, 126–7

Lamoureux, Kevin: resignation of from Manitoba Liberal caucus 159–60

Land, Gerald: and educational reform (Newfoundland) 229–30

Landry, Bernard: budget of (Quebec) 133; Dion and issue of Quebec's boundaries 58; referendum/sovereignty issues 127

Lang, Daniel: death of 245

Langdon, Oliver: cabinet position of (Newfoundland) 228

Lastman, Mel: wins Toronto mayoralty race 115

Latimer, Robert: sentencing of for mercy killing xxxi

Leblanc, Nic: resignation of from BQ 18

LeBlanc, Roméo: and constitutional amendment 230; reads Throne Speech 30–1

Lee, Iain: NB Power problems 150

Lee Soo Sung: and labour laws in South Korea 78

Legault, Albert: report of on Canadian Forces 84

Lemmon, George: on health-care cuts 150

Lennon, Eileen: and withdrawal of teachers' services in Ontario 104

Letourneau, Gilles: and Somalia inquiry xi–xii, 49–50, 87–8, 90–1, 90n, 93

Leung, Sophia: runs for election 17; wins seat in election 174

Lincoln, Clifford: loses election for Speaker 30

Lingenfelter, Dwain: cabinet position of (Saskatchewan) 190, 200

Livingston, Doug: becomes Speaker (Yukon) 235

Lockyer, James: and education in New Brunswick 151–2

Longfield, Judi: runs for election 17

Lord, Bernard: wins leadership of New Brunswick PC Party 154

Love, Rod: resignation of 213

Lueders, Pierre: winner of bobsledding title in Nagano Olympics 187

MacAulay, Lawrence: cabinet appointment of 29; and CUPW labour problems 46; and ousting of Weathergill 35; wins seat in election 183

MacBeth, Nancy (formerly Betkowski): and Alberta Liberal leadership race 216

Macdonald, John M.: death of 245

MacDonald, Michael: and Romania's extradition request 137

MacEachern, Dave: winner of bobsledding title in Nagano Olympics 187

MacEwan, Paul: dismissal of as Nova Scotia House leader 140

MacIntyre, Roland: and unionization 149

MacKinnon, Janice: cabinet position of (Saskatchewan) 190

MacLellan, Russell: becomes premier-designate of Nova Scotia xxiii, 16, 138; Calgary Declaration and 144; controversy over by-election call 138; on cuts to CHST 145; and dismissal of House leader MacEwan 140; and HST's impact 144; oil and gas sector 141–2; opposition fails to criticize 141; restoration of protected status to Jim Campbell's Barren 139; toll road issue 139

MacPhail, Joy: on tobacco companies and health-care costs xxii

MacPherson, James: and Ontario teachers' strike 105–6

Major, John 80

Malouf, Albert: death of 245

Manley, John: cabinet appointment of 28

Manning, Preston: on early election call 14; election campaign 19, 174; and Klein 213; and leak of Red Book Two contents 15; move to Stornaway of xxii, 27; and status of Official Opposition 18; and united-right alternative 27

Mar, Gary: cabinet appointment of (Alberta) 209; and education bill 215

March, Fraser: loses election 228

Marchi, Sergio: cabinet appointment of 29

Marleau, Diane: cabinet appointment of 29; on downloading of social housing 61

Marois, Pauline: on constitutional change 135; and Quebec educational reform 134

Martin, Lawrence 128

Martin, Paul: budget of 40–1, 60–2; cabinet appointment of 29; and Canada Pension Plan xiv, xxvii; and Canadian Airlines 170; and child poverty issue 42; CPP reform 41–2; on Employment Insurance surplus xxvi; federal-provincial relations 170; pre-election budget of xv; and rumours of Chrétien's retirement 27; and tax cuts xx

Massé, Marcel: cabinet appointment of 28; on Employment Insurance fund xv; and influence-peddling charge against Corbeil 53

Mathieu, Carole: and Somalia inquiry 90–1

Matthews, Bill: wins seat in election 228

Matthews, Lloyd: cabinet position of (Newfoundland) 228

McCain, Fred: death of 245

McCain, Peter: death of 245

McDonough, Alexa: election campaign xxi, 23, 174; election results 12, 138; in the House 27; NDP election platform xix; and NDP leadership change 19; wins seat in election 25

McGuire, Joe: wins seat in election 183

McKay, Peter: and influence-peddling charge against Corbeil 53

McKenna, Brian: loses PEI by-election 183

McKenna, Frank: education and francophone rights 152; endorsement of partition of Quebec 58; and funding for information technology 154; and HST bill 149; and job creation 155; NB Power problems 151; resignation of as premier of New Brunswick xxviii, 5, 146, 153

McKenzie, Lewis: as election candidate 20; on Perron incident 95; and Somalia inquiry 92

McKinnon, David: on health-care cuts (Ontario) 117; on health-care job losses (Ontario) 110

McLaughlin, Audrey: does not seek NDP re-election 19

McLellan, Anne: cabinet appointment of 29; election campaign 217; re-election of 218; unveils details of Firearms Act xxviii

McQuade, Alice: co-chair of BC Unity Panel 172

Melenchuk, James: Saskatchewan Liberal leadership of 191

Mella, Pat: budget of 182

Mercredi, Ovide: loses leadership of AFN 201; replaced as AFN national chief xxiv; and Royal Commission on Aboriginal Peoples report xv

Mifflin, Fred: announces opening of East Coast cod fishery xix, 225; cabinet appointment of 29; cabinet position of 174, 228; re-election of in Newfoundland 228; TAGS and 226

Milgaard, David: compensation for wrongful conviction of xxv, 203; Saskatchewan apologizes for wrongful conviction of xxiv

Miller, Gail: and Milgaard's wrongful conviction of murder xxiv

Milliken, Peter: on Helms-Burton law (U.S.) 72

Miltenberger, Michael: election confirmation of by NWT Supreme Court 239–40

Mitchell, Andrew: cabinet appointment of 30

Mitchell, Grant: election campaign (Alberta) 204, 207; Liberal losses in Alberta election 208; resignation of as Liberal leader (Alberta) 216

Montgomery, Lucy Maud 187

Moores, Frank: Airbus affair 52

Morin, Don: cabinet shuffle of (NWT) 240

Morin, Guy Paul: wrongful conviction of xiii, xx

Morris, Chris 148

Morrison, Nancy: mercy killing issue xx, 136

Morton, Desmond: report of on Canadian Forces 84

Mowat, Farley: on Newfoundland seal hunt 227

Mulroney, Brian: Airbus affair xi, xxvii, 51–2; on Liberals' handling of national unity xviii; on Plan B 57

Munro, John: and the Wilson Report 171

Murkowski, Frank: and 'hail and stow' laws 167

Murphy, Mitch: human-rights legislation 184

Murray, Larry: on low morale in the CF 96; replaced as acting CDS xxvi; retirement of 93; and Somalia inquiry 49–50, 51, 89–90, 90n

Murray, Phillip: on Krever report 47–9

Nemetz, Nathan: death of 245

Newman, Peter C. 84

Newman, Sidney: death of 245

Nicol, Ken: and Alberta Liberal leadership race 216; re-election of in Alberta 208

Noel, Simon: and Somalia inquiry 90

Normand, Gilbert: cabinet appointment of 30; election confirmed by judicial recount 28

Nunziata, John: loses election for Speaker 30; seeks re-election 17, 21–2; on statuary on Parliament Hill 31; wins seat in election 25

Nystrom, Lorne: wins seat in election 195

O'Brien, Lawrence: re-election of in Newfoundland 228
Ondaatje, Michael: on Newfoundland seal hunt 227
Osborne, Sheila: wins seat in Newfoundland election 229

Paghtakhan, Reis: declines leadership of Manitoba Liberal caucus 160
Palladini, Al: unsafe trucks problem xxi
Palliser, Brian: loses election 159
Pannu, Raj: wins seat in election (Alberta) 209
Parent, Gilbert: elected Speaker 30; rules BQ remains the Official Opposition 18
Parizeau, Jacques: and the 1995 referendum 57; campaign and referendum/ sovereignty issue 22–3, 131; refusal of to join 'Team Canada' trade missions 54
Parrish, Carolyn: cabinet appointment of 28
Parry, Roger: Westray Mine inquiry and 136
Payne, Jean: loses re-nomination bid 16
Péladeau, Pierre: death of 123, 245
Pelletier, Gérard: death of 53, 123, 245
Pelley, Marvin: Westray Mine inquiry and 136
Pépin, Lucie: Senate appointment of 32
Percy, Mike: retirement of 208
Perrault, Danny: escape from prison of and affect on Hogg 175
Perron, Sandra: sexual harassment of in military 95
Peterson, James: cabinet appointment of 30
Petter, Andrew: economic projections of 177; federal-provincial relations 170; and the NDP promise of a balanced budget (BC) xiii
Pettigrew, Pierre: cabinet appointment of 29; and child poverty issue 42, 62; federal youth employment strategy xiv; and opposition charges of influence peddling 52–3; on TAGS program 43, 226
Philip, Prince, Duke of Edinburgh: on celebration of 500th anniversary of Cabot's landing 221
Phillips, Gerald: Westray Mine inquiry and 136
Philp, Margaret 122
Pickersgill, Jack: death of 229, 245
Pocklington, Peter: and Edmonton Oilers 220
Porter, Tim 148
Power, Charlie: wins seat in election 228
Praznik, Darren: Manitoba health care 163
Proud, George: wins seat in election 182
Pugliese, David 96
Pupatello, Sandra: and Ontario health cuts 108

Rainville, Michel: and harassment of Perron 95; and Somalia inquiry 89
Rakoff, Vivian: psychiatric assessment of Bouchard by xxv, 128
Ramsey, Paul: and BC recall legislation 176
Reay, General: and Somalia inquiry 92
Redman, Karen: runs for election 17
Regan, Gerald: and sex-related charges against 137
Resnick, Phil 173–4
Richard, Bernard: and Andersen Consulting 146–7; education and francophone rights 152
Richards, Peter: Westray Mine inquiry and 136
Riel, Maurice: retires from Senate 32
Ringma, Bob: does not seek Reform re-election 19
Rizali, Ismail: and United Nations reform 73
Rizzuto, Pietro: death of 245
Robichaud, Ely: house leader of New Brunswick PC Party 154
Robichaud, Fernand: Senate appointment of 33
Robillard, Lucienne: cabinet appointment of 29
Robinson, Dave: on split-run magazines 74
Roblin, Duff: and Duff's Ditch 160–1
Rochon, Jean: and Quebec blood supply xxviii

Rock, Allan: Airbus affair 52; and 'anti-biker' legislation 47; cabinet appointment of 29; child-support payments issue 43; on Krever report 47–9; and Supreme Court reference 125; and tobacco company sponsorships 45

Romanow, Roy: cabinent shuffle of (Saskatchewan) 190; Calgary Declaration and 36, 200–1

Romkey, William: and report of Somalia inquiry 51

Roux, Jean-Louis: steps down as lieutenant-governor (Quebec) 123

Ruby, Clayton: on Newfoundland seal hunt 227

Ruckleshaus, William: and Pacific salmon treaty 44, 70, 168

Runciman, Robert: and young offenders facility xiv, 119

Saint-Laurent, Bernard: leaves caucus after conviction of eavesdropping 53

Sale, Tim: and Manitoba NDP leadership 162

Sampson, Sandra: on halt to Somalia inquiry 50

Savage, John: and auditor general's critique (Nova Scotia) 140; resignation of (Nova Scotia) xvii, 137

Schreiber, Karl-Heinz: Airbus affair 52

Scott, Andy: cabinet appointment of 29

Scrivener, Margaret: death of 245

Secord, David: loses BC by-election 175; runs for election 175

Segal, Hugh: on Carney's separatist remarks 173

Sewell, John: fights Toronto amalgamation 113

Sgro, Judy: runs for election 16–17, 21

Shafer, Esau: and election tie in Vuntut Gwichin (Yukon) 235

Shatner, William: on Newfoundland seal hunt 227

Shelton, Jev: and Pacific salmon treaty 166

Silye, Jim: does not seek Reform re-election 19

Simard, Jean-Maurice 153

Simmons, Roger: loses seat in election 228

Simpson, Sandra: on halt to Somalia inquiry 88

Sinclair, Duncan: chair of Ontario Health Services Restructuring Commission 107, 110

Skoke, Roseanne: and Nova Scotia Liberal leadership race 16, 138

Sloan, Linda: and Alberta Liberal leadership race 216

Smith, Bill: and Alberta bid for 2001 World Championship 220

Snobelen, John: introduces elementary school standards xxii; on length of school year in Ontario 104; replaced by Johnson as Ontario education minister 104

Solana, Javier: Ottawa visit of and NATO enlargement 77

Solomon, Art: death of 245

Sommerville, David: National Citizens Coalition president 19

Sopinka, John: death of 34, 57, 245

Speaker, Ray: does not seek Reform re-election 19

Stackhouse, John 80

Sterling, Norm: announces mandatory emissions testing for automobiles xxv

Stewart, Christine: approval of Terra Nova project by 224; cabinet appointment of 29

Stewart, Jane: cabinet appointment of 29, 232; cabinet position of 174; and Osoyoos Indian Band land-claims xxxii

Stockell, David: and BC recall legislation 176

Stockholder, Kay: and pepper spray use by RCMP at APEC 169

Strangway, David: and Pacific salmon treaty 44, 70, 168

Stringer, Alf: death of 245

Strong, Maurice: Canada as knowledge broker 80; and United Nations reform 73

Suharto, Raden: at APEC summit 6

Sullivan, Loyola: steps down as PC Party leader (Newfoundland) 229

Tannas, Dan: loses election for Speaker (Alberta) 213–14

Taylor, Charles: death of 245
Taylor, Ken: steps down as Liberal Party leader (Yukon) 235
Taylor, Lorne: cabinet appointment of (Alberta) 209–10
Theriault, Camille: and Amdahl Corp. 154; and job creation 155; and tourism 155
Thibault, Lise: appointment of as lieutenant-governor (Quebec) xiii, 123
Thomas, Lowell: report of on military police services 85; and scandal at Bosnia's Bakovici Hospital 94
Thompson, Andrew: refusal of to resign from Senate 33
Thompson, Ralph: impaired driving sentencing and 185
Thompson, Robert: death of 246
Thompson, Susan: thanks Prime Minister for flood assistance 14
Thorsteinson, Randy: election campaign (Alberta) 207
Tobin, Brian: cabinet shuffles of 227–8; and educational reform (Newfoundland) 229–30; and Pacific salmon treaty 70; public sector cuts of (Newfoundland) 221; on revenue from Hibernia 224
Todd, John: budget of (NWT) 239
Toews, Vic: and Manitoba police services 164
Tulk, Beaton: cabinet position of (Newfoundland) 228
Turnbull, John: on aboriginal rights to Crown land 156
Turp, Daniel: and BQ leadership race xi, 17
Twinn, Walter: death of 246

Valcourt, Bernard: resignation of as leader of New Brunswick PC Party 153–4; and video gambling issues 147
Vanclief, Lyle: cabinet appointment of 29
Vanstone, Ann: co-chair of Ontario Education Improvement Commission 102
Vastel, Michel 22, 131
Vautour, Angela: wins seat in election 154
Venne, Pierrette: and BQ leadership race xii, 17

Walesa, Lech: visit of to Ottawa 76–7

Watson, Kathy: re-election of as mayor of Whitehorse 235
Weathergill, Ted: sacking of 35
Webber, Linda Katherine: appointment of as judge (PEI) 185
Weir, Elizabeth: filibuster against HST 149; NB Power problems 150
Wells, Al: and Somalia inquiry 90
West, Steve: cabinet appointment of (Alberta) 209–10; and VLT issue 212
Widdowson, Frances: and aboriginal land settlements 241
Wiens, Bernie: cabinet position of (Saskatchewan) 190
Williams, Bryan: and BC recall legislation 176
Williams, Jodi: Nobel Peace Prize winner 7, 83
Wilson, Gordon: and the Wilson Report 165, 171–2
Wilson, Jim: announces privatization of Ontario Hydro xxix; and Ontario health cuts 108; replaced by Witmer as Ontario health minister 110
Witmer, Elizabeth: and pay equity in Ontario 120; replaces Wilson as Ontario health minister 110
Wong, Victor: runs for election 174
Woodman, Fred: of Fisheries Resource Conservation Council (Newfoundland) 225–6
Wright, Robin: and Pacific salmon treaty 71

Yankowsky, Julius: re-election of in Alberta 208
Yeltsin, Boris: and G7 participation 75–6; and nuclear-arms control 83
Young, Doug: on CF personnel problems 95; defence policy of 84–5, 86; loses seat in election 25, 67, 85, 154; and Maritime Road Development Corporation 156; and NFTC contract with Bombardier 77; and scandal at Bosnia's Bakovici Hospital 94; and Somalia inquiry xi, xvii–xviii, 49–50, 87–8, 92

Zed, Paul: loses seat in election 25
Zeidler, Margaret: death of 246
Zimmerman, Paul: death of 246

Index of subjects

Abegweit 186

aboriginal affairs and issues: First Nations Bank 201; health care in Yukon 231; Innu community at Davis Inlet 230–1; land claims xxxii, 223; Mohawk crisis xxv; national unity issue xxvi; OPP officer charged in death of George xix; population in Manitoba 157; and Quebec separation issue 63; and right to cut trees on Crown land xxix; Royal Commission on Aboriginal Peoples xv, 203; Saskatchewan studies of 202; and Voisey's Bay project xxv, 222–3

Africa 81

AIDS/HIV xiv; and health care 109–10

Air Canada: strike at xi

Air Ontario: strike at xi

Airbus affair xi, xxvii, 51–2

Alaska Highway repairs 232

Albania 74–5

Alberta: and 2001 World Championship bid 220; agricultural sector in 219; Bre-X Minerals saga 219; budget of xiv, 205–6, 214; cabinet shuffle in 209–10; Calgary Declaration 213, 216; credit rating xxviii; economic boom in 218; economy 218–20; education in 215; election campaign 205–7; election in xvi–xvii, 5, 204–9; election of Speaker 213–14; environmental issues 212; Growth Summit 211; health-care issues xx, 206, 215–16; housing starts 218; and interprovincial migration 218; job growth in 218; Klein's television address 205; Kyoto agreement 212–13; labour relations

and unions in xxii, 206, 216, 219–20; legislation in 214–15; legislature of xxiii, 213–16; Multi-Corp scandal 208; oil and gas sector 218–19; privatization in xx, 210, 216; rape shield law struck down in xxix; shopping-centre loiterers in 215; surplus in 211; Throne Speech of 205, 214; and tobacco smuggling 215; unemployment rate in 218; video lottery terminals in 206, 211–12

Alberta Treasury Branch 210

Amnesty International 78

Andersen Consulting 146–7

anti-personnel land-mines ban xxii, xxvi, xxix, xxxi, 6–7, 68, 82; legislative approval of 31

APEC 78, 79–80, 165, 168–9; protestors at and RCMP xxx, xxxii, 5–6, 80

Asia: financial crisis of 5

Asia-Pacific 78–81

Asia-Pacific Economic Cooperation. *See* APEC

Assembly of First Nations (AFN): leadership change in xxiv, 201–2; protests and Royal Commission on Aboriginal Peoples xv

Atlantic Highways Corp. xxx

auditor general: reports of xxviii, xxxi, 34–5, 145

Balkans: peacekeeping in xxxi

Bank of Canada: rates set by 39; and rise in household debt xxi

Bell Canada: workforce reductions at xxiv

Bloc Québécois: and the election 12, 13; election loss of xxi, 130, 131–2; election platform 18; leadership change in xvii, 17–18, 131; and leadership race xi, 17–18, 130–1; loses status as Official Opposition xxi, 3, 12, 27; overview of 17–18; party standing of 15, 18, 132; retains Official Opposition status after tie with Reform 18

Bombardier Inc. xxxii; sale of jets to Southwest Airlines xi

Bosnia: Bakovici incidents 94–5; Canada in 77; NATO in 75; peacekeeping in xxxi

Bowater and Minas Paper 143

Brazil: trade issues with xxxii

Bre-X Minerals xvii, xx, 219

British Columbia: APEC 168–9; BC Unity Panel 172; blockade of Alaskan ferry *Malaspina* 168; bond rating xx; budget issues in xiii; by-election in 175; Calgary Declaration 172; Canada Pension Plan (CPP) 170; child benefit program in 62; and compensation from tobacco companies for smoking-related health costs xxii; courthouse closures in xiv; debt and deficit of 177; economic projections 178; economy 176–8; federal election results in (table 1) 175; federal-provincial relations 169–70; fisheries 63–4, 173; forestry sector 177; Gustafsen Lake stand-off xx–xxi; job loss in 177; labour relations and unions in 177; land claims in xxix–xxx; lawsuit alleging election fraud by NDP government xv, xxix, 176; and lease at the torpedo test range at Nanoose Bay 167–8; Mifflin plan 173; national unity issue 170–3; overview of 164–5; and Pacific salmon treaty xxiii, xxiv–xxv, xxvi, 6, 165–8; place in Confederation of xxvii; recall legislation in 176; same-sex couples as legal spouses in xxi; and separatist option for 172–3; taxes in 171; threat to evict U.S. Navy xxiii; unemployment rate in 177; welfare residency rule xvi; Wilson Report 171–2. *See also* Canada-U.S. relations

British Columbia Human Rights tribunal: on breast-feeding children in public xxiv

budget (federal) xv, 40–1; pre-election 60–1

budgets (provincial/territorial). *See* provincial/territorial entries

Burma (Myanmar) 79; trade sanctions on xxiv

by-elections (provincial/territorial). *See* British Columbia; Manitoba; Newfoundland and Labrador; Nova Scotia; Ontario; PEI; Quebec; Yukon

cabinet shuffles (federal) 27–30, 174

cabinet shuffles (provincial). *See* provincial/territorial entries

Canada Action Party xii, 21

Canada-Asia Working Group 78

Canada Pension Investment Board: establishment of 42

Canada Pension Plan (CPP) xiv, xxvii, 31, 41–2, 60, 170

Canada Post: and CUPW strike xxx, xxxi; labour relations and 46

Canada-U.S. relations 67; and border controls xxix–xxx; and disparaging remarks at NATO summit xxiii; and Helms-Burton law 71–2; and lease at the torpedo test range at Nanoose Bay xxiii, xxiv–xxv, 45, 69–71, 167–8; Pacific salmon dispute 69–71; and Pacific salmon treaty xxii, xxiii, 6, 43–4, 63–4; toxic waste at NORAD bases 232. *See also* trade disputes (U.S.)

Canadian Action Party 195

Canadian Airlines: restructuring of xv, 169–70

Canadian/Dutch AgraWest 180

Canadian Human Rights Commission: on Report of the Royal Commission on Aboriginal Peoples xvii

Canadian Police Association: and call for return to death penalty xxv

Canadian Security Intelligence Service. *See* CSIS

Canadian Union of Postal Workers xxx, xxxi, 46

Canadian Wheat Board 31, 46–7

Central America: relations with 72–3

Channel Lake Petroleum 200

Cheviot mine xxii

children: content rating system and television viewing of xx; custody of by same-sex couples xxi; mortality rates xvii; and poverty 42–3, 62, 198–9; and prostitution 215; youth crime in Yukon 236; youth unemployment issue 63

Christian Heritage party 21

CIDA: announcement of human rights observers to Rwanda xiv

Cominco 235

Communist Party: court challenge of 21

constitutional initiatives: on Newfoundland educational system 38; on Quebec educational system 38

Corrections Canada: and Prison for Women xxxii

crime: Bernardo case xiii; and call for return to death penalty xxv; DNA identification of convicted criminals 31; mercy killing issue xx, xxxi, 136; rates xxiv

Crown Investments 197, 199

CRTC: and territorial plans 232

CSIS: and industrial espionage xiii

Cuba: Canada's relations with 71–2; and Canada-U.S. relations 71–2; and human rights xiii

CUPE: in New Brunswick 149

Curragh Inc. 136

Czech Republic: and NATO 7, 75–6

defence issues and policies xxvi, 69; arms control and 82–4; assessment and review of 83–6; budget of 85–6; and contract for armoured personnel carriers 86; court martial of military officer for Haiti incident xxiii; helicopter purchase 45–6; Nanoose Bay testing facility 64; nuclear weapons 83–4; observers to Guatemala 73; organization of 95–6; pay levels xviii; and personnel 95–6; and Red River flooding emergency xx, 96, 161–2; review of Canadian Forces 84–5; on role of military police 85; submarines and 86. See also peacekeeping; Somalia inquiry

DynaTek 143–4

East Isle Shipyard 180

economy: Asian crisis and the 5, 177; average incomes 39–40; bankruptcies xiii, 233; debt (national) and deficit 40–1, 60–2; dollar 39; economic statement 40–1; foreign currency debt rating xv; growth rate xvii, xxii, 39, 157–8, 178–9; housing starts xiii, 180; IMF projections xxvi; indicators 39–40; inflation rate 39; personal bankruptcies xiv, 233; poverty 40; rise in student debt levels xiv. See also budget; provincial/territorial entries

HMCS Edmonton 86

Edmonton: and the Alberta election 207–8

Edmonton Oilers 220

education: federal funding for post-secondary students xxvii. See also provincial/territorial entries

election (federal) 3, 11–30, 69; and aboriginal issues xix; in Alberta 216–18; announcement of tax cuts xx; in BC 165, 173–6; campaign 22–4, 61; Chrétien calls xix; distribution of seats and share of votes by party and province (table 2) 26; leader debates 23; in Manitoba 5, 159, 161; NDP on national unity xxi; in New Brunswick 154; in Newfoundland 228; in Nova Scotia 138; in Nunavut 232; in Ontario 101; party standings after recent elections (table 3) 28; in PEI 182–3; in Quebec 126; in Saskatchewan 194–5; voting results by party, projected and actual (table 1) 25; in Yukon 232

elections (provincial/territorial): Alberta xvi–xvii, 5, 204–9; British Columbia (by-election) 175; Manitoba (by-election) 159; Nova Scotia (by-election) 138; Ontario (by-election) 101; Prince Edward Island (by-election) 183; Quebec (by-election) 130; Yukon (by-election) 229

Embraer xxxii

Employment Insurance 179; and deal in NB 155; name change from Unemployment Insurance xi; surplus xv,

xxvi, 40–1; and TAGS program 226.
See also Unemployment Insurance
environmental issues: and trade 79
Euro-Atlantic Partnership Council 77
Europe: relations with 74–5
European Union: and fur trade xxiv, 232
exports: to Asia 79

federal-provincial relations 31, 63;
aboriginal leaders and national unity
issue xxx; Calgary Declaration 4, 35–7,
58–9, 132, 135; and coal mining near
Jasper National Park xxii; and constitutional change xxx, 134–5; devolution of
responsibilities 61; first ministers' conference 31–2, 63; 'hail-in and stow
laws' in BC 165–8; health care 64–5;
and Hôpital Montford (Ottawa) 108–9;
Klein on the Kyoto negotiations 31–2;
labour force agreement 134; and lease
at the torpedo test range at Nanoose Bay
167–8; national unity issue xviii, xxvi,
58; and Pacific salmon treaty 169; and
personal-income-tax systems 62; Plan
B 56–8; and social housing 61; and
social programs xxxii; social union
agreement 32; Supreme Court reference on unilateral secession 123–7,
129; transfer payments/cutbacks xix;
youth employment strategy xiv. *See
also* Supreme Court decisions
Federation of Saskatchewan Indian
Nations (FSIN) 201–3
fisheries: cod quota 43; East Coast cod
xix; Pacific salmon xxii, xxiii, xxiv,
43–4; TAGS program and Atlantic
fishers xxviii, xxxii, 43, 145, 225–7
Fletcher Challenge Canada 177
foreign policy: assessment and review of
67–9; and human security 80–1
France: and Quebec xxvii
HMCS *Fredericton* 77
Friede Goldman International 224
fur trade: and the European Union xxiv,
232

gambling issues: in Nova Scotia 139;
video lottery terminals in Alberta 206;
video lottery terminals in New Brun-

swick xxvii, 147; video lottery termi-
nals in PEI 183–4
Golf PEI Inc. 185
Green Party 21
Greyhound Air xxvi
Grupo Acerero Del Norte 142
Guatemala 73
gun control legislation: Firearms Act
xxviii; and Metropolitan Toronto police
xxi; in NWT 231; in Saskatchewan 195;
in Yukon 231
Guyana Power 189, 199

Haiti: court martial of military officer in
xxiii; peacekeeping in 72–3
Harmonized Sales Tax. *See* taxation
(GST/HST)
health care: lung cancer deaths among
women xvi; murder charge on death of
cancer patient xx. *See also* provincial/
territorial entries
Hibernia project xxx, 221, 223–4
human rights: age discrimination in CAF
xii; and Cuba xiii; sexual orientation
and 230; and trade 79–80
Hungary: and NATO 7, 75–6

Inco Ltd. 222–3
India 80
International Campaign to Ban Land-
mines 83
International Fund for Animal Welfare
(IFAW) 227
International Monetary Fund: projections
by xxvi
Inuit: leadership of 238
Inuit Tapirisat: leadership of 232
Iraq: crisis in 77–8
Irving Whale xxiv; raising of xviii
Israel: ambassador recalled from xxvii;
Mossad agents and counterfeit Cana-
dian passports xxvii, xxviii
Isuma Productions 238
Italy: refugees in 75

Krever inquiry xii, xxx, 4, 47–9

Labour Relations Board: firing of head of
xxxi

labour unions: CUPW dispute with Canada Post 46. *See also* provincial/territorial entries

language issues: anglophones in Quebec xviii; announced closure of Montfort Hôpital (Ontario) xv; francophone communities outside Quebec xviii; and Quebec xxi

legislation (federal): anti-biker xix, 14, 46–7; anti-personnel land-mines ban treaty 31; banning gasoline additive MMT 14; Canada Pension Plan xiv, 31, 41–2; Canadian Wheat Board 31; child poverty and 42–3; copyright 14; CUPW back-to-work bill 46; DNA identification of convicted criminals xviii, 31; free trade with Chile 14; 'person' case, statue on Parliament Hill to commemorate the women 31; on tobacco advertising 14; on tobacco company sponsorships xvi

Liberal Party (federal): and alleged fundraising irregularities xxviii, 52–3; and appointment of female candidates 174; budget surplus of 13; and the election 11–12, 174, 218, 232; election campaign 5, 15–17; election win of xxi, 24, 69; party standing of 3, 15, 132, 138, 154, 161, 194–5

Liberal Party (provincial): (Alberta) as Official Opposition 208; election campaign of 205, 206–7; election loss of xvi–xvii; leadership race of 216; (Manitoba) and leadership review 159–60; (Nova Scotia) by-elections win by 138; changing leadership of xxiii; (Ontario) by-elections win by 101; (PEI) by-election win by 183; (Quebec) by-elections win by 130; (Saskatchewan) as Official Opposition 189; leadership in 191–2; loses Official Opposition status 191; (Yukon) leadership of 233

Maersk Dubai: and Romanian stowaways 137

Manitoba: budget of 162; by-election in 159; call centres in 157–8; debt reduction in xvii; economic growth of 157–8; economy 156–8, 161; education in 163–4; employment in 157; federal election call and the flooding 161; health care in 162–3; inflation rate 157; legislative session of 162–4; out-migration 157, 158; Plan B 57; police services in 164; politics and political parties in 158–60; population in 156–7; Red River flooding in xx, 5, 14, 156, 160–2; revenues and expenditures 162; and sale of telephone service 162–3; taxes in 162; and university funding 163–4; youth unemployment issue 157

Manitoba Telephone System (MTS) 162–3

marijuana issue xxxi

Marxist-Leninist Party 21

Mercosur customs union xxxii

Michelin Tires 143

Middle East 77–8

Mobil Oil: and Hibernia project 223–4

Multi-Corp 208

NAFTA: gasoline additive ban xviii

National Action Committee on the Status of Women (NAC): election campaign debate 23

National Citizens' Coalition xii, 19, 217

National Council of Welfare: benefit reductions from provincial cost-cutting xiv

Native affairs and issues. *See* aboriginal affairs and issues

NATO: and Bombardier contract xxxii; enlargement of 75–7; membership offered to eastern European members 7; NFTC 77; SFOR 75; STANAVFORLANT 77

Natural Law Party 21, 195

NB Power 150–1

New Brunswick: and aboriginal property rights over trees xxix; and Andersen Consulting 146–7; auditor general's report 146–8; and Blue Cross 147–8; budget of 156; call centres in 148, 154; economy 154–5; education in 151–2; francophone rights in 151–2; health-care cuts in 149–50; and HST xvii; and IBM 148; job creation in 155; labour relations and unions in 149; leadership change in 153–4; legislation in 148–50,

153; municipal amalgamation and protests 152; NB Power 150–1; police services in 153; Potacan mine xxviii, xxxii; public-private partnerships 146–8; Sable Island gas pipeline 155; taxation (GST/HST) 149; Throne Speech of 155–6; tourism in 154–5; VRTs in 147

New Democratic Party (federal): and the election 11–12, 13, 174, 228, 232; election campaign xxi; election platform xix, 20; leadership change in 19–20; overview of 19–20; party standing of 15, 138, 154, 194–5; regains official party status xxi, 3, 24

New Democratic Party (provincial): (Alberta) election campaign of 206–7; election results for 209; returns to legislature after absence xvi–xvii; (Nova Scotia) by-election win by 138; (Ontario) by-election win by 101; (PEI) by-election loss of 183; (Saskatchewan) internal dissensions in 190–1

Newfoundland and Labrador: agricultural sector in 224; appointment of lieutenant-governor to 229; budget of 221; by-election in 228–9; cabinet shuffles in 228; call centres in 225; celebration of 500 years of history in 221, 231; constitutional amendment and education 38, 56, 229–30; on discrimination against gays and lesbians 230; economy 221–5; educational reform in 229–30; environmental issues 222–3; fishery in 225–7; Hibernia project xxx, 221, 223–4; and HST xvii, 221–5; land-claims settlement xxix, 223; politics in 227–9; population decline in 227; public sector cuts in xvii, 221; seal fishery in 227; shipbuilding in 224; shrimp sector in 226–7; substance abuse at Davis Inlet 230–1; Terra Nova offshore oil project xxv, 224; tourism in 221; unemployment rate in 222, 231; Voisey's Bay project 222–3

NGOs: role of 83

Nigeria 81

Nobel Peace Prize 68; anti-personnel land-mines ban 83; awarded to ICBL and Williams 6–7

Northern Telecom xxvi

Northwest Territories: and 1995 election 239; aboriginal affairs and constitutional development 240–1; abuse in 242; alcohol in 241–2; Aurora Fund 239–40; budget of 239; cabinet shuffle in 240; diamonds in 232, 237; economy 236–9; fisheries in 238; fur trade 232, 238; Inuktitut-language broadcasting in 238; labour relations and unions in 239; land claims 241; national unity issue 231–2; oil and gas sector 237–8; out-migration 236; overview of 231–2; policy and politics 239–40; population 236; rate of natural increase 236; society in 241–2; and transfer payment/cutbacks 231; world markets and 232

Northwestel 232

Nova Scotia: abuse in 137; auditor general's report 139, 140; budget of xix, 139–40; by-election in 138; Calgary Declaration 144; call centres in 143; changing leadership in 137–8; economy 141–4; environmental issues 137, 138–9; extradition request from Romania 137; film industry in 145; fisheries 142; forestry sector 142; gambling issues in 139; health care in xxiii; housing in 145; and HST xvii; intergovernmental affairs 144–5; leadership change in xxiii; legislature of 139–41; mining sector 142; patronage issues in 141; politics in 137–9; racial brawl at Cole Harbour school xxvii; Sable Island gas pipeline 140, 141–2; software producers in 143; taxation (GST/HST) 144; Throne Speech of 140; toll road in xxx, 139; tourism in 142; unemployment in 142; Westray Mine inquiry xxxi, 4, 136, 145

Nunavut: health care 242; issues 239, 240–1; process 238–9

Nunavut Corporation 238

Nunavut Tunngavik Inc. 240, 241, 241n

NWT Air 233

O'Leary (PEI): potato statue in 187

Ontario: auditor general's reports 120,

122; bail program in 118–19; budget of 121–2; by-elections in 101; cabinet shuffle in 104, 111; calls for merger of PC Party and Reform 101; current value assessment 100, 112, 115; on discrimination against gays and lesbians 101, 120; downloading in xii, 100, 112, 114; economy 121–2; Education Improvement Commission 102–3; and education reform xii, xxii, xxviii, xxx, 99–100, 101–7; elections in 115; emissions testing for automobiles in xxv; health-care restructuring in xv, xxiv, xxvi, 100, 107–11; Health Services Restructuring Commission xv, xvi, 100, 107; hospital closures in 108–11; and impact of cuts to legal aid system xxvi; justice system in 120; labour relations and unions in xxi, xxx, 104–7, 117; legislation in xxiii, 99, 101, 106, 113, 115, 116–17, 118, 122; legislature of 99; marijuana issue xxxi; and Megacity (Toronto) xvi, xxiv, 100, 111–16; municipal affairs in 100, 111–18; Ontario Parent Council 103; pay equity in 101, 120; police and material for DNA analysis xxviii; police services in 118; and police shooting of aboriginal protester xxiii; property-tax reform 100, 111–12; protests against government in xxviii; provincial-municipal relations in 100; public sector restructuring in 99; rent-review legislative changes 100; review of wrongful convictions for murder and manslaughter in xx; social assistance reform in 122; and standing of Liberal Party (federal) in 101; taxes in 100, 121–2; Toronto police and sex-slave ring xxvi; and unsafe trucks on highways xxi, 119–20; workfare in 101, 122; young offenders facility in xiv, xxv, 101
Ontario Child Mortality Task Force xvii
Ontario Hydro: privatization of xxix
Orenda Aerospace 143
Osoyoos Indian Band: land claims xxxii

Parliament Hill: security on xiv

Parti Québécois: by-elections win by 130; on reference to Supreme Court 37–8
peacekeeping: in Bosnia xxxi; in Haiti 72–3; and Zaire 81
Pearson Airport xix
Philippines: Team Canada trade mission in 40
Point Lepreau Nuclear Plant 150
Poland: and NATO 7, 75–6
population: as percentage of from Quebec xviii
Potacan potash mine xxviii, xxxii
Potash Corp. xxxii
poverty: in Canada 40; of children 42–3
Prince Edward Island 183; agricultural sector in 179; Basin Head's bridge protest 187; bombing incidents in 187; budget of 182; by-election in 183; Confederation Bridge xxi, 181, 185–7; debt and deficit of 182; economic growth of 178–9; economy 178–81; exports from 180; fire damage to Green Gables 187; fisheries 179–80; forestry sector 180; gambling issues 183–4; golf course development controversy 185; health care in 183; housing starts 180; impaired driving sentencing in 185; legislative session of 183–4; literacy of youth 182; manufacturing in 180; patronage issues in 184; population in 179; public sector in 181; retail growth 180–1; revenues and expenditures in 181–2; seasonal workers and compensation xxx; statue of potato in 187; Throne Speech of 183; tourism in 178–9, 181; unemployment rate in 179
Progressive Conservative Party (federal) 154; and the election 11–12, 13, 174, 228, 232; leadership of 20; overview of 20–1; party standing of 15, 138, 154, 194–5; platform of 21; regains official party status xxi, 3, 24
Progressive Conservative Party (provincial): (Alberta) election in 204–5; election win of xvi–xvii, 5, 208–9; (Manitoba) and federal election campaign 158–9; (Newfoundland and Labrador) by-election win of 229;

changing leadership of 229; (PEI) by-election loss of 183; (Saskatchewan) and PC-Reform alliance 192; opposition of 189; scandal over misuse of funds xiii, 191; votes itself out of existence xxix, 191
Progressive Democratic Alliance (BC) 171

Qikiqtaaluk 238
Quebec: appointment of amicus curiae to respond to Supreme Court for 126, 127; appointment of lieutenant-governor to 123; blood supply in xxviii; budget of 133; bus accident near Quebec City 135–6; by-elections in 130; cabinet shuffle in 130; constitutional amendment and education xxx, 38, 55; economy 133; education reform in 134–5; Fête Nationale and violence at xxii; language issues xxi; and Ottawa 54–5; partitionist movement in 129–30; politics and political parties in 123–34; population xviii; psychological profile of Bouchard 128; referendum/sovereignty issues xviii, xxii, xxxi, 3–4, 38, 59–60, 123, 126, 127–30; sale of information on black market in xvi; and social programs deal xxxii; spending reductions in 132–3; and Supreme Court reference 123–7, 129; taxes in 134; unemployment rate in 133
Quebec Political Action Committee: dissolution of xi

Rassemblement pour une Alternative Politique (RAP): founding of 133
RCMP: Airbus affair xxvii; and alleged Liberal fund-raising irregularities xxviii, 52–3; and APEC summit xxx, 80; and APEC summit protestors xxxii, 6, 169
Reform Party (federal): and Alberta election 207; and the election 12, 13, 159, 217–18; election loss of xxi; Official Opposition status of xxi, 3, 12, 24, 69, 174; overview of 18–19; party standing of 15, 18, 194–5; platform of 19;

Saskatchewan-based 193–4; and Stornoway issue xxii
Registered Retirement Savings Plans xiv–xv
Report of the Royal Commission on Aboriginal Peoples xv, 203; Canadian Human Rights Commission on xvii
RIGCO North America 224
Romania: extradition request from 137
Roughriders football club 188
Royal Commission on Aboriginal Peoples. See Report of the Royal Commission on Aboriginal Peoples
Royal Oak Mines 237
Russia: and G7 Summit 75–6; and NATO enlargement 75–6
Rwanda 81; announcement of human rights observers to xiv

Sable Island gas pipeline 140, 141–2, 155
Safeway xxii, 219–20
Saskatchewan: aboriginal affairs 201–3; agricultural sector in 197–8; auditor general's report 194, 197, 200; budget of 188, 196–8; cabinet shuffle in 190; Calgary Declaration 200–1; child poverty in 198–9; Crown sector 189, 199–200; debt reduction in 188–9, 197; economy 197–200; employment rates 198; globalization and 199; GRIP crop insurance 198; health care in 189–90; judges' salaries in 203–4; justice sector 4; labour relations and unions in 189; land claims 203; midwifery in 189; and national unity issue 200–1; natural resources sector 197–8; Official Opposition in 189, 190; parties and elections 190–6; Plan A and Plan B 57, 201; political fund-raising practices in 194; Potash Corp. xxxii; progressive neo-conservatism in 188; salaries for in-house babysitters 189–90; Saskatchewan Party as Official Opposition in xxv; taxation issues in 203; Throne Speech of 188–9; transportation system 198; unemployment rate in 198; wrongful conviction of David Milgaard xxiv, xxv, 203
Saskatchewan Party xxix; creation of

xxv, 191–4; Official Opposition status of 190, 191

SaskPower 189, 197, 199

Senate appointments xxx, 32–3

sexual harassment: in military xii, 95

Sherritt International Corp. 72

Social Credit Party (provincial): (Alberta) election campaign of 206–7; (Alberta) election results for 209

Somalia inquiry xii, xvi, xix, xxiii, 49–51, 86–94; halt to xi–xii, xvii, xvii–xviii, xxviii, 4, 67

South America: relations with 72–3

South Korea: economy of 39; Team Canada trade mission 40, 78

Speaker: selection of federal 30

HMCS *St John's* 77

Stora Forest industries 142, 143

Strathcona Mineral Services xx

Summit of the Eight xxii, 75–6

Supreme Court: reference on unilateral secession 37–8, 56–7

Supreme Court decisions: on aboriginal land rights xxxi–xxxii; gender-bias ruling 239; and judges' salaries 184–5; legal rights of fetus xxix; on private records of sexual assault victims xiv; on Quebec's referendum law and spending limits xxviii; reference on unilateral secession xv–xvi; right of inquiries to assign blame xxvii, 48; on Westray Mine trial 136

Supreme Court of Canada: appointments to xxvii

Sydney Tar Ponds 137

taxation: personal-income-tax systems 62

taxation (GST/HST): implementation of xvii, 65–6, 149, 221–2

Team Canada trade mission 40, 78–9; Bouchard joins the 54

T. Eaton Company: and bankruptcy protection xv; restructuring of xvii

television: children's content rating system xx

Terra Nova offshore oil project xxv, 224

Thailand: Team Canada trade mission in 40

Throne Speech (federal) xxvii, 30–1

Throne Speech (provincial). *See* provincial/territorial entries

Time magazine: on UN ranking by of Canada as best place to live xx

tobacco: advertising 14, 45; and company sponsorships xvi, 45; smuggling of 215

Torngat Mountains National Park 223

Toronto Stock Exchange: delisting of Bre-X xx

trade disputes (U.S.): split-run magazines 73–4. *See also* Canada-U.S. relations

trade (international): with Asia 78–9; with India 80

trade missions: Team Canada trade mission to East Asia 40, 54

Trans-Canada Highway xxx

Ukraine: and NATO 77

Ultramar Oil Refinery 143

Unemployment Insurance: eligibility requirements change xi; increases in payroll taxes 60; name change to Employment Insurance xi. *See also* Employment Insurance

unemployment rate 39

United Nations: Conference on Disarmament (CD) 82; Iraq and weapons inspection 77–8; reform of 73; sanctions against Iraq 78; U.S. withholding of dues from xviii

United States: withholding of dues from UN xviii. *See also* Canada-U.S. relations; trade disputes (U.S.)

Vancouver (BC): and strike by sanitation workers xxvi

Voisey's Bay project xxv, 222–3

Wal-Mart: sale of Cuban pajamas by 72

war crimes xii, xxxii

Westray Mine inquiry xxxi, 4, 136, 145

HMCS *Winnipeg* 77

Winnipeg (Manitoba): Canadian Forces cheered for work in flood-ravaged areas xx

women and women's issues: and appointment of female candidates to run as Liberals in federal election xvi, 174;

elected federally 25; and Kingston Penitentiary xii, xxxii; lung cancer deaths among xvi; in the military xii, 95; sexual harassment in military xii

World Trade Organization (WTO): ruling on beef xxv; split-run American magazines 73–4; and split-run U.S. magazines xv

York University: strike at 106–7

Yukon: aboriginal affairs and constitutional development 235–6; budget of 234; economy 232, 233–4; Faro mine 233, 235; fur trade 232; health care 235; housing in 233; inflation rate 233; job growth in 233–4; legislature of 234; minimum wage in 235; municipal election in 235; oil and gas sector 231; overview of 231–2; policing in 236; policy and politics 234–5; population of 232; Porcupine caribou herd 232; resource sector 232, 233; society in 236; strike at Whitehorse Hospital 235–6; substance abuse in 236; taxation in 234; and transfer payment/cutbacks 231; Workers' Compensation Health and Safety Board 234; world markets and 232

Yukon Energy 234

Yukon Party 235

Zaire: and peacekeeping mission 81